FAITH, UNITY, DISCIPLINE

For my children:
Stefan (†), Andreas, Natasha and Emma

HEIN G. KIESSLING

Faith, Unity, Discipline

The Inter-Service-Intelligence (ISI) of Pakistan

HURST & COMPANY, LONDON

First published in the United Kingdom in 2016 by
C. Hurst & Co. (Publishers) Ltd.,
41 Great Russell Street, London, WC1B 3PL
© Hein G. Kiessling, 2016
This work is an expanded and updated version of *ISI und R&AW,
Die Geheimdienste Pakistans und Indiens. Konkurrierende Atommächte,
ihre Politik und der internationale Terrorismus*, Berlin: Verlag Dr. Köster, 2011
All rights reserved.
Printed in India

Distributed in the United States, Canada and Latin America by
Oxford University Press, 198 Madison Avenue, New York, NY 10016,
United States of America.

The right of Hein G. Kiessling to be identified as the author
of this publication is asserted by him in accordance with the
Copyright, Designs and Patents Act, 1988.

A Cataloguing-in-Publication data record for this book
is available from the British Library.

ISBN: 9781849045179

This book is printed using paper from registered sustainable
and managed sources.

www.hurstpublishers.com

CONTENTS

CONTENTS

AUTHOR'S NOTE ON SOURCES

This book seeks to present an objective history of the ISI, its origin and development, tasks and objectives, successes and failures. Since the ISI also works, de facto, as an internal intelligence agency, the domestic political environment in Pakistan has also been extensively scrutinised.

The author's observations and analysis are drawn from personal experience, based on the years he lived in Pakistan (1989–2002). He spent three years with his family in Quetta and Loralai in Balochistan and later another nine years living in Islamabad. A special permit allowed him to travel all over the country, including the Tribal Areas, and working as the representative of a German political foundation enabled him to establish good contacts with Pakistan's political and military elite. Journeys to the rest of South Asia, to China and to Central Asia, and contacts with the political elites there helped to broaden the knowledge gleaned in Pakistan. Since 2004, the author has traveled at least twice a year to Pakistan and to India to maintain his local contacts.

Details of his interviewees and personal conversations with serving and retired military and intelligence personnel are not listed here in detail, for reasons of confidentiality.

The author is grateful to Michael Dwyer and his colleagues at Hurst for their excellent editing of the manuscript.

Last but not least, special thanks goes to my wife, Irene Kiessling, for assisting me in my research and translating the book from German into English.

LIST OF ILLUSTRATIONS

1. Brigadier Syed Raza Ali, former Director of the Special Operations Bureau in the ISI and head of the Afghanistan Office.
2. Ex-DG ISI Lt. Gen. Ziauddin.
3. Ex-DG ISI Lt. Gen. Javed Ashraf Qazi.
4. The author with Ex-DG ISI Lt. Gen. Ziauddin, Lahore 2008.
5. The author with Ex-DG ISI Lt. Gen. Mahmud Ahmed, Lahore 2008.
6. Ex-DG ISI and Ex-CJCSC Gen. Ehsan ul-Haq, Islamabad 2009.
7. General retd. Mirza Aslam Beg, Rawalpindi 2010.
8. The author with Ex-DG ISI Lt. Gen. Hamid Gul, Islamabad 2011.
9. The author with Ex-DG ISI Lt. Gen. Asad Durrani, Islamabad 2011.
10. Ex-DG ISI Lt. Gen Shamsur Rehman Kallue.
11. The author with Col. (retd.) Imam, Rawalpindi 2008.
12. Ex-COAS Gen. Mrza Aslam Beg and Col. Imam, Rawalpindi 2008.
13. Brig. (retd.) Shaukat Qadir with the author, Rawalpindi 2010.

INTRODUCTION

The countries of South Asia constitute one of the most conflict-prone areas in the world. India and Pakistan, with their well-equipped military forces, face each other in a politically volatile situation. Since their successful nuclear tests in 1998, both states have rapidly expanded their arsenal of nuclear armaments. The number of operational nuclear warheads on both sides is now estimated to be over 100; both states also possess short-, middle- and long-range rockets. There is therefore a possibility of tactical and strategic nuclear weapon deployment from both sides, especially given the absence of a "no first use" agreement. India has a "no first use" doctrine against non-nuclear weapon states; but Pakistan does not even abide by this restriction. There, the military is extremely influential and has so far blocked political leaders from committing to any such "no first use" doctrine.[1]

The security of nuclear weapons storage in both countries has been discussed by international experts, and frequently questioned. In Pakistan's case, in particular, it is feared that nuclear weapons could one day fall into the hands of extremists, with potentially deadly risks for the region and beyond. Pakistan's nuclear warheads are currently stored separately from the carrier weapons and are guarded by a selected special force. The deployment decision rests with the National Command Authority (NCA)—ultimately the President and the Prime Minister. However, observers agree that it is ultimately the Army chief and the Director of the Strategic Plans Division, now a serving lieutenant general, who are the functional authorities in the NCA and they will decide. Each has a briefcase with special codes for the release of the warheads. The possibility that terrorists could simultaneously seize both men and their briefcases seems small. Nevertheless, Taliban terrorists have attacked the GHQ in Rawalpindi, the regional HQ for the security agencies, as well as the military and the civilian airports in Karachi, leaving behind dead or wounded and substantial damage to property. This provides some justification for anxiety amongst the international community in relation to the security of Pakistan's nuclear force, though of course risks associated with atomic storage facilities are a global phenomenon.[2]

There have been ongoing conflicts between the two powers ever since Partition in 1947, many concerned with the perennial dispute between Pakistan and India over the status of Kashmir, to which no end seems in sight. Military confrontations occurred in 1947, 1965, 1971 and 1999, with the Indo-Pakistan war of 1971 resulting in the separation of East Pakistan and its birth as the new independent state of Bangladesh. The 1999 war, commonly known as the Kargil conflict, prompted the United States to exert diplomatic pressure on Pakistan to back down, as the danger of a nuclear war between the two neighbours appeared to be a distinct rather than a remote possibility.

In 2002 the President of Pakistan, General Pervez Musharraf, traveled to India for talks with the Indian Prime Minister, Atal Behari Vajpayee. Musharraf had concluded that the Kashmir border issue could not be solved by military means alone; negotiations should be opened to find a solution that would allow everyone to save face and silence the radical elements in Pakistan and Kashmir. Since Islamabad was also impressed by India's economic recovery since economic liberalization in 1991, the government also wished to explore economic cooperation and indeed intensified cooperation between all seven SAARC states: India, Pakistan, Nepal, Bhutan, Bangladesh, Sri Lanka and the Maldives. Benazir Bhutto had already suggested this strategy as Prime Minister during her second period of office (1993–6). However, as both her Ministry of Foreign Affairs and intelligence service, the Directorate for Inter-Services Intelligence, more commonly known as the ISI, opposed the separation of the Kashmir conflict from potential economic cooperation with India, she had to back down.

Musharraf's visit to India in July 2001 for what became known as the Agra summit should have been a first step in the improvement of bilateral relations. Pakistan was prepared for concessions and presumed that India's then Prime Minister, Atal Behari Vajpayee, would also seek to complete his political life's work with a Kashmir solution. But the error on Pakistan's side was to present Kashmir as the core issue of their visit, thereby making the success of the trip effectively predicated on success in resolving the Kashmir question. The entire composition of the Pakistan delegation looked tailored for such discussions. Because of this overt negotiation strategy, Vajpayee came under pressure from Indian hardliners and a solution was not forthcoming.

Islamabad however reduced its direct backing for insurgents in Kashmir, in support of a dialogue between both governments, which continued from 2003 till the terrorist attacks in Mumbai in November 2008, but with no solution to the Kashmir question. Also in 2008, immediately after his investiture as the new President of Pakistan, Asif Zardari sought once more to focus on trade promotion with India and the other SAARC states, leaving the solution of the Kashmir problem to later generations. Zardari was strongly criticised by nationalistic circles in Punjab and by extremist groups in Kashmir for his stance. They cited the fact that Pakistan's river system originates in Kashmir, and that even the nation's founder, Muhammad Ali Jinnah, had referred to Kashmir as Pakistan's jugular vein.

Indeed, water resources remain a geo-strategic issue to this day. The Indus is one of the longest rivers in the world, and its five eastern tributaries—the Jhelum, Chenab, Ravi, Beas and Sutlej—all play a significant role in the water conflict between India and Pakistan. The Jhelum originates from the Indian part of Kashmir, the Sutlej from Tibet, and the other three from the Indian Himalayan region. The Indus Waters Treaty of 1960 provides that India can only interfere with the two upper tributaries—the Jhelum and Chenab—by making "run of the river" projects which do not affect their water flow. Nevertheless, India has built two dams on the Chenab to generate electricity (Baglihar 450 MW, Sedal 690 MW), and three more on the Suru, Indus and Jhelum rivers. Pakistan remains concerned that any damming of rivers within India will deprive it of water for irrigation and hydro-power along its part of the Indus.

Against this background, the late Mr Majid Nizami, a veteran Muslim Leaguer and publisher of the well-established Pakistan daily *The Nation*, said in an interview in March 2008 that he did not rule out a possible deployment of nuclear weapons for the liberation of Kashmir. In reaction, articles appeared in India's newspapers warning of Pakistan's naive policy. The National Security Advisor in New Delhi, M. K. Narayanan, observed later that month that: "We have seen no change in ISI's attitude to mentor terror groups like Lashkar-e-Taiba and Jash-e-Mohammed... Attacks on India from Pakistan's soil are likely to continue."

Over the last three decades, there have been several proposed solutions to the Kashmir conflict—experts speak of over a dozen models, but none has proved successful. Today, many international observers are of the opinion that the Kashmir question can only be resolved by following the status quo, in which India controls about 50 percent, Pakistan 30 percent and China (with

Aksai Chin and another smaller area) about 20 percent of the former principality of Jammu and Kashmir. Whoever governs in New Delhi refuses any changes to the boundaries, except for minor border corrections, as to do otherwise would be politically suicidal; however, it is evident that Pakistan will not accept a status quo solution. Therefore the conflict drags on and on, guaranteeing continuing uncertainty in the region.

The other serious issue for the SAARC countries is China, their huge and powerful neighbour to the north-east. India in particular feels particularly threatened. It sees itself as being well on the way to becoming a world power but is confronted by the People's Republic which has already achieved that status. Territorial disputes between China and India also strain the bilateral relationship. The first altercation, known as the Sino-India border conflict, occurred in October 1962, when the People's Liberation Army (PLA) went on the offensive on two fronts, 1,000 km apart from each other. The western theatre was in the Aksai Chin area of Ladakh, which the PLA occupied within a month—a situation that still obtains to this day. The eastern theatre was centered on Sikkim and Arunachal Pradesh, where the PLA penetrated up to 48 km inside Indian territory, but later withdrew to 20 km, leaving a legacy of border patrols that still create tension between India and China decades later. On official Chinese maps, parts of Arunachal Pradesh are still shown as "Southern Tibet" and within Chinese territory. Altogether, China currently claims an area of 90,000 sq km; whereas India treats 38,000 sq km in Jammu and Kashmir as illegally occupied by China. Both parties have been in discussion about the issue for years but are no closer to a solution. China has been deliberately dragging its feet on resolution of the border dispute. It remains to be seen whether the Indian government of Prime Minister Narendra Modi, who has set himself the goal of a huge expansion in trade with China, can solve the border conflict.

China's other threatening area of expansion has been in the Tibet Autonomous Region. A railway line has been built from Lhasa to Qinghai, now being extended to the Indian border in Arunachal Pradesh. There are reports that China plans a second line from Qinghai to Lhasa, primarily dedicated to freight. Third, after expanding and developing the port of Gwadar in Pakistan, China is now studying plans to improve and expand a Gwadar–Karakoram-Kashgar freight corridor, which will pass through Gilgit–Baltistan or the parts of Azad Kashmir that India calls Pakistan-Occupied Kashmir (POK). In April 2015 the Chinese President Xi Jinping visited Pakistan and agreements for a Chinese—Pakistan—Economic—Corridor (CPEC) were signed, comprising road and railway infrastracture, energy infrastructure and trade zone agreements worth $45 billion. The CPEC leads from Kashgar in North-West China to the Pakistani port of Gwadar on the Arabian Sea. It is part of China's Silk Road initiative and seeks to deepen and broaden economic links between China and Pakistan.

China has also expanded its civil aviation infrastructure in Tibet with several new airports, making Tibet a hub for air traffic in western China. New Delhi is also worried about the military maneuvers being conducted by the PLA in Tibet. During the first China Great Maneuver "Stride" in 2009, the agency responsible for Tibet Military Region, Chengdu, was excluded; but in three maneuvers in 2010, two in Tibet and one in the military regions of Chengdu and Lanzhou, this was no longer the case. It is obvious that China cares little if anything for Indian sensibilities regarding Tibet.

China is also expanding its navy and extending its area of maritime operations. Since 1960, Beijing has argued that the name Indian Ocean is unjustified and indefensible. China's priority is to expand and secure its presence in the Indian Ocean, the Arabian Sea and in the Persian Gulf. It is anxious to attain port rights along the coasts of Burma, Malaysia, Bangladesh, Sri Lanka, Mauritius and even the Seychelles, and has been reasonably successful in seeking these objectives. China has obtained access to the ports of Sittwe in Burma and Chittagong in Bangladesh. In 2008, Beijing gave Sri Lanka US$1 billion for the development of the south coast port of Hambantota. In the same year, US assistance to Sri Lanka amounted to US$ 7.4 million, from Great Britain £1.25 million. In comparing these figures one appreciates why Colombo under the former Rajapaksa regime paid so little heed to Western criticism of its human rights violations of the Tamil population. Meanwhile, the Pakistani port of Gwadar, located on the Makran coast of Pakistan on the Arabian Sea, is now under Chinese management. From there, Chinese reconnaissance units monitor the passage of tankers through the Hormuz Strait and the movements of the Indian and US navies in the Indian Ocean.

India's response over the last four years to China's growing presence in Tibet has been to expand its own infrastructure in Arunachal Pradesh and double its military deployments there. Apart from in Arunachal Pradesh, Indian security experts also keep a watchful eye on the six north-east Indian states of Assam, Manipur, Meghalaya, Mizoram, Nagaland and Tripura. Since the mid 1950s, the ISI has cultivated and backed underground separatist organizations like the United Liberation Front of Assam (ULFA), the People's Liberation Army (PLA) and the National Liberation Front of Tripura

(NLFT), giving them money, weapons and training. Indian security agencies have noticed a decrease in ISI activities in the North East over the past two decades, but there is evidence that Chinese intelligence now supplies weapons to ULFA. Previously it had been losing ground, but has revived with Chinese assistance. Beijing's cover intervention in the region is thus the top priority for New Delhi's military and intelligence agencies.

On the other hand, China is closely monitoring India's new "Look East" policy, which while initiated by Prime Minister Narasimha Rao in the 1990s, has only really taken effect in the last three years. The trigger was the anxiety in India's political and military circles about "China's Threat Theory." In September 2010, the Defense Minister A. K. Antony called China's increasing assertiveness "a serious long-term threat", the then Prime Minister, Manmohan Singh, urged the Indian armed forces to strengthen the security of the country's borders and the country's military chiefs categorised China as a "long-term threat"—comparable to that from Pakistan.

In 2010 and 2011 Indian governmental and military missions visited Vietnam, Korea, Japan, the Philippines, Indonesia, Thailand and Singapore. An Indian naval flotilla also undertook a month long voyage to the Pacific, visiting Australia, Indonesia, Singapore and Vietnam. Delhi's political and military leadership are now employing tactics to counterbalance support for China's neighbours as a long-term defence strategy, raising its diplomatic profile in East Asia in an effort to stymie China's strategic advances, and fashioning a "Look East" policy in order to forge concrete military partnerships with its Asian partners.

India has invested special efforts in its relationship with Vietnam: for nearly twenty-five years projects over oil and gas exploration focused mainly on the mainland. But Hanoi has now signed contracts with India for exploration also in the South China Sea. Although these are for projects located in the alleged Vietnamese maritime zone, angry reactions from China were forthcoming. For example, the Chinese newspaper *Global Times* proposed the use of force to protect China's "core interests" in the South China Sea, though it is not clear whether this reflects the opinion of the Chinese government.

China is now in a strategic alliance with Pakistan, which is to some degree directed against India, as explained in Andrew Small's recent book, *The China-Pakistan Axis*. This alliance began with military assistance in 1966 and has evolved over the years: China is now Pakistan's largest supplier of arms and its third-largest trading partner. The military and nuclear sectors see the greatest cooperation: together they cooperate in producing armaments including fighter jets and guided missile frigates. China has also assisted Pakistan in developing the Chashma Plutonium Separation Plant located at Kunshab in Punjab. In February 2015 it was officially confirmed that Beijing is now involved in a further six new nuclear power projects in Pakistan.

China is also looking for trading partners for its increasing imports and exports: to the east it wants to develop a new land route through Burma; to the west a new land route through Pakistan to Gwadar. However, the western route runs through the unstable parts of Afghanistan and the restless province of Balochistan. The simmering insurgency there has lately been spearheaded by many of the young population who have lost confidence in the veteran political leadership of tribal chiefs and sardars. Groups from the lower middle classes became active in a political underground, especially the Balochistan Liberation Army (BLA). They targeted the Punjabis living and working in Balochistan (many of them doctors, academics and businessmen), who subsequently fled. They also targeted pipelines, power lines and transformer stations, and attempted assassinations and kidnappings of foreign experts working in the province, mainly the Chinese.

Beijing therefore withdrew most of their personnel from Balochistan, which has become the problem child of Pakistan's politics—as much as Karachi and the Federal Administrated Tribal Areas (FATA) are. To date, neither economic assistance from the Federal government nor measures by the security agencies have proved effective. The ISI has tried to infiltrate the various resistance groups and tacitly encouraged the elimination of their leadership cadres. Press reports of corpses discovered in gunny sacks, suggesting extra-judicial execution, are unambiguous in their intent, which is to intimidate the local population. The response has been fresh attacks on migrants and the state's economic infrastructure by the Baloch opposition.

Gwadar's importance lies in it providing the shortest connection between the Indian Ocean and western China, via Pakistan, Afghanistan and Central Asia. It was financed and constructed by China, which contributed 80 percent of the overall costs. Construction phase II was completed in 2008, after which Gwadar was operated by a subsidiary company of the Port of Singapore Authority until 2012. During this time only a few ships anchored, with little freight being handled as yet, given the ongoing instability in Afghanistan and the hinterland of Balochistan. However, Islamabad remains confident that ultimately it can pacify Balochistan.[3]

Gwadar has been operated since 2013 by the state-owned China Overseas Port Holding (COPH). Their land route plans to skirt Afghanistan and strike a strategic passage through Balochistan and the Karakoram Highway (KKH) to the old west Chinese town of Kashgar. There are currently several thousand Chinese engineers working in Pakistan, according to information from Beijing. The KKH is being upgraded to become winter-proof and there are plans for oil and gas pipelines along the highway. Pakistan's dreams of a working railway connection to China, parallel to the Karakoram, might be unrealistic due to the winter weather conditions in Karakoram. Gwadar is planned to be a free trade commercial zone. In this way, Gwadar might be developed and expanded until it becomes indeed a real gateway to Afghanistan, Central Asia and western China.

Ever since Afghanistan voted against the inclusion of Pakistan in the United Nations in 1948, there have been numerous latent political tensions between the two neighbours. There are also specific border issues, such as the Durand Line, namely the colonial era boundary between the two countries, which was never officially recognised or ratified by any government in Kabul.

In the wake of the Soviet invasion of December 1979, Afghanistan became the new faultline in the the Cold War. Thousands of mujahideen, who saw themselves as defenders of the Islamic faith and warriors for freedom, fought the godless invaders in a resistance campaign of guerrilla warfare, for which they received considerable material support from the United States, Saudi Arabia and Pakistan, initiated and controlled by the American CIA and its Pakistani partner, the ISI. This was one of the biggest and most successful covert operations in history, and was largely hidden from the world. Only in the latter phase of the war did more detailed reports become available, with pictures taken by mujahideen making their way into the world press: of shot-down helicopters, destroyed tanks, dead Russian soldiers and huge camps full of Afghan refugees.

Global press coverage continued after the withdrawal of Soviet troops from Afghanistan in February 1989. Media reports focused on the Afghan civil war of the 1990s, and then the rise of the Taliban in 1994–5. Articles were published explaining the background of these new Islamist fighters, followed by stories about their inability to govern the country, their religious beliefs, their treatment of women and their destruction of anything they deemed un-Islamic, such as the blowing up of the historic Buddha statues in the Bamiyan valley, which precipitated a universal outcry. Only a few reporters investigated the interests of external players in Afghanistan at the time, such as the Western oil companies who were planning a gas and oil pipeline from Central Asia via Afghanistan and Pakistan to the Arabian Sea.

On 11 August 1988, in Peshawar, Pakistan, seven men met to discuss the future course of the post-Soviet jihad in Afghanistan. There were four Egyptians, one Iraqi Kurd and two Saudis present, one of whom was Osama bin Laden.[4] The result of the three-day conclave was the formation of a new group, to be called al-Qaeda. At first it had only thirty fighters, but their numbers soon increased. They participated in attacks against the Najibullah regime in Afghanistan and in the unsuccessful storming of Jalalabad in March 1989.[5] For a long time al-Qaeda acted secretly, and at first accomplished little. Then in March 1997 bin Laden invited a team from the American TV station CNN for an interview in Afghanistan, during which he identified al-Qaeda as the initiator of terrorist attacks. They claimed responsibility for the attacks in Mogadishu in 1993, in Riyadh in 1995 and at the Khobar Towers housing complex in Saudi Arabia in 1996. Bin Laden declared war on the USA and the Saudi royal family in Riyadh, blaming them for the presence of US troops in Saudi Arabia after the First Gulf War of 1991.

Then in February 1998 bin Laden and six other people (two of whom were Pakistanis) issued a fatwa in the name of an International Islamic Front for Jihad against Jews and Crusaders, according to which every Muslim was obliged to kill Americans and their allies, both those in uniform and civilians. The justifications cited were the Gulf War of 1991, America's role in Israeli politics and the presence of US troops in Saudi Arabia.[6] On 28 February 1998 the London based Arabic newspaper *Al-Quds al-Arabi* published the fatwa, even though it was later dubbed invalid by noted Islamic scholars. On 7 August 1998 terrorist attacks were carried out on the US embassies in Nairobi (Kenya) and Dar es Salaam (Tanzania); the US retaliated by firing tomahawk cruise missiles at an al-Qaeda camp at Khost on the Afghan–Pakistan border. The subsequent developments are well-known, culminating in the terrorist attacks on New York in 2001, on 9/11.

The other major event of this era was the collapse of the Soviet Union, in December 1991, which precipitated a strategic reorientation between Pakistan and India. The latter decided to forge closer ties with the West, in particular by opting for a liberalised free market system and a nuclear energy pact with the US. New Delhi realised that the US would be leading the world of science and technology for many years to come, and that India must seek to profit from an opening to the West. The old friendship with Moscow was maintained in principle, but gradually new economic and trade, technology and security agreements were made with Western states.

For Pakistan, the end of the Cold War also precipitated a turning point. The United States chose to shun its long-time ally and treated Pakistan's nuclear armaments as a pretext for leaving the country to deal with its financial and development policy alone. Islamabad realised that without massive US aid, bankruptcy beckoned and was forced to seek financial help elsewhere, in particular from China, the emerging global power; that enduring friendship only became stronger.

India and Pakistan both carried out nuclear tests in 1998, which again brought South Asia into the focus of international attention, as other states in the international system realised that the previous non-proliferation policy had failed and they would have to deal with the new nuclear realities. The devastating attacks on the US embassies in Kenya and Tanzania in August 1998 and events of 9/11 finally made it clear that the cradle of this new terrorism was located in the Hindu Kush. In response, Pakistan's President, General Musharraf, had no alternative but to place his country on America's side in the fight against this ominous international threat.

The US launched its military action in October 2001 and ISAF troops arrived in Afghanistan from December 2001 onwards, with the result that Pakistan and Afghanistan were also besieged by the international media. In Islamabad, Peshawar and Kabul, hotel rooms were hard to come by and the simplest accommodation commanded exorbitant prices. Even when the invasion of reporters and politicians eased over time, Afghanistan and Pakistan remained a special focus of the world's press.

In Pakistan, the country's prime intelligence agency, the Inter-Services Intelligence (ISI), was particularly affected by such reporting. Its involvement in Kashmir and in Afghanistan from the beginning of the 1980s came under greater scrutiny and it was soon portrayed in journalistic shorthand as a state within a state—as an intelligence agency that was influencing and controlling Pakistan's domestic and international politics. Reports proliferated that the ISI did not shy away from kidnapping and liquidating individuals it considered undesirable.

Such assessments of the ISI might have been true in some cases, but they were also often circulated by politicians and journalists in Pakistan without any substantial proof, and then adopted unchecked and republished by their international colleagues. Another common statement was that within the ISI various groups existed which pursued their own political agendas. They were allegedly "out of control", even beyond the reach of the agency's own leadership, and were undermining official policy, harming the government's reputation and hindering the democratic development of the country. Since then, and to this day, politicians, journalists and analysts in Pakistan and elsewhere look to the ISI whenever there is a kidnapping, a killing or a major terrorist attack in the region. Even if no proof or connection to the ISI is revealed, suspicions of its involvement still remain.

The ISI also remained in the international spotlight through Pakistan's aforementioned entry into the alliance against international terrorism in late 2001, the return of the neo-Taliban in Afghanistan in 2004 and revelations of the transfer of nuclear technology to Pakistan by its nuclear weapons guru, Dr A Q Khan, in 2004. Terror outrages like that in Mumbai in November 2008 and the attacks on the Indian embassy in Kabul in 2007 and 2008 only added to the international interest. The climax was the killing of Osama bin Laden by American Navy Seals in a house in Pakistan's military cantonment town of Abbottabad in May 2011. The ISI thus remains a subject of frenzied and often ill-informed discussion, providing sufficient material for speculation, accusations and conspiracy theories of all kinds.

By contrast, India's equivalent to Pakistan's ISI, the Research and Analysis Wing (R&AW), acts as India's foreign intelligence service in the region and has attracted hardly any international attention. This was not from any lack of activity on its part, but rather because its consistent isolation from the press ensured the successful concealment of its structure, objectives and operations. The long friendship between New Delhi and Moscow rubbed off on India's intelligence agencies. In structure, R&AW is more similar to the KGB of the Soviet era than to Western intelligence services of the twenty-first century.[7] The country's journalists and authors know how much the quest for secrecy dominates thinking in Indian national security circles. In early 2007, the monthly magazine *FORCE* was declared to have compromised national security by publishing a photograph of the then Indian Army chief. In the opinion of the powers that be, the magazine was available to the public and so the enemy now knew what the Indian Army chief looked like. *FORCE* then published the following cautionary statement:

> Everyone can be arrested under the pretext of national security without charge and thrown into prison. There is no information on what is seen as a threat to national security, the whole concept is subjective and depends on the sentencing of the men in uniform.[8]

1

THE FIRST DECADE

The Historical Background

The ISI was established in 1948 and is generally described as a consequence of the first Pakistan–India war over Kashmir, when there were supposedly substantial reconnaissance gaps on the Pakistan side.[1] However, as shown during the course of the war, both sides were gathering inaccurate information. In any case, by the end of 1948 the front line in Kashmir ran approximately as it does today along the Line of Control (LoC), where units from both armies confront each other in perennially hostile mode. Pakistan's troops in the 1947–8 war were not as badly defeated as is often described in the published sources. Azad Kashmir[2] is on Pakistan's side of the LoC; and Pakistan also controls Baltistan and Gilgit, known as the Northern Areas, where on 3 November 1947 the Gilgit Scouts raised the Pakistan flag. Thus Pakistan had gained about a third of the former principality, a definite indication of military success. Further developments did not bring any substantial changes. Today, of the former princely state of Jammu and Kashmir, Pakistan controls about 32 percent, India with Jammu and Kashmir 48 percent, and China with Aksai Chin about 20 percent.

The traditional version of the creation of the ISI therefore needs to be reevaluated. Was its establishment only the result of perceived failings of military intelligence? Historians also refer to the "Great Game" of the colonial era between Great Britain and Russia,[3] which continued to some extent after the Second World War, when the former colonial powers were preoccupied in seeking intelligence and information about Central, South and West Asia. The creation of the ISI was therefore not only a consequence of the 1947–8 war over Kashmir but also a result of British political interests in the post-colonial region. This was spelled out in a letter from Sir Francis Mudie, Home Secretary during the British Raj and afterwards Governor of Sindh. Engaged in the service of Pakistan after Partition, he wrote to a friend in Lucknow:

> The facts of the situation are that Pakistan is situated between hostile—a very hostile—India on the one side and ... an expansionist and unscrupulous Russia [on the other]. As long as the relations between Pakistan and Britain are good and Pakistan remains in the Commonwealth an attack by Russia—and also I am inclined to believe an attack by India—on Pakistan brings in the UK and the USA on Pakistan's side.[4]

Stephen P. Cohen, a prominent American South Asia expert, wrote on the creation of the Pakistan Army as follows:

> One long range problem was clear to all of the military professionals who had studied the issue: Pakistan alone did not have the strategic depth or resources to withstand serious pressures from the northwest, although the immediacy of a Soviet threat had evaporated by 1948.[5]

Major General Walter Joseph Cawthorne

The founding father of the ISI is considered to be Walter Joseph Cawthorne, who headed the ISI from January to June 1948. The Indian ISI critic Bhure Lal wrote:

> Gen. Cawthorne developed the blueprint for the structure and functions of ISI, as of several other interservices organizations. He had opted to serve with the Pakistan Army after independence as Deputy Chief of Staff, with his headquarters in the Ministry of Defence in Karachi. He was a close confidant of Maj. Gen. Iskander Mirza, who was then serving as Defence Secretary, and Gen. (later Field Marshal) Ayub Khan, first Pakistani C-in-C of the Army. Gen. Cawthorne served as a liaison between the Ministry of Defence and the three Services Headquarters.[6]

The founding of the ISI reads similarly in this version by S. K. Ghosh, another Indian author:

> Whether the Australian born British Army officer called Major General Cawthorne, who opted to serve the newly formed state of Pakistan, was instrumental in the birth of the ISI is not known. What is certain is that he had the honour of drawing up the ISI's initial organisational structure.[7]

Indeed, the Melbourne-born Cawthorne was an experienced intelligence expert. The future Major General (Kt, CB, CIE, CBE) fought in the First

World War with Australian troops in Turkey (Gallipoli), France and Belgium. In 1919 he joined the British Indian Army and participated in fighting in the North-West Frontier Province against the Mohmand tribes in 1930 and 1935. During the Second World War he was Head of Middle East Intelligence Centre 1939–41; then Director of Intelligence, Indian Command 1941–5; and Deputy Director of Intelligence, South-East Asia Command 1943–5.

After Partition in 1947, Cawthorne opted for service in the new Pakistan Army; in 1951 he was promoted from Major General to Deputy Chief of Staff.[8] The future British Lt. Gen. Sir James Wilson described his former superior Cawthorne as follows:

> Douglas Gracey was fortunate to have as Deputy Chief of Staff Bill Cawthorne ... a brilliant staff officer with a flexible mind. He worked in Karachi, where he provided professional advice to Iskander Mirza and Liaquat, obtained their instructions and passed these to us in Rawalpindi ... Bill Cawthorne was a fine teacher, assuming always that one was more intelligent than I often appeared. I am grateful for what he taught me and also for the way he relied on me to keep Douglas Gracey briefed about Karachi affairs.[9]

Cawthorne remained connected with Pakistan even after leaving military service in 1951. After an interlude as Director of Joint Intelligence Bureau, Department of Defence, Australia he was posted as the first Australian High Commissioner in Karachi, 1954–8. His last posting was as High Commissioner in Ottawa, Canada, 1959–60. He died in 1970 in Australia.

The ISI's Leadership in the First Decade

Since Cawthorne, there has always been an Army professional heading the ISI as Director. His successors until the mid 1960s were brigadiers, appropriate for the modest size of the service and its manageable field of activities. One exception was from May 1951 to April 1953 when a colonel headed the ISI. At that time and until the end of the 1950s the norm was a two-year term of office. The first longer tenure was in October 1959 when Brigadier Riaz Hussain headed the ISI for over six years. The first two decades of ISI Directors were: Brigadier Syed Shahid Hamid (July 1948–June 1950), Brigadier Mirza Hamid Hussain (June 1950–May 1951), Colonel Muhammad Afzal Malik (May 1951–April 1953), Brigadier Syed Ghawas (April 1953–August 1955), Brigadier Sher Bahadur (August 1955–September 1957), Brigadier Muhammad Hayat (September 1957–October 1959), and Brigadier Riaz Hussain (October 1959–May 1966).

Structural Concepts 1948–1958

With the establishment of Pakistan's new armed forces, it became apparent how poorly they compared with India's. Cohen wrote as follows about the allocation of the military inventory between India and Pakistan:

> Pakistan received six armored regiments (to India's fourteen), eight artillery regiments (to India's forty), and eight infantry regiments (to India's twenty-one). Of the fixed installations, it received the Staff College, situated at Quetta; the Royal Indian Army Service Corps School (at Kakul); and a few other miscellaneous facilities, as well as several regimental training centres, important naval facilities at Karachi and Chittagong, and the obsolete defensive infrastructure of the Northwest Frontier.[10]

The initial plan was for an Army of 150,000 soldiers led by 4,000 officers, but only 2,500 were available. Directly after the proclamation of the new state, on 15 August 1947, there was only one Pakistani major general, two brigadiers and six colonels, as compared to the 13 generals, 40 brigadiers and 53 colonels that were required. The gap was partly filled by about 500 contracted British officers, of whom 355 were already in Pakistan and 129 were newly recruited from England.[11] Moreover the first two commanders of the new Army were British generals, Sir Francis Messervy and Sir Douglas Gracey. Only from January 1951 under Ayub Khan was the first Pakistani Commander-in-Chief (C-in-C) appointed.[12]

Cawthorne's composition of the ISI included not only military but also Muslim civilian personnel from the former Indian Intelligence Bureau. These civilian experts formed the backbone of the ISI in its early years.[13] The initial model for the structural design of the ISI was possibly the Iranian SAVAK, as Winchell describes:

> Created from the three branches of Pakistan's military, and modelled after Iran's intelligence service, the SAVAK, the ISI coordinates with the Army, Navy and Air Force intelligence units of Pakistan's military in the collection, analysis, and dissemination of military and non-military intelligence, focusing mainly on India. After receiving its training from the Central Intelligence Agency (CIA) and the French intelligence service, the SDECE, the ISI originally had no active role in conducting domestic intelligence collection activities, except in Pakistan Occupied Kashmir (POK) and Pakistan's Northern Areas (NA) of Gilgit and Baltistan.[14]

But in fact SAVAK was not set up until 1950 and the French SDECE till 1947, so neither can have been the actual model for the ISI. Instead Pakistan's military historians prefer to cite the British Secret Intelligence Service, MI6, as the blueprint for the ISI, partly because the first training and equipment assistance came from MI6 and from the CIA.

The initial tasks of the new agency were intelligence (reconnaissance) work outside Pakistan's borders in India and Kashmir. In addition, there were the planning and coordination of the first Pakistan Military Attachés for foreign postings. But internally, apart from the Northern Areas and Azad Kashmir, the ISI had no intelligence mandate.

2

THE ERA OF THE FIRST GENERALS, 1958–1971

The ISI and Ayub Khan

At the beginning of the 1950s, Pakistan had two agencies for external and internal intelligence: the ISI and the Intelligence Bureau (IB); in addition, the Army, Air Force and Navy had their own intelligence wings responsible for tactical intelligence. Formally the IB came under the Ministry of Interior and reported to them direct; whereas the ISI came under the Ministry of Defence but reported to the head of government. In reality, however, the Army chief (C-in-C) decided what information from ISI was passed on to the political leadership.

Altaf Gauhar, a member of the Prime Minister's Secretariat from 1957, wrote years later that Prime Minister Feroz Khan Noon (1957–8) was aware that some members of the military had conspiratorial contacts with various politicians. The Prime Minister actually had no way of counteracting this, since President Syed Iskander Ali Mirza, who was closely connected to the armed forces, and C-in-C General Ayub Khan, were already pursuing their own political agenda.[1] Ayub Khan later admitted spying on Prime Minister Feroz Noon, justifying it with his concerns about extending his service, due to expire in 1959. He explained more frankly to Altaf Gauhar: "The fellow was under the influence of his wife. He wanted to promote General Sher Ali. My boys were keeping tabs on him."[2]

President Syed Iskander Mirza proclaimed Martial Law on 7 October 1958, with the support of his C-in-C. The 1956 Constitution was suspended and Ayub Khan was appointed Chief Martial Law Administrator (CMLA) by Mirza. The people of West and East Pakistan accepted this development, because the majority saw the former politicians as corrupt and obstructing the development of the country. From the military leadership they expected political regeneration: the generals were considered to be patriotic, efficient and possessing political integrity.[3] However, the new leadership duo survived for only three weeks. The ambitious Ayub Khan was alert to signs that President Mirza was not content with just a representative role and was looking for allies in military, political and legal circles. The daily paper *Dawn* from Karachi quoted Mirza on 16 October 1958 as follows:

> I shall run Martial Law for the shortest duration possible... Then we shall have a national council of not more than twelve to fifteen persons, and run on that basis for some time, to clean up the country. Thirty or forty men of goodwill and experience would be asked to frame a constitution. The censorship would be lifted, and the constitutional debate would be in the open.[4]

President Mirza was not able to carry out his plans. Late in the evening of 27 October 1958 he was visited by three generals, forced to resign and then flown with his wife to Quetta in Balochistan on a freight airplane. Only the American Ambassador Langley and the Australian High Commissioner Cawthorne received permission from the new powers to bid farewell to Mirza at the airport. But for unknown reasons Cawthorne missed Mirza's departure flight.

On 2 November 1958 the Mirzas were brought back to Karachi and left immediately on a KLM flight for exile in London. It was here that Cawthorne saw the deposed President once again. This time only he and his colleague from Portugal were present at the airport. It is also known that Cawthorne had approached Ayub Khan seeking that his friend Iskander Mirza be treated humanely while under house arrest in Quetta. Years later Mirza's son Humayun wrote:

> During the early days of Pakistan, Major-General Sir Walter Cawthorne was Iskander Mirza's Deputy Chief of Staff at the Defence Ministry. His wisdom and good judgment were invaluable in building Pakistan's armed forces... After he left Pakistan's Service, he joined the Australian Diplomatic Service returning as Australian's High Commissioner. Both he and U.S. Ambassador Langley made repeated calls on Ayub and maintained pressure on him to ensure that no physical harm came to Iskander Mirza. Without their efforts, it is quite possible that the generals would have arranged a convenient accident to kill the unfortunate President.[5]

Iskander Mirza, who had been Governor General, 1955–6, and the first President of Pakistan, 1956–8, lived for a further ten years in South Kensington, London, in straitened circumstances. He was never to see his homeland again, and died on 13 November 1969.

At the beginning of Ayub Khan's time as C-in-C a covert action division was created in the ISI that was supposedly involved during the 1960s in supporting militant groups in northeast India and from the mid 1970s in helping insurgent Sikhs in the Indian Punjab. However, their prime task was the consolidation of the political situation at home. To achieve this, the reporting structure of the intelligence agencies was changed. Now MI reported to the Chief of General Staff (CGS), who forwarded what he judged as important information marked "Eyes Only" to Ayub Khan. The ISI and IB reported directly to the Martial Law Administrator.[6] Additionally, political and military opponents were kept under observation, a task undertaken by the ISI's Colonel Khawaja Muhammad Azhar. As acting ISI Director during the interim phase, Azhar often carried out interrogations personally, apparently to the satisfaction of his superiors. At the end of his military career he was a three-star general under Yahya Khan and afterwards became Governor of NWFP.

Internal political intelligence thus became a focus of activity for the ISI. The agencies became an early warning system for the political leadership and tried to surpass each other in their professional dedication. Those under observation were individuals, parties, organisations, universities and the press. The ISI was responsible for applying pressure and delivering warnings. Even the physical elimination of political opponents could be considered, as when Ayub Khan suggested such a solution for his political critic, Nawabzada Nasrullah Khan. However, ISI Director Brigadier Riaz Hussain (1959–66) managed to prevail upon the dictator to change his mind.[7]

But it was some years before the ISI would become the most important and most powerful secret service of the country. Ayub Khan still listened more to the IB and MI; the text of his diary published in 2007 mentions the ISI only once during a period of six years. These few references were overwhelmingly negative: on 21 May 1967 he accused the ISI of neglecting a conspiracy being hatched against him, after it was uncovered by the Karachi police: "DIG Tareen and his associates have done excellent job whilst on the naval intelligence and ISI were nearly asleep… it just shows that we are babes in intelligence network."[8]

Indeed, six naval officers led by Faiz Hussain had planned to assassinate Ayub Khan while he was on a fishing trip and assume power. After the coup they intended to appoint Maulana Maudoodi, founder of the Islamist Jamaat-e-Islami, as Minister of Law; Maulvi Farid to be Governor in West Pakistan; and General Azam as Governor in East Pakistan. These names indicate the conservative religious background of the coup plotters.

Ayub Khan's scepticism about local security was matched by his general distrust of his compatriots in East Pakistan; he also doubted the loyalty of the Bengali police officers in the Subsidiary Intelligence Bureau (SIB) in Dhaka. Therefore he decreed in 1960 that the collection of internal political intelligence in East Pakistan be transferred to the ISI. In this case the IB and ISI squared off against each other. In the run-up to the 1965 presidential elections, the IB gave "...a detailed assessment of his prospects in the election..." and ISI and MI "...kept him informed of the trend of public opinion based largely on gossip."[9] However, despite Ayub Khan being confirmed as President in January 1965, the close result of the election showed that all the services had underestimated the popularity of the opposition candidate Fatima Jinnah and had anticipated an overly optimistic result for Ayub Khan.

The next major political event was the war against India in 1965, which proved a real fiasco for MI and the ISI. The ISI joined the secret Kashmir cell in the Foreign Office to draft a plan for groups of armed men, disguised as freedom fighters, to infiltrate Kashmir and carry out a campaign of sabotage in the territories under Indian occupation.[10] This "Operation Gibraltar" was based on the likelihood of persuading the Kashmiris to launch a wider general rebellion against Indian rule. It was presented to a cabinet meeting of the Intelligence Committee in February 1965 by the ISI's Deputy Director, T. S. Jan. The President initially rejected it, saying: "Who authorised the Foreign Office and the ISI to draw up such a plan? All I asked them was to keep the situation in Kashmir under review. They can't force a campaign of military action on the Government."[11]

However, in May 1965 Ayub Khan agreed to an extended version of the plan called Operation Grand Slam, revised and adapted by the commander of XII Corps, General Akhtar Malik. At the end of July, at five different locations, groups of twenty to thirty infiltrators sneaked across the LoC into Indian-held Kashmir. The original Operation Gibraltar had begun. Then Operation Grand Slam swung into action, bringing additional deployment of larger units across the international border. But both operations proved to be disasters,[12] bringing only significant losses and no territorial gains.

MI had failed largely because of a technical fault. They were relying on the transmission of their radio program Voice of Kashmir, with propaganda material encouraging rebellion. After Voice of Kashmir experienced transmission problems, MI had to change over to the Azad Kashmir transmitter, which could be heard by the Indian side. The Indian reprisal was to present four arrested Pakistani army personnel on All India Radio, who revealed details of their orders. When MI director Brigadier Muhammad Irshad was informed, he expressed his shock with the words: "Oh my God, the bastards have spilt the beans."[13]

In comparison with MI, the ISI Director Brigadier Riaz Hussain had felt better prepared for Operation Gibraltar. His office possessed its own sophisticated equipment and well-trained personnel. Additionally, there were contacts, or rather agents, in Kashmir as well as in India itself, from whom he hoped to get a flood of information. However, after the operation was launched, the ISI found that their contacts had gone underground. The ISI had become blind politically as well as militarily and could not carry out any substantial intelligence work. Later on, in discussions with Ayub Khan, ISI Director Riaz Hussain is said to have justified their failure with the words: "All these years we were not doing our real work of counterintelligence, because we were too busy chasing your domestic political opponents."[14]

Thus the 1965 war over Kashmir was a total failure for the Pakistan intelligence services. More used to being involved in internal monitoring and shadowing their own politicians, they failed in enemy intelligence. The ISI and MI appeared unable to locate and pinpoint the movements of Indian troops. Later reports on the 1965 war often referred maliciously to the fact that the ISI had lost contact with a whole Indian division and could not determine where they were.

To get to the bottom of these shortcomings Ayub Khan set up a committee of inquiry headed by Yahya Khan. In the subsequent interviews GHQ tried to portray the IB in a bad light, thereby deflecting the errors and incompetence of the military services.[15] Yahya Khan also managed to include in the commission report a recommendation for the future appointment of an ISI and MI expert at local (district administration) level. This was a highly controversial demand which the civil servants of the commission and IB Director A. B. Awan rejected out of hand. President Ayub Khan then refused an increase in the military budget, which finally thwarted any plans for penetration of the local administration. The ISI had to be content with continuing to monitor those politicians and civil servants classified as undesirable.

President Yahya Khan 1969–1971

At the end of March 1969 the Ayub Khan era came to an end. His decline had begun with the unsuccessful 1965 War and the Tashkent Declaration on February 1966. The latter saw thousands of prisoners of war return home but the Kashmir question, at least for the Pakistani side, remained unresolved.

The last years of Ayub's rule were characterised by political unrest in West and East Pakistan. He had also become a sick man, after suffering a cardiac arrest in 1968. This prompted Ayub to agree to resign and return power to the army. On 25 March 1969 there was another Martial Law proclamation, with the new Chief Martial Law Administrator (CMLA) being the former C-in-C General Yahya Khan. In Pakistan's short history the military had taken over for a second time. A newly created National Security Council, headed by Yahya Khan himself, was set up to control the intelligence agencies. Together with the Information Ministry and the intelligence services, these formed the pillars of the new regime. However, the unfolding tragedy in the eastern part of the country would be misjudged by all.

The generals deemed that a balanced parliament seemed the best way to keep the politicians in check as they wished to avoid at all costs dominance by a single political party. So they authorised free elections countrywide at the end of 1970, which is still considered to be Yahya Khan's major legacy. To guide the elections in East Pakistan they allocated the sum of 29 lakh rupees[16] and Major General Ghulam Umar, the second highest ranking officer in the army hierarchy, was assigned to supervise the ISI's activities in East Pakistan. Additional to the ISI office in Dhaka, new bureaux were attached to the army regiments in Comilla, Chittagong, Mymensingh, Rajshahi, Pabna and Bagura, and to all other ISI offices in East Pakistan, all of which were staffed solely by West Pakistanis.

Aware of the growing influence of the secular-leaning Bengali Awami League, emphasis was placed on religion as the anchor for the country's unity. So the agency's priority became the support of the Islamist Jamaat-e-Islami (JI) in East Pakistan, a task that failed due to self-delusion and wishful thinking. This became clear in a report from the Dhaka office on 31 May 1970 when the Islamist parties celebrated the "Glory of Islam Day" with rallies. The headline of the corresponding situation reports from the ISI read: "Massive show on Shaukat-e-Islam Day by Muslims indicate their unflinching faith in Islamic cum Pakistan ideology."[17] The ensuing developments showed that this ideal of linking religious with political ideology was simply unrealistic. The ISI revised their predictions for JI downwards in the run-up to the election campaign, but they always believed in a final balanced result. The ISI's chief, Major General Muhammad Akbar Khan (1966–71), predicted the haggling of politicians after the elections, describing them as *"bandar bant"* (monkeys dividing the spoils).[18]

The final results of the December 1970 elections were a shock for the ISI. In the East Pakistan parliament Sheikh Mujibur Rahman's Awami League won 298 out of the 300 seats; the ISI supported Jamaat-e-Islami was left with the remaining two seats. Similarly in the National Assembly, the parliament of the country as a whole, the Awami League held the majority with 167 of the 313 seats. This should have been the signal for a transfer of power to the new leading party, or at least the provision of greater political autonomy for East Pakistan. But the majority of the military and political elite of West Pakistan could not accept this and showed callous arrogance towards their Bengali brothers. So ensued the tragedy of the 1971 Bangladesh War of Liberation, in which ISI agents were implicated in betraying Bengali academics and journalists and infiltrating the Awami League. Later, Altaf Gauhar was to write:

> General Akbar, who was the head of the ISI and with whom I had good relations when I was in service, requested me that I should introduce him to some Bengali academics and journalists... Had I given him any names they too [would] have been put on Rao Farman Ali's hit list of Bengali intellectuals.[19]

In their attempts to control political developments in East Pakistan, the ISI resorted to the harshest of means, including the assassination of prominent Bengali politicians.[20] Army intelligence failed to make a correct assessment of the situation, and senior generals offered poor leadership and decision-making.[21] Also, the ISI now had to confront a new adversary. In India, the Research & Analysis Wing (R&AW) had been created in 1968 and developments in East Pakistan, resulting in the creation of Bangladesh, was to be the first major success story for New Delhi's foreign intelligence agency.

Although the ISI was ill-informed about the political scene in East Pakistan, they were better primed on New Delhi's military intentions. As early as 6 September the ISI had forwarded copies of the Indian Chief of Staff General Sam Manekshaw's operational instructions, issued in mid August,[22] to the President, the three service chiefs and the Secretary for Defence; one month later they furnished precise information about the forthcoming invasion. Without a formal declaration of war, Indian troops crossed the border to support East Pakistan against the Pakistan Army in the first week in November; the main invasion with eight divisions took place on 21 November 1971. On

3 December the ISI was able to supply the military with a copy of the latest Indian combat instructions. However, this had little influence on the actual conduct of the war. Years later Zia's former Chief of Staff K. M. Arif wrote, "Notwithstanding the timely availability of strategic and technical level intelligence, there was something lacking in putting together of the Pakistani act."[23]

Yahya Khan's failings were not only in the military arena; it was said later that his capabilities were up to division commander level, equivalent to just a two-star general. His misfortune was that Ayub Khan exaggerated his abilities by making him first his C-in-C and at the end also CMLA. Khan also liked to drink, and was not averse to the company of attractive women. Nevertheless, the elections he instigated in December 1970 are still seen even today as the freest that Pakistan witnessed until 2008. Yahya Khan's real failure was his inability to accept the need for the political reforms deemed necessary by the election result. In March 1971 he ordered the first military operations in East Pakistan, in which thousands of Bengalis died. Then in December the Pakistan Army in Dhaka had to surrender to the encircling Indian Army, and 93,000 Pakistan soldiers were captured. For Yahya Khan the loss of East Pakistan meant the end of his Presidency.

In the ISI, however, the change had already taken place some months before. In June 1971 Major General Muhammad Akbar Khan was replaced by Major General Ghulam Jilani Khan.

Structural Changes in the Leadership and Activity Areas

After Cawthorne's leadership in 1948, the directorship of the ISI was generally held by a brigadier. The service was regarded as relatively small and compact. But after the failures of Operations Gibraltar and Grand Slam, it was felt that the ISI needed a stronger leadership. Even more so after the final loss of East Pakistan, the new President Zulfikar Ali Bhutto realised that the dejected military leadership needed a boost in self-confidence. So in the 1970s for the first time the ISI was headed by a three-star general. From 1966 up to the beginning of the Zia-ul-Haq era the ISI leaders were Maj. Gen. Muhammad Akbar Khan (May 1966–June 1971), Lt. Gen. Ghulam Jilani Khan[24] (June 1971–October 1977), and Maj. Gen. Muhammad Riaz Khan (October 1977–April 1979).

Over two decades the ISI's fields of activity had also expanded considerably. By the end of the Ayub Khan and Yahya Khan period they consisted of:

– collection of external information

– coordination of the secret work of all three armed services
– monitoring of their own military cadre
– observation of foreigners in the country
– monitoring of media and political groups
– diplomatic activities abroad
– collection of technical information
– execution of secret operations

However, in counter-espionage they still had little experience. The Soviet KGB had already succeeded in winning over informants both in the Foreign Office and in Pakistan's diplomatic corps to help them spy on foreign policy during Ayub Khan's era. The former KGB member Vasili Mitrokhin, who defected to England in 1992, reported there being a number of sources in Pakistani ministries and also among diplomats stationed abroad.

Among them were "Gnom", "Kuri", "Grem" and "Gulyam". Gnom provided diplomatic cables, photographed with a miniature camera. After returning to Pakistan in 1967 he broke contact with his controller. Kuri was a cipher clerk who provided information until the 1970s both from his posting in Washington and from the ministry itself. Grem was the most senior Pakistani diplomat, recruited in 1965. He later became an ambassador and provided valuable information. Gulyam was the only agent whose identity became known: he was Abu Sayid Hasan, recruited in 1966, who worked as Third Secretary at the High Commission in Bombay, Second Secretary in Saudi Arabia and Section Chief in the ministry's Administration department. One of the biggest KGB catches was the recruitment of "Ali", who held a senior position in the military communication centre in Rawalpindi. He was recruited in 1965 by G. M. Yersafyev, a KGB operation officer masquerading as a German radio engineer. Ali delivered classified information for ten years, though he soon realised for whom he was working. Overall, the main purpose of KGB activities during Ayub's time and after was to spread suspicion and mistrust of the United States.[25]

ISI and CIA: Intensified Cooperation

President Mirza had served as the first President of Pakistan from 1956, when the position of Governor General was replaced by that of President. Only two years later, a military coup was plotted against him. On 7 October 1958, three days before the anticipated putsch, Washington was informed that it was likely to go ahead. While the Americans saw no justification for such a step and advised against it they were unable or incapable of stopping the coup. Eisenhower and Dulles apparently understood why General Ayub Khan acted as he did. The 1950s and 1960s were overall a period of sound cooperation between the ISI and CIA as became evident when the American pilot Francis Powers was shot down over Soviet territory on 1 May 1960, after having taken off from Peshawar on his U-2 reconnaissance flight.

From then onwards, the bilateral relationship was fairly restrained during Kennedy's government (1961–3) and Johnson's (1963–8); but during the Nixon administration the cooperation between the CIA and ISI intensified. As documents in the public domain reveal, Nixon liked Yahya Khan, whereas on the other hand he referred to Indira Gandhi as an "old witch" in discussions with Kissinger. Kissinger's secret flight from Rawalpindi to Peking on 9 July 1971 was a masterpiece of cooperation between the CIA and ISI. The allegedly ill Secretary of State was able to fulfil his mission without attracting the attention of local journalists.

The CIA and ISI also cooperated in working against the Indira Gandhi government after she signed an agreement with Moscow on 7 August 1971 confirming peace, friendship and cooperation between India and the Soviet Union.[26] Articles 8 and 11 of the agreement included military cooperation and a common obligation for defence, in the case of a threat to the territorial integrity of either partner. Washington did not know the exact contents of the agreement, but they were concerned about the naval facilities offered to the Soviet fleet in Visakhapatnam (Andhra Pradesh) and the Andaman and Nicobar Islands.[27] On the other hand, India complained about the assistance of the ISI and CIA to secessionist groups in Punjab, in Kashmir, and their supporters in Europe and the USA campaigning against violations of human rights in India. Only after the murder of Prime Minister Indira Gandhi in 1984 did the joint CIA–ISI campaigns come to an end.

First Operations Against India

At the beginning of Ayub Khan's time, a covert action division was created in the ISI. During the 1960s it was involved in the support of local militant groups in north-east India, and from the mid 1970s it also helped insurgent Sikhs in Indian Punjab.[28]

As early as 1957 Indian sources had noted the beginning of the ISI's involvement in north-east India: Naga rebels were being provided with retreat and training facilities in the Chittagong Hill Tracts (CHT) in East Pakistan and also assistance with logistics. On their way there the Nagas had to cross the Burmese territory of the Chin Hills Special Division of Myanmar. Under pressure from New Delhi, the government in Rangoon despatched their army in 1962, which partially closed the route from 1965 onwards. From 1968 the ISI then used their contacts with Beijing and China's intelligence agencies to furnish training camps for the Nagas in Yunnan. Thereafter, the Nagas found support and training in southwestern China.

Another group who found shelter in East Pakistan were the rebels of the Mizo National Front (MNF) who from 1966 were fleeing from Indian Mizoram. They similarly established their headquarters in the Chittagong Hill Tracts (CHT) and were supported by the ISI. In December 1971 during the East Pakistan war an Indian Army command found the MNF headquarters abandoned. The Mizo leader Laldenga had set off with his supporters for Akyab in Burma (Arakan Division) from where the ISI brought them through Yangon to Karachi. Laldenga left Pakistan in 1975 and set off for Kabul, going through Peshawar and later to Geneva, where he began peace talks with the Indian government.

After the debacle of the 1965 war over Kashmir, the ISI began to strengthen its ties with the seccessionist Sikhs in Indian Punjab who were seeking autonomy. The new leader of the Sikh Homeland Movement was Charanjit Singh Pancha, appointed during his exile in London. His group were frustrated by the lack of support from the British government, so were open to new friends and backers just at the time they were first contacted by the ISI. Meanwhile in Indian Punjab the United Front Government, in office since 1967, was toppled and Dr Jagjit Singh Chauhan, a former cabinet minister, also moved to London in 1970. He succeeded in seizing the leadership of the Sikh Homeland Movement and renamed it the Khalistan Movement. The ISI was delighted by this development and invited Chauhan to Pakistan in 1971, where Yahya Khan portrayed him as the "Father of the Sikh Nation". In the same year Dr Chauhan also travelled to the US, where he was cordially received by Henry Kissinger and appeared on the television networks. In publicising India's alleged excesses offences in Punjab, Islamabad sought to counter Indian propaganda about human rights violations by Pakistan during the 1971 Bangladesh war. In this manner was the CIA-ISI cooperatiom cemented and for the next fifteen years New Delhi was confronted with a Sikh separatist insurgency in Punjab, which culminated in the assassination of Indira Gandhi after Operation Blue Star.

3

ZULFIKAR ALI BHUTTO, 1971–1977

As the 1971 war ended in defeat for West Pakistan, President Yahya Khan stepped down on 20 December 1971 due to civilian and military pressure. He proposed as his successor as President and CMLA Zulfikar Ali Bhutto, who had been Minister of Foreign Affairs in Ayub Khan's government, 1963–5. Bhutto had founded the Pakistan People's Party (PPP) in December 1967 and had competed successfully in the 1970 elections in West Pakistan. Bhutto also felt political guilt at the loss of East Pakistan, but now became the beneficiary of the situation. He remained President and CMLA until August 1973. With the introduction of the 1973 Constitution, Bhutto became Prime Minister.

Cherat—Army Combat School

At the end of the 1950s in Cherat, a hill station close to Peshawar in NWFP, the establishment and training of Pakistan's elite unit Special Service Group (SSG) began. The rationale behind its establishment was the danger of a Soviet occupation of Afghanistan and subsequently an attack on Pakistan, which the country could not have withstood with conventional means. With the support of the US, the Pakistani government decided to prepare for a guerrilla war. Under the umbrella of US military aid to Pakistan, CIA and US Special Forces specialists started to arrive. They helped their ISI friends train underground fighters who would resist the Soviets in the event of a Communist invasion of Pakistan. So Cherat became the centre for the elite

31

SSG brigade, which years later would boast an impressive roster of graduates. The columnist Ikram Sehgal writes:

> SSG prides itself in wearing the winged dagger and having the universal motto of Special Forces everywhere, "Who Dares Wins". Having done two SSG tenures, prime product General Pervez Musharraf is presently SSG's Colonel-in-Chief...among the instructors were Chuck Lord, Robert Buckley, Robert Dunn, Maj Murray, Lt Hicks, Sommers etc. Pakistani SSG officers travelled to Fort Bragg and/or Fort Benning for advanced training. Robert Dunn knew most of the SSG personnel by name, having spent almost his whole life in this area. Casey chose him to be CIA's Operations Chief for the Afghan War.[1]

The SSG officers were trained firstly to blend in with the population and build undercover structures; and then, step by step, to move into operational mode. To locate their initial positions and areas for deployment, small groups of officers received orders to explore clearly defined geographical areas. They examined the political views of the inhabitants, the economic and social conditions for a guerrilla war, the educational situation, the experience of local people in handling weapons, historical aspects and tribal traditions, as well as the infrastructure and topography of the areas in question. Lastly a plan had to be compiled on how resistance was to be organised. This ambitious training objective meant that all of Pakistan had to be mapped and researched.

After the Soviet Army invaded Afghanistan in 1979, the Cherat base was redesignated as a commando training camp. Of the former SSG officers, however, only thirty-five were placed under the command of the ISI in Afghanistan, where they played an important role in the battles of the 1980s and 1990s. They were not regarded as foreigners by the Afghans, and indeed worked hand in hand with them, and some of them remained there. These operatives had a global reach as they maintained contacts with jihadis in many countries.

Years later, when in 1998 the US compelled Benazir Bhutto's government to break off all contacts with the Taliban, this special ISI unit was dissolved. The cadres dispersed but still maintained contacts in the respective areas inside. There are voices in Pakistan that imply that the marginalisation of this special force has resulted in the ISI losing vital knowledge of what actually takes place in Afghanistan.

Focal Point Balochistan

Balochistan is the largest of Pakistan's four provinces in terms of area, and in 1972 it experienced separatist unrest again. Just as Ayub Khan had felt little confidence during the 1960s in the local personnel in the IB's offices in East

Pakistan, Bhutto felt the same about the IB bureau in Quetta. Thereafter the ISI assumed responsibility for monitoring the province.[2]

Between October and December 1972, gangs of *lashkars*, or tribal fighters, from the Marri, Mengal and Bizenjo tribes, supported by the local police troop, the Baluchistan Dehi Mahafiz (BDM),[3] clashed with 7,000 Jamoto people in Balochistan. The Marri–Bizenjo–Mengal government in Quetta had accused the tribes of Jamoto, Zehri and Bugti of siding with the central government, thereby behaving disloyally towards their own province. The conflicts were bitter, the mutual animosity being fueled by new laws regarding the mining of natural resources in the province, which the Balochis feared would be extracted from their homeland with all the benefits flowing to Punjab. More radical elements became active. In the irrigated parts of the province, the so-called Feeder Areas, the farms managed by non-Baloch settlers were set on fire. In February 1973 a large cache of weapons was found in the Iraqi embassy, destined for the Marri tribe.[4] Bhutto accused his opponents in Balochistan of having separatist intentions and dissolved the provincial parliament. Nawab Akbar Bugti, Chief of the Bugti tribes, was appointed governor, which the Marris and Mengals saw as a betrayal. They reacted with intensified rebellion, and in solidarity with them the North-West Frontier Province government also resigned.

In neighbouring Afghanistan these events were followed with great interest. The Durand Line was never recognised as the state border by Kabul and there were dreams of a greater Afghanistan which would include all of Pakistan's Pashtun areas. The rebellious groups in Balochistan were soon receiving covert assistance from Kabul. Bhutto could only settle the situation in Balochistan with the help of the Army, and so cooperation was forged between the ISI and SAVAK. Shah Reza Pahlevi was afraid of Balochi rebellions in the eastern part of his own country and provided Bhutto with economic aid, helicopters and pilots to repress the rebellion. ISI personnel went to Iran for coordination work, in which the CIA was also helpful. They were present both in Iran and in Pakistan and cooperated with the ISI as well as SAVAK. At the end of the conflict the Marri Chief, Khair Bakhsh Marri, and his fighters fled to Afghanistan into a decade-long exile. Many of them were trained there by KGB and KHAD experts in sabotage techniques and carried out attacks in their former homeland. Even in Balochistan, the population no longer felt in control. The phrase "Punjabi imperialism" was frequently used and even today is strongly ingrained in many Balochi and Pashtun minds.

The Birth of the Afghanistan Office

At the beginning of the Bhutto era the ISI was led by Major General Ghulam Jilani Khan, appointed by Yahya Khan. Jilani was an infantryman from the Frontier Force, a kind of active veteran. Sitting at the desk was not his thing; he loved to move among the people. Sudden and unannounced appearances were his typical style, and over a cup of tea he would listen to the concerns and opinions of interlocutors. Jilani had a successful ISI debut issuing reports on increased Indian troop movements in the Bengal border areas and dispatches about Soviet weapon supplies to India.[5] Like the Army, the ISI was also deeply demoralised at that time about the loss of East Pakistan.

Since the KGB and KHAD had taken care of the exiled Balochis in Afghanistan, the ISI was soon compelled to make a move in Pakistan. In particular, Naseerullah Khan Babar, Inspector General of the Frontier Constabulary in NWFP, pushed Bhutto into a more aggressive position against their neighbour. With the goal of preventing Afghan trouble-makers joining the Pashtuns in the borderlands, on Bhutto's instructions the ISI set up a 5,000-strong Afghan guerrilla troop, trained by Babar's people in NWFP. Among their first members were figures such as Gulbuddin Hekmatyar, Burhanuddin Rabbani and Ahmed Shah Masood, whose names would become world-famous in the 1990s.

One consequence of the Balochistan events was the creation of a Special Operations Bureau in the ISI in 1973, which later became the cradle of the legendary Afghanistan Office. The head of the new office was Colonel Syed Raza Ali, who later wrote as follows about his assignment:

> I was required to raise and simultaneously run an organization that was needed to advise the Government on the multiple facets of counter insurgency operations in Pakistan and to coordinate activities of various (different) elements of state power onto a given direction that was designed to initially contain and subsequently to eradicate the menace. That is how it all began. The first phase of the Afghan War was now on.[6]

The era of the ISI's actions in Afghanistan now began. A first large-scale operation in 1975 was the encouragement of a rebellion in the Panjshir valley. Though unsuccessful, Kabul realised it could ill afford to underestimate the Pakistan card. Raza Ali reported how the ISI had become aware of people like Hekmatyar, Rabbani, Khalis and Masud and used them for their own purposes:

> These individuals in their own right had commanded a level of influence in various colleges and universities of Afghanistan, particularly in Kabul. Their

rightist-cum-religious orientations and their opposition to Communism rule had brought them into direct conflict with the Government in power...They frequently crossed and recrossed the border into Afghanistan, where they organised an uprising that took place in Pansheer valley in 1975. This event shook Daud out of his slumber and mellowed him down to realise the gravity of the situation. He began to mend his fences with Pakistan. From that point onwards real politic and diplomacy took the front stage. Daud condescended to look into the issue of the Durand Line and to stop infiltrating terrorists from across the Pak-Afghan border into Pakistan.[7]

Meanwhile, in the Special Operations Bureau Colonel Syed Raza Ali had accomplished his assigned task to the satisfaction of the COAS and DG ISI. In 1977 he returned to the barracks as a brigadier. Two years later, the new CMLA Zia-ul-Haq recalled him. Espionage, sabotage and how to counter such tactics were once again in demand.

Zia-ul-Haq 1976–88

With the introduction of the 1973 Constitution, the new Army hierarchy retitled the Commander-in-Chief (C-in-C) as Chief of Army Staff (COAS). In February 1976 Mohammad Zia-ul-Haq was appointed COAS as successor to General Tikka Khan, which proved to be President Bhutto's fateful move. A later comment on his decision by Lieutenant General Chishti, an intermittently trusted friend of Zia, was that Zia was "the best sycophant to win over Mr Bhutto."[8]

Pakistani historians now maintain that the US as well as the ISI had endorsed the appointment of Zia in advance, and only the Chinese embassy had advised against it.[9] The American vote for Zia is explained by his time in Jordan; and in turn Zia's close cooperation with the CIA was a reason for the ISI leadership to opt for him. Zia's posting to Jordan was as a brigadier with his unit for two years, where it is said he was acted with great toughness against Palestinians opposing King Hussain. Raja Anwar wrote:

> When Bhutto became president he promoted Zia from Brigadier to Major General, after King Hussein of Jordan had put in a word for him. Had that not happened, Zia would probably have retired as a Brigadier. Zia, who was in Jordan in 1970 at the time of the Black September operations against the Palestinians, was believed to have taken part in the massacre on the orders of Hussain, in blatant violation of his charter of duties as an officer seconded to Jordan from the Pakistan army. Hussein had now returned the favour. It was a signal to Bhutto that Zia was the kind of man who would go to any length for him too.[10]

Years later, the ISI chief Jilani maintained that he had suggested to Bhutto that in appointing the next COAS he should consider the seniority list of the generals, where Zia-ul-Haq then stood in eighth place. All the top candidates on the list were suitable for the Army leadership post and bypassing them might lead to rumblings amid the higher officers' corps, which could prompt their resignation, according to tradition. When Bhutto directly asked Jilani about Zia-ul-Haq, he answered: "As compared to others, I do not really know him as a person, and therefore, it would not be fair to comment on him...the last time Zia and I had served together was when we were both captains in Kohat in 1950."[11]

However, there are still murmurs in Pakistan to the effect that the DG ISI had explicitly endorsed the appointment of Zia. It is indeed improbable that Jilani, as intelligence chief, did not have a dossier regarding Zia's time in Jordan and therefore had no detailed information about him. It is a reasonable assumption therefore that Jilani conferred with his CIA friends regarding the appointment of Zia. As a consequence, the reasoning that the ISI under Jilani tried to influence Bhutto's decisions in internal affairs is not far off the mark.

Internal Political Entanglements

The successful crushing of the Balochistan rebellion did not result in the political pacification of the whole country. In 1973 there was a conspiracy among younger officers of the Army and Air Force who blamed Bhutto and the generals for the loss of East Pakistan and their defeat by India. They succeeded in persuading a brigadier and a colonel to lead their plot but the ISI received well-timed information about the case, which came to be known as the Attock Conspiracy, and observed the group for months undercover until they struck. Major General Zia-ul-Haq headed the subsequent court martial and used the opportunity to inform Bhutto about the proceedings and to offer his services to him. The conspirators received life sentences; Bhutto and some generals demanded the death penalty but they did not get a court majority in favour of capital punishment.

The vast majority of the people, having given President Bhutto a convincing mandate in the 1970 elections in West Pakistan, fully supported Bhutto's internal and foreign policy. His high point in office was 1974; but then his despotic governmental style and a disappointing general performance meant that he became increasingly unpopular. Bhutto reacted in his own way. In 1975, through a directive from the Prime Minister's office, the ISI was boosted by the setting up of an internal political cell. The cell, already secretly installed by Ayub Khan, was now formally endorsed and expanded quickly. Bhutto then allowed the IB to furnish a parallel special cell, in order to be informed about tendencies and developments within the military, the IB cell to be headed by Colonel (retd.) Mukhtar. Its attempts to install a network of informers in the cantonments among former officers had little success. ISI and MI recognised what was up and relayed appropriate reports to the GHQ. The active officer corps was warned, which resulted in Mukhtar's people being mocked. With obvious satisfaction the brigadier heading the ISI Counter-Intelligence office (JCIB), Syed A. I. Tirmazi, later wrote this about Mukhtar's operation at the time of martial law (ML):

> When ML was declared, his office was sealed and then searched. Of course, they had no clue to things which were brewing up towards imposition of Martial Law but what other information his men had collected on some of the senior officers, provided a lot of amusement to those who read it. Mukhtar was the first person to be served with dismissal orders at his residence.[12]

By the time Zulfikar Bhutto had been in office for six years, elections were overdue and the ISI was well aware of it. The author Hussain Haqqani, who later served as advisor to two Prime Ministers and after 2008 was Pakistan's ambassador to the US, wrote about the situation at that time:

> In April 1976, soon after Zia-ul-Haq's appointment as army chief, the ISI prepared a position paper for Bhutto, recommending that he hold early elections and renew his mandate. In October, Lieutenant General Ghulam Jilani Khan, the ISI chief, sent another paper to the Prime Minister that spoke of him in glowing terms and repeated the proposal for holding elections.[13]

Bhutto agreed, still believing that the majority of the people were behind him. The intended date for the national parliament elections was set for 7 March 1977, and three days later the provincial parliaments would be selected. However, the results on the evening of 7 March gave the Prime Minister cause for concern. Of the 200 parliamentary seats, the PPP won 155 and the opposition Pakistan National Alliance (PNA) 36. Bhutto knew that such a result could only be the result of manipulations by an assiduous election bureaucracy and he treated the victory with mixed feelings. His question on the election evening as to why he was gifted with such a mandate is still quoted today within PPP circles.[14] His premonitions did not deceive him however.

The PNA opposition boycotted the provincial elections scheduled for 10 March 1977 and staged other rebellions. They demanded the resignation of the government, the appointment of a new electoral commission and new elections under the supervision of the legal authorities and Army; they backed their demands with continuous protests in the larger cities of the country.

The government meanwhile convinced itself that the opposition was being financed from abroad. Jilani later reported on how the Prime Minister and his Foreign Secretary Aziz Ahmad exerted pressure on the ISI and IB to uncover the flow of foreign funds. They lamented during a cabinet meeting "that the intelligence agencies had failed in anticipating foreign intervention... The intelligence agencies merely provided information, often out of date and without any analysis or forecast."[15] However, neither Jilani nor Rashid could furnish any proof of foreign funding; any such evidence had melted into thin air. They held the view that the PNA alliance was supported by Pakistan's commercial sector, and offered a reward for such evidence. Brigadier Tirmazi, chief of the Joint Counter-Intelligence Bureau in the ISI, who was responsible for the observation of internal affairs, was of a different opinion. He wrote ten years later in his memoirs: "Funds to JI and individually to the families of some of the leaders were coming in from foreign sources in a clandestine manner. Some businessmen and industrialists who had resented ZAB's nationalization polices also contributed funds to the movement."[16]

As a result of the continuing unrest, on 19 March 1977 DG ISI Jilani handed the Prime Minister another report proposing new elections. Jilani later claimed that he also advised the Prime Minister against proclaiming martial law as a tool against internal political unrest, for the reason "... that once the army comes in, it might hang around for a long time which would not be good for either side." He recommended instead "to resolve the issue through political dialogue."[17] However, Bhutto distrusted his ISI chief and ignoring his advice on 21 April 1977 proclaimed martial law in the troubled cities of Karachi, Hyderabad and Lahore. Just weeks later he had to withdraw his actions: on 9 June the Lahore High Court announced that the procedure was unconstitutional. As a result, 1,700 opposition supporters were released. The PNA later claimed that 200 of their followers had died, which further strengthened their resistance.

From now on the Prime Minister distrusted the ISI's reports relating to the opposition and instead listened to sycophants. His alternative measures in May 1977 included the closure of gambling houses, prohibition, the introduction of Jumma (Friday) as the day of rest, re-instalment of the Council of Islamic Ideology and the announcement of the introduction of the Sharia within six months, on the advice of Zia-ul-Haq. Bhutto later defended himself by saying that Zia had predicted these measures would usher in a truce in Pakistan's domestic political scene. In retrospect it seems that he may have had his first initial suspicions about the General's deceitfulness.

When he was later deposed by Zia and brought before the court, Bhutto insinuated a possible conspiracy had been hatched against him among the military leadership and the intelligence agencies. There is no conclusive proof for this, although the existence of such a conspiracy cannot be dismissed. Haqqani writes hypothetically:

> This conspiracy, if it existed, would have begun with the ISI proposal for an election, advanced through Pakistan National Alliance (PNA) agitation against the fairness of the election, and finished up with the overthrow of Bhutto in the July 1977 military coup d'état.[18]

Downfall of a Prime Minister

Jilani later maintained that in 1977 both he as ISI chief and Rao Abdul Rashid as IB chief together warned Bhutto of a *coup d'état* by the military:

> We met Mr. Bhutto together on 3 July and apprised him of our fears and assessments based on our observations and analysis. By then, there had also been reports of some opposition party leaders encouraging/conniving with the military for a possible take-over to end the agony. After listening to both of us, Mr. Bhutto, in our presence, spoke to each of the corps commanders on telephone individually. In a subtle manner, he enquired from them if all was well and whether anything unusual was happening! Mr. Bhutto was no wiser after the conversation and there ended the matter.[19]

Rao Abdul Rashid, Bhutto's secretary for many years and by this time head of the IB, might have had genuine fears of a military *coup d'état*. Whether Jilani also feared a military coup remains doubtful. Benazir Bhutto remembered the situation quite differently. According to her, Prime Minister Bhutto was warned by the chairman of the Joint Chief of Staff Committee (JCSC) General Sharif that Army General Zia-ul-Haq "...was up to no good, and might be planning some kind of coup." After receiving this warning, Bhutto called the DG ISI himself in order to obtain the truth about this information. Jilani "... showed his total ignorance of any such move or plan, and attributed General Sharif's warning to his alleged ill will toward General Zia; because General Sharif was not made the army chief."[20]

DG ISI Jilani's later statement that he first heard of Zia's *coup d'état* on the night of 5 July is therefore to be treated with scepticism. Zia had launched the coup in the early evening of 4 July. General Arif later wrote about that particular day:

> At 6:30 p.m. on 4 July 1977, Lieutenant-General F.A. Chishti and Major-General Riaz Muhammad arrived at my residence, unannounced, in a private car. Pleading urgency, they took me to the Army House. A relaxed Zia told us that the military contingency plan—Operation Fair Play—was to be implemented that night. "The government and the PNA have agreed to disagree," said General Zia, adding, "There is no light at the end of the negotiating tunnel. The corps commanders agree with my assessment.[21]

Lt. Gen. Faiz Ali Chisti, Commander of the X corps in Rawalpindi, with his personnel then arrested "almost all the leaders of the PNA as well as the Prime Minister and his closest PPP advisers and cabinet ministers."[22] Even if, as is stated in Pakistani military circles, for the seizure of power only one battalion is necessary, Lt. Gen. Ghulam Jilani would have been an inferior intelligence chief had he been unaware earlier of such an operation. Also, General Arif's reference hardly contributes to Jilani's removal as ISI chief after Zia's *coup d'état*. The new post of Secretary for Defence represented a key position and under no circumstances can it be considered as a dismissal. Besides, contradictory theories are in circulation regarding the timing of the DG ISI's transfer. While in published sources it is predominantly reckoned that the transfer took place after the coup, the ISI dates the change in the ISI's hierarchy to June 1973, still within Bhutto's time. This is unquestionably wrong and poses the question: what was their intention? The change of leadership in the agency is anyhow ineffectual as proof of the non-participation of the ISI leadership in the coup.

As counter-evidence, it can be proved that Zia-ul-Haq was warned of his forthcoming displacement by the DG ISI. For Bhutto, the attitude of his Army General concerning the unrest in internal affairs was no longer suspicious. He was determined to see a change in the Army hierarchy. His widow, Nusrat Bhutto, later expressed the same thoughts.[23] The renowned monthly magazine *Newsline* also wrote:

> It has now been confirmed in several published accounts of Bhutto's last days in power, that is was the then ISI Chief Major General Ghulam Jilani who tipped off General Zia that he was about to be removed. This precipitated the coup of July 5, 1977 that ousted Bhutto. Ironically only months earlier, General Jilani was involved in the prolonged negotiations between Bhutto and the opposition PNA movement.[24]

The ISI was also involved in Bhutto's fate after his toppling. Zia had authorised the agency to compile a report about the public's reaction to a conviction and execution. The agency employed two psychologists: one from GHQ, the other the Secretary for Education. Both specialists saw no dangers for the new ruling power, although the Army psychologist was of the opinion that Bhutto could be more dangerous dead than alive for Zia in the long term. The General remained unimpressed by the findings. He allowed Bhutto to go through a dubious appeal process and on 4 April 1979 he was hanged. Zia ignored all requests for clemency from foreign Heads of State and Prime Ministers.

The ISI was implicated in the verdict by applying pressure on witnesses and judges.[25] The former ISI chief Ghulam Jilani Khan was by then already Governor of Punjab at the time of Bhutto's execution. In Lahore, he also acted as a political talent scout and it was he who discovered the young Nawaz Sharif and recommended him to Zia as a potential candidate.

4

AN INTERIM BALANCE SHEET OF THIRTY YEARS, 1948–1977

If one were to imagine a balance sheet on the ISI at the end of Bhutto's era, then in its early years the service was seen as a small reconnaissance unit, "a low profile organisation with a strictly professional mandate."[1] Its role began to grow after the coup by Ayub Khan, who was determined to change the course of the new nation's history. In the 1950s the general allowed the establishment of a covert action division in the ISI, and the scope of the service's activities grew larger and more aggressive.

During Ayub Khan's tenure the ISI was also used for internal intelligence information, both in East and West Pakistan, a development which continued under Yahya Khan. The years of military rule showed that the ISI was already deeply involved in domestic politics. However, former COAS General Mirza Aslam Beg testified years later in June 1997 before the Supreme Court that only from 1995 onwards did the ISI become involved in internal affairs. Beg stated:

> ISI is an Inter Services Intelligence organisation created by the government of Pakistan and had been directly answerable/responsible to the three services through JCSC till 1975. In 1975, the then Prime Minister of Pakistan through an executive order, created a political cell within the organisation of the ISI, and by virtue of this change in the working of the ISI it came directly under the control of the Chief Executive, particularly on political matters, and for all the security matters concerning the armed forces, ISI reported to Joint Chiefs of Staff Committee. This status continues till today. ISI is virtually divided into two parts, one is the political wing and (the) other concerns matters relating

to counter and strategic intelligence of the armed forces. During the days of Zia martial law, the ISI was reporting in all matters to the president, who, by virtue of his office as chief martial law administrator and president of Pakistan, controlled its office.[2]

Beg's statement showed that the Internal Security wing within the ISI was officially created by Zulfikar Ali Bhutto. But in reality a political cell for the observation and manipulation of the internal political scene had already existed under Ayub and Yahya, and was diligently employed.

In Pakistani and international historiography today, the meddling of the ISI in internal politics in the 1950s-60s at the behest of the Army leadership is attributed predominantly to the political ignorance and power ambitions of the military. This point of view seems one-sided and does little justice to the actual history of the newly founded state. After the death of Mohammad Ali Jinnah in 1948 and the murder of Liaquat Ali Khan in 1951, no great political personality presented themselves for the next few years.[3] From 1951 to 1955 it was Ghulam Mohammad, a bureaucrat, who stood at the top of Pakistan's hierarchy as Governor-General. With no post of Prime Minister he tried to lead the country with the help of bureaucrats and officious politicians, but with little luck. There was no political culture with functioning parties and competitive programs, and the urgently needed constitution did not materialise. In the end, the enfeebled man had to be removed from his office through pressure. His successor Iskandar Mirza officiated as President after the introduction of the 1956 Constitution, yet he bypassed the Constitution by proclaiming martial law. As a former Defence Secretary and having personal contacts with parts of the military, he looked to them for support, primarily for the security and development of his own position and power. In 1956 Mirza appointed Ayub Khan as his Defence Minister while he was the serving C-in-C, thus voluntarily ceding political authority and accepting the Army's role in politics. Mirza basically sowed the seeds for the military coup against him two years later.

After January 1951, beginning with Ayub Khan, a Pakistani served as head of an Army, which was still being established. From the outset he was confronted with a political coup attempt, known as the Rawalpindi Conspiracy. This was uncovered by the IB and not the ISI, and included a major general, some brigadiers and colonels as well as a commander of the Air Force, all of whom were dissatisfied with the course of political developments since 1948. Army chief Ayub Khan was loyal towards the government; for the conspirators, the courts and dismissal from the military service awaited them.

In 1952 language riots broke out in East Pakistan. The Dhaka Parliament declared their Speaker insane. On 21 September 1958 his deputy was beaten to death in the Senate. In West Pakistan, anti-Ahmadi unrests led to the proclamation of Martial Law in Lahore in 1953. The Khan of Kalat, in Balochistan, declared the sovereignty of his principality, a threatening regional situation that could only be settled by the deployment of the Army. Such a development must have worried the generals, and triggered the need for better intelligence and information. From that point on, it was only a small step to involve the ISI in clearing up the internal political situation.

In the late 1960s, with Sheikh Mujibur Rahman in East Pakistan and Zulfikar Ali Bhutto in West Pakistan, influential political figures once again emerged, but they could not find a way to match their political ambitions with the interests of the state. The generals were not experienced in the ways of politics, and so they hung onto their political control as a form of national survival. They could not see beyond the threat of India, a powerful, unfriendly and hostile neighbour on their doorstep, and so deployed the ISI on both the external and the home front, as a necessary and legitimate step in the fight for Pakistan's existence.

Even under the subsequent democratic rule of Zulfikar Ali Bhutto, there was to be no U-turn for the ISI. The young Bhutto had studied international relations in the US, a subject in which he maintained a close interest throughout his political career. He understood the importance of a good foreign intelligence service. Consequently, he encouraged the ISI to adopt a strong profile in South Asia, as it implied getting a grasp on the region's intelligence. Additionally, the development of nuclear armaments, starting with procuring the necessary technology from abroad, gave a key role to the ISI.

The internal political role of the ISI also increased under Bhutto. On his directive, the Internal Security wing was formally created in the mid 1970s. Its task was the monitoring of the political opposition and his party colleagues. An insider at that time later said:

> Even his ministers' phones and offices were bugged, and their personal lives monitored, since Bhutto trusted no one and relished re-playing tapes in front of those who had fallen from grace.[4]

Thus, the Bhutto years were a time of intensive internal political deployment of the ISI, something PPP supporters often forget today. Bhutto also created the Federal Investigation Agency (FIA), intended to counter the ISI. Furthermore, distrusting both military and the police, Bhutto set up a paramilitary body, the Federal Security Force (FSF), which served him as a

Praetorian guard.[5] He had more confidence in the director of the FSF than the ISI chief.[6] On the other hand, it was Zulfikar Ali Bhutto who helped a demoralised secret service regain its self-confidence after the disaster of 1965 and the 1971–2 war. He did this by upgrading the position of the ISI head to that of a three-star general, increased the budget of the service substantially, and installed the Internal Security wing. The internal political conflicts in the mid-1970s created a boom for this new department. It could be seen as an irony of history that the ISI would not let down its benefactor; at the crucial juncture, the ISI's military officer corps remembered their origins and stood shoulder to shoulder with GHQ.

The developments in Afghanistan at the end of the 1970s ushered in a new era for the ISI. The FSF created by Bhutto had already been dissolved, but the ISI now became far more than just an intelligence service for the country.

5

THE ISI UNDER ZIA-UL-HAQ, 1977–1988

The End of the 1970s

General Zia-ul-Haq had no political power base except that of the Army, and therefore he required reliable information about political developments in Pakistan. A resurgent PPP had to be avoided at all costs, and so the intelligence services gained in importance. In the ISI the monitoring of the country's political scene was already a top priority during Bhutto's time, and the work of the Internal Security wing intensified under Brigadier Tirmazi and later Brigadier Imtiaz Ahmed. A leader of the Muslim League later described the ISI's commitment at this time as follows: "General Jilani spent a great deal of time hobnobbing with political leaders thus putting a whole generation of politicians in contact with the agency."[1]

According to ISI sources, Ghulam Jilani Khan was replaced in October 1977, though others say this occurred in March 1978. Irrespective of the actual date, his later appointments as Secretary for Defence and later Governor of Punjab indicate that he had the full confidence of Zia-ul-Haq: "Jilani remained one of the most trusted Zia lieutenants for a number of years, both as the DG and later as the governor of the Punjab."[2] The author could find no conclusive proof for the awkward rumours that persist even today in Pakistan that Jilani, in Lahore, pressured the judges during the Zulfikar Ali Bhutto case so that Zia could obtain the desired sentence. It can certainly be verified that, as Governor, Jilani became attentive towards the young Nawaz Sharif and groomed him as a new political candidate.

47

Jilani's successor in the ISI was Major General Muhammad Riaz Khan, who was previously Adjutant General in the Pakistan Army in GHQ. One source, M. K. Arif, reports that he pushed for Riaz to become Principal Staff Officer (PSO) and thus one of the closest daily assistants to Zia. This was rejected, apparently because Riaz had no experience in the functioning of a CMLA Secretariat.[3] However, he was considered qualified enough to take over the ISI. Riaz held this post for only one and a half years. Brigadier Syed A. I. Tirmazi, serving under him as Director of the Counter-Intelligence Bureau, wrote this about him: "He was religious minded, scrupulously honest, thoroughly professional and a committed soldier...a man of unimpeachable honesty and integrity."[4] DG ISI Muhammad Riaz Khan died of a cardiac arrest in the same year as Bhutto, 1979; however, his death was probably more merciful than that suffered by the former Prime Minister.

Riaz Khan's term of office fell during a time when Pakistan–US relations deteriorated sharply. Two days after Bhutto's execution the Carter administration began an attempt to halt Pakistan's nuclear activities and announced the discontinuation of foreign aid. The burning of the US Embassy in Islamabad in November 1979 marked a low point in relations.[5] However, despite the Embassy's destruction and the aid embargo, relations between the ISI and CIA remained amazingly constant and consistent: they knew each other intimately, and also the advantages of a mutual cooperation. This was not however the case for the entire ISI staff: in the late 1970s a majority of its officers had become strongly antipathetic towards the US, which they resented, though there was always a small pro-American group in place. More important than the ISI's attitude was the government's chosen course: this was increasingly against America during Bhutto's time, but more pragmatically steered by Zia. This explains how it was possible that, after the onset of the Iranian revolution in October 1978, and even before the Shah's downfall, the CIA moved its Near and Middle East operational control centre to Pakistan. They needed a replacement position for the electronic listening posts formerly stationed in Iran. Zia was approached and immediately recognised the opportunity it presented to his country and agreed to it. As a consequence, the CIA supplied electronic equipment and also trained ISI specialists, so that together they could eavesdrop on the Soviet Union.

Months before the invasion of Soviet troops in Afghanistan, in July 1979 President Carter had agreed to covert assistance to the Afghan resistance against the communist regime in Kabul. According to American information, it was mainly propaganda materials that were supplied, including copies of the

Koran. Initially, the Frontier Constabulary in NWFP was responsible for their distribution to the Afghan underground network. However, from late 1980 the ISI took over this task. At Brzezinski's suggestion, the CIA approved US$ 500 million for their Operation Cyclone; the aim was to destabilise the Soviet Union by promoting Islam in the Central Asian Republics. On the day of the Soviet Army's invasion of Afghanistan, national security advisor Zbigniew Brzezinski wrote to President Carter that: "we now have the opportunity to give the USSR their Viet Nam war."[6] According to one journalist, he said in 1998: "we did not force the Russians into intervention, but we have consciously increased the probability for it ... this secret operation was an excellent idea. The goal was to lure the Russians into the Afghan trap."[7] Just four days after the invasion by the Soviet Army, President Carter expanded the American program for Afghanistan: now weapons and ammunition were also to be procured and delivered.

The Afghanistan Option

Seen in Washington as a chance to make amends for the loss of face in Vietnam, a partnership of unprecedented scale between the CIA and ISI took place in the 1980s over Afghanistan. It was crucial for Zia that such cooperation would stabilise his authority. As a devout Muslim believer, Communist ideology was anathema to him. President Carter, hoping to improve bilateral relations, offered Zia in 1979 an initial US$400 million in military aid. This was rejected by Zia as "peanuts"; he knew that more money was likely to follow and indeed could be expected. In February 1980 Brzezinski came to Pakistan in order to discuss larger covert efforts in Afghanistan with Zia. This was agreed to and the US security advisor flew on to Riyadh where the Saudis consented to support dollar for dollar the American commitment to Afghanistan. For Pakistan, Zia's cooperation paid off. At the beginning of 1981 Ronald Reagan increased US military aid to US$3 billion and brought Zia-ul-Haq fully on board again.

Today, we know that in the two last years of the Carter administration the CIA was less convinced of success in Afghanistan. Senator Gordon J. Humphrey, Chairman of the Congressional Task Force on Afghanistan, later reported that the Agency had only reluctantly got involved in Afghanistan. Nevertheless, in May 1979 a CIA agent travelled to the border to one of the ISI's arranged meetings with Afghan resistance leaders, marking the beginning of a large undertaking. Zia himself was attending the meeting too, together with his confidant, Lieutenant General Akhtar Abdul Rehman, the DG ISI who now headed the agency from April 1979 until March 1987. Zia, who was from the armoured corps, and Rehman, a gunner, had developed a close and confidential working relationship which would continue for years.

The 1992 bestseller, *The Bear Trap*, written by Brigadier (retd.) Mohammad Yousaf, was the first substantial report on the ten-year guerrilla war in Afghanistan.[8] Yousaf writes that after the Soviet invasion Zia requested from the ISI chief a situation assessment report with particular consideration of the effects on Pakistan. In his analysis, Akhtar suggested that Pakistan should support the mujahideen. This would make them defenders of Islam and also, in a forward strategy, satisfy their own security requirements. Otherwise, a Soviet-controlled Afghanistan would sooner or later tempt Moscow to risk a march to the Indian Ocean. Just as Brzezinski did, so too did Akhtar Rehman believe that Afghanistan would become the graveyard of the Soviet Union. He urged Zia-ul-Haq to accept the guerrilla option. Zia had a similar view: three years after Brigadier Syed Raza Ali's transfer back to barracks, Zia recalled him, and in 1980 assigned him "to take over from the point where I had left off earlier."[9]

Later on Raza Ali gave an interesting description of the reactions in Pakistan to the Soviet invasion at that time; its originality merits this long quotation:

> Somewhere in the first half of January 1980 a high level conference was held in Islamabad, to look into the situation created by the Soviet invasion... Less the President (also the COAS) and the Foreign Minister, anyone else who mattered attended... The first speaker making his point by saying that "the Soviets have come, they have come to stay, they are a super power, they have never left a country which they have occupied." "It is only a matter of time before they will be sitting on our border," said the other speaker, "the game is over..." And so the debate went on and on.... "The Soviets will simply bulldoze their way through with their tanks. These rag tag groups of ill-equipped, ill-disciplined and disorganized bands of Afghan Mujahideen will not be able to resist the Soviet occupation. The game is over. We need to reassess our policy towards Afghanistan", said one of the speakers who was followed by others who conveyed similar messages... Only one lone voice spoke up against the general consensus: I said, "the game has only just begun...the longer the Soviets stay in Afghanistan the more serious will their problem become."[10]

Naturally, Zia consulted the heads of the military, the Foreign Office, the provincial governors and a number of other experts and counselors regarding the Afghan question. M. K. Arif later wrote that only few would have half-heartedly argued that Pakistan was "... too small and weak to challenge Moscow."[11] The majority was of the opinion that Pakistan or Iran was the real target of the Soviet invasion and it was better to defy the aggressor in the Afghan mountains.[12] General Arif, a four-star general and one of the closest colleagues of Zia-ul-Haq, gave a very glossy picture of events in the 1980s. Raza Ali's description regarding the first fearful reactions of the Pakistan elite seems to be more realistic. In any case, Zia decided upon the Afghan adventure: he saw the chance to stabilise and intensify Pakistan's relationship with the US and also become the champion of the Islamic world. His head of the Intelligence Service, who supported him in this strategy, later became the most powerful general in the Pakistan military.

The ISI Afghanistan Bureau

Contrary to Zia's suggestion to work out of the CMLA Office, Brigadier Raza Ali recalled the successful secrecy of the earlier years and the cooperative atmosphere under Ghulam Jilani Khan, and so opted for the ISI Directorate as his base. He wrote:

> Even though the President had desired that I should work from the Chief Martial Law Administrator (CMLA) Secretariat, yet for purely security, operational and protocol reasons alone I had opted to work from the ISI Directorate based on my pleasant experience of (earlier) working with General Ghulam Jilani Khan the DG ISI at that point in time, an experience that I cherish even today. Thus the Special Operations Bureau came to be housed in the ISI Directorate. It is now an integral part of that organisation (ISI) and has continued to be there ever since.[13]

Meanwhile the new head of ISI, Lieutenant General Akhtar Abdul Rehman, was one of the most interesting, most successful but also the most controversial of all ISI directors. Like Zia, Rehman also was originally a product of the Indian Army, having enlisted in 1946 and in early 1947 received his commission. He became an artillery man (gunner) and underwent training at Pakistan Military Staff College Quetta in 1957. He was an instructor and company chief at the Pakistan Military Academy Kakul 1961–4, and in the late 1960s as a colonel attended the Joint Services Staff College in England for one year. In 1973 he graduated from the Pakistan National Defence College (NDC).

Akhtar Rehman participated in all the military conflicts against India and proved to be a good officer. His career proceeded normally as far as the rank of colonel, and then it buckled. He was initially ignored in promotions to brigadier and also two- and three-star general. In *Silent Soldier*, his biographer Yousaf commented:

> this was partly due to his introspective nature, and refusal to cultivate "political" favours or seek out influential friendships. He did his job and he did it well, but often more than this was needed to ensure accelerated advancement... Akhtar was a difficult man to get to know well. He had a complex character with many facets. In his relations with his superiors he was a model of obedience and loyalty, but his handling of subordinates could at times be rough.[14]

In *The Bear Trap*, published one year later, Yousaf upgraded Akhtar's personality and wrote: "His success in reaching such high rank had been due to his energy, his boldness and his readiness to drive his command to its limits."[15] For Brigadier Tirmazi, heading counter-intelligence in the ISI under Akhtar Rehman, this was not enough. In seeking explanations for Akhtar's late promotions, he saw Akhtar as:

> a victim of professional jealousy... His professionalism paid him dividends as he ultimately attained the highest rank and appointment that Pakistan Army can offer. I have not known an officer who was more respected at the international level than General Akhtar.[16]

In discussions with the author, other contemporaries referred to his predeliction for sycophancy. They quote a letter written by Akhtar to Zia, assuring him of his continuous loyalty even without promotion. Its tone is said to have implied that even without his personal advancement he considered it an honour to serve under Zia. This fell on fertile ground with the CMLA. In June 1979 he appointed Akhtar Rehman, then serving in GHQ as Adjutant General, to head the ISI.

It was difficult for DG ISI Akhtar Rahman to have someone working in the midst of the ISI who did not report to him but to the President directly. He suggested to Raza Ali to report to Zia through him. Raza Ali clarifies today that due to his continuous travelling he had no choice but to agree with the suggestion. Often he was unable to obey Zia's call to report due to his absence. He trusted in his own competence, experience and his good reputation with the President. This explanation of how he lost his personal and official independence shows his frustration over a change that did not suit him personally:

> In the meantime the situation in Afghanistan was moving at a very fast pace. The need for briefing, updating and coordinating programs at the highest level was becoming imperative if not critical. General Akhtar Abdul Rahman who was overtly keen to act as the front man and take over the role of liaison between the President and the Special Operation Bureau (myself) was readily

available. On my part I remained committed to Jehad and concerned myself with the winning of the war. After all that was the assignment given to me by the President. "All well that ends well". This situation was amicably settled to the satisfaction of all concerned, but as time passed, interference, distortions and snags appeared in the working of the system. Being away from the center of gravity, it was not possible for me to update the President on the day to day progress of Jehad. Perforce under the circumstances the reins of command of the Operational Bureau gradually and (but) imperceptibly shifted from me to the General. With the passage of time this change became discernable and institutionalized.[17]

Akhtar Abdul Rehman built on this advantage. An incident at Quetta in 1983 eventually gave him the opportunity to replace Raza Ali as head of the Afghanistan Bureau. At the ISI Quetta base, three ISI men were charged with corruption for selling weapons to Afghans. All three were accused, transferred and sentenced. Raza Ali, reproached for neglecting his supervisory duties, was dismissed as Director of the Afghanistan Bureau, though he remained connected to it as a kind of Chief of Staff.

The new director selected by Akhtar was Brigadier Mohammad Yousaf, who later laconically wrote about the background to his appointment and new assignment:

> Later, I learned that it was the so-called Quetta incident that had resulted in that call being made. Some months before there had been a corruption scandal within the ISI, involving three Pakistani officers who had been arrested for accepting bribes from Mujahideen Commanders in exchange for the issue of extra weapons, well above their allocation. These arms would fetch high prices in the frontier areas of Pakistan. The officers were court-martialled and imprisoned, while the Brigadier, whose job I was to take, was moved sideways... I was answerable only to General Akhtar, he reported to the President—it was as simple as that.[18]

In October 1983 Yousaf took over an already well-established bureau which consisted of departments for Operations, Logistics and Psychological Warfare. Operations was headed by a colonel and was responsible for operational planning, including the selection of target objectives and which mujahideen groups would go launched in to the fray. The department was further responsible for the collection of all operational information and the combat training of the mujahideen. Logistics was similarly headed by a colonel and was responsible for the storage of weapons and ammunition as well as their distribution to the mujahideen. The Psychological Warfare department was run by a lieutenant colonel and controlled the operation of three radio sta-

tions, the printing of flyers and other propaganda and the broadcasting interviews and recordings.

The ISI Afghanistan Bureau had in total 60 officers, 100 JCOs and 300
NCOs.[19] They trained over 80,000 mujahideen through the 1980s and distributed thousands of tons of weapons and material. Officially Pakistan denied
giving material support to the Afghan resistance, but it was no secret either in
Kabul or Moscow that the mujahideen were trained on Pakistan soil and that
the supply channels ran through Pakistan.

The message to the US from Zia and Akhtar was that only the ISI was
responsible for the distribution of weapons and ammunition to the Afghans,
as direct contact between the Americans and the mujahideen commanders
was not to the Pakistanis' liking. So the ISI was in no way acting as junior
partners of the CIA; on the contrary, the ISI was leading the struggle for
Afghanistan in the 1980s. Their personnel planned the missions, trained the
mujahideen and often accompanied them in operations deep inside
Afghanistan. The latter had little or no direct contact with CIA personnel, but
this did not diminish the role of the US services. Apart from the financial
contribution of the US, estimated at US$3 billion plus, American specialists
offered training activities which made possible and successful the cooperation
between the ISI and the Afghan mujahideen.

Logistics and Corruption

The Afghanistan Bureau had its headquarters at Ojhri Camp, located in the
northern outskirts of Rawalpindi, 10 km. from Islamabad. Besides the educational and administration buildings, the 80 acre complex consisted of a mess
hall for 500 people, garages for 300 civilian vehicles, training sites, a school for
psychological warfare and, starting from 1986, also the training centre for the
famous "Stinger" ground to air rockets.

Ojhri also served as a transit camp for 70 percent of all of the weapons and
ammunition assigned to the mujahideen. Besides the Ojhri camp, weapons
and ammunition were channelled to the mujahideen through other bases: a
White Paper published in Kabul in 1986 listed 16 weapon and ammunition
depots as well as 67 camps for military equipment and supplies on Pakistan
soil.[20] The logistics of supplying weapons, ammunition and equipment on
such a huge scale was an enormous challenge to the organizational abilities,
commitment and honesty of all those involved. The Quetta incident had

revealed the problems of corruption, which were difficult to dispel. Such rumours persisted, some funds did disappear and 15–40 percent of the weapons intended for the mujahideen never left Pakistan.

In Washington, in mid 1986, it was ascertained that:

> In Afghanistan the US cash flow exceed those for all other covert actions. Since 1979, commencing before the Soviet invasion at the end of the year, a billion dollars were already imparted to the rebels secretly. Informed observers say that 30 or more percent of the assistance were stolen on the transportation routes which run through Pakistan.[21]

In his written accounts, Brigadier Yousaf takes personal credit for having established the supply procedures for weapon logistics. Initially, weapons and ammunition were given directly to the commanders of roughly 300 resistance groups, but from 1984, in order to stabilise control and influence over these disparate fighters, supplies were given only to those who belonged to an alliance of seven parties, cobbled together with the assistance of the ISI. Each mujahideen commander was therefore forced to be affiliated and subject to one particular party.

Within the alliance there existed two camps: a fundamentalist one for religious zealots and a conservative one for monarchist and civil-liberal forces. The first group included Hezb-i-Islami (Islamic party I) under Hekmatyar; Hezb-i-Islami Chalees (Islamic Party II)[22] under Yunnus Khalis; Jamiat-e-Islami Afghanistan (Islamic Society Afghanistan) under Burhanuddin Rabbani; and Edehad-i-Islami Mujadin Afghanistan (Islamic Liberation Organization) under Rassul Sayyaf. The second group included Mahaze Melli Wa Islami Afghanistan (National Islamic Front) under Said Ahmad Gailani; Jabhai-e-Nedjate Melli Afghanistan (National Liberation Front) under Sebghatullah Mujaddadi; and Hezb-e-Harakat Enqelab-e-Islami Afghanistan (Party of the Islamic Revolution) under Maulvi Mohammad Nabi.

Corruption continued despite the new system. Late in 1987 the Western press revealed the commander of a party who sold weapons that were assigned to him, thereby becoming a millionaire. It was known that another group sold six truckloads of rockets for multiple rocket launchers to Iran. The distribution chain from production through to the deployment of the weapons offered many profitable opportunities. A publication from East Berlin in 1988 lists types and manufacturers of the weapons which were used in Afghanistan.[23] It is ironic that the 100-page East German study does not mention the weapons from Eastern manufacturers, such as the rocket launchers from China, the Czech machine guns, or the famous Russian Kalashnikovs. In fact the CIA purchased weapons and ammunition according to availability and price, including from non-Western countries like China, Turkey, Egypt and Israel. Friendly intelligence agencies helped to procure Soviet-produced weapons to conceal the Western commitment in Afghanistan.

The Egyptian President, Anwar Sadat, revealed in an NBC interview two weeks before his death: "The first moment the Afghan incident took place, the US contacted me here and the transport of armaments to the Afghans started from Cairo on US planes."[24] Egypt supplied Soviet Kalashnikovs and anti-tank missiles; in exchange they received the most modern air defense rockets from the US. Shortly afterwards, Afghan fighters were also trained in Egypt. The People's Republic of China, unhappy with Moscow's show of power in Afghanistan, likewise supplied weapons; the Chinese military even came to Pakistan in order to train Afghan fighters.

It was a missed opportunity that the Stinger rockets were only deployed in later years, due to the hesitancy of both Pakistan and the US. Ronald Reagan had already mentioned in his 1981 election campaign that "those shoulder-launched, heat-seeking missiles" should be supplied to the Afghan rebels.[25] The Stinger system had been operational since 1982 in the hands of select US units, but first came to Pakistan only in 1986. Washington had feared that the weapon system might fall into hostile hands and be used against their own aircraft, and they therefore lost their headstart in technical research and development.[26] Zia-ul-Haq in Rawalpindi was also fearful that the Stingers might be used against his own airplane, recalling two unsuccessful attempts on his life by the Al-Zulfikar group.

1987: Departure of Akhtar Rehman and Yousaf

By March 1987 the ISI had seen seven years under Akhtar Abdul Rehman and was ready for a change. Akhtar obtained his fourth star and became Chairman of the Joint Chiefs of Staff Committee (CJCSC). But why did Zia jettison his closest confidant and move him to the higher, yet powerless, post of CJCSC before victory was secured in Afghanistan? According to one view it was simply the right time for a change in the ISI. The Afghanistan victory was in sight and Akhtar had earned his fourth star. Also, Zia wanted to have a familiar face in the vacant post of CJCSC. Another opinion suggests that the ever distrustful Zia no longer had faith in Akhtar and transferred him before the likely triumph in Afghanistan would make him more powerful. A third explanation is that over the years Akhtar was involved in an enormous scale in financial corruption which was too much even for Zia to stomach, who was not innocent in this regard himself. This version relates to the considerable fortunes amassed by relatives of both generals and questions the source of their wealth.

According to Brigadier Yousaf, US pressure was the reason for Akhtar's transfer. Washington was extremely concerned that a fundamentalist regime might one day take power in Kabul, similar to what happened in Iran, with all the attendant consquences for the Americans. In their eyes, DG ISI Akhtar's many years of close cooperation with people like Hekmatyar made him suspect in their eyes. His well-known and oft-stated ambition to pray at the largest mosque in Kabul after the retreat of the Soviet army prompted further American distrust. Their doubts overlapped with Zia's paranoia. He had no wish to share the imminent triumph in Afghanistan and felt that the time had come to push aside his closest colleague. For two weeks the new CJCSC endeavoured to maintain responsibility for the Afghanistan operation and bring it within his new domain. But Zia refused. In Yousaf's words, Akhtar "... was being kicked upstairs to a sinecure ... to a job that carried little authority or influence."[27]

All four interpretations are to some extent valid. Relations between the CIA and ISI, despite their many years of co-operation, were at times strained, with distrust and opposing assessments of situations often a part of the daily agenda. The Americans never deviated from their opinion that the fair distribution of equipment and ammunition and clear selection of operational goals directly assigned to individual commanders would result in more effective control and influence. Moreover their endless complaints about corruption became ever more irritating to the ISI. Akhtar could not be brought to heel on the issue and set his own independent course. So from Washington's point of view and also that of CIA in Langley, Akhtar's time had come to an end. According to Yousaf, the American Ambassador's protest against Akhtar's transfer was merely a formality.

Brigadier Yousaf's observations were made close to the end of his career. On 27 April 1987 the Army Promotion Board bypassed his promotion to a two-star general. The explanation in his memoirs is that his work and services were not acknowledged because of the necessary secrecy of the Afghanistan undertaking. He must have seen it as an irony of fate that on 27 April the USSR ambassador in Islamabad protested to the Minister of Foreign Affairs, Sahibzada Yaqub Khan, threatening tough consequences from Moscow against Pakistan in the case of further attacks by Afghan mujahideen on Soviet territory. In his memoirs he writes how for three years ISI-trained guerrillas crossed the Amu River, which marked the international border, and penetrated 25 km into the Soviet Union where they carried out various acts of sabotage. Propaganda about Soviet excesses against the local Uzbek population, as well as thousands of copies of the Koran, were distributed under the cover of psychological warfare to the Uzbekistan and Tajikistan underground from 1985. Bomb attacks were carried out on bridges, roads around the Soviet frontier were sporadically mined, and Russian patrols were lured into ambushes. During 1986 two guerrilla groups carried out rocket attacks on hydro-electric power stations using rocket-launchers from China and Egypt.[28]

Inspiration for such ventures had come from the personal intervention of CIA chief William Casey; he was convinced "that stirring up trouble in this region would be certain to give the Russian bear a bellyache. He suggested to General Akhtar that a start could be made by smuggling written propaganda material across, to be followed by arms to encourage local uprisings."[29] Both the ISI Director and his Afghanistan Bureau chief shared the same opinion but followed Zia's instructions "not to overcook the Afghanistan kettle." A particularly spectacular attack was carried out in December 1986 when a three-man group attacked a fuel camp in Nizhniy Pyandzh. The CIA station controller in Islamabad warned their ISI partners not to let the situation escalate any further, and Prime Minister Junejo ordered the new DG ISI, Hamid Gul, to end all activities beyond the Amu River.

As CJCSC, Akhtar had no more influence on Yousaf's promotion, and Zia obviously had no interest in bestowing any special acknowledgment on him. Yousaf must have been deeply disappointed. He resisted the pressure from his former boss to remain in the ISI and left the Army on 8 August 1987. In *The Bear Trap* he justified his retirement, saying it was his intention to return to Afghanistan as a civilian and to continue fighting for the common cause. According to his own account, after a stay in Peshawar he once again crossed the border in 1992, a flying visit probably made for research purposes. Yousaf moved with his family to Karachi and in 1991 wrote *Silent Soldier*, a book replete with lavish praise of the Mujahideen and Akhtar. In Rawalpindi and Islamabad the rumour is that the book was commissioned by the Akhtar family, since it is dedicated to the memory of the father and their wider reputation. But it did not satisfy their aspirations and was therefore followed up by *The Bear Trap*, this time co-authored with Mark Adkin.

Yousaf's predecessor in the Afghanistan Bureau, Syed Raza Ali, commented on Yousaf's separation from the ISI and the Army as follows: "I saw it as my duty to carry on. Why did Yousaf go, if he was so committed to the cause, as he is telling us in his book?"[30] Raza Ali remained as Chief of Staff in the ISI's Afghanistan Bureau, but no further promotion materialised. Today he lives as a pensioner in Rawalpindi, working on his memoirs.

6

TURBULENCE AT THE END OF THE 1980s

From Akhtar Rahman to Hamid Gul

The new ISI head to succeed Akhtar Rahman was Major General Hamid Gul. He came from the armoured division and, as former director of MI, was accustomed to the work of military intelligence services. Among his close personal contacts were the American Ambassador Arnold Raphel and CIA station chief Milton Bearden. Those ISI personnel who had felt sidelined or unfairly treated by Akhtar Rahman, or for whom promotions were unattainable, hoped for a new broom in the service. And indeed everything was to change under the new ISI head.

Replacing Akhtar Rahman, Hamid Gul became the second ISI maestro in the Afghanistan circle. Gul was a Pashtun whose family had migrated to Punjab at the end of the nineteenth century, where his grandfather, who had served in the British Indian Army, was granted a plot of land close to Lahore. Hamid Gul attended two Christian schools in Lahore and joined the Pakistan Army in 1956, which he was to serve for a total of thirty-six years. He was selected as DG ISI by Prime Minister Junejo from a panel selected by the GHQ. Zia-ul-Haq had no objection to the appointment of Gul. These days the ISI chief is described by former comrades as different from other military men, reference being made to his intelligence, conceptual and analytical ability as well as his zest for action. However, his political preoccupation and his unrealistic conception of the world also get a mention; his analyses were not always immune to wishful thinking, and he was ambitious and sometimes stubborn, but always loyal. Never hiding his own opinions, he was a Pashtun polished by the army who often thought like a Pashtun.[1] However, some former comrades have a different opinion: that Gul was Pashtun in name only, and failed to pick up more than a few words of Pashto.

In Afghanistan, Gul maintained the ISI's cooperation with Gulbuddin Hekmatyar, though he later professed that he respected Ahmed Shah Masud more and endeavoured to give him the same support as Hekmatyar.[2] According to Yousaf, the former ISI agent in Afghanistan, Hamid Gul's tenure began with a series of spectacular errors, though he regarded the wider circumstances, rather than the general himself, as being responsible. Yousaf assessed the ending of guerrilla attacks in the Amu Darya river region as mistakes, since Gorbachev's Soviet Union was already in no position to opt for outright war against Pakistan. DG ISI Akhtar would have seen it this way too and therefore allowed the actions to run their course, albeit on a small scale. The Afghanistan Bureau within the ISI was, according to Yousaf:

> ...the only military headquarters in over 40 years to have planned and coordinated military operations inside the communist superpower. The great majority were successful; they wounded the bear and they proved the effectiveness of well led guerrilla attacks to be out of all proportions to their size.[3]

Gul's decision to return to the system of distributing weapons to individual Afghan commanders was also seen as mistaken by Yousaf. It resulted in disruption of the logistics system and a loss of political control over the seven parties' alliance. Yousaf attributed the responsibility for this reorganization to pressure from Washington. The US did not believe in the long-term survival of the Najibullah regime and was horrified at the possibility of people like Yunnus Khalis, Rasul Sayyaf, Burhanuddin Rabbani or Gulbuddin Hekmatyar becoming the future leaders in Kabul. They favoured the return of the former king Zahir Shah from his exile in Rome to Afghanistan as head of a reconciliation government with the cooperation of Najibullah, a plan which met with vehement rejection from the Mujahideen commanders. The fact that both the Pakistan political and military leaders were of the same opinion as the Mujahideen leaders is one of Afghanistan's tragedies.

The Ojhri Camp Catastrophe

One year after taking over the ISI, Major General Hamid Gul was confronted with a catastrophe when in April 1988 the Ojhri Camp went up in flames. According to Pakistan's version, the new logistics system was experiencing a backlog of deliveries to the individual Afghan commanders, which explained why the camp was bursting to the seams with supplies. Rockets, bombs, mountains of ammunition, anti-tank mines and Stinger rockets went up in flames, generating an impromptu firework display that lasted for three whole days, something that had never been experienced Pakistan before.[4] The official statistics claimed that 100 people died and 1,000 were injured, although there was probably a higher number of victims. The ISI lost five of its men and up to thirty were hurt.

The disaster generated an intense blame game in Pakistan with many hard questions being asked. The then Prime Minister, Muhammed Khan Junejo, and other politicians picked on Generals Akhtar and Gul. In self-defense, the Army accused the ISI of incompetence. Akhtar Rehman, who had selected the Ojhri site and who had been responsible for the camp for seven years, was questioned as to why he had allowed huge quantities of explosives to be stored in close proximity to civilian residential areas over such a long period of time. The former DG ISI, then CJCSC and a four-star general, must have feared for his reputation and position.

President Zia, being both COAS and Army chief, was fully aware of the existence of Ojhri for many years and had visited the camp several times, and therefore had no choice but to stand by Akhtar and the ISI. A Commission of Inquiry, under the leadership of Lieutenant General Imranullah Khan, Corps Commander of Rawalpindi, was obviously overworked or short-staffed because their report was never published. The end of the affair was marked by the dismissal of Prime Minister Junejo in May 1988, for being far too sharp in his criticism of the Ojhri camp debacle and of the presiding generals.[5] His dismissal represented merely the climax of a period of distrust and political enmity between Junejo and Akhtar Rehman; as DG ISI the latter had already spoken against the Prime Minister in the President's presence.[6]

In the debate over the main cause of the Ojhri disaster, the two theories of deliberate sabotage and an accidental conflagration both have their partisans, with both sides offering good supporting arguments. The accident theory relies on the possibility of spontaneous ignition of live rockets supplied by Egypt. Contrary to transport and storage regulations, the fuses were inadvertently not disabled. In addition, there was initially not enough fire-fighting done; everyone concentrated first on the casualties instead of containing the fire. The sabotage theory is based on the fact that the rockets were supplied in a non-disabled state. Potential saboteurs would have known that temperatures in Pakistan from April onwards would be high enough for spontaneous combustion. Potential culprits for this theory are the Russian, Afghan, Indian or American intelligence agencies, who supposedly worked together with the terrorist group Al-Zulfikar, created by Zulfikar Ali Bhutto's two sons.

An alternatie version of the sabotage theory, often heard in Pakistan even today, views the ISI itself as the culprit through its obeying of Zia's instructions. The supporters of this version, among them particularly PPP followers, refer to the fact that an extraordinary American inspection of the depot stocks was planned and would have brought to light the considerable shortfalls in Stinger rockets being held there. The Stingers had been sold in significant numbers to Iran, not only to smooth political negotiations with Tehran but also for the personal enrichment of some Pakistani generals.[7] As a public smokescreen for what really had happened, arson was mooted, and this scapegoat worked fine. The Americans, who had recently arrived in Pakistan, could not prove anything else and left frustrated a short time later.

The Ojhri Camp disaster remains unexplained to this day. Whether the actual events will ever be known is doubtful. Meanwhile, the area has been re-modelled, renamed and today accommodates parts of the ISI's infrastructure, such as classrooms and accommodation for its personnel.

A Plane Crash and its Consequences

An even bigger tragedy in 1988 was the crash of the presidential plane *Pakistan I*, a Hercules C-130 aircraft, close to Bahawalpur in Punjab on 17 August. For the first time since dismissing Prime Minister Junejo three months earlier, President Zia-ul-Haq left his heavily guarded residence.[8] Those who died in this incident included President Zia and CJCSC Akhtar, the American Ambassador Arnold Raphel, the Senior Pentagon figure in the US Embassy in Pakistan at the time, Brigadier General Herbert Wassom, as well as eight Pakistani generals with their accompanying officers and the entire flight crew, a total of thirty-one deaths. The mysterious crash has never been explained, with theories of accident versus sabotage or attack vying with each other for credibility.

The most prevalent explanation is assassination. As with the fire at the Ojhri Camp, supporters of this version believe in a conspiracy theory directed towards Russian, Afghan, Indian, American or Pakistani perpetrators. They refer to the alleged delays, omissions, inconsistencies and errors in the investigations of the Americans as well as the Pakistanis and the non-publication of reports. A special piquancy to the assassination theory is that there must have been military assistance from the Pakistani side in order for it to have succeeded.

The advocates of the assassination theory suggest an ingenious plan to release a highly effective nerve gas on the crew. The ignition of a gas cartridge, previously installed in the cockpit, would have taken place during the plane's ascent after take-off. The two pilots and the flight engineer would have been suddenly immobilised, forcing the aircraft to stall, then a tailspin and finally the crash. The key question is who had that type of gas at their disposal at the time, and all fingers point towards the Americans. Another theory is that Shias in the Pakistan Air Force installed the cartridge in the cockpit. Just weeks before, one of their highest religious leaders had been assassinated, suggesting the deed was a revenge attack motived by sectarian hatred.[9]

One key supporter of the assassination theory was the US ambassador in India, John Gunther Dean. He was convinced of an Indian–Israeli plan, assisted by the KGB and the Afghan secret service KHAD, with help from Pakistan. According to him, Israel was responsible for the perfect planning, their motive being the conviction "that Gen Zia was becoming very dangerous to the region."[10] When Dean made his theory public, he was ordered back to the State Department; and when he held strongly to his conviction, he was declared mentally incompetent and prematurely dismissed from the diplomatic service.

Then there are the theories of Indian involvement. A. K. Verma, chief of India's intelligence service, R&AW, 1987–9, reported on the talks between Zia-ul-Haq and Rajiv Gandhi in 1988, aimed initially at improving the situation on the Siachen Glacier and later including the Kashmir problem.[11] As proof of the progress of these discussions, Verma points to the four Sikh deserters from the Indian Army whom the Pakistanis sent back to India for court martial. However, the increasingly positive tone of the discussions made the generals in Rawalpindi nervous. For them Zia was about to overstep their negotiation mandate. Zia-ul-Haq had his accident in August 1988, and Rajiv Gandhi died in May 1991 from a female Tamil suicide assassin. Just hours before his death, Rajiv gave an interview to the renowned American journalist Barbara Crossette, in which he spoke of shattered dreams. The *New York Times* published this discussion a day after his assassination, including this quotation from Rajiv Gandhi:

> But I know who would have solved these problems with us, he said: "General Zia. We were close to finishing agreement on Kashmir; we had the maps and everything ready to sign. And then he was killed." As Prime Minister from

1984 to 1989, Mr. Gandhi had a good working relationship with President Mohammed Zia-ul-Haq, who died in an unexplained plane crash in Aug. 1988. Mr. Gandhi said there was evidence that General Zia had been murdered, but he would not say more.[12]

The remarks of the former R&AW chief are surprising. In other SAAG papers, Zia was always portrayed as a hardliner, especially on the Kashmir case. Also, there are hardly any clues in other sources regarding the supposed good relationship between Zia and Gandhi. Verma's remarks stand as the sole evidence for those particular allegations about Zia's death.

Supporters of the accident theory, among them experienced former pilots of the Pakistan Air Force, believe the aircraft was brought down by a technical error.[13] They say that the Hercules C-130 is a tried and tested plane with stable flight characteristics, and that in a deviation from a normal flight path the aircraft would revert to normal without pilot input because all transport planes are designed for positive stability. So if the pilots were incapacitated the C-130 would continue to fly normally as it was already in a climing mode.

The erratic behavior of Pakistan-I observed by people on ground would indicate either a hydraulic flight control problem or a rearward shift in centre of gravity. The former could possibly be brought about by fluid loss in the hydraulic accumulator; the latter by a shift in the cargo to the back as the aircraft was climing. There was no evidence of explosion, engine failure or structural separation before impact.

The C-130 is not a comfortable aircraft for VIPs. Lockheed, the manufacturer, had designed a capsule to be fitted inside the cargo area whenever needed. PAF had built their own capsule locally made to seat a number of VIP passengers. It is possible that in the case of the fateful flight the fitting of the capsule was not properly anchored so it could have broken loose while climing. Had this happened the centre of gravity would have shifted back and stalled the C-130 in mid-flight.

In the recorded flight movements, after take off observers saw the plane careening three times with fully powerd engines, signifying erratic flight. After that they saw the aircraft going into a dive and crash followed by a fire.[14]

Indeed, historically the Hercules C-130 has not been problem-free: there have been twenty instances of accidents due to rudder malfunction. Also *Pakistan-1*, the President's flight, had a history of previous technical problems; Mahmud Ali Durrani, Pakistan's former ambassador in Washington, reported:

> I had travelled many times on it with the President and many times we had mechanical, electrical problems. On three, four occasions, we had to abandon

the aircraft for one reason or another. This is what I regret very deeply, that a proper scientific investigation was not done.[15]

Contrary to all conspiracy theories, an accident could well have happened on 17 August 1988. The American side of the joint investigation report blamed a mechanical malfunction as the cause of the accident; while the Pakistani side speaks of a criminal act or sabotage leading to a loss of aircraft control.

The death of General Akhtar, the CJCSC and former DG ISI, was tragic as he was included only at the last minute and at his own instigation to accompany the President. Akhtar had asked for a discussion with Zia and it was proposed that he accompany Zia on the day trip to Bahawalpur.[16] According to Brigadier Yousaf, an advocate of the sabotage theory, Akhtar became a *shaheed*, a martyr in the Holy War. Akhtar would miss the triumphs of 1988: the Soviet Army began to withdraw from Afghanistan in May 1988 and had fully left by February 1989. For the mujahideen and their leaders this was the confirmation of Allah's will; for the ISI it was also the cause for increased self-confidence and self-assessment.

The Disaster in Jalalabad

We now turn back to Hamid Gul as DG ISI, and his policy of directly seeking to influence military developments in Afghanistan. Gul had managed to become Chairman of the Military Committee, the union of the military heads of the seven parties' alliance. This was the first step in a new strategy, approved by Zia, aimed at breaking away from the guerrilla war and moving towards conventional warfare. However, this was a premature decision, one that led to the Jalalabad disaster.

In 1987, Akhtar and Yousaf had agreed that the guerrilla campaigns in Afghanistan should be kept going even after the departure of the Soviet Army. But under Hamid Gul from 1989 there was a change in strategic thinking in the ISI. The goal was to demoralise both the political and military leadership in Kabul through individual military actions, in this way forcing the other cities of the country to collapse as a consequence.

Thus from December 1988 the ISI strove to bring in an Afghan Interim Government (AIG), and it looked as if the goal was about to be reached in February 1989. In an earlier consultative *shura* in Rawalpindi, and after long drawn out negotiations, it seemed possible that a cabinet was about to be formed. The Saudi secret service provided US$ 25 million for this difficult task. The leadership role would rotate every six months, both to secure the weaker leaders of the alliance and to prevent the future emergence of a strong and independently minded leader in Kabul who might be inimical to Pakistani interests. Hekmatyar left Rawalpindi in high dudgeon, while Ahmed Shah Masud behaved with far more intelligence. He knew that leaders like Mujaddedi and Rabbani would ultimately have to fall back on him and his fighters. He was assigned a key role as Minister of Defence.

The Afghan Interim Government's seat of power was to be transferred from Peshawar to Jalalabad, 50 km across the border. Both the ISI's and Pakistan's political leadership believed that the transfer to Jalalabad would relieve Peshawar from being overpopulated by Afghans. So from the beginning of March 1989, 5,000–7,000 mujahideen were sent to besiege Jalalabad for three months, enduring much bloodshed. The resistance of the Afghan defenders in Jalalabad had been severely underestimated. They were aware of the fates of previous defectors, who had often been cruelly abused and killed, so for them their only chance was holding out or death. Besides that, Hekmatyar had promised much for Jalalabad. Over the years he had received money and equipment from the ISI for over 30,000 mujahideen, who were trained by his people and also by the ISI and were, allegedly, ready to storm Jalalabad.[17] In reality these were men who had accepted Hekmatyar's offer of training, which included subsistence, pay and weapons, but who afterwards returned to their home villages. They only partially followed now the call to storm Jalalabad. It became clear that Hekmatyar was simply a leader of mercenaries rather than a tribal head with a devoted retinue of traditional followers.

Four months after the withdrawal from Jalalabad, a body count revealed that the attackers had suffered 3,000 dead and wounded, thereby confirming JFK's proverb that "Victory has a thousand fathers, but defeat is an orphan". Today, Jalalabad stands as a huge blunder on the part of the ISI and is considered a blemish on Hamid Gul's military career. However, as a matter of fact, many other actors were involved. In a crucial meeting of the ISI Afghanistan Bureau on 6 March 1989 in Peshawar, where no Afghan representatives participated, Prime Minister Benazir Bhutto and her Minister of Foreign Affairs, Sahibzada Yaqub Ali Khan, were present and agreed with the decision to attack Jalalabad. According to the latter's opinion, the newly exiled government had to show that they were not only "some Johnnies riding around Peshawar in Mercedes."[18] The US Ambassador Robert Oakley was also present and agreed to the storming of Jalalabad; the CIA and ISI had already jointly prepared a detailed military plan of attack. All this does not absolve both the Afghanistan Bureau and Hamid Gul personally of direct responsibility for the

Jalalabad affair; but it also shows the prevailing lopsidedness of the prejudice over Jalalabad to this day.

After Jalalabad, Benazir Bhutto made a U-turn and shifted responsibility for interfering in politics in Afghanistan from the ISI to Army GHQ, which had not been previously involved previously in the Jalalabad operation. She called Beg and explained that she wanted him "to work out the military and political strategy for transfer of power in Afghanistan."[19] Beg remembers that at the time he received the new directive he was consumed with the preparations for the large Zarb-e-Momin manoeuvre. Nevertheless, he invited Afghan politicians and field commanders to Rawalpindi for discussions from November 1988 to March 1989. Northern Alliance leader Ahmed Shah Masud also came.

In pursuit of a lasting solution, COAS Beg took his Afghan guests also to Teheran. There the Iranian leaders suggested a political division of Afghanistan, the North being administerd by the Northern Alliance, the South by the Mujahideen councel. Ahmed Shah Masud agreed but the other Mujahideen leaders did not.

On the basis of their exhange of views, Beg and his team compiled plans for a future Afghanistan policy for Pakistan, which they forwarded to the Bhutto government in spring 1990.

In a speech to Pakistani officers on 28 January 1991, Beg reported:

> As you know, the first phase of this war ended about two years back, and with the retreat of the Soviet troops from Afghanistan yet nobody has dared intervene, because it is the Afghans alone who will manage their affairs, and in their own style—the tribal way, where the time and space dimensions are very different. They have taken a long time but you have seen that a few months back they all collected here—field commanders and political leaders—for the first time in 10 years. They worked out a common strategy—a military and political strategy—to resolve the Afghan issue. The process has started and Insha Allah it will reach its culmination by the middle of this summer. You can say that the turning point will be somewhere in June, July or August. Simply stated, the strategy is that the military offensive and the political efforts will be launched simultaneously. They must move parallel, because that is the logical thing. Once the military creates a situation, the political process must take over.[20]

However, six months before this speech, in August 1990, Benazir's government fell and the storm clouds of the first Gulf War began to gather. Afghanistan receded into the background for the time being at least and with the accession to power in Islamabad of Nawaz Sharif in November 1990 little official interest was shown in Pakistan's neighbour.[21]

After the end of the Jalalabad fighting, Benazir Bhutto forced a change in the ISI leadership, in June 1989. While the Jalalabad fiasco provided her with a pretext to do so, the dismissal of Hamid Gul was an attempt to bring the ISI more directly under political control, an objective which was never realised. For the ISI's Afghanistan Bureau and for Hamid Gul himself, Jalalabad represented a pause rather than the end of its activities in Pakistan's neighbouring country. Gul was promoted to Lieutenant General and posted as Corps Commander to Multan, but was forced into early retirement in January 1992. As advisor to and mentor of the Islamic parties and jihadi groups, he continued to influence developments in Afghanistan and Pakistan. International press reports and think tank commentary on the region often featured statements about or by Gul, who was often exaggeratedly portrayed as one of the most dangerous men in Pakistan. Hamid Gul died, aged 78, in August 2015, from a brain haemorrhage.

After Jalalabad, the ISI experienced a series of setbacks in Afghanistan, before striking out again from 1995 with new partners for a further round in the struggle for influence and power there. To understand these external manoeuvres and machinations, we need to address the role of the ISI in internal affairs in Pakistan in the post Zia-ul-Haq era.

7

DOMESTIC POLITICS, 1988–1991

General Mirza Aslam Beg

As Vice Chief of Army Staff (Vice-COAS), General Beg was present on that fateful day in August 1988 at the army tank test site near Bahawalpur, to which he had travelled in a smaller aircraft. Beg is said to have politely declined Zia's invitation to take the return flight on board the President's plane with the excuse that he had to make an official stop in Lahore on his way back and therefore had to fly in his own plane. Aslam Beg himself gives another account of the last crucial minutes before the aircraft's fateful departure. After he had thanked Zia-ul-Haq for his invitation to accompany him and was already ascending the steps of the Presidential flight, Zia happened to notice the aircraft that Beg had taken to Bahawalpur. He impulsively decided that Beg should fly back together with his escorts on that plane—an order which saved Beg's life.

Critics and foes of General Aslam Beg still dismiss this version of events as an attempt at rehabilitation, which neglects the reality at that time. Aslam Beg could hardly refuse the honour of travelling with the President and the US Ambassador Arnold Raphel without attracting attention. So General Beg's statement that Zia finally instructed him not to fly with the President's plane is more believable than the version that claims he turned down the President's offer to accompany him on the return flight. Beg's predecessor as Vice-COAS, K. M. Arif, who can hardly be counted as one of Beg's close friends, nevertheless vouches for him:

> Before boarding the plane, Zia shook hands with the military officers on the departure line. While meeting Beg, he offered him a lift. Beg thanked the

President. Zia had a look at the jet prop and said, "You have your own plane also here".[1]

Vice-COAS Beg took off minutes after the presidential flight Pakistan-I. and did not realise for some time that Pakistan-I had crashed. On hearing the news of the accident on the radio transmitter, he ordered the pilot to turn back and circled over the crash site. Informed through ground radio telephone that only debris and smoking ashes remained, he decided against landing.[2] Aware of the new power vacuum in Pakistan, his top priority was to quickly reach the army's GHQ.[3]

In 1988, the way to power was open for General Beg; and he was urged to take the helm of the nation on 17 August and again later. A contemporary witness, Hussain Abbas, wrote later: "Many of Zia's former colleagues made it clear that they would be prepared to pay homage to him should he decide to move into the presidency."[4] Beg's decision to opt for a different route came from his conviction that the era of military dictatorship had come to an end and that democracy was the need of the hour. As Vice-COAS, he had observed the political developments in Pakistan and had drawn his own conclusions.

Beg came from the former United Provinces in colonial India, today's Uttar Pradesh. His biography reveals him to have been a political animal through and through: even when at college, he was President of the Muslim Students' Association, at a time when the quota of Muslim students was just 9 percent. Before Partition, in 1945–47, he actively supported the Pakistan movement, and in 1949 he migrated to Pakistan. That same year Beg was admitted to the Pakistan Military Academy and in January 1950 joined the army.

Stationed in East Pakistan in 1971, he had pleaded for a political solution and was opposed to the Army's involvement in the political events that unfolded there. This resulted in an immediate transfer back to West Pakistan and the threat of court martial.[5] During his later military career Beg was seen as a sociable man, never shy, and was considered to hold fast to his own opinions. Thus, in 1985, he advised Zia-ul-Haq "to have a rendezvous with history and to democratize the country." According to Beg, the President laughed and asked him, "General Beg, do you want the noose around my neck?"[6] In the book *Pakistan's Drift into Extremism*, by Hassan Abbas, the author portrays General Mirza Aslam Beg as follows:

> Beg was an infantry officer who had also served in the elite Special Service Group. Of average height and medium build, he was soft-spoken, had an easygoing air around him, and was well liked by both his subordinates and superiors. His baby face hid an acute mind and an ambition to match. He was also not averse to the odd scotch.[7]

In 1987 President Zia became distrustful of Beg and wanted Lt. Gen. Zahid Ali Akbar as Vice Army chief. The journalist Zahid Hussain, one of the best informed experts on Pakistan's military, wrote in 1991 about the decision:

> Although he had a reputation as an able professional soldier, General Beg was not among General Zia's inner coterie, and his promotion to the position of Vice-COAS owed largely to former Prime Minister Mohammad Khan Junejo. Beg's appointment to the post was one of the few independent decisions taken by Mr. Junejo, and it contributed to widening the gulf between him and Zia.[8]

Beg's opponents and critics argued later that had he tried to seize power in 1988, the corps commanders would not have followed him. And yet, after more than eleven years under a military dictator, the generals would hardly have changed overnight and opposed another soldier as commander. All of them were still numb from the tragedy of Zia's death. Opposition towards any new boss was bound to occur, whatever the circumstances. So just supposing that in August 1988 it had been possible for General Mirza Aslam Beg to seize power, then it is likely that the disciplined, British-style Pakistan Army would have followed him obediently.

Elections and the Formation of a Government

On the afternoon of 17 August, a crisis meeting was convened at GHQ. Those present included General Aslam Beg, Lt. Generals Imranullah Khan and Imtiaz Warraich, as well as Maj. Generals Jehangir Karamat and Hamid Gul.[9] On Beg's recommendation it was agreed that the President of the Senate, Ghulam Ishaq Khan, was to become Acting President in accordance with the Constitution. Afterwards, the heads of the Air Force and the Navy were invited to the Army GHQ and they too agreed with this decision. Ghulam Ishaq Khan was informed, and at 19.30 arrived at GHQ. General K. M. Arif, who retired in 1988 and was a close colleague of Zia's, later wrote in his book *Working with Zia*:

> It was improper for the military brass to call Mr Ghulam Ishaq Khan to the General Headquarters. Instead, they should have called on him to express their grief and loyalty. Ishaq had the constitutional right to become the President and the military had shown him no favour. He was too nice a person to fuss about the protocol and that too in an hour of national tragedy. It would have been prudent for the top military hierarchy to show him due courtesy.[10]

In reality, the generals in conclave at GHQ had proposed to call on Ghulam Ishaq Khan in Islamabad the next morning, but it was he who opted to come to Rawalpindi that very evening. Ghulam Ishaq Khan was an experienced bureaucrat. In his years in office as President he also proved to be a clever and power-orientated politician, who was to hound two Prime Ministers, Benazir Bhutto and Nawaz Sharif, from office. On 17 August 1988 he insisted on coming to GHQ in Rawalpindi for a situation assessment. He showed himself to be submissive and suggested that the Army, in other words the COAS, should control the situation by remaining in power for the time being. Realising that it had already been decided otherwise, he quickly seized his chance. His rapid arrival in Rawalpindi had paid off, and that very night he gave a broadcast over radio and TV, informing the nation about the President's death and announcing that he was taking office. A ten-day state mourning was proclaimed and elections confirmed for November. General Mirza Aslam Beg was sworn in as COAS in accordance with the Presidential order under the Constitution of Pakistan; and the caretaker cabinet, already appointed by Zia-ul-Haq, was installed in office.

However, a difference of opinion soon emerged from within the conservative camp. The Pakistan Muslim League (PML) toyed with the idea of restoring parliament and Junejo's government that had been dismissed by Zia.[11] Anxious that an election victory by the PPP would propel Benazir Bhutto into power, they tried to thwart such a development through administrative and bureaucratic pressure. The new President, Ghulam Ishaq Khan, agreed with them. He belonged to the majority in the bureaucracy who had been silent during the condemnation and execution of Zulfikar Ali Bhutto, had supported Zia-ul-Haq's system for many years and had profited from it.[12]

Benazir Bhutto was aware of this situation and went to the courts in order to secure the holding of elections.[13] On 27 September 1988 the Lahore High Court passed judgement that, in the interests of democracy and political accountability, new elections were to be held that November.[14] Neither President Ghulam Ishaq Khan nor the PML group around Junejo and his followers admitted defeat. They now went to the Supreme Court of Pakistan, knowing that the majority of the judges stood close to the establishment.

It soon appeared that the Supreme Court would overrule the Lahore decision in favour of the applicants. In the cities the order books of reputable men's tailors were full as the politicians of the old guard stood by, ready to take their new place in office. Among the dissatisfied observers of this chain of events was Aslam Beg, who knew the establishment's agenda[15] but was nurturing political ambitions of his own. Benazir Bhutto later recounted that an arrangement was made between Beg and her whereby he guaranteed the holding of fair elections in November if she endorsed his position as COAS.[16]

On 6 October 1988 General Aslam Beg utilised his position and power and summoned the Minister for Justice Wasim Sajjad to come to GHQ early that day for the pronouncement of the court ruling. Through him, Beg sent an urgent message to the Court, making it clear that an over-ruling of the Lahore Court's judgement would be unacceptable to him, and as a consequence he would then have news of his own to convey to them. Beg also discussed this with the chiefs of the Air Force and the Navy and together they paid a call on the President. Ghulam Ishaq Khan immediately understood the situation, as did the twelve judges of the Supreme Court. In the end they decided to hold elections in November on a political party basis. However, the actual strength of Benazir Bhutto's and the PPP's opponents' influence can be seen by the pronouncement of the court's ruling: originally set for 14.00 hrs, it was finally announced only at 17.00 hrs.

Beg realised that through his actions he had lost the sympathy of the establishment and some of his generals and that at the senior levels of the Army a general anti-PPP feeling prevailed. He therefore decided to keep the door open to both sides of the political divide. To keep himself up to date about developments during the election campaign, he invited members of the conservative camp to his house on 24 October and 6 November, the core topic for discussion being Pakistan's political scene. The situation report was delivered by the DG ISI, Lt. Gen. Hamid Gul,[17] who told the gathering that the PPP was heading for an election victory. The military establishment, which doubted the political integrity of the PPP leadership, found themselves in a tight spot. Patriotic forces had to be strengthened against their secular opponents, and thus it was that, with the COAS's blessing, the ISI once again rejoined the fray.

DG ISI Hamid Gul was the one person who had a good relationship with both the President as well as with the Army chief; so together with Brigadier Imtiaz Ahmed and Major Aamer from the Internal Security Wing of the ISI, they cobbled together the party alliance that became known as Islami Jamoori Ithad ("Islamic Democratic Alliance", IJI)[18] as a political counterweight to the PPP. It was a project that Gul was originally entrusted with by Zia. Assistance came from Ijlal Haider Zaidi, a top bureaucrat and a close and trusted friend of President Ghulam Ishaq Khan; Zaidi also acted as political advisor to Nawaz Sharif, the hopeful candidate from Lahore.

In later years Gul justified his actions as follows:

> I think it was necessary that this group came together—who put it together is not the point. This kind of a grouping was necessary. Look at the situation at

that time when the 1988 elections were to be held. The top brass of the army was gone. There was a great deal of confusion in the country, there was no cabinet because of a judgement of the Supreme Court. There was no National Assembly, there was a president who was not sworn in and there were the politicians, particularly those in the right wing, who thought that the forces opposed to them would win a walk-over. And these forces in the right were hellbent on, let us say, impeding the process of elections and restoration of democracy. There was a demand that the elections be postponed, that an emergency should be imposed. Then there was the carnage in Hyderabad on September 30. There were heavy floods which affected 65 constituencies of the National Assembly. And in that situation, there was definitely a need to create a balance so that we could go to the polls. This was very important. It was not easy because we were bitten by the experience of 1971, when we were unable to transfer power to a party which had won a clear majority.[19]

COAS Aslam Beg was also on board. He later defended his commitment in the IJI matter with similar words to those of his intelligence chief:

Otherwise the army, perhaps, would not have allowed the transfer of power to Benazir Bhutto. So to ensure that power is smoothly transferred to Benazir Bhutto and democracy restored, the IJI was formed by the ISI knowing full well that it wouldn't stop the PPP from forming the government.[20]

Naturally Beg's and Gul's critics and opponents see such explanations as a defence of their illegal measures: for them the army leadership was clearly guilty of election manipulation. They believe that "General Mirza Aslam Beg took the decision in principle but left the nuts and bolts to Hamid Gul, who completed the job within weeks of the polls."[21] In doing so, they ignore the conservative camp's readiness at that time to prevent by all possible means the seizure of power by Benazir Bhutto. Against this background, the creation of the IJI, controlled by the ISI, was the best way to keep the situation under control. In fact, both Beg and Gul had realised that a PPP election victory could not be prevented; the internal ISI reports made that very clear. Their intention was to avoid a one-sided distribution of political power. As in 1971, a balanced parliament suited the the military best as it would allow them to exert influence over the politicians. The ISI screened the available candidates: Ghulam Mustafa Jatoi, hailing from a Sindhi family with huge landholdings and long used to exerting political power, was selected as the senior candidate of the IJI. In the election campaign two well-known personalities from the same province competed against each other, thereby splitting their constituency.

The IJI alliance consisted of nine parties with different ideologies and programs, united only in opposing the PPP. However, in the eyes of most voters this was not enough for them to succeed. On 14 November 1988 the PPP became the largest party in the National Parliament.[22] Together with the MQM, which was successful in urban Sindh, as coalition partner they obtained the necessary majority to form the government in Islamabad and Karachi. However, the machinations of Hamid Gul and his associates were not completely unsuccessful. In the elections for the four provincial parliaments, Punjab, Pakistan's most densely populated and most important province, went to the IJI. Here Nawaz Sharif, as IJI candidate, was victorious. As Chief Minister, he would soon launch his agitations against Benazir Bhutto and the PPP governments in Islamabad and Sindh.

On 22 November President Ghulam Ishaq Khan met with the election winner in order to discuss the formation of a new government and to put his terms and conditions on the table. His previous talks with other politicians had resulted in deadlock, due to a lack of a parliamentary majority. Independently from the President, Aslam Beg had invited the Mrs Bhutto and Mr Zadari to dinner at his home in Rawalpindi that very evening. Before the meal, Benazir and Beg had a two-hour private talk. Later on, Benazir commented:

> It was a private social dinner to break the ice. I was a leader who was unknown to most of them. They had never met me before. Yet due to the support of the people of Pakistan, I had to be sworn in as the chief executive of the country, the person whom they have to salute.[23]

By seeing it purely as a private social occasion, the prospective Prime Minister had misjudged the purpose of the meeting. Beg not only wanted to become acquainted with Benazir Bhutto; he also wanted to form a first impression of how political cooperation between them might be possible. He made no demands other than to advise the new government to leave Zia-ul-Haq's family alone. His personal objectives, even if he did not spell them out, may have been to do with extending his tenure as COAS beyond August 1991, or perhaps a later political career.[24] Years later a biographer of Benazir Bhutto was to write about their get-together:

> The General told her that the reservations or apprehensions of the army emitted from a variety of reasons ranging from her brother's alleged involvement with an organization like Al-Zulfikar, to fears about her future policies on Afghanistan and Kashmir.[25]

It is correct that in his discussions General Aslam Beg was neither arrogant nor demanding. He saw himself in the role of a friendly counselor. However, the prospective Prime Minister, Benazir Bhutto, missed the chance to develop a bond of trust with him; on the contrary, she soon surrounded herself with people who were not counted among Beg's friends.

On 1 December President Ghulam Ishaq Khan proposed Benazir Bhutto as the new Prime Minister to Parliament. She took the oath of office the next day and on 12 December 1988 won the vote of confidence by 148 to 55. On the same day that President Ishaq Khan was approved for the next five years in office, he also received the backing of the PPP. For their own candidate, the PPP could muster no majority. Besides, some of Benazir Bhutto's advisors pleaded for Ghulam Ishaq Khan, expecting an impartial administration from the experienced bureaucrat—but these hopes were soon dashed.

The consenual view among experts on Pakistani politics and senior PPP supporters is that the new Prime Minister had to make huge concessions to the establishment in order to have her exercise power. According to her former fellow colleagues, she agreed to the MQM as coalition partner in Islamabad and in Sindh, to Sahibzada Yakub Ali Khan's appointment as Minister Foreign Affairs, to no political interference in policies affecting Afghanistan or Kashmir and to having no role whatsoever in Pakistan's nuclear policy.[26]

Former top military personnel disagree. According to them, pressure was neither imposed nor was it necessary. On the Afghanistan and Kashmir issues, there existed a broad consensus; and economic policy was, from the outset, always a matter for the politicians only. But even as far as the nuclear question was concerned the truth was more complicated: the Prime Minister belonged, *ex officio*, to the Pakistan Nuclear Command Authority, participated in their meetings and was included in and responsible for all decisions.[27] Interesting to note is this contemporary CIA analysis, from a report of 3 May 1989:

> ...because of the broad consensus in Pakistan on acquiring nuclear weapons, Benazir Bhutto will not try to abolish or significantly cut back the weapons programme... however she will be more sensitive and responsive than the military to US concerns over the nuclear issue... In the longer run we expect the military will retain firm control over nuclear decision making in Pakistan, leaving little room for Bhutto to gain significant additional influence on the nuclear weapon issue.[28]

Beg soon came to realise that the new Prime Minister attached little importance to his advice and was purposefully seeking to extend her influence over the Army, without consulting him. Under the pretext of a political clean up, she demanded from her Army chief a list of military personnel who had been closely linked to the Zia regime. Benazir conveyed her request to Beg through her Defence Advisor, Major General (retd.) Imtiaz Ali Khan, who had served under her father as Secretary. Beg rejected the request, saying that the Army had its own agenda regarding such things and advised her not to interfere in its internal affairs. In his reply he ironically suggested starting with him, as he also had worked closely with Zia. The Prime Minister abandoned her unjustifiable demand; but the first clear disagreement between her and the Army chief had been noted.

Iqbal Akhund, Foreign Affairs Advisor in Benazir's first government, was one of those who was against the creation of a National Security Council, as suggested by Beg, and he accordingly advised his Prime Minister. According to Beg, the most frequent cause of past Army coups was the lack of consultation between politicians and the military within top committees. Akhund saw things differently: for him a Security Council would be an attempt by the military to control and determine national politics.[29] Beg could not insist on his idea being put into practice, though a Security Council would be created several years later by a general who would seize power in a *coup d'état*: Pervez Musharraf. This development would run its course; but it was with the ISI that Benazir Bhutto made her first major mistake.

From Hamid Gul to Shamsur Rahman Kallue

Aslam Beg enjoyed a three year tenure as Chief of Army Staff, until August 1991, but Hamid Gul did not benefit from such a secure situation. According to the Constitution, the appointment of the head of the ISI was the responsibility of the Prime Minister. The new government knew of the ISI's biased partisanship in favour of the IJI during the election campaign; and they also knew about the ISI chief's political viewpoint, which a former Minister for Foreign Affairs described to the author as follows: "Hamid Gul was out and out pro-Army and pro-ISI. He was completely anti-civilian politicians. He was pro-Jamaat-e-Islami and one of his remarks about Benazir Bhutto was, 'Prime Ministers like her we make and unmake.'"[30]

Gul is known to have kept Prime Minister Junejo and Minister of Foreign Affairs Yakub Khan under close observation at Zia's behest during the 1987 UN negotiations for Afghanistan in Geneva, thereby using the ISI to discredit the Geneva Accords. Benazir Bhutto may even have recalled the fate of her younger brother, Shahnawaz Bhutto, who died mysteriously of poisoning in southern France in July 1985. Even today, a majority of Pakistanis are convinced that the ISI, under the leadership of Akhtar Rehman, had a hand in that tragedy. It is therefore understandable that now, as Prime Minister, she wanted to have someone whom she could trust as head of the most powerful intelligence agency in the country.

Hamid Gul sensed this and tried to hang onto his position. At the request of the Prime Minister, he sent four Sikhs who were Army deserters, held in ISI custody, back to India, where court martial waited them. President Gulam Ishaq Khan would strongly reproach Benazir for this a year later after she was dismissed.[31]

The military fiasco in Jalalabad gave Benazir the opportunity to replace Hamid Gul, which duly happened in June 1989. She told Beg on the telephone that she wanted a change in the ISI's leadership and was considering the retired Lt. Gen. Shamsur Rahman Kallue as the new chief. Beg felt he had been deliberately misled, if not deceived, as the head of the Army chief would normally have been involved in making such a decision. Prime Minister Junejo had selected Hamid Gul from a panel of five proposed names given to him by GHQ. Beg called on Benazir to persuade her of the problems that would ensue if she appointed a non-serving general. In his view, such a move would upset the communication system of the Army which followed the rule "In is in and out is out." Ergo, no retired military man was invited to commanders' meetings, graduation board meetings and so forth. Also, under a civilian leader the ISI would become estranged from the Army, a development which was wrong and dangerous for GHQ. Beg may also have been thinking how Hamid Gul kept contact with him while simultaneously becoming one of the President's men. In this way, Ghulam Ishaq Khan had won considerable influence in the ISI. So Beg submitted a panel with the names of three active generals whom GHQ considered suitable to be head of the ISI. The Prime Minister sent her regrets: her decision was already made.

Beg accepted her decision: within a week Hamid Gul was replaced and the changes in ISI leadership were carried out. Gul was promoted and as Lieutenant General took command of the important Army corps in Multan. He commented to Beg on his dismissal with the words "today it is the DG ISI, tomorrow the lady will challenge the Army chief." Here Gul's intuition proved true: soon it became known that Benazir was planning to move Beg to the less powerful post of Chairman of the Joint Chiefs of Staff Committee. As Prime Minister she now wanted a man of her own as COAS. However, President Ghulam Ishaq Khan blocked these plans, especially since the tenure of the present CJCSC, Admiral Sirohey, was ongoing and he was loudly insisting on a full term in office. Benazir had to abandon her plans; she wrote a kind of apology letter to Beg in which she assured him of her full confidence in him as Army chief. But Beg had got the message; he now knew that Benazir was no ally of his politically.

Hamid Gul's successor, Shamsur Rahman Kallue, was a retired officer from the armoured corps. He was seen by many as a professional soldier and a good commander, intelligent and well-read, a man with his own views. According to these opinions, he would have carried this up to COAS level and, when necessary, would contradict even Benazir Bhutto. Other more critical views were that Kallue was indecisive, lacked determination and was even hedonistic, even though he was a teetotal bachelor. Together with General Rafi Alam, he was considered close to Zia-ul-Haq. It was expected that after M. K. Arif's retirement, Kallue would take over the vacant post of Vice-COAS in May 1987. Abbas explains why Aslam Beg was selected instead: "Kallue was not given the coveted slot because he had refused to hold any appointment in having anything to do with martial law, and in this preference there was a message Zia could not have been comfortable."[32]

In fact, in 1987 Kallue had never been in the running for the Vice-COAS slot; Zia had Lt. Gen. Zahid Ali Akhtar in mind for this. He was related to General Akhtar Rahman who had lobbied Zia on his behalf. However, the persistence of Prime Minister Junejo in gunning for Beg was finally the decisive factor here.

The appointment of Kallue as head of Pakistan's prime intelligence agency was an attempt by Benazir to domesticate and control the ISI, thereby increasing the security of her own office. Consequently, parts of the former staff from the Internal Political Division were removed and the department was reduced in size but not dissolved. Put simply, the temptation to spy on the country generally and especially on their political opponents was more than the PPP government could resist. But the attempt at exerting greater control over the ISI failed, mainly because of the wrong choice of leader. Kallue's appointment proved to be a mistake, for the job did not correspond to his disposition. He had neither the cold aloofness of Akhtar Rehman nor the energy-driven subservience of Hamid Gul. According to the opinion of many ISI personnel, his time in office proved a lost opportunity for the agency.[33]

The Army leadership reacted in its own way to this new ISI regime. There was a feeling that Kallue was more loyal to politics than to the military; some even saw him as a turncoat. Kallue was not invited to meetings of the corps commanders and nor was he informed about important decisions. The boycotted DG ISI was not even in charge in his own "house". Under his leadership the ISI was no longer a source of information and inspiration for the government. In the Prime Ministerial Secretariat he was seen as naive and was mockingly referred to as "no-clue Kallue". Benazir later called his appointment the biggest mistake of her first period in office; it was definitely the first crucial step in the separation between the Prime Minister and the Army chief

During Kallue's tenure the Afghanistan Bureau was not however transferred from the ISI to MI, led at that time by Assad Durrani. The MI was in structure and agenda not equipped for this. On the other hand, the Afghanistan Bureau within the ISI was fiercely independent and could easily bypass Kallue if necessary. On the positive side of the balance sheet, it was Kallue, according to hints from Rawalpindi and Islamabad, who first informed Benazir of the stange business practices of Dr A. Q. Khan.

Pakistan's Intelligence Bureau (IB)

If the ISI is considered to be the prime military intelligence agency in Pakistan, then the Intelligence Bureau (IB) is the state's most important civilian intelligence service. According to their charters each has different tasks, but in practice they overlap in their work responsibilities and authority. In 1992 two senior Pakistani journalists offered this critical description of the IB:

> From the corner of Islamabad's elegant Constitution Avenue, a road winds across the secretariat blocks and leads to a rather desolate and nondescript building. This is the "K" block—headquarters of the Directorate of Intelligence Bureau (DIB). Although Pakistan's premier civilian intelligence agency is believed to be modestly staffed, its role has far exceeded its prescribed function of counter-espionage and monitoring the activities of hostile foreign powers and their diplomatic missions in Pakistan. "K" block has been involved not just in keeping tabs on opposition politicians and tapping telephones, but recruiting informers among journalists, and, above all, manipulating politics. Its activities have included blackmail, harassment, disinformation campaigns against oppositions as well as keeping watch over other intelligence agencies. Eclipsed during the martial law years by the better known and more awesome Inter-ServiceIntelligence (ISI), the DIB has acquired greater notoriety in the past two years, especially after December 1990, after Brigadier (retd.) Imtiaz Ahmed took charge.[34]

In the 1950s and 1960s, the top levels of the IB included G. Ahmed, A. B. Awan, Anwer Ali and N. A. Rizvi, all experienced civil servants of the old school, trying to keep the service out of party politics. The situation changed when General Yahya Khan appointed his brother Agha Mohammad Ali as head of the IB in 1969; then its political use became obvious. Under

Zulfikar Ali Bhutto, this trend strengthened: the IB became a tool in the government's internal affairs. "It was not only used to harass and intimidate political opponents but also to suppress dissent within his own party… The agency was also used to prepare dossiers on ministers and other officials."[35]

The position and importance of the IB in internal affairs changed in the mid 1970s when, by decree, Zulfikar Bhutto created the Internal Security Wing in the ISI. From then on, both services cooperated but also competed with each other. Zia-ul-Haq again took complete control of the IB by placing Major General Nek Mohammed in charge of it. In turn, Prime Minister Junejo disassociated the IB from the military's clutches by replacing Nek Mohammed with the experienced police officer Zafar Iqbal Rathore. Knowing that the ISI was formally disposed to him, but in reality fully controlled by the military, Junejo tried to precipitate a new arrangement. He wanted the Interior Ministry to take over control of the IB again to make it more useful to the government, "but the bureau could never regain the power it enjoyed during the initial Bhutto years."[36]

During Benazir Bhutto's government 1988–90, the IB worked under their director Noor Nabi Leghari, son of the future President Farooq Khan Leghari, who was loyal to the government. However, Nabi Leghari was considered by insiders as only a figurehead chief. The strong man in the IB was his deputy, Major (retd.) Masud Sharif, a schoolmate of Asif Zardari, Benazir Bhutto's husband. Against this background, in September 1989, there erupted a political scandal in which both services were involved.

The "Midnight Jackal" Affair

The entire drama unfolded in September and October 1989. The first part of The "Midnight Jackal" Affair was the attempt by two ISI officers to bribe government parliamentarians to cast their votes against the Benazir Bhutto government in an upcoming vote of no confidence. It is still unclear on whose instruction they acted. In the second act of the drama, the government tried to catch the culprits with the help of the IB. The Opposition tabled in Parliament a vote of no confidence against Benazir's government and attempts were made to corrupt PPP parliamentarians. The IB attained video recordings of conspiratorial meetings in which the two ISI men tried to bribe the parliamentarians. However, the goal of luring the Opposition leader Nawaz Sharif into the trap failed. At the last minute, he stayed away from the meeting.

The two culprits offering bribes were Brigadier Imtiaz Ahmed and Major Mohammad Aamer, both still active in the army.[37] In the ISI, Aamer was responsible for Islamabad real estate properties; Ahmed was with the Engineer Corps in Risalpur, but was associated with the ISI for many years. Ahmed was posted to Karachi during DG ISI Akhtar Rehman's time, as Colonel in charge of the Intelligence Bureau. Later he was promoted to chief of the Joint Counter Intelligence Bureau (JCIB) at the ISI's headquarters in Islamabad. In this capacity, he had helped Hamid Gul to cobble together the IJI electoral alliance. After the assumption of Benazir Bhutto's government, Imtiaz Ahmed remained subversively active. In December 1988 he tried to form a new coalition against the new government. Due to complaints from Major General (retd.) Naseerullah Babar, the security advisor to the Prime Minister, Imtiaz was finally rotated back to the Engineer Corps. However, his willingness, skills and talent for undercover operations remained available for hire. The man was a born conspirator, considered by many as the Pakistani James Bond, an opinion not shared by all. According to Brigadier Tirmazi, his former boss and predecessor in the JCIB, Ahmed had, "like his friend Aamer, the habit of building himself up through publicising cooked-up feats of derring-do."[38]

Even today, it is not clear who encouraged Imtiaz and Aamer. Were they acting on top-level instructions from GHQ, or cooperating with the political opposition? Or was DG ISI Kallue himself behind all this? Supporters of the first version note that Ahmed and Aamer were involved in the creation of the IJI as far back as 1988. Soon, rumours surfaced that Ahmed had told a third party that he had acted on direct instructions from Aslam Beg and Hamid Gul.[39] However, this scenario is highly improbable: Beg was far too experienced and careful to get involved in such an operation with two subordinates. In this connection his statement that "no political activities were undertaken by the army" can be taken as credible.[40]

The second version, the more probable one, suggests that Nawaz Sharif, after becoming Prime Minister in autumn 1990, compensated Ahmed and Aamer in the best way he could. At that time, both had been dismissed from the Army. Ahmed was now Director of the IB and, as such, was one of his most important aides. Aamer became Director of Immigration in the Federal Investigation Agency (FIA). By autumn 1989, both guessed correctly that Nawaz Sharif would be the next political leader of Pakistan. If they helped him to achieve this in the shortest possible time, they would both be the beneficiaries in their retirement. According to this narrative, thanks to a last-minute warning, Nawaz Sharif missed the conspiratorial meeting where he would have been filmed and recorded by the IB.

The third Kallue version does not exclude the previous versions. It relies on a statement made by Aamer before an Army disciplinary committee. Aamer stated that he had acted on Kallue's instructions, with the idea "to pose as an anti-government person in order to collect information about the black sheep among the PPP."[41] This statement is plausible: Kallue apparently tried to help Benazir Bhutto, who feared a vote of no confidence. However, in Aamer he had trusted the wrong man and had overlooked his close working relationship with Imtiaz Ahmed. Both decided to double-cross Kallue, most probably after consultations with their former boss Hamid Gul.[42]

In the wake of the scandal and complaints from the Prime Minister's Secretariat over the affair, COAS Aslam Beg handed over the matter to the Adjutant General responsible for Army disciplinary matters, who had the accused face a three-man committee. Beg later referred to their testimony as follows:

> Major Aamer took the plea that he was acting under instructions from the DG ISI, General (retd.) Shamsur Rahman Kallue, to undertake such a mission and find out who among the PPP MNA's were hobnobbing with the opposition. Imtiaz was not in the ISI then, so his plea was that, being an old colleague of Aamer, he helped him perform this task. No reply came from Kallue.[43]

Imtiaz Ahmed and Muhammad Aamer were dismissed from the Army; "retired on fault" was the official reason given. For critics of the Army and opponents of Beg, this was deemed an inappropriate reaction and punishment. The fact that no proper military court was convened was considered by some as proof that the Army leadership was involved in the scandal, an opinion which is still held today.

Even after the dismissal of Benazir Bhutto's government, in August 1990, the "Midnight Jackal" affair refused to die down. On 10 August 1992 Salman Taseer, the PPP's Central Secretary for Information, made public additional audio recordings. His source was the ISI, now using the tapes against their erstwhile disgraced protégé, Nawaz Sharif. Asad Durrani, who headed the ISI from August 1990 to March 1992, is said to have known about this operation.

The "Midnight Jackal" affair is often used by politicians and journalists alike as a stick with which to beat the Army and the ISI. Thus, an editorial in the *Friday Times* in early 2001 described "the role of a serving corps commander and Nawaz Sharif in persuading Osama Bin Laden to help finance a no-confidence motion against her by sending a cheque for US\$10 million to General Aslam Beg personally."[44] Benazir Bhutto later gave this version of events in a speech to the World Leaders Summit in Abu Dhabi in November 2005:

> My opponents turned to a then not so well known Osama Bin Laden for help. They called him back from Saudi Arabia where he had returned after the

Soviets withdrew from Afghanistan in 1989. They asked him for $10 million to bring down the government I lead. In return they promised to legislate a religious bill turning Pakistan into a theocratic state.[45]

When interviewed by the author, Aslam Beg vehemently denies having receiving any money. He sees the payment story for what it probably was, namely a means of defaming political opponents and using a smokescreen to hide one's own errors.

August 1990

Army chief Beg is considered by most Pakistanis today as the key actor in Benazir Bhutto's downfall in August 1990, following the corps commanders' meeting held on 21 July 1990. While it is true that Pakistan's political situation was always discussed on such occasions, it was the COAS who always made the final decision. Beg had the habit of listening carefully to his generals:

> As a matter of policy, I always allowed my corps commanders to speak their mind. Invariably, almost all, with very few exceptions, confirmed the commitment that the government should be allowed to continue, but the person who should give an ultimate judgement is the president.[46]

In reality, the decision to topple the Bhutto government reveals Beg more as a follower than an instigator, whereas the driving force was the President. He knew that most of the establishment shared his skepticism about Benazir. Soon after taking office, Ghulam Ishaq Khan had shown himself to be a head-strong politician. On 8 August 1993 the columnist Altaf Gauhar wrote the following in the daily newspaper *The Nation*:

> When he was sworn in as President, after the sudden death of his mentor General Ziaul Haq, he refused to appoint a Caretaker Prime Minister in clear defiance of the constitutional requirement. The Chiefs of Services, who had put him to power, tried to persuade him to act accordingly to the Constitution but he told them that any politicians appointed as Prime Minister would cause unnecessary complications which might result in the postponement of the elections. What he really meant to convey was that he had no trust in politicians as a class. He had seen them cringe before three military rulers and knew that they had no understanding of the problems of the country and their commitment to democracy was merely a façade behind which they could conspire to seek public offices and enrich themselves. When the Supreme Court criticised President Ishaq for not appointing a Caretaker Prime Minister, he took the plea that it was General Ziaul Haq who had not considered it necessary to appoint anyone as Prime Minister. He had inherited that situation and did not want to disturb the status quo.[47]

Ghulam Ishaq Khan never had any confidence in Benazir Bhutto, and nor did a majority of the top military. He found allies amongst Pakistan's elite, among the feudal class, landowners, top bureaucrats and industrialists, as well as in the religious lobbies, for whom a woman as head of government was anathema. Naturally, there was also support from the ISI. According to one insider, Ghulam Ishaq Khan held considerable sway in some parts of the agency. In any event, authorization to topple the government came from him; he was the decision-maker. Beg later explained to journalists that he had received from Ghulam Ishaq Khan excerpts from letters of complaint which he (Khan) had written to the Prime Minister. In a meeting of the commanders Beg read these out and "the general consensus among the corps commanders was that the President should take the final decision since he was the best judge of this."[48]

General Beg had initially hoped to cooperate with the new Prime Minister, but his overtures were rebuffed. Benazir Bhutto relied on other supporters. ISI spies eavesdropped as Benazir phoned her American friends the night after her first meeting in Beg's house and reported on her discussions with Ghulam Ishaq Khan and Beg. She let it be known that they did not want to entrust the government to her, and asked for political pressure to be exerted by Washington. *Voice of America* duly reported on the issue the next morning. Beg felt betrayed for, as Benazir admitted years later, at the beginning he was on her side. In the monthly magazine *Herald* she wrote: "Beg was with me till the intelligence worked on him and convinced him that 'she wants to remove you and replace you with General Imtiaz as COAS'. It was a ridiculous story but he believed it."[49] In this quote she forgot that her attempt to deprive Beg of power by transferring him to the post of CJCSC is well-known and on record.

Another incident that engendered Benazir no sympathy among the security establishment was the attendance at the December 1988 SAARC meeting in Islamabad of the Indian Prime Minister Rajiv Gandhi. There was an official announcement concerning a non-aggression treaty covering the nuclear plants in both countries and an agreement to solve the Siachen dispute through discussions. However, the ISI's interception of official communications revealed another story. Soon rumours circulated that the Indian and Pakistani Prime Ministers had agreed that for the economic and social advancement of their two countries a substantial reduction in the armed forces was required, a proposal which naturally met with a frosty reception at the respective military headquarters. In addition, they reported on Rajiv Gandhi's recommendation to Benazir Bhutto that she replace Beg. In New Delhi, Aslam Beg was seen as a hardliner: he had implemented the Zarb-e-Momin manoeuvres in 1989, in which he broke from prevailing Pakistani strategic planning and switched to an offensive stance. His plan for columns to penetrate quickly and deeply into the enemy's territory in order to gain ground for later use as leverage in negotiations caused little joy in Delhi. As Benazir did not publicly reject Rajiv's recommendation about Pakistan's senior military commander, she lost even more sympathy within GHQ.

The ISI was not slow to respond. Soon accusations of betrayal haunted Pakistan. On instructions from Benazir Bhutto, so rumour had it, the PPP Minister for the Interior Aitzaz Ahsan handed over to the Indians a list of all ISI contacts with insurgent Sikhs in East Punjab—a betrayal which most of them paid for with their lives. An intensive pursuit of the Sikh rebels in East Punjab, beginning in spring 1989, was considered proof of the authenticity of these accusations, though in fact there is no conclusive proof of the accuracy of these rumours and accusations. PPP supporters assume that it was an ISI smear campaign, arguing that Benazir would not be foolish enough to expose herself to blackmail by New Delhi. Besides, they argue, it is improbable that the ISI would have delivered a list of their Sikh contacts to the government, since this would mean endangering many years' work. No intelligence agency would sell out its agents in such a manner. However, supporters of the betrayal theory even today believe that the list was acquired by Benazir Bhutto through her trusted General Imtiaz.[50] Benazir and the PPP vehemently denied all such accusations, but the ISI campaign achieved its objective; the betrayal rumours survived and are not forgotten, least of all in East Punjab.

Benazir Bhutto's first period in office lasted only one and a half years; it was hardly successful and, from the outset, had very little chance of lasting any longer than it did. The establishment found both time and the opportunity to block if not sabotage her government, availing the services of the ISI and MI, which later prompted Benazir to remark: "the security apparatus has run amok."[51] According to her, from the beginning Hamid Gul sanctioned the bugging of her phone, and from January 1989 made substantial efforts to induce PPP members in Sindh to defect in order to bring about the fall of the PPP-MQM government in Karachi. In autumn 1989 these efforts succeeeded when the coalition partner, Altaf Hussain, agreed to switch sides and join the opposition camp.

The Prime Minister tried to counterattack. She commissioned the former Air Force Chief Air Marshal (retd.) Zulfiqar Ali Khan in spring 1989 to investigate the overall situation of the secret services in the country. His report had little impact and ended up being shelved. Only years later did the contents become known after the monthly magazine *Herald* in August 1994 published an extract with comments and recommendations from the Commission entitled "The Forgotten Report."[52]

In a report on the MI in 1992, Maleeha Lodhi and Zahid Hussain, both journalists at the time, wrote about the political activities of the MI:

> Meanwhile, almost all the political tasks that had been assigned by GHQ to the ISI were shifted to Military Intelligence. In undertaking these, the MI too extended itself beyond its stated function of counter-intelligence within the military and gathering information about hostile neighbouring countries. Like the ISI, the MI now added these prescribed duties, a political role. Under Maj. General Asad Durrani, a trusted associate of Beg, the MI involved itself in political surveillance. Meeting politicians, and evolving strategy to deal with a government with which the army became increasingly estranged.[53]

Aslam Beg disputes such statements and sees articles of this kind as being designed to damage his reputation and establish the notion that he was against Benazir as Prime Minister from the outset. Actually Beg, like his predecessors and successors as COAS, had spoken with people of different political affiliations and had maintained contact with them in order to be informed about what was really going on in political circles. Years later, he still believes that had he not done this, the elections of 1988, for example, would not have taken place.[54]

8

THE ISI AND NAWAZ SHARIF, 1990–1993

A Change in GHQ

On 6 August 1990 the first Benazir Bhutto regime petered out; Nawaz Sharif (PML), former Chief Minister of Punjab, became the new Prime Minister on 1 November. With the end of the Bhutto government, Shamsur Rahman Kallue's term of office also drew to a close and the DG ISI "left as a gentleman."[1] In the ISI itself there was very little mourning over his departure; many felt his time there had represented a period of stagnation for the service. Like the previous DG ISI Akhtar Rehman, Kallue had not signed any ACRs,[2] and thus he blocked the promotions of some of his colleagues. His successor was Major General Asad Durrani, who was recommended by Beg and accepted by the caretaker Prime Minister Ghulam Mustafa Jatoi. Durrani had expected to be in command of an Army corps after his term in the MI; but in a private discussion he was persuaded by Beg that he could better serve his country as head of the ISI.

The new Prime Minister Nawaz Sharif liked neither Beg nor Durrani and his political sympathies lay with some of the generals lining up for the new COAS post in August 1991. Beg played into the new Prime Minister's hands by publicly opposing the government's Iraqi politics. Nawaz Sharif was ready to comply with Washington's request to deploy Pakistani combat troops to Iraq in the first Gulf War, which his Army chief opposed. As a compromise, Pakistani troops were sent to Saudi Arabia to protect the holy sites.[3] As Saddam Hussein's Iraqi army collapsed Beg forecasted in the Pakistani press that Washington would experience a second Vietnam in Iraq, for which he was widely mocked. However, even today Beg thinks he was falsely interpreted and unfairly attacked over this matter. According to his story, he travelled to Saudi Arabia to visit the Pakistani troops at Nawaz Sharif's behest: "the trip was a try by Nawaz Sharif and Washington to appease me."[4] In Riyadh he met with the US Commander General Norman Schwarzkopf and was given a full military briefing on the situation. The US General explained that while the Coalition had not yet attained its goal, Washington's final intentions in Iraq remained unclear. "They are shifting the goalposts," Schwarzkopf said. In the case of a prolonged occupation of Iraq, Beg foresaw a guerrilla war which the US could never win.[5] He admitted that after his return, in his dealings with the press, he became increasingly anti-US: like Benazir Bhutto he was also afraid that in international politics the inexperienced Nawaz Sharif would concede to America's desires and demands.[6]

Pakistani observers detect another reason for Beg's attitude. It was not his belief that Saddam Hussain could win the "mother of all wars" that motivated Beg. Rather the general was disappointed about political developments in Pakistan, which drove him to oppose the government's Iraq and US policy. Nor did Beg appreciate the young upstart from Lahore, whom he saw as politically only average. He knew that he could not expect any support from Sharif for his own plans, and seeing his career coming to an end, he became irrational. The mass demonstrations held in Pakistani cities at the beginning of the first Gulf War were unfolding before him and he hoped to jump on the political bandwagon by allying with Benazir. Beg had hoped that his statements at the peak of these protests would propel him to the zenith of power.

As plausible as such explanations seem, there were deeper reasons that explain Beg's behaviour in 1990. During Zia's time, Aslam Beg was seen as American-friendly; in Washington circles he was even known as "our man." However, with the departure of Soviet troops at the end of the 1980s, the American attitude towards Pakistan's nuclear policy hardened and the US put pressure on its former partner. According to Hussain Haqqani,

> Beg had argued even during Zia-ul-Haq's life that 'Pakistan needs to show its spine' to the United States. The Americans could not afford to ignore Pakistan, their only ally in a turbulent region, he maintained. General Beg also believed that Pakistan's nuclear capability was its greatest strategic asset. Instead of postponing the development of nuclear weapons to avert US sanctions, Beg proposed accelerating the nuclear program and going public about it. He believed that the United States would not abandon a nuclear-armed Pakistan;

in fact, a demonstrated nuclear capability could become the new reason for continued U.S. interest in supporting Pakistan. The United States was more likely to accept Pakistan's choice of leaders for Afghanistan if Pakistan stayed the course. In Beg's view, Pakistan could compensate for crossing the nuclear Rubicon by simultaneously taking steps towards democracy.[7]

The more Washington applied pressure on the nuclear question, the more Beg's dislike of American politics grew, and he knew that he had most of his countrymen behind him. He made no secret of his opinions and Washington reacted to that too. In the US press, Beg was increasingly represented as being anti-Western, an irrational hardliner, viewpoints that persist even today. Liberal Pakistani journalists jumped on the bandwagon; after thirteen hard years during which they had endured press restrictions under Zia, the dam against criticism of the Army leadership burst and Beg became the target of their long accumulated displeasure. In addition, there were writers for hire linked to certain political and religious circles who now directed their vitriole against him. Many of them were already on someone else's payroll; even top journalists and columnists were "on board". Also, highly regarded freelance journalists often wrote biased articles under third party pressure. In this way, they kept some of their independence and were able to further utilise their channels of information and contacts.

In 1990, through the MQM leader Altaf Hussain, Beg tried to win over the President as an ally. He failed: primarily because the Pathan Ghulam Ishaq Khan already had his own political ideas. It must have given him some satisfaction that, free from military oversight, he was now a decision-maker and kingmaker on his own terms. Nevertheless, he acted carefully: in early 1991 the President offered Beg a one year extension as COAS as well as a three-year term of office as CJCSC. Beg rejected the first offer and set conditions on the second. The usually well-informed monthly magazine *Herald* reported in June 1991:

> Sources say that General Beg, through the GHQ, laid down the condition that he would be willing to accept the offer provided that the post was made more powerful, on the pattern of the commander of the joint forces in the United States.[8]

When the President rejected this and also Beg's suggestion to form a National Security Council, Beg announced his intention of retiring in August. He handed the President a list of four potential candidates as his successor: Shamin Alam Khan was at the top and Asif Nawaz Janjua at the bottom. Beg felt he had acted fairly, and to the best of his knowledge. Months before this, the press and political circles had speculated who would succeed him, and it was reckoned that Shamin Alam had not yet commanded a corps and Asif Nawaz lacked HQ experience. Shamin Alam was replaced as CGS and took over the corps in Bahawalpur, while Asif Nawaz gave up the corps in Karachi and became the new CGS in GHQ. Both of them now had the same qualifications and opportunity, so the final decision lay with the President.

Prime Minister Nawaz Sharif expressed his preference for Asif Nawaz Janjua to the President, because as corps commander in Karachi, he had already worked with the Prime Minister. Janjua had reported to Lahore regarding the situation in Karachi and had also done little to ease the difficulties of the Benazir Bhutto government in Sindh. In July 1991 *Newsline* reported:

> Janjua shot to prominence after Benazir Bhutto came to power mainly because of his high-profile role as corps commander in Sindh. Janjua made no secret of his distaste for the PPP government and its policies. When bloody clashes erupted between the PPP and the MQM in February last year, and the two sides exchanged hostages under his aegis, Janjua reportedly strolled into a meeting and said to PPP members, 'You people are totally immature and, therefore, incapable of running a government.'[9]

Ghulam Ishaq Khan had no reservations against the general, who hailed from Jhelum in Punjab, and was said to have contacts in Washington through a brother living in the US. This conforms to the finer points of Pakistan's internal policy: that not only did the President and Prime Minister go against the recommendation of the COAS and decide on Asif Nawaz, but they also let Asif Nawaz know that he was their preferred choice while the serving COAS had put him last on the list. In this way, they ensured that the relationship between the new appointee and his predecessor soured and that after his retirement Beg no longer had any allies or interlocutors in GHQ.

Beg was not surprised by Ghulam Ishaq Khan and Nawaz Sharif's decision, as he knew that he was being watched carefully. Kallue had already set his people from the ISI on him, and in GHQ there was an informer in Beg's immediate circle who reported about him to the President's office, the Prime Minister's Secretariat or the PML or PPP leadership. He was aware of the career ambitions of CGS Asif Nawaz, MI head Javed Ashraf Qazi and his own PSC Brigadier Ziauddin. In this way, Aslam Beg became the first Army chief of Pakistan whose telephone was tapped by his own people. Only a concern about the Army's reputation kept Beg from launching a disciplinary action against "the gang" as he called them.[10] The fact that Beg had placed the Sandhurst graduate Asif Nawaz in fourth place as his successor may have been one of the reasons here.

On 21 August 1991 Mirza Aslam Beg's active tenure and successful military career came to an end. Beg had been CGS 1980–85, Corps Commander in Peshawar 1985–7, Vice-COAS 1987–8 and COAS 1988–91. He had advanced the modernization of the army and re-defined their morale, self-image and reputation. The number of officers with an academic education had risen during his time and 450 officers were sent by him for further training to the US.[11]

In 1991, General Aslam Beg still enjoyed a mainly positive public reputation. After the censorship and secrecy of the Zia-ul-Haq era, his handling of the press brought him the nickname "General Glasnost". It only required the political comeback of Benazir Bhutto in 1993, the initiated Mehrangate affair and a purposeful press campaign to wreak damage to Beg's reputation. Thereafter, he became the target of sharp criticism and cheap polemics over the years, his political interventions and all round openness usually goading his opponents to act.

An Un-military Goodbye—General Hamid Gul's Fall

In the months before Beg's retirement, President Ghulam Ishaq Khan and Prime Minister Nawaz Sharif were worried that, despite his public announcement, the former COAS might still take power through a *coup d'état*. In turn, Asif Nawaz had reservations about Hamid Gul, the corps commander in Multan. He confided to Beg that he believed that Gul had assigned his "bearded" friends in Afghanistan to murder him. Hence Nawaz slept every night in a different room in his house, yet still wanted additional security. Beg offered him a security troop and the newly renovated official residence of the Vice-COAS, which was in a secured area. Asif Nawaz moved in immediately and had this temporary residence additionally guarded with more than a hundred soldiers in three concentric security rings.

It remains questionable whether from 21 August 1991 onwards the new COAS Asif Nawaz slept better at night. The appointment of Lt. Gen. Shamim Alam Khan as CJCSC and the award of his fourth star were accepted by the corps commanders. However, there was still the bogeyman figure of Hamid Gul sitting in Multan. Even when COAS, Asif Nawaz did not forget his alleged enemy. Gul continued to enjoy a high reputation among the Afghan Mujahideen leaders, many of whom visited him in Multan and reported about the situation in their homeland.[12] Additionally, numerous Pakistani politicians sought his advice, because for many of them Gul was still a powerful and influential figure. Asif Nawaz waited for his chance, which came in December 1991. In the third week of the month, Alexander Rutskoi, Vice President of Russia, came for an official visit to Pakistan. Beforehand, Islamabad, in coordination with the Afghan jihadi leaders, had assured the visitor of the release of Russian soldiers who were held by Hekmatyar's men. However, Hamid Gul recommended his Afghan friends to renege on this promise, and indeed none of those imprisoned were released. In Pakistan, the government and army felt duped and disgraced.

Asif Nawaz reacted two days after Rutskoi's visit by giving Hamid Gul his marching orders. Gul was transferred to be head of the Heavy Rebuild Complex in Taxila, a military administrative post. Gul obeyed only one of his orders: he handed over the corps in Multan to Jehangir Karamat, but did not take up the post in Taxila. Nor were his attempts to win the support of Ghulam Ishaq Khan and Nawaz Sharif successful. Indeed, the Prime Minister promised Gul a transfer back into the Army mainstream, but could not get Asif Nawaz to acquiesce to the move. And President Ghulam Ishaq Khan, who had watched Hamid Gul quietly from the sidelines during the removal of the first Benazir Bhutto government, now refused to receive him. Hamid Gul, the armoured tank general, was a man steeped in professional honour. Two years before the end of his service, Taxila was not an acceptable finale to his brilliant officer's career. Nawaz seized his chance and Gul was sent packing.[13]

Pakistan's Islamists talked of a betrayal; the Jamaat-e-Islami and the Urdu press elevated Hamid Gul next to Zia-ul-Haq and Akhtar Rahman as the third hero in the Afghan jihad and explained "that General Gul's forced exit from the army was part of a move to compromise on the Afghan Jihad and clear evidence of the shift in the army's ideological position."[14]

Even if he never sported a beard, Hamid Gul was known as a born-again Muslim. The suicide of one of his two daughters in the early 1990s was said to have been the catalyst for his newfound religiousity. The young woman wanted a divorce, but her parents were against it; thereafter her younger daughter was raised by her grandparents. Even today, reports about Gul are biased. Here is an appraisal of Gul's personality by an experienced local political analyst:

> Very clear vision and clarity of thoughts. He is convinced of what he is saying, doesn't talk to the gallery on what our politicians are doing. He believes in a social justice based on the fundamentals of Islam. Isn't a bigot, is no cleric but he is anti-USA. Gul is an asset to the religious parties, he has the ability and the knowledge for training in organising things. In overthrowing

a government through sabotage he can also deliver the goods, here he can do a fine job.[15]

DG ISI Asad Durrani

Under Asad Durrani, the ISI was soon better organised. The fact that Durrani, as Beg's man, continued as ISI head under Asif Nawaz demonstrated the trust that the new COAS had in Durrani's professionalism. Also, Durrani was able to create an image of being a "safe player" and an "institutional" man. Asif Nawaz trusted him and, for the time being, Nawaz Sharif had other priorities. The Prime Minister saw the President's executive powers—that permitted him to dismiss governments and dissolve parliaments—as a potential danger to his government and toyed with ways to abolish the 8th Amendment of the Constitution, a project which would set him on a collision course with Ghulam Ishaq Khan. Therefore Nawaz Sharif avoided annoying and thereby pushing the new COAS into the presidential camp. A demand for a change at the top of the ISI so early in his tenure would have been unwise.

For Asad Durrani, the plane crash of August 1988 brought an end to the block in his career. As brigadier and a leader of a study group at the National Defence College (NDC), he had given a lecture on democracy in summer 1988 which had incurred Zia-ul-Haq's strong disapproval. In a meeting of the Promotion Board the President had struck back, blocking Durrani's promotion. Durrani knew that he would have no opportunity for advancement under Zia; so the dictator's death was a stroke of luck for him. COAS Aslam Beg did not have any reservations about him, Durrani received his second star and the two began cooperating closely thereafter. After the departure of Kallue, at the end of the first Bhutto government, Durrani, then a major general, became head of the ISI. He received his third star towards the end of his ISI tenure.

Once Asad Durrani was ISI chief, political observers in Pakistan welcomed the fact that they had an expert heading the bureau, as the new DG had MI experience. According to an insider, if Durrani had enjoyed a longer term in office, he would have revamped the ISI.[16] Durrani saw this quite differently. He said that he neither gave the order nor was there a need to reorganise the service. During his tenure he transferred only a few people, whether internally or outside the office.[17] Durrani also arranged special courses for ISI personnel in mathematics and computer science at Quaid-eAzam University in Islamabad. Additionally, he permitted two internal studies on the efficiency of the service, which pointed to an imbalance between quantitative and qualitative analysis; ideally an 80:20 relationship should exist, but in the ISI exactly the opposite obtained.[18] The fear of Indian infiltration and sabotage had led to a predominance of counter-intelligence at the expense of operational recon-naissance; "the ISI was weak in Human Intelligence (HUMINT)", one ISI man commented to the author.

Durrani headed the ISI from August 1990 to March 1992, a period when Kashmir, Afghanistan and internal affairs were the ISI's main concerns. For Kashmir, this was when the ISI became more deeply engaged in events there, starting in 1990. The Line of Control between India and Pakistan became more permeable for the so-called jihadis. Two secret meetings between Durrani and his R&AW counterpart, G. S. Bajpai, failed to calm the situation.[19]

In Kabul, Najibullah was still in power, which was a challenge for the ISI. After the storming of Jalalabad failed, the jihadis fell back on the guerrilla tactics of the 1980s. They planned a takeover of the city of Khost in eastern Afghanistan as the next stage in weakening the Najibullah regime. With the help of the ISI, Hekmatyar made contact with the Afghan Secretary of Defense, Shahnawaz Tanai, and was able to win him over in a conspiracy against Najibullah. Tanai permitted Afghan pilots to bomb Najibullah's offi-cial residence in Kabul on 9 March 1990, hoping to kill him at his desk. At the same time, with the help of loyal armoured troops, Tanai tried to open a pas-sage for Hekmatyar's troops from south of Kabul to make the conquest of the capital possible. The conspiracy failed and Tanai fled to Pakistan. But the redoubled ISI assistance to Hekmatyar continued, under Durrani as well.

In October 1990 the ISI organised a convoy of 700 trucks to drive from Peshawar towards Kabul carrying a cargo of 40,000 rockets intended for Hekmatyar. The Hizb-e-Islami commander was planning to soften up the capi-tal by an intensive rocket bombardment in preparation for a final attack. The expected high civilian losses were taken into consideration. But all Afghan com-manders, with the exception of Hekmatyar, were against the shelling of Kabul.

The CIA station in Islamabad was aghast at the prospect of the fundamen-talist Hekmatyar seizing power. Even before the failed Tanai putsch, they had supported the Northern Alliance of Ahmed Shah Masud with an immediate cash injection of US$500,000 on 31 January 1990. If there were to be rocket attacks on Kabul, US experts estimated there could be 2–300,000 casualties.[20] The US Ambassador Oakley handed over a letter from President George Bush in which he threatened profound effects on the bilateral relationship should the convoy not be recalled and Hekmatyar's project halted. The ISI caved in. Tanai Two, as the project was known in the US embassy, was abandoned and the trucks ordered back. As a result, Durrani's attitude to the US became increasingly hostile; while in Washington, where Durrani was initially not regarded as anti-American, scepticism about him similarly increased. The developments in Kashmir and Afghanistan were an eye-opener regarding his leadership of the ISI.

On the other hand, after Hekmatyar's failed attempt to attack Kabul, Durrani was flexible enough to participate as an observer in a Shura of the Afghan commanders, from which Hekmatyar was excluded. Durrani also contacted Ahmed Shah Masud, who was later invited to Islamabad, in the hope of including the Northern Alliance within a stronger anti-Najibullah alliance. For the first time too Masud received Stinger ground to air rockets.[21] In March 1991 Durrani met secretly with Najibullah's Security Minister and Intelligence chief, Ghulam Faruq Yaqubi, something which he always denied to both the Americans and the distrustful Afghan commanders. Information about the background and course of the meeting is impossible to obtain. Most likely the ISI tried to persuade the Afghans to defect.

The late Agha Shahi, who was during Zia's period in power first FO Secretary and later Minister of Foreign Affairs, explained to the author that at that time Afghanistan politics were a matter for the ISI and he (Shahi) was not involved. But contrary to the 1980s, Afghanistan politics in the 1990s were no longer handled by the ISI alone. At the end of 1988, the Foreign Office's participation increased and joint meetings began. These started with a paper presented by the FO Secretary, so that the opinions of politicians and diplomats were heard. Even more communication ensued when Prime Minister Nawaz Sharif started chairing such meetings, so that he could contribute to and influence policy outcomes.

Normally the meetings ended in mutual agreement, but twice there were exceptions. After the departure of the Soviet Army, the FO demanded an evaluation of the situation and new objectives for Pakistan's Afghanistan policy. The ISI opposed this as they saw no reason to change their current strategy. A meeting held on 25 January 1992, the last one which Durrani participated in, precipitated a second disagreement. Nawaz Sharif had refused to implement the resolutions of the previous meeting, in which he had agreed to strengthen Afghanistan's position by diplomatic means rather than force of arms. Consequently Siddique Kanju, Minister of State for Foreign Affairs, announced two days later that Pakistan would support a 5-point UN plan which enlisted a *Loya Jirga* for the installation of an interim government, which would also include representatives of the Najibullah government. At the same time Kanju announced the cessation of further weapon supplies to the Afghan mujahideen. Only days later, however, Nawaz Sharif, obviously under pressure from the Jamaat-e-Islami, demanded a revision of these resolutions from the ISI and the continuation of support for the commanders. He also pleaded for intensified cooperation between Hekmatyar and Rabbani, which was rejected by Durrani, as Hekmatyar's usefulness had sunk to zero in the ISI. Besides, Rabbani had made it clear that for the other mujahideen groups, continued cooperation with Hekmatyar was no longer possible. However, for Nawaz Sharif the resistance of his intelligence chief was too much; a few weeks later he would respond in kind.

Up to March 1992, when Afghanistan politics were in a critical phase, COAS Asif Nawaz could still shield Asad Durrani; but then Nawaz Sharif acted. His intention was to distance the ISI from GHQ and bring it closer to the Prime Minister's Secretariat. Under this dispensation, there was no place for Asad Durrani. Durrani was recalled to barracks, where GHQ made him Instructor General for Training and Evaluation (IG T&E); with the transfer came his promotion to three-star general.[22]

Altaf Hussain: A Political Career

Lt. General Asif Nawaz tried to be an un-political Army chief, in contrast to his predecessor. In his first executive order as COAS he announced the Army's abstinence from politics. In the relationship between the government and opposition, the military should henceforth stand neutral, thereby supporting Pakistan's democratization process. However, he soon realised that he had misjudged the pitfalls of Pakistani politics and the risks that came with political neutrality.[23]

When the Army's "Operation Clean Up" in Sindh started in summer 1992, he was already confronted by a myriad of domestic conflicts. The six-month campaign was an attempt to crack down on the MQM and bandit groups who were protected by various politicians in the province. As Corps Commander in Karachi, Asif Nawaz, in pursuit of his own career, had reported to Nawaz Sharif from Karachi on the MQM's activities in Sindh. At that time, the Mohajir party was a partner of the Punjab Chief Minister in his struggle against Benazir Bhutto. Now that he held power in Islamabad, Nawaz Sharif saw himself confronted with a brutal and highly demanding former ally, whom he now had to cut down to size. He gave the directive *"paijau"* to his COAS; in other words, "finish them off".[24]

Even today, the Mohajir Qaumi Movement (MQM), which had emerged during Zia's time, remains a problematic issue. A majority of local observers still regard the ISI as its original patron.[25] In the 1970s and 1980s, the Jamaat-e-Islami (JI), then strong in the cities of Sindh, was unable to destroy the Bhuttos' political base in the province. On the contrary, in 1983 the PPP-propelled Alliance for the Restoration of Democracy (ARD) called for resistance against Zia-ul-Haq's regime. Benazir Bhutto threatened to return from exile and to play the Sindh card. Zia was worried by this political threat and instructed the ISI to organise and mobilise the Mohajirs politically to his advantage. The build-up of the MQM began in 1985 through mufti bazaars, where clothes, shoes and food were either sold cheaply or given free to the poor. The money came from the ISI; they only withdrew when what they had instigated became a hugely successful grassroots movement.

However, by the 1990s the MQM could no longer be controlled by the ISI. It was radical in terms of its political platform and criminal in its daily business. Kidnappings with ransom demands, extortion and political assassination soon became part of daily life in Sindh.[26] In 1991 Altaf Hussain proposed renaming the party the Muttahida Qaumi Movement (United People's Movement), "marking the party's aspiration to grow beyond the limitations of an ethnically based movement of Muhajirs only."[27] In addition, he loudly championed his dreams of a homeland for the Mohajirs, which immediately made him a political outcast in Islamabad. Once again, the ISI was asked to rein in its former protégé.

At the end of the 1980s, the ISI started supplying Sindhi nationalists with weapons in order to support them in their fight against the MQM. At the same time, they started to look for opponents to Altaf Hussain within the MQM itself. They knew there were internal critics of the party leadership among the Mohajirs from Bihar, and they banked on that faction. In summer 1991 their strategy bore fruit: three leadership cadres publicly announced the establishment of the MQM Haqiqi, or true MQM. Altaf Hussain's idea of all-Pakistan national expansion of the party was branded as a betrayal of the Indian migrants' cause. The MQM Haqiqi demanded to be seen as the only true representatives of the Mohajirs.

Altaf Hussain reacted by declaring the Haqiqi founders to be renegades and a tool of the ISI, a critique which was accepted by his followers. The splitting of the party was based on ethnic lines: the Haqiqi faction comprised people who originated mainly from Bihar, while Altaf Hussain's followers came from Uttar Pradesh. The latter formed the majority among Mohajirs, so the old

MQM camp therefore remained dominant. In a skilful political strategic move, Altaf Hussain also appointed himself as spokesman for the Biharis from former East Pakistan—an approach which endeared him to many Biharis now living in Sindh. An attempt by the ISI to split the MQM along sectarian, Sunni versus Shia, lines in the Altaf Hussain camp failed also to produce the expected results.[28]

It was nevertheless a dangerous situation for Altaf Hussain, and in spring 1992 he went into voluntary exile in London. He had spent the last days before his escape in different hiding places, fearing for his life. The ISI allowed him to go; the febrile situation in Sindh was such that a new political martyr was the last thing the agency needed. The MQM-Haqiqi could never become the dominant force in Mohajir politics, given the stigma of cooperation with the ISI that attached to them. Instead they gradually gained control of certain districts in Karachi, so-called no go areas, where for over a decade they would hold out against their former and now hostile MQM comrades and the national intelligence bodies. These districts became known as havens of criminal intrigue. The Haqiqi factor diminished in significance when Musharraf, who came to power in 1999, needed a partner for the planned destruction of the Bhuttos' political base in Sindh, just as Zia had. He opted for Altaf Hussain, who decided to remain in London. Meanwhile, thanks to the right contacts, he now possesses British nationality and receives more than adequate financial support from his followers.[29] Over the last twenty years in exile he has kept his party firmly in his grip by holding internet-based political rallies and conferences and, as believed by many in Pakistan, when necessary even using his own strongmen.

A Heart Attack and its Consequences

On 28 May 1992 the army launched "Operation Clean Up", directed against Altaf Hussain's MQM in urban areas and against the bandit culture then prevalent in the hinterland of Sindh. Asif Nawaz succeeded in bringing the situation in Sindh under control and accomplished the operation without harming the Army's image. The reputation of the military even rose among Sindhis who had long demanded firm action against the MQM. However, in Islamabad Prime Minister Nawaz Sharif was not altogether happy with what his COAS had done. According to Ahmed Rashid, the Army chief wanted

> ...free elections in Sindh, and he was quite prepared to see the PPP take over the province if it won. In fact, Prime Minister Nawaz Sharif's real paranoia in

dealing with Asif Nawaz was not that the army would declare martial law in Sindh or take over the province. Rather, Nawaz Sharif feared that the army would simply act with common sense and hand the province to the most popular party.[30]

The relationship between the Prime Minister and Asif Nawaz began to deteriorate and had gone altogether within the year. Nawaz Sharif sent a brand new BMW as a personal gift to the COAS, but it was returned. Apparently, in his last meeting with the corps commanders the COAS had warned against such moves by the government.

In Afghan politics, Asif Nawaz supported the turn away from Hekmatyar, which therefore improved relations with the US, and he also endeavoured to maintain goods contacts with the Pentagon. He held conversations with the US Army or with CENTCOM without Ambassador Abida Hussain being present, who wrote angry missives to Islamabad. Prime Minister Nawaz Sharif, now becoming alarmed, sent a message to his Army chief via Chaudhry Nisar Ali Khan and Malik Naim who warned him to "watch your step".

The outwardly calm and self-assured style of the COAS disguised the obvious heavy political stress and frustrations associated with his office. Before his appointment as Army chief he had suffered a cardiac arrest, which he kept secret, but in December 1992 he had a second heart attack and died. His many obituaries were gracious in describing him as a true officer and a gentleman. His family, however, believed that a political plot had been hatched and the Pakistani press spent weeks reporting an alleged poisoning rumour. Nawaz Sharif's government could only absolve themselves by arranging an exhumation, carried out by foreign specialists, after which the natural cause of death was confirmed. The poisoning story still persists, however, not least because of a book published in 2008, written by one of Asif Nawaz's brothers.

Javed Nasir: The Bearded Spymaster

The appointment of Lt. Gen. Javed Nasir as the DG ISI on 2 March 1991 was a decision Nawaz Sharif took alone; as was Benazir's in the appointment of Kallue. Months before, the Prime Minister had stated to the COAS his intention to make a replacement and asked for a list of names of three suitable candidates; afterwards, however, there was an impasse. In a meeting on 1 March, the Prime Minister casually communicated his decision to the Army chief; witnesses speak of a perplexed Asif Nawaz. Just two months prior, the military had transferred Javed Nasir to be head of Pakistan's Ordnance Factory in Taxila; so his appointment to the top slot of the ISI took them completely by surprise. As had happened in the Kallue case, it was accepted by GHQ that the right to appoint the spy chief was the prerogative of the Prime Minister.

The personal decision of the Prime Minister also roused the public's attention, as the new ISI head had the reputation as an Islamic fundamentalist; he was a born-again Muslim. When a brigadier he had done the party rounds, and on the social circuit he was regarded as a bon vivant. The death of his mother in 1982 is said to have prompted a change of heart and much reflection: Javed Nasir let his beard grow and became deeply religious.

Like Nawaz Sharif's family, his parents also came from Kashmir but had migrated to Lahore and Gujranwala before Partition. He was related to Brigadier Imtiaz Ahmad, also a Kashmiri, by marriage. Besides that, they both came from the Engineer Corps where they had been coursemates. The former "Midnight Jackal" was now head of the IB and the most important supporter of Nawaz Sharif. He was known for carrying out his new job with great relish. Soon the phones of even senior officers in the Army were bugged by the IB. It is probable that Imtiaz Ahmad had influenced the Prime Minister in his decision to appoint Javed Nasir as DG ISI.

Besides Javed Nasir's image as a born-again Muslim, he also had the reputation of a highly competent officer. Together with Hamid Gul, he had completed the 18th course at the PMA, having achieved only one point less than him in the final results, since which a certain rivalry prevailed between them. At the NDC, he had been an instructor for nine years. He was seen as an experienced and self-assured officer, deeply entrenched in his religious faith. An engineer officer as head of the secret service was no novelty in Pakistan; in 1985 Nek Mohammad's appointment by Zia had put someone similar at the top position of the IB.

Before Javed's appointment as ISI chief, he was already involved in the big and influential Islamic reform and mission group Tablighi Jamaat (TJ), which in Pakistan and Bangladesh was classified as a purely religious organization. Government servants were permitted to become members and take part in TJ activities. Both during and after his ISI tenure, Javed Nasir was, as Amir of the TJ, its official leader for several years. Among the members of this group were officers of every sort, from members of the intelligence services to nuclear and rocket scientists. Many of them spent their summer holidays accompanying TJ preachers on journeys, both domestic and overseas. It is well-known that during his tenure as head of ISI, Javed Nasir participated in TJ proselytisation missions abroad, particularly in Southeast Asia. After completing his military service in May 1993, he undertook additional journeys, for instance to Cambodia to support its resurgent Islamic groups.

One mission led Nasir in 1992 to Pyongyang in North Korea, where he visited Factory 125 at the Changgwang Sinyong Corporation, where Russian R-19 rockets were modified to Nodongs.[31] In his baggage Nasir took with him American Stinger rocket blueprints and parts from Pakistan's army depot. He also signed an agreement with his North Korea colleagues for the manufacture of Stingers and their batteries and in a supplementary agreement Iran took over the financing of Stinger battery production.[32]

This trip to North Korea was not an isolated case of high-ranking Pakistanis visiting the country. As early as 1971 Zulfikar Ali Bhutto had visited North Korea and made the first contacts and agreements between the two countries. During his daughter Benazir Bhutto's second term of office, she also travelled secretly to the communist country, which contradicts her persistent claims that she was never informed about the full scope of Pakistan's atomic program. Another frequent visitor to North Korea was Dr A. Q. Khan.

ISI chief Javed Nasir also gave assistance to Bosnia, in cooperation with Iran, and supplied anti-tank rockets, bazookas, 3-inch mortars, Kalashnikov rifles of Russian and Chinese production, landmines and other small weapons, flown to the Balkans by the Pakistan Air Force (PAF).[33] ISI personnel also cooperated with al-Qaeda in order to help their Bosnian brothers-in-faith with manpower: Pakistani fighters from Harkat-ul-Ansar, Harkat-ul-Mujahideen and other groups, as well as al-Qaeda's notorious 055 Brigade, were smuggled to Bosnia via Turkey and Croatia. The brigade consisted of both Arab and non-Arab fighters, the latter drawn from Bangladesh, Indonesia, Malaysia and Kashmir.[34] ISI personnel were responsible for the transport, which was carried out in chartered planes as well as in PAF airplanes right under the noses of NATO and the CIA. But why wouild the ISI, already fully engaged in Pakistan and elsewhere in the region, concern themselves with the Balkans and the Caucasus? The answer is simple: it was all about stabilising and improving Pakistan's position in the Islamic world, in pursuit of a leadership role in the Ummah.

In March 1993 a series of bomb blasts hit Mumbai, killing 257 people. They were a response to the destruction of the Babri Masjid in Ayodhya by a Hindu mob, and can be attributed to the ISI, as they occurred on the watch of the bearded general. On the other hand Washington was now becoming increasingly concerned about what the ISI was up to in North Korea, Bosnia and Mumbai and there was growing unease over ISI operations in Kashmir and the growing number of Arab jihadis in Peshawar. Pressure was put on Nawaz Sharif for a political change, and he was urged to dissociate himself from his subversive general. On 12 May 1992, the US Secretary of State, James Baker, wrote to Nawaz Sharif to criticise Pakistani support of "militant elements operating in Kashmir." US Ambassador Nicholas Platt brought up this letter together with "talking points," which also spoke a clear language:

> We are very confident of our information that your intelligence service, the InterServices Intelligence Directorate, and elements of the Army are support- ing Kashmiri and Sikh militants who carry out acts of terrorism... This support takes the form of providing weapons, training and assistance in infiltration... We're talking about direct, covert support from the Government of Pakistan... Our information is certain. It does not come from the Indian Government. Please consider the serious consequences to our relationship if this support continues... If the situation persists, the Secretary of State may find himself required by law to place Pakistan in the U.S.G. [United States Government] State sponsors of terrorism list... You must take concrete steps to curtail assis- tance to militants and not allow their training camps to operate in Pakistan or Azad Kashmir.[35]

In a meeting chaired by Nawaz Sharif on 18 May 1992 to discuss America's threatening missive, Javed Nasir explained: "We have been covering our tracks so far and will cover them even better in future." However, the dilemma of Pakistan's situation was clearly expressed in the words of Asif Nawaz: "...it is not in Pakistan's interest to go into a confrontation with the US but we cannot shut down military operations against India either."[36]

Washington was also frustrated at the lack of cooperation from the ISI in the Stinger affair. Christina B. Rocca, Assistant Secretary of State for South Asia, was assigned to buy back 300 of these rockets that were supplied to the ISI in the late 1980s and to commission these highly effective weapons for use in Afghanistan. DG ISI Javed Nasir showed little readiness to cooperate, so Rocca recommended to her superiors that Pakistan be added to the control list of "suspected state-sponsors of terrorism."[37]

The Nawaz Sharif camp finally recognised the danger, and decided to replace the bearded intelligence chief with a less controversial figure. President Ghulam Ishaq Khan and the new COAS Waheed were informed of the deci- sion.[38] Sharif's right-hand man Chaudhry Nisar travelled as Special Envoy to the US, where he offered to sacrifice the ISI chief and offered to close the jihadi training camps and ultimately to clamp down on the activities of the Jamaat-e-Islami in Kashmir. Washington remained sceptical and Nawaz Sharif could not in any case fulfil any of these promises, even if he had wanted to do so. The abrupt end of his government came on 18 April 1993, before the dismissal of the ISI chief in May.

The Downfall of Nawaz Sharif

After the death of Asif Nawaz, the new COAS was Lt. Gen. Abdul Waheed Kakar, who was produced like a rabbit out of a hat by President Ghulam Ishaq Khan. The Corps Commander of Quetta was fifth in seniority and at the time of his appointment had been ready to pack his bags for retirement. He too was just as surprised as others to learn of his appointment, given that a number of hot favourites had hoped to be promoted to the top job. However, Ghulam Ishaq Khan proved to be a cool poker-player and surprised everyone, including Nawaz Sharif.

The new Army chief was from the Kakar tribe from the area around Zhob[39] in Balochistan, and was the third COAS after Ayub Khan and Yahya Khan to speak Pashtu, the language of the population of southern Afghanistan and the Pathan belt of Pakistan. However he was no political animal; rather, Waheed was considered an apolitical general, which is why he was selected by Ghulam Ishaq Khan. In his debut speech at GHQ, Waheed acknowledged his predecessor's achievments and expressed his hopes of doing likewise in the coming three years. Waheed envisaged his command as an extension of Asif Nawaz's tenure, in which the Army would avoid politics. But very quickly Waheed would find out that he had delivered a difficult promise. Political developments caught up with him quickly.

As mentioned above, President Ghulam Ishaq Khan and Prime Minister Nawaz Sharif had started to drift apart during autumn 1991, the core issue at stake being the political power struggle. Above every government hung the Damocles sword of the 8th Amendment of the Constitution, which was endorsed by Zia. This troubled every Prime Minister but was defended by the President. Besides that, there arose political differences between the two men. Ghulam Ishaq Khan was troubled by the economic and financial policies of the Nawaz Sharif government. He manifested the scepticism of an old, experienced and power-conscious civil servant, against what he saw as an inexperienced new political generation, as exemplified by the opposition from Benazir Bhutto. In December 1992 the then 77-year-old President sought a second five-year term of office, but Nawaz Sharif wanted to have his own man in that post. In the first half of 1993 the decision had to be shelved and the President carefully considered his options.

In the final months of his term in office and his life, COAS Asif Nawaz had worked hard to reconcile Ghulam Ishaq Khan and the Opposition leader Benazir Bhutto. His goal was to bring the PPP together with the PML-Junejo group in order to create a workable political majority. It was Ghulam Ishaq Khan who acted first. On 18 April 1993, the President dismissed the Nawaz Sharif government. A five-week caretaker government under Balakh Sher Mazari followed. The Pakistan Supreme Court declared the overthrow of Nawaz Sharif as unconstitutional on 26 May, so the Prime Minister and his team found themselves back in office. The President did not give up that easily however and three days later dissolved the PML government in Punjab, and a day later that in NWFP. Even when all sides spoke to and negotiated with everyone else, political chaos prevailed, which precipitated a situation where, almost automatically, the third pillar of the country's troika was forced to act. On 1 July Waheed went first to the Presidency and then to the Prime Minister's Secretariat to submit the Army's formula: the men in khaki demanded new elections. Nawaz Sharif yielded and finally stepped down on 18 July; he could not deploy the Supreme Court against the Army.

At the onset of the three-month election campaign, however, Nawaz was handicapped by the President remaining in office. Benazir Bhutto as PPP leader had issued the public avowal, "I will be able to work with Ghulam Ishaq Khan." Nawaz Sharif, however, hit back by saying, "I will fight this power-hungry President." During the three-month interregnum, the overseas Pakistani Moin Qureshi led a technocrat cabinet. The subsequent elections, held on 6 October 1993, were won by the PPP, and Benazir formed a coalition government on 19 October: a second chance for her. For a frustrated Nawaz Sharif, life in Opposition had just begun.

Sudden Farewells

As COAS, General Abdul Waheed Kakar had to stay politically neutral. From the outset he had supported Ghulam Ishaq Khan, to whom he owed his ascent. Benazir also wanted a peaceful relationship with Ghulam Ishaq Khan, and was closer to him than were Nawaz Sharif and his men. In this Sharif followed the line of his predecessor, Asif Nawaz. However, at the commander level, not everyone was happy with this state of affairs. At a meeting in April 1993 criticisms were aired and demands made for the COAS to hold to the neutrality initially announced by him.

The corps commanders had two reasons to speak their mind. Firstly, in their view, the President had become too involved in politics over the last few years and had often overstepped the framework of the Constitution. Secondly, they were particularly annoyed about his response to the murder allegations raised by the family of the deceased COAS against the Nawaz Sharif camp. They thought that Ghulam Ishaq Khan's attitude appeared to support rather than reject these accusations. The commanders were aware that Nawaz Sharif enjoyed great sympathy within the whole officer corps. He was seen as a dynamic politician who, while in government, had pushed through large-scale projects like motorway construction and setting up Pakistan's optic fibre system, both projects that were of great use also for the armed forces. The credit for these achievements was given to Nawaz Sharif.

Waheed sought to limit this damage in two ways. Firstly, he prematurely promoted Maj. Gen. Iftikhar, the brother of Sharif's trusted man Chaudhry Nisar Ali Khan, to be a three star general; he also extended the tenure, by one year, of two of his closest three-star generals, thereby gaining their loyalty.[40] Secondly, he dismissed Generals Asad Durrani and Javed Nasir prematurely from the Army. Thus, he made use of the singular power of his office to sack three-star generals on the spot without having to account for his decision.[41]

At the beginning of May 1993, a short communication from GHQ made it known that DG ISI Javed Nasir was to be replaced by Lt. Gen. Javed Ashraf. Some days later, he was given the status "struck from duty," meaning that the former ISI chief was dismissed from the Army eight months before the expiry of his regular military service. In the previous case of Lt. Gen. Asad Durrani, his dismissal had happened at almost the same time and in an even shabbier manner: the then NDC commander and former ISI chief was returning from a journey abroad when he learnt from one of his junior officers, in the early morning at the airport, that with immediate effect he was no longer serving in the Army. Durrani had been dismissed from the military two years before the end of his normal service.

The removal of Javed Nasir as ISI chief had been publicly expected in the wake of the fall of the Sharif government. Even the compulsory parting from the Army did not surprise local observers, as they knew of the criticisms levelled against him. Maleeha Lodhi wrote in *Newsline*, "during Lt. Gen. Javed Nasir's tenure, GHQ seemed to have lost control over the ISI. Not just the Americans but several friendly Arab countries had discreetly complained about Nasir's activities."[42] And in Islamabad, a source at the Ministry of Foreign Affairs labelled Javed Nasir's activities as irresponsible. In Washington the CIA Director during the Clinton era, James Woolsey, reported, "that the ISI was fanning conflicts in the region."[43]

New Delhi had submitted strong evidence about ISI-backed operations in Kashmir and East Punjab, and they also pointed to the hand of the ISI in the Mumbai blasts. The ISI's connections with the Sri Lankan Tamil Tigers, or LTTE, were also disclosed.

Washington was afraid of an escalation of tensions in South Asia, and as there was solid proof that linked the ISI to multiple terrorist attacks in India, questions were asked as to whether Nawaz Sharif had sanctioned Javed Nasir's actions. The US State Department also urged Nawaz Sharif to part with his ISI chief.[44]

After Waheed's actions, local observers then asked themselves what had led to the dismissal of Asad Durrani. Just one month prior, the lieutenant general had taken over the important post of commander of the National Defence College (NDC) in Islamabad. An initial clue seemed to lie in the words of the visiting senior US diplomat John Malott, who explained to the press in Islamabad on 15 May "that Pakistan had taken certain steps to allay American concerns on the terrorism issue" and mentioned the dismissal of the two generals as such a step. According to Malott, both were responsible "for having the terrorist label stuck on Pakistan," and it remained to be seen "whether it would have any impact on the ground."[45] But Durrani had left the ISI over a year earlier, and local observers asked themselves whether there was another explanation for Waheed's actions. In fact, the reason was the aforementioned discontent among the commanders that prompted Waheed Kakar to do what he did.

Durrani was always a man with his own entrenched political opinions. Even in the Ministry of Foreign Affairs, a stronghold of sceptical views of the military's policies, the ISI chief had been respected. In the Afghanistan case, he was known and valued as "one of the brightest officers in the army."[46] However, while at the ISI Durrani had become introspective, and distanced himself from Ghulam Ishaq Khan and Nawaz Sharif. The politics of the Sharif government were, in the general's mind, ill-conceived while he regarded the President's actions as those of a power-hungry individual. In short, Durrani, who as MI chief had been against Benazir Bhutto, "developed from 1992 on a soft corner for Benazir Bhutto and the PPP".[47]

Critics will refer here to the fact that Durrani, as a former general, could expect future civilian employment only in the PPP camp and had acted accordingly. To some extent, they might be right. Durrani was not a wealthy man and there were no rumours of corruption against him. In such a situation, a three-star general strives for office after retirement; particularly in Durrani's case, since he still had two children in school. It suited his disposition and experience to keep his position secure, yet in the turbulent first half of 1993, due to his strong convictions and feelings, he found himself in the Opposition camp. Benazir Bhutto, waiting for her second chance, welcomed him in. For her, it was useful to have the former not so friendly MI and ISI head as supporter and election advisor now in her own camp.

Durrani's political transformation did not go unnoticed in GHQ. Waheed seized his opportunity. Superficially on disciplinary grounds, but actually to strengthen his own position, Waheed sacked Durrani. The former DG ISI was the sacrificial pawn. Maleeha Lodhi, Islamabad's acknowledged expert on ISI affairs, wrote in *Newsline* about what lay behind GHQ's actions:

> Reliable sources cite an "unauthorised" conversation with a key political leader as the cause of army chief General Abdul Waheed's ire and his decision to send Durrani home. In March, General Durrani is said to have had a telephonic conversation with a leading political figure then abroad, which was recorded by one of the intelligence agencies. The tape was handed over to the chief of army staff in late April soon after the fall of the Nawaz Sharif government. General Waheed is said to have told his close aides that by engaging in political activities without authorization, the general was committing a grave breach of discipline that could not be tolerated. However, it was in early May when the politician in question paid a courtesy call on General Waheed to congratulate him on assuming command that Durrani's fate was sealed. The political leader cited General Durrani on a number of issues that came under discussion, innocently assuming that the general had been speaking on GHQ's behalf. For the army chief, this was final confirmation of Durrani's "non-mandated" behaviour.[48]

Most of those in the military could live with this statement, in particular Waheed. The eavesdroppers on Asad Durrani's conversations were the IB sleuths of the Midnight Jackal affair, and the tape was later given to the men in uniform by Nawaz Sharif's people. Indeed, Durrani not only telephoned Benazir Bhutto, but also offered his assistance in her election campaign. He had banked on a PPP victory and his advice and knowledge were welcomed by Benzair. As commander of NDC and former DG ISI, he still had access to inside military information. However, unauthorised reporting from within GHQ was deemed inappropriate by COAS Waheed; he used Javed Nasir's dismissal to give Asad Durrani the boot as well—because of his hobnobbing with Benazir.

Both Nasir and Durrani were dismayed at the premature end of their military careers. However, Javed Nasir would be the first to regain his inner equilibrium, given that he had much to do on behalf of Tablighi Jamaat, of which he had been a leading figure even when heading the ISI.

Nawaz Sharif returned to power in 1997 and made him his security advisor, a post which he lost in 1999 due to his criticism of the Prime Minister's role in the Kargil affair.

For a year Asad Durrani was put on ice until the new Benazir Bhutto government packed him off as Pakistan's ambassador to Germany, a position he held from May 1994 to May 1997, when he once again came under fire in the Mehrangate scandal. Having the ear of Musharraf, in September 2000 he became ambassador to Saudi Arabia, the place of exile of Nawaz Sharif. Back again in Pakistan four years later, Durrani parted from Musharraf after publicly criticizing the military operation in South Waziristan. In doing so he made common cause with two other former DG ISI heads, namely Hamid Gul and Javed Nasir.

A Dialogue with Javed Nasir

In a three-hour talk with the author in Lahore in 2005, the then 69-year-old Javed Nasir gave the impression of a calm but religious man. For him all events were in Allah's gift, including his own removal from the military.

Thanks to Allah's help he was able to demonstrate his courage in dealing with the Ojhri Camp disaster. Praying before the wall of fire, he received a sign from Allah; the fire suddenly died down and the heat became bearable. With his colleagues he then managed successfully to put out the fire and reported back to Zia and Junejo that, due to contact with Allah, the situation was under control and that no new fires would erupt. American, French and German observers at the scene estimated that the extinguishing and clean-up work would take three to four months, but "we did it with our own hands in fifteen days."[49]

There were other difficult assignments where he could feel Allah's helping hand, such as the construction of the Skardu airfield runway. He had been given responsibility for it in 1989, as DG Frontier Works Organization, with Allah's blessing. He managed to accomplish the dangerous, 11,000 feet high assignment thanks to the late onset of winter. He had prayed and, thanks to Allah, snow that would under normal conditions have started falling from mid-September only fell on 11 November, after work was completed.

After his tenure, Javid Nasir alleged, the ISI made several grave errors. In his view the priorities of the service should have been:

> to evaluate the threat to Pakistan, But today they are doing what others are doing too, a total sell-out of Pakistan's interests. ISI is today sneaking around

the people, they should talk with them. Their real job should be counter-intelligence. They should do threat evaluation. During my time at ISI our plan was threat evaluation. President Nixon wrote in one of his books that fundamentalistic Islam is a threat. USA will therefore not allow an Islamic bloc to be formed... Washington gave in writing to the Government of Pakistan that Javed Nasir had to be replaced as DG ISI... Musharraf today is a stooge of Mubarak but nobody can remove him until Allah does it, see what happened to the Shah of Iran.[50]

Javed Nasir's views on the 2005 world geo-political situation focused mainly on America's policies towards North Korea, Iran and India. He did not mention China. Nasir's remarks reflected his experience and an appraisal of years of active service. According to the former DG ISI, for many years the United States gave US$ 5–6 billion in aid to North Korea. Today Pyongyang says that the Americans lie about the range of North Korea's rockets and that therefore Washington today is in a weaker position than hitherto against North Korea: they are unable to impose their will on the country and have little effect on their politics.

Nasir's position on Iran was also clear: "Now comes the situation in Iran, Israel fears it. If they attack Iran they [the Iranians] will literally slaughter every American in every country outside the USA."[51] He showed his sound grasp of contemporary politics when one year later the *Washington Post* reported on a similar situation analysis by American experts:

> As tensions increase between the United States and Iran, U.S. intelligence and terrorism experts say they believe Iran would respond to U.S. military strikes on its nuclear sites by deploying its intelligence operatives and Hezbollah teams to carry out terrorist attacks worldwide. Iran would mount attacks against U.S. targets inside Iraq, where Iranian intelligence agents are already plentiful, predicted these experts. There is also a growing consensus that Iran's agents would target civilians in the United States, Europe and elsewhere, they said.[52]

The former ISI chief manifested great pride when mulling his country's achievements in the nuclear field of nuclear armaments:

> Despite restrictions, Pakistan has outnumbered India in nuclear matters as they possess modern and effective rockets. The first step on the way to a nuclear war will be a conventional war. Now what is USA doing? They are arming India conventionally. In a conventional war with Pakistan after 5–6 days India will be clearly have the upper hand. For whomever then rules in Islamabad the nuclear holocaust will be inevitable. Pakistan is seen as a dangerous country because of her nuclear capability. She doesn't depend on nuclear power plants because of her centrifugal techniques. We have 4000 depleted uranium anti-tank shells and no limit on uranium. Pakistan is able to build

100 nuclear bombs and outnumbers India's potential. The West also sees her as threat to Israel, therefore Pakistan is today the most dangerous country in the eyes of the West.[53]

When discussing geo-politics with Javed Nasir, Afghanistan is a perennial underlying theme. He prefaced his opinions by citing one of his predecessors:

> Afghans are not people for a conventional war. I had to talk with Afghans for hours to convince them about operations. Therefore, Hamid Gul was not a good strategist. You shouldn't plan an operation like Jalalabad. It would have been better to have ambush tactics. Hamid Gul took us for shooting practice to Afghanistan. The Afghan fighters didn't have any shooting ranges, they were using rock walls. But after 10 days of training their shooting accuracy was better than ours. The stinger accuracy quota was 80 percent. Dostum und Masud were without any wealth or possessions. Masud didn't have a single private drawer. I ordered clothing for him in Pakistan. Hekmatyar was a selfish man. Rabbani's biggest weakness was money, he kept 50 percent for himself. Mujadeddi was the best man of the whole lot.

> Masud had developed a strong friendship with me. For the Islamabad Accord I arranged a meeting between Dostum and Masud in Islamabad. The helicopter was waiting, a message was sent to Masud but he didn't show up. Hekmatyar was against the Islamabad Accord which was never implemented although they all went to Mecca where they declared they would obey it. During my time as ISI Chiethe USA sabotaged our Afghanistan policy with money. Iran was against the Taliban. I said we should give them what they need.

Our meeting ended at noon as the general had to go for Friday prayers. Before doing so he reflected on religion again. For him the Koran is original; the Bible is not. Therefore, there are a billion Christians today ranged against 1.25 billion Muslims. According to Nasir, Islam is a peaceful religion; the suicidal assassination attempts current today are forbidden, and likewise prayers at the perpetrators' graves. "Islam is misused in every aspect; today you don't find true Islam. Allah will not help this world. I'm 69 years old, I wait for the day to go."

9

HISTORY REPEATS ITSELF

An Overview of the Second Benazir Bhutto Government

The second Benazir Bhutto government's term began in autumn 1993. In the elections on 6 and 8 October the PPP had emerged as the winner against the PML led by Nawaz Sharif. One month later, Benazir appointed Sardar Farooq Leghari, "one of her trustworthy associates for the last many years," to the Presidential office. For thirty years Leghari had been a faithful and active activist and the political future of the PPP seemed bright at this juncture. There was little to suggest that barely three years later there would be a repetition of her fall in 1990. In late 1996, the second Benazir Bhutto government came to a premature end. Like Ghulam Ishaq Khan in 1990, President Leghari also dismissed Benazir's government by decree on 5 November and dissolved the national and provincial assemblies. He justified his actions by stating that the government could no longer function according to the constitution. Corruption, nepotism, disregard of High Court decisions and lack of financial discipline made it inevitable that he would have to intervene. The President knew also that he was reflecting the majority of voters who were disappointed with the government and dismayed by the endless newspaper articles that caricatured Benazir as "Alice in Plunderland".

In analyzing what explains her repeated failures, much blame lies with her government, given their own maladroit political manouevring. One must also not overlook the machinations of the establishment, the military syndicate, bureaucrats, the feudal class and business magnates. Even though the personnel in the top ranks of the military had changed, distrust of the PPP and of the Bhutto family name remained an entrenched attitude. Negative information about the family was disseminated in parallel with and uncovering of alleged cases of corruption.[1]

The ISI also succeeded in sowing distrust between the President and Prime Minister, which evolved into political rivalry and personal enmity. A video was leaked to the press which showed the President's married daughter in a compromising situation. The tape, allegedly prepared by the IB at the request of Zardari, was to be used as a bargaining tool. Indeed, the video, which was later passed on to Leghari, proved to be authentic. The question remains, however, who authorised it? The opinion prevailing in Pakistan today is that Zardari had the video in his possession to use as leverage against the President's interference in government politics. However, there is one school of thought that contends it was an ISI operation which successfully ensnared the President, who was deeply affected by the affront to his family's honour and which turned him into an embittered and ardent opponent of the Bhutto–Zardari regime.

Two events in particular during Benazir Bhutto's second term need to be mentioned. One is the emergence of the Taliban in 1994, which will be dealt with in-depth later. The second event, which was only uncovered by chance, was a planned *coup d'état* by a group of officers and Islamists whose goal was the violent overthrow of the government and army leadership. The plotters' objective was truly radical and included the murder of Prime Minister Benazir Bhutto, Army Chief Waheed Kakar and some generals, with the goal of establishing a Pakistan–Afghan Islamic caliphate.

The ISI's role in uncovering the conspiracy remains unclear. According to one version it had, like the MI, messed up. It was only the coincidental search of a jeep, on its way from NWFP to Rawalpindi, that launched the investigations which unearthed the conspiracy.[2] Another version states that the conspirators had been under observation for several weeks before the vehicle was stopped and the plot uncovered. This version is less likely however.

Major General Zaheer ul-Islam Abbasi, the leader of the revolutionary conspirators, was a former ISI officer. In the late 1980s he was a brigadier and military attaché to New Delhi, and as such an active ISI station leader.[3] Relieved of that post, for reasons that remain unclear, he was later appointed to the command of a division in the Northern Areas, as a two-star general, where he once again strove to perform with pizzazz. In an unauthorised attack on Indian military posts in the Siachen area, his unit suffered huge losses.

COAS General Asif Nawaz disciplined Abbasi and had him transferred to logistics, where Abbasi nurtured his antipathy to the less religious circles of the army leadership and broadened his contacts with Islamist radicals. After the revolutionary plan was uncovered, Abbasi and his co-conspirators were sentenced by a military court to harsh detention for several years. They were prematurely released after the coup by Musharraf in 1999.[4]

To recap, the main cause for the downfall of Benazir's second government was that its minor achievements were overshadowed by corruption scandals and mismanagement. The toppling of a transparent and economically successful government would have been difficult for the President and the intelligence services. But the absence of development and the constant bombardment of political corruption stories meant that the majority of PPP voters, who had blamed the establishment for Benzair's fall in 1990, now abandoned her. Benazir herself ascribed her defeat in the 1997 elections to the corruption charges against her, her husband and her government. As she put it, "some of which might be right and some wrong."[5] In addition, Benazir deflected the charges by describing them as the country's usual practices, saying "...corruption is used as a pretext...to defame politicians and parliamentarians."[6] She could have added that those who live in glasshouses should not throw stones. For the sake of fairness, here is her former advisor, Iqbal Akhund, who summarised the achievements of both Benazir Bhutto's governments as follows:

> Her first term was notable for its focus on human rights and, especially, the attention paid to the condition of women. The government took action against drug barons, against terrorism in the cities and banditry in the countryside; in her second term, the economy showed promise and foreign investors were beginning to discover Pakistan. An objective assessment of her performance does not leave one with an impression of exceptional wrongdoing and malfeasance.[7]

The voters saw it differently: the elections three months later ended in a defeat for Benazir and the PPP. Nawaz Sharif and the PML triumphantly returned with a secure majority. The diligent staff of the ISI had worked so well together that they far exceeded their planned objective. However, the new Prime Minister inherited a convincing mandate and on the back of that soon struck out on his own, ultimately veering well out of control, as the ISI saw it. History was about to repeat itself.

Intentions with Consequences

Benazir Bhutto returned as Prime Minister in October 1993, assuming office with the resolution not to repeat the errors of her previous reign. In her relations towards the Army's leadership she showed that she was anxious to avoid confrontation and would not derail the political agenda of the men in khaki.[8]

Exercising restraint against former military personnel did not however feature on her agenda; here old accounts had to be settled. One was with Brigadier (retd.) Imtiaz Ahmed who was to pay for his role in the "Midnight Jackal" affair and as head of the IB. Her request for a prosecution was not resented by her political opponents so much as how it was manipulated. On an evening news bulletin in August 1994, Pakistani TV viewers saw the former brigadier paraded in chains, with the obvious intention of public humiliation. No one in Benazir's camp posed the question whether such a spectacle would be counter-productive in military circles, considering that he was an officer with a long service record. They were only annoyed that they could not also exhibit the former Major Aamer to the public, as he had managed to avoid arrest. Imtiaz was accused of "illegal activities during his tenure in the ISI, including the alleged murder of a member of a leftist party."[9] A Lahore court eventually acquitted him of this accusation in 1997, after the fall of the second Benazir Bhutto government.

Another old score for Benzair to settle was with Mirza Aslam Beg, who in Benazir's eyes was the prime mover behind her first fall from power. A bank scandal in March 1994 involving Beg's name seemed to offer her the opportunity to seek revenge and finally bury the general politically.

The Mehrangate Bank Scandal

The revelations of the Mehran bank scandal in 1994 prompted a reassessment of the ISI's involvement in internal affairs, especially in the 1990 elections. "Mehrangate", as the scandal was soon called, was a methodical arrangement by which a small stratum drawn from the political class, bureaucracy and military had been making money over the past fifteen years. In comparison to the transfers of money that went on during the Afghanistan war and those associated with the drug trade, Mehrangate scarcely compares. However, the explosiveness of the scandal lay in the fact that many high-ranking people from both main political camps were involved, and that money was the motivating force for political intrigue from 1988 to 1990.

The financial scandal revealed that the Chief Operating Officer Yunus Habib had used unfair, irregular and fraudulent business transactions, first in the Habib Bank and later as head of the new privately owned Mehran Bank, over a period of five years, either to embezzle or to misappropriate the sum of 5.6 billion rupees (then c. €160 million). This amount was 80 per cent public administration money given to the bank under political auspices. It was also revealed that the ISI's directors, Asad Durrani and Javed Nasir, had deposited US$39 million in foreign currency reserves with the Mehran Bank, though according to state regulations such funds should have been held exclusively in a national bank. This was money that had been collected worldwide for jihad, and on which a high interest rate was illegally paid. For quite some time the State Bank of Pakistan was aware of Yunus Habib's practices, but he remained protected from prosecution since both the first PPP government under Benazir Bhutto and also Nawaz Sharif and members of his cabinet were beneficiaries of the cashflow in the form of donations, gifts, bribes or low interest long-term loans.

The malpractice surfaced when the ISI's Lt. Gen. Javed Ashraf, who had succeeded Javed Nasir as DG ISI, wanted to transfer the funds to another bank in January 1993. Yunus Habib was at first unable to comply, and later could pay only in instalments. In an attempt to save his skin he circulated to six senior politicians a copy of an audiotape on which he named those who benefited from his "generosity," including the amount of money and the date of the allocation of funds. In the process the name of the former Army chief Mirza Aslam Beg was mentioned, who confirmed a donation from Yunus Habib of 140 million rupees (then about US$4 million) made in favour of an election cell within the Presidency.[10] The scandal was made public as Aslam Beg, now retired, joined the PML-Chatta group in 1994 in coalition with Benazir's PPP. Beg made it known that he wanted to re-unite the PML. This would have set him at odds with Benazir Bhutto's camp, who believed that with Yunus Habib's mention of Beg's name they had a tool to fend off a future political opponent. Others who for various reasons wanted to settle old debts with Beg joined the fray.[11]

Of the more than 100 names mentioned, former COAS Aslam Beg was the only one who had to deal with direct accusations. In a statement to a Parliamentary Committee of Inquiry he contended that:

> After the general elections of 1988, ISI was completely free from the influence of the Army and since then ISI is virtually under control of (the) chief executive while remaining responsive to JCSC. In 1990, when money was donated by Younus Habib, ISI was acting under directions from higher authorities.[12]

Beg's intentions were clear: the Army was not to be dragged into this scandal. For him, those responsible were the politicians, including President Ghulam Ishaq Khan. The role of the intelligence service had been to support the politicians, according to Beg. He expressed this clearly by saying, "although the Director General ISI is an officer in uniform, the Chief of Army Staff has no authority to take action against him."[13] Asad Durrani, DG ISI from August 1990 until March 1992, sought to exculpate the ISI. He told the author that the ISI had no involvement whatsoever in the Mehrangate scandal.[14]

The truth surfaced when the money trail revealed the 140 million rupees given to Aslam Beg. As stated previously, before the elections in autumn 1990 Beg had backed Mustafa Jatoi; at this stage his support was short of any financial underpinning. Yunus Habib then entered the fray, unaware what notoriety his donation would later achieve. A portion of the cash went to Jatoi and his immediate political circle. In addition, Beg had a list of a further forty names who he wanted elected to the new parliament in order to safeguard his position against the future Prime Minister. These allies also had to be supported financially. The ISI was assigned to execute this operation, which is rather at odds with Durrani's later statement in the Mehrangate affair.

The dynamics of the Mehran Bank scandal and the investigations initiated in 1994 threatened to trigger a serious political crisis and to lay bare the morass of corruption that implicated Pakistan's leading families, the main political parties and their representatives, the intelligence agencies and the military. The political advisors around Benzair, including COAS General Abdul Waheed and the ISI head Lt. General Javed Ashraf, did not take these consequences into account in their determination to present Mehrangate to the Pakistani public. Efforts to cover up the scandal soon followed. The government authority, the FIA, was instructed not to conduct investigations against Aslam Beg while GHQ confirmed that no funds had been transferred to his accounts. Also the rumoured involvement of Altaf Hussain, chairman of the MQM party, was soon forgotten, since the PPP in Sindh needed the MQM as its partner in order to control the chaotic security situation in the cities.

To isolate the process against Yunus Habib, a deal was made—a Pakistani form of compromise. From the 100 plus implicated individuals, some were selected to deflect the proceedings through their statements—to take the rap, in common parlance.[15] Yunus Habib took all the blame, said very little and received a sentence of eight years', which he served out in comparatively pleasant prison conditions. A portion of his sentence was later dropped, and after only five years in prison he was released to live as a free man in Karachi. The missing money was compensated by the State Bank and the scandal put to rest.

The Mehrangate issue surfaced again on 31 May 1994 when Nawaz Sharif counter-attacked in Parliament where he accused President Leghari of being deeply involved in the scandal. There was uproar when the Opposition leader explained: "We have documentary evidence that the President is involved in Mehrangate. He received 7.5 million rupees from Mehran Bank through fake accounts."[16] Leghari, who was in the US at the time these accusations were made, produced a jumble of controversial explanations in his own defence, claiming that he had sold some plots of land to six unknown people from Karachi, with Yunus Habib acting as his broker and banker to facilitate the business transaction on his behalf. The majority of his countrymen were sceptical of his claims and Mehrangate resulted in a loss of prestige and respect for President Leghari from which he would never fully recover.

Durrani played a special role in the Mehrangate affair. Benazir appointed him as Ambassador to the Federal Republic of Germany in May 1994, which seemed on the surface to be compensation for his former services to her. In reality, however, the ambassadorial post was offered in order to put him under pressure. Days after Durrani's departure, the IB Director Malik travelled to Bonn with papers prepared to push Durrani into a corner. The latter had to swear an affidavit stating who were the beneficiaries of the Mehrangate affair. Major Gen. (retd.) Babar, the then Minister of the Interior, submitted the declaration to the court, including a letter from Durrani to Benazir Bhutto. The aim was to prove that of the cited 140 million rupees, Beg had passed on only 60 million to the ISI and had retained 80 million in favour of his think-tank "friends."

So to recap, when Benazir Bhutto returned in 1993, her advisors saw Beg as a political threat. He had joined the Hamid Nasir Chatta group of the PML and became their Secretary-General, his avowed goal being the re-emegerence of the Chatta group in the Muslim League, which Chatta had left in 1993 to form a coalition with the PPP. Beg left the PML-Chatta group and withdrew from the political scene after the Mehrangate scandal. To this extent, Mehrangate was helpful for Benazir's government, in that his image was permanently damaged. Even today the names of Beg and Durrani usually crop up when the scandal is discussed; all the others involved have retreated into the shadows or fallen into oblivion. The cost of Benazir's revenge on Aslam Beg was however disproportional to its outcome. A large part of the political system suffered damage that would last for many years.

One special role in Mehrangate was that of Air Marshal (retd.) Mohammad Asghar Khan. In 1996 he submitted a human rights petition to the Supreme Court against Beg and Durrani, his accusation concerning the criminal use of public funds for political purposes. The court took up the lawsuit, tried it only once and put the case on ice, where it remained for many years. Asghar Khan insistently demanded that the army leadership subsequently court martial the two generals. Only General Musharraf could calm down the headstrong old fighter, who enjoyed a reputation as an unsuccessful but honourable politician. He made the Air Marshal's son, Omar Asghar Khan, a cabinet minister in 1999, but he mysteriously committed suicide in 2003. Asghar Khan went on to publish a book in 2005 entitled *We've Learnt Nothing from History*, of which a large part focused on Mehrangate and listed the beneficiaries of the scandal.

After Musharraf's fall from power in 2008, Asghar Khan re-opened the case in January 2012. In October 2012, a three-judge bench of the Supreme Court of Pakistan concluded that the then president Ghulam Ishaq Khan, along with General (retd.) Mirza Aslam Beg and Lt. Gen. (retd.) Asad Durrani, distributed funds among various political quarters to influence the 1990 general elections. The SC's verdict asked for action against the two retired generals and also against all beneficiaries of Mehrangate. General (retd.) Mirza Aslam Beg has filed a review petition against the verdict.

During the court proceedings in 2012, two interesting matters came to light. First, the old friendship between Aslam Beg and Asad Durrani was clearly over—both went their separate ways in countering the court challenge to them. Second, that at the time of former Prime Minister Zulfikar Ali Bhutto's imprisonment, Asghar Khan had fanatically demanded the death sentence for Bhutto. In a letter to Zia-ul-Haq, the Air Marshal had even offered to hang Bhutto with his own hands from a flyover in Rawalpindi.

DG ISI Lt. Gen. Javed Ashraf Qazi (1993–1995)

Javed Nasir's successor as head of ISI in May 1993 was Lt. Gen. Javed Ashraf Qazi, who was previously DG MI and Master General of Ordnance. His father, who originated from the circle of generals hailing from Rawalpindi, had been assistant financial controller in the Ministry of Defence before 1947. Javed Qazi himself joined the Pakistan Army in 1962 where he became an artillery gunner. He was recommended by Waheed for the position of ISI chief and appointed by the caretaker Prime Minister, Balakh Sher Mazari. The general was considered to be a professional officer, but according to his critics he swayed with the wind, his primary ambition being to become Army chief, which he knew required good relations with the Prime Minister. Therefore he also strove to maintain close ties with Asif Zardari, her influential husband.

As DG ISI he delved so deeply into Pakistan's internal affairs that the PML Opposition soon accused him of trying to manipulate the Senate elections. In a discussion with the Opposition leader, Nawaz Sharif, he tried to secure the deputy post in the senate presidency for the PPP candidate.[17] The deal did not materialise, which was symptomatic of Qazi's maladroit handling of the Opposition. Then in 1994 the New Delhi Parliament announced that the entire area of Jammu and Kashmir was an integral part of India; Qazi contacted the PML on behalf of Benazir Bhutto to find out whether Pakistan could and should absorb Azad Kashmir. The DG ISI reported back to Benazir that the Opposition leader had only one question: what was in it for him?

The most remarkable act of Javed Qazi as ISI chief was the reorganization of the Afghanistan Bureau of the ISI. This move, which was obviously ordered by the Prime Minister, was designed to rid the organisaiton of an unwanted inheritance from the Zia era. Primarily controlled by officers sympathetic to Jamaat-eIslami and Hekmatyar's Hizb-e-Islami, the Afghanistan Bureau had become too independent-minded, out of control. Javed Qazi carried out a harsh purge: numerous brigadiers and colonels had to go, most of whom were retired or returned to barracks. The columnist Ikram Sehgal, who is well-informed about GHQ and intelligence matters, later wrote:

> Qazi went at ISI like knife through butter, bringing in another artillery officer Maj Gen Iftikhar...to handle the External Wing. The ISI's priceless intelligence network was dismantled, all Afghan veterans were posted back to the Army, most headed into retirement. By 1995, the ISI had been totally purged, except for a handful of favourites; no officer who had served in Afghanistan remained in ISI. Lacking either Afghan or combat experience, the ISI hierarchy developed an inferiority complex that made them petty, including ordering the surveillance of those patriots who had fought so hard for their country, risking life and limb without asking for reward or recognition.[18]

Years later, Javed Ashraf Qazi told the author that there was no other way to carry out a personnel or structural overhaul of the ISI in 1993 and 1994. He had taken over an intelligence agency that resembled a rudderless ship, where everything was a complete mess. Javed Qazi saw his predecessor Javed Nasir as a man who had no time for office procedures and paperwork. His officers had adjusted themselves to the situation—no one wore their uniform, they sought to please their boss—many ISI personnel accompanied the deeply pious ISI chief for prayers. The prevailing atmosphere in the bureau was inharmonious, and the deputy directors were not respected.[19]

Javed Qazi's first orders of the day were that the armed services would wear uniform in the ISI, and the office hours would start punctually at 7.30 am. New rules were introduced for daily financial transactions that were then largely made in cash. Payments were now to be by cheque with an officer countersigning each one. Next was the goal of structural reform, with a new classification for the main ISI departments: Internal, External, Analysis, Technology and Administration. This rationalization aimed to put all subsections (or wings) under one roof to avoid friction and inefficiencies.

But it was the changes implemented in the ISI's leadership echelons that was Javed Qazi's most effective act. He replaced his three deputies (two-star generals) and a large number of brigadiers and colonels. At the lower levels, a number of older functionaries were replaced. So he asked himself, "why are we wasting so much money on people we don't need any more?"[20] He had in mind the corrupt, religious sections and the so-called Afghans in the ISI staff, with whom Hamid Gul had maintained contact over the years. Their dismissal was to reduce Gul's influence within the ISI to nil.

On instructions from the new DG, a training academy was created within the ISI, so that civilian co-workers could get promoted to Grade 21. In retrospect, according to Javed Qazi, the ISI was "reorganized, restructured, retrained and reoriented."[21] Actions and efficiency shaped Qazi's leadership style for the two years and three months of his tenure as ISI chief, but he spent less time on diplomacy. For example, he let one of his deputies look after a Russian secret service delegation led by Yevegeni Primakov, while he remained in the background. In sending the delegation, Moscow hoped to restructure the relations between both states, bringing Pakistan on to a friendlier course towards Russia. They were working on a new strategic Russia–China–India triangle, and the purpose of the delegation was to allay Pakistan's fears regarding this plan. Additionally, through an improvement in bilateral relations, the Russians were hoping to facilitate future arms dealings. After a realistic appraisal of the ongoing political power struggle in Islamabad and to maintain good relations with India, the visit was arranged through intelligence channels. The Russians, sensitive in protocol matters, were piqued that they were demoted to the level of second fiddle in the ISI, and so the visit led to no tangible results. Apparently, the DG ISI's behaviour towards the Russian delegation was discussed by the Prime Minister and COAS. The Russians' annoyance was also noticed in New Delhi, and for a while their bilateral relationship was strained. But in Pakistan the overall feeling was that Washington was more important to them than Moscow.

Today, Lt. General (retd.) Javed Ashraf Qazi is critical of the role of jihadi organizations. In a television discussion he called all of them fakes or terrorists, with the exception of two groups active in Kashmir. However, he ought to explain why the ISI did not move against these groups during both his tenure and later. In fact, during his time in office the ISI's involvement in Kashmir and the Balkans continued. According to India's former intelligence agent B. Raman, during the bloody conflicts in Bosnia in 1991–5, some 200 British Pakistanis went for training in Harkat-ul-Mujahideen (HUM) camps and later to boost the HUM contingent in Bosnia.[22] Both Prime Minister Benazir Bhutto and the British and American secret services were informed. They were apparently interested in replacing the original primarily Arab HUM fighters in Bosnia with ones from Britain.[23] Former DG ISI Hamid Gul, who travelled to Bosnia himself, assisted in the training in the HUM camps.[24] Besides Gul, another former ISI chief was active in the Bosnian operations. Retired Lieutenant General Asad Durrani, coordinated from Bonn teams of young Muslims from the Ummah for the Bosnia assignment. Gul and Durrani also worked together with the Turkish Insani Yardim Vakfi (IHH), established in 1992, which organised the first so-called aid convoys to Gaza in June 2010. The events made headlines in the world media.

As well as in Bosnia, Pakistan also had an impact in Kosovo. The former Indian intelligence official Maloy Krishna Dhar, who worked for the Indian IB and later wrote books and articles on intelligence issues, reported:

> In 1994, the ISI linked Harkat-ul-Mujahideen and Lashkar-e-Tayeba volunteers numbering about fifty had left for Albania through Turkey. They were lodged in Kosovo by the Kosovo Muslims to fight against Serbian army and militia. These Pakistanis were grouped under the Al Qaeda banner and had established linkages with Kosovo Liberation Army (KLA) elements. Two more groups of Pakistani mujahideen belonging to Markaz-al-Dawa-al-Irshad were deputed to Kosovo in a flight chartered by the ISI. The flight took them to Turkey, from where they were smuggled into Kosovo. Their leader was known as Mullah Saraf-ud-Din.[25]

There is little reason to doubt Dhar's report. In summer 1995 foreign observers estimated there were over 4,000 Muslim fighters in Kosovo, standing shoulder to shoulder with the KLA. These volunteers came from Egypt, Saudi Arabia, Iran, Pakistan, Bangladesh and Southeast Asia, and with them were some hundred or so Muslims from Great Britain, France, Italy and Germany. Camp Donja Koretica, close to the Albanian city of Maglaj, offered accommodation and a deployment centre. Here, at one time, local observers counted forty-five Pakistanis, fifteen Bangladeshis and forty or so fighters from Southeast Asia. Polish sources reported journeys made by certain KLA leaders to Pakistan, where questions about weapon supplies were discussed with the ISI. The supply line ran through Turkey, Ukraine and Bulgaria—a route which was also used by Iran. After the events of September 2001, the US put pressure on their Pakistani partner to stop this supply route to Kosovo. However, it continued, albeit sporadically, through Turkey and Macedonia.[26]

Besides the Balkans, the ISI's handiwork can also be found in the Caucasus, Chechnya and Dagestan during the Javed Qazi era. During the Gorbachev era, Dzhokar Dudayev, a former Soviet Air Force general, had launched a separatist revolt in his Chechen homeland. As a Muslim, he portrayed his fight as Jihad, thereby incurring a wave of sympathy and a willingness to help throughout the Islamic world. Hundreds of Arab fighters rushed to assist their Muslim brothers, travelling through Azerbaijan, Turkey, Cyprus and Iran. Money and weapons came from Iran, Libya, Saudi Arabia, Sudan and Turkey. Because of their success in Afghanistan, the CIA and ISI believed they would be able to strike another blow at Moscow, and secretly supported the Chechen insurrection. The Americans' pretext was human rights, Islamabad's that of jihad.

The other internationally well-known Chechen rebel of that era was the notorious "Field Commander", Shamil Basayev. As a young man he had fought in Afghanistan, where he attracted the attention of the ISI through his courage and skill. In the early 1990s he appeared in Abkhazia, in Georgia, where he was once again noticed by the ISI. Basayev was one among a 1,500-strong Afghan mujahideen contingent in oil-rich Azerbaijan, which fought under Pakistani command against Armenia in the war over the Nagorno Karabakh enclave. In April 1994, the ISI arranged a refresher course for Basayev and some of his NCOs in guerrilla warfare and Islamic learning in the Amir Munawid Camp in Khost province in Afghanistan. As part of this course, ISI arranged special training in Rawalpindi, Peshawar and Muridke near Lahore.[27] The Chechens were trained to handle Stingers and anti-tank rockets as well as advanced explosives.

Basayev also met the Pakistani cabinet ministers Aftab Shahban Mirani (Defence) and Naseerullah Babar (Interior), as well as the DG ISI Javed Ashraf Qazi. As a result of their discussions, Stinger ground to air missiles from ISI stocks found their way into the Caucasus and were used to shoot down three Russian SK-25 combat airplanes and six helicopters. Additionally, it was agreed that a hundred or so Chechen fighters would be trained in guerrilla techniques and mountain warfare in camps in Khost province in Afghanistan. The running of the camps and implementation of the training were entrusted to Harkat-ul-Ansar, and the ISI contributed nine experienced trainers, among whom was the well-regarded Abu Abdullah Jaffa, who once served in the Pakistani Northern Light Infantry and now imparted his expertise to the Chechens. He and Basayev worked together closely and Jaffa is thought to be the strategist who planned Basayev's later invasion of Dagestan. Moreover some of the spectacular assassination attempts by Chechen separatists in Moscow are said to have been rehearsed in the Afghan camps.[28] By late 1997 several hundred Chechen fighters had undergone training in Afghanistan. Naseem Rana, Qazi's successor, continued these operations in the Balkans as well as in the Caucasus.

In August 1995 Lt. Gen. Javed Ashraf Qazi left the ISI and took command of the XXX (or Triple X) army corps stationed in Gujranwala. He might have expected that all preconditions to his becoming COAS had now been fulfilled, but in January 1996 General Jehangir Karamat succeeded Waheed Kakar as the new Army chief. It was President Farooq Leghari who had the decisive word here. The former PPP loyalist and friend of Benazir Bhutto had subsequently emerged as one of her most vociferous critics, and a crucial confrontation was already brewing between them. Farooq Leghari had no interest in promoting a henchman of the Prime Minister as he was cultivating the Army's Pashtun generals, seeing them as the most reliable support base in his ongoing conflict with Benazir and Zardari. Together they pursued the goal of ensuring that the leading Pashtun contender Ali Kuli Khan, who was CGS under Karamat in the GHQ, was appointed COAS as of January 1999. In this set-up there was no place for Javed Ashraf Qazi.

Javed Ashraf Qazi was barely troubled by financial concerns in civilian life: eight development plots in Islamabad's premier locations had been transferred to the DG ISI as a kind of back-up pension plan in 1994, their market value alone making him a wealthy man.[29] His role as a civil servant also continued after his departure from active military service: Benazir Bhutto appointed him as Secretary for Defence in August 1996, an office which he held on to after their downfall in 1998. After Musharraf's coup in 1999, he appointed Javed Ashraf Qazi to every one of his cabinets: first as Minister of Railways; eight months later the additional post of Minister of Communication (holding both offices until October 2002); in April 2003 he became a Senator, and as such the Senate's Chairman of the Defence Committee; then in Prime Minister Shaukat Aziz's cabinet, Qazi was Minister of Education.

DG ISI Lt. Gen. Nasim Rana, 1995–1998

Nasim Rana's family originated from Jullundher in East Punjab but moved to West Punjab after Partition. He joined the Army in 1961, initially in the Signal Corps. Promoted to Major General in 1990, he commanded a division in Lahore, before moving to the ISI in 1993 and later becoming DG for Counter-Intelligence. Referring to his time in the ISI, he remarked to the author about the good understanding that existed with the intelligence agencies of the Army, Air Force and Navy as well as with the IB. His appointment to the ISI's top post, which was agreed by Benazir Bhutto and Kakar, came with his promotion to Lieutenant General. In retrospect, Rana was seen as an ISI chief who operated by the book and had no political preferences or party affiliations. Thus, there were no difficulties in his official relations with Benazir Bhutto and Nawaz Sharif, the two prime Ministers during his ISI tenure, nor with Waheed and his successor Karamat.[30] The reports from his office went directly to the Prime Minister through the Military Secretary or Private Secretary, following regular procedure. In exceptional cases the reports also went through the Ministry of Defence, the CJ, the CSC or the COAS.[31] After leaving the ISI in October 1998, Rana returned to GHQ where he spent his remaining military career as Master General Ordnance and Principal Staff Officer (PSO) to the COAS. In September 1999, at 57 years old, Nasim Rana reached the retirement age of a three-star general and left the Army. His final posting 2001–3 was as Pakistan's Ambassador to Malaysia.

During Rana's time as ISI chief there was a murder conspiracy in Karachi, which was quite unusual even for that politically restive and usually crime-ridden city. On 20 September 1996, Murtaza Bhutto, the eldest son of Zulfikar Ali Bhutto and brother of Benazir, and six men in his entourage were killed in the street. A detachment of police was waiting for Murtaza's car close to the Bhutto residence in Clifton to ensure that there were no survivors.

Before the attack there had been a week-long series of press stories about political rivalries, such as the private disputes between the Bhutto siblings, in a way preparing the ground for the killings that were to follow and aimed at casting suspicion on Benazir and her husband Asif Zardari. There had inevitably been clashes between Zulfiqar's children over their father's financial and political legacy. The Prime Minister was certainly hardly delighted by the return of her brother Murtaza in November 1993 after seventeen years spent abroad; however, his continued exile was also no longer a feasible option. Nusrat Bhutto, their mother and the PPP's chairwoman, was happy about her son's return: the family would regain its equilibrium and the Bhutto name would recover some of its lustre. Benazir, as sister and Prime Minister, could hardly oppose this. Murtaza demanded his inheritance; as the eldest son he also saw himself as his father's political heir. On his return he was initially arrested, then released in May 1994—a stage-managed drama to show that no one was above the law. However, there seemed to be no procedure for political power-sharing between the siblings, who squared up to each other in early 1996 for the first time since his return from exile. In the meantime Murtaza had founded his own party, PPP-Bhutto Shaheed (Martyr), and attributed the differences with his sister primarily to Asif Zardari's malign influence.

Against this background, it was a straightforward matter for the ISI to organise a purposeful press campaign targeted at the Bhuttos. Both actual and fake incidents were reported so fancifully and with such bias that most people, not only in Pakistan, believed that Murtaza Bhutto was liquidated on the orders of his sister and/or brother-in-law. My research revealed that most of the Islamabad diplomatic corps in Islamabad were sold this version of events, which they then recycled.[32] They probably felt less sure of that account six weeks later, when President Leghari dismissed Benazir's government, thereby revealing the contours of a broader political conspiracy. And the day after the events in Karachi, the police officer who led the task force mysteriously committed suicide at home in the middle of the night.

Still in shock, Benazir's government set up an independent investigation of the incident, led by former Scotland Yard detectives, headed by Roy Herridge. The official local police version was that Murtaza's death was "accidental" rather than being the result of a conspiracy.[33] They claimed it resulted fom an exchange of fire started by his entourage, prompting the police to shoot back in self-defence: two policemen were injured in addition to the seven dead in Murtaza's group who were killed. However, the Herridge Commission issued an interim report stating that there was "evidence of a police conspiracy, and of an unidentified gunman at the scene."[34] The government meanwhile fell, and the Commission was paid off and dismissed. It has still not been proved which accomplices worked together. Was it the police and Asif Zardari, as many Pakistanis alleged? Or were other players involved?

As the Murtaza Bhutto tragedy unfolded, experts in Pakistan's political history looked towards the ISI HQ in Islamabad. It was clear to them that this incident could be manipulated to settle outstanding accounts. After the execution of Murtaza Bhutto's father in 1979, his son had left Pakistan and set up the guerrilla resistance group Al-Zulfikar, which was responsible for the hijacking of a PIA plane from Karachi to Kabul in March 1981 and also various political murders and assassination attempts.[35] Murtaza had lived in

Afghanistan, France and Syria. Well-known also were his sojourns in India, where some of his cadres were trained by India's intelligence agency R&AW. Raja Anwar later wrote about that episode as follows:

> The Indian Research and Analysis Wing, RAW, was the prime espionage agency of the country, and far more efficient than the amateurish KHAD, its Afghan counterpart.
>
> As Al-Zulfikar men began to arrive in India from Pakistan and Afghanistan from the beginning of September 1982, RAW set up a reception centre and camp for them in the city's [Delhi's] Surya Nagar locality. It was under the charge of Sardar Salim, a PPP worker from Rawalpindi. Every new arrival was fingerprinted and photographed by RAW and given a code-name that was always Hindu. The agency did not want the junior training staff to know that these men were Pakistanis or Muslims. Sardar Salim's name was Kashi Ram, while Yakub Cheena was Ashok and Umar Hayat was Deepak. Sohail Sethi was Prakash and Murtaza Bhutto the leader was Kumar.
>
> RAW was not only careful with code names; it took security seriously. For instance, it knew that some of the men would eventually be caught by Pakistani agencies such as Inter-Services Intelligence (ISI), and so it took steps to prevent them from knowing where they were trained in India. These men were transported to and from their camps by helicopter. Where the training camp was located they did not know, except that in was in a hilly area about three to four hundred miles from New Delhi. Actually the training centre lay in the city of Bhuj. What they learned there included the use of light weapons and techniques of sabotage, including bomb-making. When they were ready, the men were brought back to the Surya Nagar facility in the Indian capital, where they were always met by Murtaza, Shahnawaz and Sohail Sethi. They were organised into groups of four and smuggled across the border into Pakistan to carry out different missions. All Al-Zulfikar affairs were controlled and guided by a RAW officer named Chawla.[36]

In January and February 1982, two members of Al-Zulfikar only narrowly failed in an attempt to bring down President Zia-ul-Haq's plane during take-off. The would-be assassins were nervous and inexperienced, and made simple operating errors with the SAM-7 rockets, which saved Zia's life.[37]

Both Army HQ andthe ISI were determined not to let this affront go unchallenged. They saw the Al-Zulfikar fighters, trained by KHAD in Afghanistan and R&AW in India, as hostile agents. The fact that armed insurgents could now move freely in Pakistan did not sit well with the ISI. In addition, there were the old political worries about the stability of Sindh to contend with. According to Anwar, in a meeting with Indira Gandhi in New Delhi on 15 December 1979, Murtaza had said to her:

The army has not executed my father; it has executed what was left of Pakistan after 1971. These generals are also a threat to your security, and the only way we can be rid of them is to divide Pakistan into four parts.[38]

Such a statement was simply unacceptable to the intelligence services of Pakistan, and they set upon eliminating the Bhutto factor entirely from the nation's politics. The moment was opportune, as the public were disenchanted with the second Benazir Bhutto government and especially with Minister Asif Zardari. Also, with the exception of some parts of Sindh, Murtaza Bhutto had no large following or political capital to draw upon. Particularly favourable, however, was the fact that the relationship between the Legharis and the Bhuttos had hit rock bottom. The time to act was now.

The counter-intelligence specialist B. Raman is considered a reliable source on the political and intelligence scene in Pakistan, even if his background as an Indian and former R&AW man suggests otherwise. His version largely reflects the perceptions of local and international experts:

> [...] sections of the ISI, close to Farooq Leghari, the then President of Pakistan, had Murtaza Bhutto, the surviving brother of Mrs Benazir, assassinated outside his house in Karachi in September 1996, with the complicity of some local police officers and started a disinformation campaign in the media blaming her and her husband, Asif Zardari, for the murder. This campaign paved the way for her dismissal by Leghari in November 1996.[39]

The fall of the second Benazir Bhutto government came on 5 November 1996, followed just hours later by Asif Zardari's arrest. The case of Murtaza Bhutto was also included in the legal proceedings made against him. Zardari became a political pawn, the bargaining chip against Benazir. He was finally released eight years later, without having been convicted of any of the many accusations brought against him. Even though many Pakistanis are persuaded that the allegations about his corruption are true, only very few believe that he was involved in Murtaza's assassination. When he was released in late 2004, Benazir was once again in political exile for some years, fighting from Dubai for her political rehabilitation and comeback, unable to withstand the political pressure in her country any longer.

Lt. Gen. Nasim Rana remained as ISI chief till October 1998, and was replaced when Nawaz Sharif returned as Prime Minister. Local political analysts advance three explanations for his replacement. The first was the increasing inability of the ISI to control the Taliban and al-Qaeda effectively, exemplified by Osama bin Laden's Khost press conference in May 1998 when he had called for jihad against the US and Israel, which was disapprovingly received in Islamabad. The second reason was that Rana omitted to report to the Prime Minister about the proceedings of an Army commanders' meeting on 19 September 1998, at which Lt. Generals Ali Kuli Khan and Khalid Nawaz had criticised the Prime Minister's style of government and stumbling economic policy. The third reason was the ISI's failure to predict the approximate timing of the Indian nuclear tests on 11 and 13 May 1998 (Pokhran II); Islamabad was surprised by the relatively early date of the tests after the advent of Atul Behari Vajpayee's BJP government in March that year.

Nevertheless, considering the ISI's involvement in internal affairs and its successful oversease operations, Rana succeeded in keeping himself mostly in the background—which is to be commended for an intelligence chief. The columnist Ikram Sehgal summarised Rana's tenure by praising him, criticising his predecessor and offering a word of warning to his successor:

> There are many things to worry about, not the least being that of the many Intelligence agencies only the inherent Armed Forces entities, i.e. Army's MI, Naval Intelligence and Air Force Intelligence have retained their credibility and effectiveness. The others seem to suffer from the time-dishonourable syndrome of creating facts according to whims, caprices and jealousies rather than faithfully reporting them and providing analyses thereof. Rather upsetting had been the systematic dismantling of the much vaunted ISI machine since 1993 though one should give credit to honest and upright Lt Gen Nasim Rana, the previous DG ISI, for having not only contained the rot after he took over in 1995 but also for restoring the morale of the organisation to quite an extent during his tenure. It is still some time before we can assess how the new incumbent Ziauddin fares and find whether he has a similar penchant for personal vendetta or aggrandisement like Nasim Rana's rather unesteemed predecessor.[40]

Apparently the CIA and FBI personnel stationed in Pakistan were not sorry to see Rana go; they regarded him as a "dull-minded time server" who had little inclination to cooperate.[41] In the hunt for the assassins who murdered two American citizens in Karachi in 1995, Rana's people showed little persistence. The same applied to the search for Mir Aimal Kansi who killed two CIA agents at its Langley headquarters. After the incident Kansi fled to Pakistan, where he was sheltered by a Baloch tribal chieftain in his home province of Balochistan. After a long search the Americans believed he was being sheltered in a housing complex in Quetta by a member of the Kansi tribe. A nighttime exfiltration operation by about 100 people, including Americans, did not lead to an arrest, and there were repercussions in the Pakistani press.[42] The ISI simply stopped the search for Kansi, leaving the CIA and FBI to their own devices. Months later, however, the tried and tested method—of a large reward—brought the desired outcome. Kansi's host arranged with the CIA to lure him into a trap; the ISI also cooperated with his eventual arrest in a hotel in Dera Ghazi Khan, thereby securing a hefty chunk of the reward for themselves.

10

FOREIGN POLICY AND THE ISI

DG ISI Hamid Gul is supposed to have said that "the Foreign Office (FO) has to convert but not to design the country's foreign policy." He went on to say of the FO, "it does not have any demands on the insights and knowledge of the intelligence agency."[1] These comments reflect the self-conception and power of the ISI at the end of the successful Afghanistan operation of the 1980s, when most of its officers saw themselves as victors over the Soviet Union. A frequently heard self-assessment was "we are second to none."[2]

It was in Geneva in 1982 at a UN-sponsored conference to contain the Afghanistan situation, that the problem with Pakistan's Foreign Office first came to light. Its diplomats appeared out of touch with events there, bewildered even, due to missing briefings. They were aware only of the successes of the mujahideen in the war, while the role of the ISI itself remained out of bounds to them. In order to change this state of affairs, one of the first initiatives of the new Prime Minister, Benazir Bhutto, in December 1988, was the establishment within the FO of an Afghanistan Cell. There were now weekly situation reviews between the intelligence agency and the Foreign Office, with the latter being represented by the Secretary General. Today, the ISI state this as proof that the FO was fully engaged in Afghanistan politics during the 1990s, and that therefore Hamid Gul's sentence was no longer valid. Formally this may be correct, but all the main decisions regarding foreign policy still emanated from the ISI. For the FO, it was inadvisable to step out of line or oppose the military's preferred policy options.

The fact remains, however, that the ISI ran its own foreign policy throughout the 1990s. "They were making their own foreign policy as they went along and as it pleased them," according to Ahmed Rashid who also wrote about "a clandestine privatisation of Pakistan's foreign policy,"[3] referring to the ISI's activities in Kashmir, East Punjab, Central Asia, the Arab world, the Caucasus and the Balkans. The degree to which the Prime Ministers were informed differs from case to case. Generally they were relatively well briefed by their military and security advisors, with little being concealed from them. Meanwhile the FO were more often than not on the sidelines, spectators in the decision-making of the 1990s, as becomes clear from developments in Afghanistan and Kashmir.

The influence of the military and the ISI on Pakistan's foreign policy is revealed in the many postings of retired generals to diplomatic missions abroad. Usually up to a quarter of these foreign positions are reserved for former military men, a right that the latter had introduced and maintained over years. In 1958 Ayub Khan was allowed to shunt off the deposed President Iskander Mirza to London, where he had to open a shop in order to survive. Zulfikar Ali Bhutto, who came to power with help from the Army and Air Force, acted in a different manner. He deposed the Army chief Gul Hasan and Air Marshal Rahim Khan in a humiliatring manner, but then sent them abroad as ambassadors.[4] Bhutto had not forgotten that Yahya Khan, despite the loss of East Pakistan, relinquished power due to the resistance mobilised against him by younger Army officers. For Bhutto it was important that these officers remain calm, and loyal to him, and he secured their loyalty by these ambassadorial posts.

The example set a pattern. In subsequent years many generals were appointed as ambassadors after their retirement, most of them in their fifties, and the practice developed into a customary right of the military. With many of the former generals, the ostensible reason given was that their pensions were not sufficient. With the increasing engagement of the military in the country's politics, these postings also were derived from political calculation. The later posting of Durrani by Musharraf to Saudi Arabia, where Nawaz Sharif was exiled, was for different reasons. The strategic partnership between the two countries now demanded an experienced military officer as ambassador in Riyadh.[5] Another example of GHQ's and ISI's political diplomacy in recent times was the posting of former COAS General Karamat as ambassador to Washington. He was a man in whom the military had full confidence. In return, Washington knew that they had been offered a fast conduit to Musharraf.[6] Again, the accreditation of Major Gen. (retd.) Mahmud Ali

Durrani was for different reasons. His nomination was the work of President Asif Zardari, and was accepted reluctantly by the Army and the ISI. Mahmud Durrani was closely linked to many different circles in Washington and hence not fully trusted by GHQ and the ISI.

Pakistan's career diplomats live with the knowledge that they are often passed over in appointments to foreign diplomatic posts because of GHQ and ISI intervention. With Kayani's decision in 2008 to return the military to barracks, an improvement in the diplomatic situation was in prospect. However, the ISI and IB continues to send their own personnel undercover to foreign embassies. In many countries the ISI representatives are officially accredited. The ISI themselves speak of connections with more than fifty other foreign intelligence services. Additionally, there are undercover ISI agents in the Pakistani embassies, consulates and other international committees and institutions. Many of them are primarily occupied with the absorption of technical data and developments. They are also active as "shoppers", as proved by the history of Pakistan's nuclear armament acquisition programme.

11

NAWAZ SHARIF, SECOND TIME AROUND, 1997–1999

An Overview

After the overthrow of Benazir Bhutto's second government, Meraj Khalid took over as caretaker Prime Minister for three months and in that short term moved responsibility for operations in Afghanistan back to the ISI.

When Nawaz Sharif returned as Prime Minister again in February 1997, he felt blessed with a "heavenly" mandate. With the PML, he had won 80 percent of all parliamentary seats, even though only 32 percent of voters had gone to the polls, but this did nothing for the new Prime Minister's self-assurance. He immediately carried out a reshuffle in the IB, replacing a group of police officers with active or retired military personnel, some of which he brought in directly from the ISI. In addition, in November 1998 he called back the former DG ISI Javed Nasir and Imtiaz Ahmed. They now worked as principal intelligence and security advisors directly from his private office.

The new government also took on the press: critical journalists were put under pressure, while troublesome editors and publishers soon saw themselves confronted with the tax office, or else they lost lucrative government press release contracts. The highest court of the country, the Supreme Court in Islamabad, came under fire as the new Prime Minister had a contempt of court proceeding pending against him. The first two summons he ignored while the third was responded to by a delegation of his supporters. A hundred-strong mob, among them one cabinet minister, parliamentarians and advisors of the

139

Prime Minister, stormed the court. Fences, doors and windows were broken, and courtroom furniture destroyed. Chief Justice Sajjad Ali Shah first went on vacation and then into retirement, and the court case against Nawaz Sharif was suspended. Newly appointed loyal judges ensured that the government would henceforward influence future legal proceedings.

Next in line was Farooq Leghari. As the President pounced on the judiciary in the controversy between the Prime Minister and the Supreme Court, he sealed his political fate. Even before the expiry of his five-year term of office, Leghari was so squeezed by the Sharif camp that he resigned in December 1997. Rafiq Tarar, a retired Supreme Court judge, took over the office of President on 1 January 1998. Tarar was close to Mian Muhammad Sharif, father of the two Sharif brothers. He was considered a friend and an acolyte of the family. As such, he consented to reducing his own political power by abolishing Article 58(2) (b) of the Constitution which had been introduced by Zia-ul-Haq and gave the President the right to dismiss the government and dissolve parliaments.

In autumn 1998 Sharif embarked on a plan that was to further boost his power. With a new Constitutional amendment, the Sharia would be made the highest law of the country. Sharif wanted to become Amir-ul Momineen, the "Leader of the Faithful". In the National Assembly this passed with the necessary majority, but was blocked in the Senate after it failed to get its two-thirds majority. Nawaz Sharif waited patiently for the next Senate elections to advance his plans.

At GHQ, after Abdul Waheed Kakar's period of office, General Jehangir Karamat had taken over as COAS from January 1996. He was considered to be a good general staff officer and analyst, a real life officer and a gentleman, not prone to recklessness or quick decision-making. He had studied closely Nawaz Sharif's policies, which filled him with concern. In a speech on 6 October 1998, at the Lahore Naval College, Karamat suggested a formal role for the military in political decision-making processes through the creation of a National Security Council (NSC). It was the same idea as had been floated by Aslam Beg, during Benazir Bhutto's first government. Then it met with strong opposition from the politicians, the same reaction that Karamat would also experience. Knowing that this COAS was no revolutionary type, Sharif responded hard and fast. He demanded from the Army chief a public retraction of the idea or his resignation; Karamat opted for the latter.

On the Prime Minister's instructions, President Tarar appointed a successor on 7 October. The new COAS, the Urdu-speaking Pervez Musharraf, was third in the seniority list. Nawaz Sharif went on the assumption that a Mohajir would prove less dangerous for him than a Punjabi or a Pashtun.[1] It seems ironic now that those who advocated most strongly for Musharraf were Sharif's father Mian Muhammad Sharif, President Tarar and former DG ISI Javed Nasir, all three of whom were members of the Tablighi Jamaat. Obviously, all of them paid little attention to Musharraf's military CV, which showed him to be an impulsive individual.

The ISI under Khawaja Ziauddin

In a repetition of history, Nawaz Sharif erred with Musharraf, just as Benazir Bhutto had done with Aslam Beg. In 1989, Bhutto had insisted on Kallue as ISI chief, thereby creating a divide between her and Beg. Sharif committed a similar blunder with the appointment of Lt. Gen. Ziauddin as DG ISI.

Musharraf knew that Nawaz Sharif had originally intended having Ziauddin, a loyal Muslim Leaguer, as his next COAS. This plan had to be put on ice because of resistance from the generals. They were piqued over the parting from Jehangir Karamat and did not trust Sharif, so they used the opportunity to show their unified strength. They referred to the fact that traditionally the COAS came from the infantry or the armoured corps, whereas Ziauddin, an Engineers Corps officer, was a non-combatant. In fact, Ziauddin had an exemplary military career in both the engineers and the infantry; as a major general he had commanded an infantry division and as a lieutenant general an infantry corps.[2] Musharraf had no doubts about Ziauddin's competence and in October 1998 offered him the CGS post, the second most important one in the Army. Ziauddin rejected this offer and opted for the Prime Minister's offer of DG ISI. This put Musharraf on alert, as both were now located in opposing camps.

The ISI comes directly under the Prime Minister's office, and the DG ISI reports directly to the Prime Minister. Therefore the Army chief has no authority over the ISI. In reality, there is close contact and cooperation between GHQ and the ISI. A COAS without an ally in the secret services would be severely handicapped. Musharraf reacted to Ziauddin's appointment by shifting the ISI files for Afghanistan and Kashmir. With this move, the control of further operations was retained by GHQ. This responsibility was entrusted to Lt. General Mohammad Aziz Khan, CGS within GHQ since early 1998. Aziz was considered to be Musharraf's man. As Major General he was DDG in the ISI, responsible for Afghanistan and India.[3]

Ziauddin began his tenure as ISI chief with his room for maneouvre curtailed. Although he replaced a group of senior and middle rank officers at the start of his incumbency, he never got a full grip on the service; his deputies and other senior officers kept their distance.[4] They were preoccupied with observing the standoff beween Musharraf and Aziz and Sharif and Ziauddin, wondering which of the two sets of allies to back. There then developed the same kind of cooperation between the Prime Minister and his ISI chief as there had been only once before, namely between Zia-ul-Haq and Akhtar Rehman. Ziauddin became a close advisor to the Prime Minister; he either accompanied him on travels abroad or made the preparations during his own solo journeys. This was the case in the second half of 1999 when he travelled first alone and afterwards with Nawaz Sharif to the US. Both trips were for a special reason. For Washington and Langley (the CIA headquarters), a new and urgent issue had arisen: the hunt for Osama bin Laden. This began after the bloody attacks on the American embassies in Kenya and Tanzania in August 1998. America had to show the world its ability to retaliate as well as to control the situation. During Ziauddin's first visit to Langley in 1998, he was shown a plan of how Osama bin Laden could be lured into an ambush. Steve Coll of the *Washington Post* wrote:

> Pakistani intelligence would schedule a meeting with bin Laden at Kandahar's airport. ISI officers would tell bin Laden that they had a message for his eyes only. The CIA would then put its tribal agents into position on the long, open desert road to the airport. There was only one way in and out, and it would be relatively easy to set up the ambush. A senior ISI officer might fly into Kandahar for the supposed meeting. When bin Laden failed to turn up, the Pakistani officer could just shrug his shoulders and fly back to Islamabad.[5]

Ziauddin first promised to review the plan, and then later rejected it. The price that the government in Islamabad had to pay seemed too high, so the ISI chief proposed his own ideas. Their next US visit was in December 1998, when Nawaz Sharif and Ziauddin took the matter forward. In talks with President Clinton they suggested the deployment of a top Pakistan unit, consisting of former members of the elite Pakistan SSG. The team would be recruited on a contract basis and arrive by helicopters or road once the CIA was sure about Osama bin Laden's whereabouts.[6] The goal was to eliminate him. President Clinton, surrounded by both sceptics and promoters of this plan, later summarised the American considerations: "We tried to get the Pakistanis involved in this, realizing that it was a difficult thing for them. They had both the greatest opportunity, but the greatest political risk in getting him."[7]

The unit was set up and an initial payment of US$25 million was transferred from Washington. However, neither Nawaz Sharif nor Ziauddin were set on an armed abduction of Osama bin Laden. Ziauddin travelled to see Mullah Omar in Kandahar to persuade the Taliban leader to cooperate with the Americans on the bin Laden case. A second topic was Islamabad's demand to move against the Sipah-e-Sahaba Pakistan (SSP) leaders, who were carrying out attacks from Taliban-controlled areas against the Shias in Pakistan. Mullah Omar refused both requests. Ziauddin had failed in his mission, just like Prince Turki al-Faisal, Head of Saudi Intelligence, who in September 1998 was unable to persuade Mullah Omar to extradite Osama to Saudi Arabia. On that occasion he was accompanied by DG ISI Nasim Rana, who played the role of a spectator.

At GHQ, the generals kept a wary eye on Ziauddin's efforts to build up a team of bin Laden hunters. His Kandahar mission had not remained secret. Counter-measures were prepared, though little could be done against a mercenary/PMC abduction option, as that was a civilian enterprise. However Ziauddin's meeting with Mullah Omar, which was not coordinated with GHQ, resulted in a secret delegation of CGS Aziz and Maulana Fazl ur Rahman to Kandahar. The Taliban Amir was asked to ignore requests from Sharif or Ziauddin and to obey only those from Aziz. Thus Mullah Omar learned who to trust and who not to trust in Pakistan.

Downfall

A rash decision by Prime Minister Sharif on 12 October 1999 precipitated the end of both his career and that of his DG ISI. It is still incomprehensible how Nawaz Sharif could ignore the numerous, relevant warning signals. After the inglorious departure of Karamat as COAS in October 1998, the corps commanders decided they would accept no further humiliation from the government. Both Nawaz Sharif and Ziauddin should have known this. Besides, the important posts of the CGS and commander of the X Corps in Rawalpindi were occupied by generals close to Musharraf. Two corps commanders, known for sympathizing with the Prime Minister, had already been transferred and neutralised.[8] But the Prime Minister ignored the warning signs. He believed he had a perfect opportunity to make a proposal to the generals during Musharraf's four-hour return flight from Sri Lanka to Pakistan. His previous successes in conflicts with the press, the law and Karamat clouded his judgement. Also, in the wake of the Kargil episode he considered Musharraf to be much weakened, which was a mistake. In fact, most generals still stood behind the COAS. They thought that Nawaz Sharif was caving in to demands from Washington and was personally responsible for the hasty retreat from their positions in Kargil.[9]

Just like Nawaz Sharif, DG ISI Ziauddin also played a high stakes game. On the fateful day, he was at the Prime Minister's side, and surrounded himself with some ISI personnel loyal to him. Perhaps some of the troops that were hunting Osama bin Laden were now deployed, albeit on a different mission. Their objectives were the close personal protection of Nawaz Sharif and Ziauddin, as well as control of Pakistan's radio and television stations.[10]

On the afternoon of 12 October 1999, at 16.30, the Prime Minister signed a document appointing Ziauddin a four-star general and COAS. At 17.00 Pakistan television broadcast an announcement of the appointment and news of Musharraf's dismissal. Over the next hour the breaking news was repeated; but from 18.00 onwards there was no further mention of it, and a little later both the radio and TV stations went off air. GHQ had reacted. Pakistan TV was now controlled by members of the 111 Brigade, who met only desultory opposition on the part of Ziauddin's men. A similar situation was repeated in the Prime Minister's official residence, which had been occupied by 111 Brigade at 18.30.[11]

The consequences of the failed replacement posting were equally serious for both the Prime Minister and the DG ISI, namely the end of their official careers. Sharif found himself in custody and before a court; the accusation against him was based on the Anti-Terrorism Act and held out the possibility of severe punishment. In his defence, Nawaz Sharif named three reasons for the split between the army leadership and the government:

– the recall of Lt. Gen. (retd.) Moinuddin Haider, a Mohajir and close friend of Musharraf as Governor of Sindh;
– his acceptance of US President Bill Clinton's demand to withdraw Pakistan troops from Kargil;
– sending DG ISI Ziauddin to Kandahar to meet Mullah Omar with the request that the Taliban leadership should cooperate with the Americans in the search for Osama bin Laden.

The court refused to let the former Prime Minister offer a defence seeking to prove counter-productive behaviour by the Army leadership in the bin Laden case and in sabotaging cooperation with the US. Sharif's defence lawyer, Iqbal Raad, had to provide a written explanation for this strategy, and in doing so unknowingly signed his own death warrant. He was killed by a hit squad in his Karachi office, his documents either stolen or destroyed; the case was never resolved.[12] Afterwards, Nawaz Sharif was convicted of tax evasion, corruption, hijacking and terrorism, with a sentence of fourteen years' in prison and a 20 million rupee fine (US$ 380,000) for tax evasion, as well as two concurrent life sentences for the actions taken regarding Musharraf's return flight from Sri Lanka to Pakistan. The court also denied Sharif the right to hold public office for twenty-one years.

Nawaz Sharif was in detention for fourteen months before President Tarar was allowed to grant him a pardon on 9 December 2000, the catch being his exile to Saudi Arabia. Under pressure from Riyadh and Washington, Musharraf chose this option, so that Sharif's extended family could take along their household.[13] A decade-long absence from Pakistan was one condition of the deal, the actual details of which remain unknown to this day. On the expiry of the first five years, the Sharifs' area of movement became wider and they were allowed to travel to Dubai, London and the US. In 2006 they were able to leave Saudi Arabia, opting for London as their new residence. However, a return to Pakistan was still forbidden.[14]

The downfall of Lt. Gen. Ziauddin was steeper and harder. The former DG ISI was held in solitary confinement for fifteen months in a safe house in Rawalpindi. Sporadic visits by his wife were permitted but not TV, radio and newspapers, though later on books were allowed. Meals and medical care were sufficient, according to Ziauddin's statement to the author. In the first months interrogation determined the day's routine, but no official accusation was ever levied at him. The former DG ISI's point of view was that he had been appointed to both the ISI and potentially to COAS by a democratically elected Prime Minister (Chief Executive) and his acceptance of either promotion could not be an illegal act. Legally there was little recourse; but Musharraf took his personal revenge.

A month-long detention was enforced to break his spirit by casting doubt on his own fate and that of his family. After this seemed successful, announcements were leaked to the press about him having suffered a nervous breakdown. The military press office ISPR briefly announced the conclusion of the investigation on 6 January 2001, and Ziauddin was dismissed. He had already been discharged from the Army; in addition he lost his rank, pension rights and all his assets, which normally would be granted to a Pakistani general at the end of his service. The reason for the dismissal, entered in his military file, was expressed as "damage done to the army's interests."

Ever since, Ziauddin and his by no means wealthy wife have been surviving on a small income, living in a modest house in Lahore which had belonged to her family. Only at the end of Musharraf's tenure did his conditions improve both economically and socially. At first he worked for a British consortium on the construction of the new Islamabad airport, and in early 2010 he became chief executive of a Pakistani construction company specializing in bridges, for which he had to renew his expired engineer's certificate. Much later the Sharif brothers remembered their former henchman and in April 2010 appointed Ziauddin as chairman of the Punjab Chief Minister's Inspection Team, a post he held for only a few weeks.[15] The restoration of his full pension rights as a former Army general is still pending.

12

AFGHANISTAN IN THE 1990s

The Birth and Rise of the Taliban

The emergence and growing resilience of the Taliban in Afghanistan occurred during the ISI tenures of Javed Ashraf Qazi (May 1993–August 1995) and Nasim Rana (August 1995–October 1998), both of whom played their part as helpers and supporters, although the main encouragement came from others.

Before the Taliban entered the political arena in Afghanistan, the country was divided into different ruling domains. In Kabul the Tajik Burhanuddin Rabbani controlled the city and the surroundings as well as the north-east of the country. In the south and the east of Kabul sat Hekmatyar, who had his sights set on the capital. In the west, three provinces around the city of Herat were controlled by Ismail Khan, who was considered Iran-friendly. In the east, bordering on Pakistan, were three Pashtun provinces governed by a so-called Shura, with their seat in Jalalabad. In the north with his office in Mazar-e-Sharif sat the Uzbek Rashid Dostum, controlling six provinces. Initially Dostum had been allied with Rabbani, but in 1994 he crossed over to Hekmatyar. Together they would bombard Kabul into debris and ash. In central Afghanistan, the Hazaras controlled the province of Bamiyan. In the south, dozens of former petty warlords divided the country among themselves. This was the situation before the appearance of the Taliban in 1994.[1]

During Benazir Bhutto's second regime, her husband Asif Zardari was a cabinet minister, though still better known for his business interests. In summer 1994 there were huge losses in Pakistan's cotton harvest after it was attacked by pests, and the country's textile industries found itself in dire straits. Zardari saw his chance and bought up almost the entire cotton harvest of Turkmenistan, assigning its transportation to a friendly entrepreneur with offices in Karachi and Hong Kong. Against the advice of the Ashgabat (Turkmenistan) government to transport the cotton by ship via an Iranian port to Karachi, Zardari opted for the overland route through Afghanistan. The plan was to send truck convoys from Ashkhabad in Turkmenistan to Herat and Kandahar in Afghanistan and from there through Chaman to Quetta in Balochistan.[2] The safety of the transportation was overseen by Major General (retd.) Naseerullah Khan Babar, then Minister of Interior. Babar did not read the danger signs, even after the first two convoys were hijacked and robbed. He began negotiations with the warlords who controlled the stretch of road to Kandahar, his goal being a functioning southern passage from Pakistan via Afghanistan to Central Asia.

On 20 October 1994, Babar travelled with six invited ambassadors from Islamabad to Kandahar and Herat, to demonstrate the future travel possibilities to the diplomats. Accompanying them were Pakistan's Minister of Railways, Minister of Communications and Minister of Electricity. At the end of October, Benazir Bhutto met Ismail Khan and Rashid Dostum in the Turkmenistan capital of Ashgabat, a safe route through Afghanistan to Central Asia being the main item on the agenda. Her government then announced the modernisation of the road from Quetta to Chaman and Kandahar,[3] even though safe passage could not be guaranteed. After unsuccessful negotiations with the dominant warlords in the south-east of Afghanistan, Babar looked around for new allies and alighted upon Mullah Omar.

Omar was born in 1959 near Kandahar and educated in local madrasahs. He fought against Najibullah's troops under Commander Khalis' Hizb-e-Islami from 1989 to 1992, during which he was wounded twice and lost an eye. After his return, he became the village mullah in Singesar in the Mewand district of the Kandahar province and opened his own madrasah. Disgusted by the goings-on of the warlords in the province, he got together with like-minded people to help the civilian population against the excesses visited upon them by local warlords who were entirely out of control. Thus it was that Rabbani's government in Kabul became aware of Omar. They offered him financial support if he agreed to fight against Hekmatyar. Pakistan's Interior Minister General Babar also decided to exploit Omar's group of fighters for his own ends and arranged with Omar to take over the Pakistani weapons depot in Spin Boldak, opposite the border town of Chaman. The guards, who were Hekmatyar's people, believed they were being attacked by the regular Pakistan Army and ran away.

Interior Minister Babar was politically experienced enough to seek support for his plans from the military and the ISI. In GHQ, Director General of Military Operations (DGMO) Maj-Gen Pervez Musharraf was sympathetic. In the ISI, the DDG ISI responsible for Afghanistan and Kashmir, General Major Muhammad Aziz Khan, also showed interest in Babar's plans. Both were conscious of the dead-end situation in Afghan politics and were open to new options. However, a majority in the ISI Afghanistan Bureau remained sceptical and preferred to continue to support Hekmatyar and his Hizb-i-Islami.

After Spin Boldak, Omar's group began to be known as "the Taliban." They possessed some artillery, large quantities of ammunition and 18,000 Kalashnikovs.[4] Babar arranged an extensive test convoy comprising thirty trucks, loaded with medicine destined for Ashgabat. The journey started on 29 October 1994, with vehicles from the National Logistics Cooperation (NLC), and drivers who were former army personnel. Accompanying them were also two ex-ISI members, one being Colonel Imam, a seasoned Afghanistan expert in the service. As expected, the convoy was stopped twelve miles before Kandahar by followers of three dominant local warlords. They demanded money and a part of the consignment for themselves. Babar called Omar for assistance. On 3 November his men, supported by a militia unit from the Ministry of Interior, freed the convoy. The warlords believed it was an attack by the regular Pakistan Army and fled. One of them was caught and hanged from the muzzle of an artillery piece, on public display.

In consultation with Babar, Mullah Omar and his people continued to march onwards towards Kandahar. After two days of fighting in the outlying areas, the city was taken on 5 November 1994 without much resistance. Mullah Naquib, the city's commander, who had over 2,500 men, was bribed with money and promises that he would retain his old position under the new leadership. His men were integrated into Omar's outfit, but he was sent back to his home village as a mullah. For the first time a tactic of the Taliban's was clearly identified: the attempt to win people over with money instead of fighting. They had learned from the Jalalabad and Khost disasters in 1992.

With the fresh troops from Kandahar, the forces at Omar's disposal grew considerably, both in personnel and equipment. They now had tanks, armoured personnel carriers (APCs), artillery, trucks, ammunition and an airport with 6 MiG-21 planes at their disposal; the Taliban were born.[5] At the ISI headquarters in Islamabad, this triggered a change in view. The fear that

Babar's Taliban undertaking was an enigmatic attempt by Benazir's government to take the Afghanistan affair out of their hands now vanished. They saw the Taliban as a new way of turning around their fortunes in Afghanistan, which had been at a dead-end since 1989. In November 1994 there occurred the first official contact between the ISI and the Taliban. A delegation led by Mullah Mohammad Rabbani Akhund[6] was received by the ISI directorate in Islamabad. According to the then DG ISI, Lieutenant General Javed Ashraf Qazi, the tenor of the first Taliban requests to the ISI was as follows: extend no further help to the mujahideen commanders, stay out, be neutral. We do not want weapons or money from you, but do not stop the food and oil supply to us, which we will pay for.

Possibilities for future cooperation were successfully discussed, and from the beginning of 1995 the ISI was a powerful mentor of the Afghan Taliban, a partnership that met a dramatic end only in the wake of the events of 9/11. However, the dubious honour of being their midwife and godfather goes to Prime Minister Benazir Bhutto, her husband Asif Zardari and her Minister of Interior Naseerullah Babar.

The Late 1990s

The nucleus of the Taliban was initially a group of students from madrasahs in Afghanistan, with the Pakistan madrasahs increasingly supplying the reserves. The Jamaat-i-Islam (JUI), who became the coalition partner of the Bhutto government, was counted among them, and their leader Maulana Fazlur Rahman became the Taliban's principal supporter. The majority of the fighters soon came from the JUI madrasahs in Balochistan. They marched on after the fall of the fall of Kandahar, seeking to capture the entire country.[7] These *talibs* had received their weapon technology and combat training in camps in the Balochistan and Afghanistan border areas. Their trainers came from the Frontier Constabulary Corps and the Sibi Scouts. Later, the Taliban came to draw on Sami-ul-Haq's madrasah in Attock and the Benori madrasah in New Town, Karachi, for further recruits.

In 1997, Western experts estimated the strength of the Taliban to be 50,000 fighters and 40,000 trained reservists, with 300 tanks, plus APCs, cannons, a squadron of MiG fighter planes and sufficient hand-held weapons with ammunition at their disposition. It was understood that such a military apparatus could not be kept functioning solely by guerrilla fighters. In the areas of training and personnel reserves, logistics, strategy and tactics, the ISI and the

1. Brigadier Syed Raza Ali, former Director of the Special Operations Bureau in the ISI and head of the Afghanistan Office.

2. Ex-DG ISI Lt. Gen. Ziauddin.

3. Ex-DG ISI Lt. Gen. Javed Ashraf Qazi.

4. The author with Ex-DG ISI Lt. Gen. Ziauddin, Lahore 2008.

5. The author with Ex-DG ISI Lt. Gen. Mahmud Ahmed, Lahore 2008.

6. Ex-DG ISI and Ex-CJCSC Gen. Ehsan ul-Haq, Islamabad 2009.

7. General retd. Mirza Aslam Beg, Rawalpindi 2010.

8. The author with Ex-DG ISI Lt. Gen. Hamid Gul, Islamabad 2011.

9. The author with Ex-DG ISI Lt. Gen. Asad Durrani, Islamabad 2011.

10. Ex-DG ISI Lt. Gen Shamsur Rehman Kallue.

11. The author with Col. (retd. Imam, Rawalpindi 2008).

12. Ex-COAS Gen. Mrza Aslam Beg and Col. Imam, Rawalpindi 2008.

13. Brig. (retd. Shaukat Qadir with the author, Rawalpindi 2010).

Pakistan Army stood helpfully on the sidelines. Former R&AW head of counterterrorism B. Raman wrote:

> The Taliban's militia is officered, trained and guided by Pakistani ex-servicemen. The Administration in the Taliban-controlled areas is largely run by retired Pakistani bureaucrats. The budget of the Taliban Government, which has no source of revenue except heroin, is heavily subsidised by the Pakistani exchequer.[8]

Ahmed Shah Masud, leader of the Northern Alliance, officially announced that he had imprisoned over a dozen Pakistani officers and ISI people. Islamabad's reply was that these were former servicemen and therefore they had no responsibility for their private activities. The fact was that in summer 2001 two dozen Pakistani officers and some hundred soldiers trained the Taliban in their fight against the Northern Alliance.[9]

Experts estimate the Taliban's monthly budget was US$70 million, financed by funds from the drug trade, backing from Saudi Arabia and Pakistan, as well as taxes which were raised along the traditional trade routes to Central Asia. Special assistance from the ISI to the Taliban came in the form of establishing a new intelligence service for the insurgents, among which the ISI placed their own agents.

After the seizure of Kandahar, other developments followed rapidly on. In a kind of blitz offensive, the Taliban occupied fourteen provinces in a few months, in this way controlling south and central Afghanistan. In their approach, they often encountered only slight resistance. Their formula for success was to bribe the local warlords and commanders, who would change sides for money. However, this did not always work. In Kabul, which was defended by Ahmed Shah Masud and his Tajiks, they fought for a year before they could move into the capital, in August 1996. The former president Najibullah and his brother, who had resided in the UN building since August 1992, were seized, tortured and killed, their mutilated corpses put on triumphant display.

By summer 2001 the Taliban controlled 90 percent of Afghanistan; only in the north did Ahmed Shah Masud hold out, supported very half-heartedly by Russia, India and Iran. The other important names were already out of the picture: Hekmatyar and Ismael Khan were in Iranian exile, Dostum in Turkey. The other former mujahideen leaders looked for protection outside their country.

The Taliban saw themselves on the verge of their goal, even if they were diplomatically recognised only by Pakistan, Saudi Arabia and the UAE by 1996. Together with their supporters and advisors in the ISI, they set about getting worldwide recognition. This presumption relied on the well-known interests of the US in Central Asia. Washington went along with the emergence of the Taliban. They expected peace in Afghanistan and believed that with the Taliban's help they would be able to implement their own plans for pipelines and strategic interests in Central Asia.

But then Osama bin Laden returned to Afghanistan in 1996,[10] and in August 1998 planned the truck bomb attacks on the US embassies in Kenya and Tanzania, which left 224 dead and 4,500 wounded.

On 9 September 2001 the Taliban were feeling jubilant. Ahmed Shah Masud was killed by two Moroccan terrorists posing as journalists and bearing Belgian passports. Today it is generally regarded that bin Laden and al-Qaeda were behind the assassination. Local experts in Pakistan maintain that they were also complicit with the ISI. The assassination required careful and long-term planning. The appropriate expertise for this came from the ISI. It is improbable that the ISI would not have been informed about the undertaking, given the relationship then existing between al-Qaeda and ISI. Also the Taliban summer offensive against the Northern Alliance had been postponed from May to August without any plausible reasons. They were obviously waiting for success in the ongoing project to assassinate Ahmed Shah Masud.

The events of 11 September 2001 and the following US reaction brought a rude awakening for the Taliban, for Osama bin Laden and al-Qaeda and also for the ISI. Ultimately, all of them, including the strategists in GHQ and the ISI, under-estimated the effects of the retalitory American air strikes. Even at the end of September 2001, five ISI officers, among them a brigadier and a colonel, went to Afghanistan, taking with them several trucks laden with ammunition. Their goal was to consult with the Taliban regarding the forthcoming defense against the American invasion. The irony is that it was Lt. Gen. Aziz Khan who, later on, had to negotiate with the Americans for the return of the Pakistani Taliban supporters who were held up in north-east Afghanistan. Three Hercules planes from the Pakistan Air Force brought back the defeated Talibs, military and ISI personnel.[11]

13

INSURGENCY IN PUNJAB

Indian Punjab

From the beginning of the 1980s and into the 1990s, the Indian state of Punjab became a special area of operations for the ISI. As New Delhi saw it the Khalistan movement supported by the ISI was:

> ...one of the most virulent terrorist campaigns in the world. Launched in the early 1980s by a group of bigots who discovered their justification in a perversion of the Sikh religious identity, and supported by a gaggle of political opportunists both within the country and abroad, this movement had consumed 21,469 lives before it was comprehensively defeated in 1993.[1]

With the Partition of the subcontinent in 1947, West Punjab went to Pakistan, Eastern Punjab to India. The areas inhabited by a majority of Muslims were awarded to Pakistan; India received the areas dominated by Hindus and Sikhs. The Sikh Panth, the religious guide and defender of the faith, stood by Nehru's vision when he said before the All India Congress Committee in July 1946: "The brave Sikhs of Punjab are entitled to special consideration. I see nothing wrong in an area and a set up in the North wherein the Sikhs can experience the glow of freedom."[2]

In February 1946, the Sikh Panth passed a resolution for the division of Punjab. The goal was the establishment of a separate autonomous Sikh state within the borders of the new India. However, developments on the ground from mid 1947 ran quite differently, resulting in forced resettlement on an unprecedented scale, the killing of one million people and the destruction of enormous material assets. Thus the dream of a special political status for the Sikhs vanished at Partition. Moreover most Sikhs in that first decade after Independence felt politically ignored and economically disadvantaged after the division of the subcontinent.

The Khalistan Dream

Throughout the 1970s and 80s support for an independent state of Khalistan (Land of the Pure) was growing, a development which was closely watched and tracked by the ISI. Help for Sikh secessionism on the part of Pakistan was nothing new however. Zulfikar Ali Bhutto had supported the Khalistan idea politically at every possible opportunity while under Zia Pakistan's engagement deepened. Superficially, the motive was revenge for India's role in the splitting of East from West Pakistan and subsequent independence of Bangladesh. Of more importance politically however was Pakistan's yearning to discredit India's global status and reputation via the emergence of a separate Sikh state, which Islamabad saw as redeeming Mohammad Ali Jinnah's two-state theory.

To attain such a goal, the ISI threw itself into its Khalistan adventure from the early 1980s. A newly created cell supported the insurgent Sikhs and channeled weapons and ammunition to the followers of Jarnail Singh Bhindranwale, who had emerged in the 1970s as the rising new star of Sikh militancy.[3] Terrorist training camps for young Sikhs were set up in Karachi and Lahore while on the Indo-Pakistan border Field Intelligence Units (FIU) were the vectors of direct ISI support. Among the key insurgent groups helped in this manner were the Khalistan Commando Force, the Bhindranwale Tiger Force, the Khalistan Liberation Force and the Babbar Khalsa. The Punjab cell in the ISI's headquarters followed a three-stage plan:

> The first phase sought to precipitate the alienation of the Sikh population from mainstream India;
>
> The second emphasised the need to subvert the state's machinery and mobilise mass agitation against the government;
>
> The third phase marked the onset of a genuine reign of terror in Punjab in which the population became victims of violence and counter-violence by the militants and the state respectively.[4]

As an additional partner, the ISI sought to co-opt the Panthic Committee, which was a body of five members elected from the centre of religious leaders of the Panth, who were the upholders of the Sikh faith.[5] They also appealed to the Shiromani Gurudwara Prabhandhak Committee (SGPC), established as custodians of all Sikh shrines through the Gurudwara Act of 1925, who had considerable financial resources at their disposal. With the SGPC overseeing the management of gurudwaras and other holy places, the Panthic Committee was responsible for the decisions in faith and political questions; together they had considerable political influence, both in Punjab and New Delhi.

On the other hand, the situation in Pakistan was very different. The Sikhs, as a tiny religious minority, were entirely dependent on the good offices of the government.[6] Also there existed three rival Panthic Committees in Pakistan, with which the ISI quickly evolved close cooperation by exploiting this situation. These local Panthic Committees soon began assisting Pakistan's propaganda campaign, becoming the willing tools of the ISI's psychological warfare. The target was the Sikh community at home and abroad and international public opinion.

From New Delhi's point of view, the situation then escalated dramatically:

> ...by delivering speeches of religious sentiments and by revealing certain incidents of torture meted out to the Sikh community in early 1980s during the course of Punjab agitation, the Pak-based Panthic Committee instigated people to take arms against the Government of India. In the name of a hypothetical autonomous Sikh nation; the young people got orders and marched on the path of no return i.e. terrorism the outcome of which was violence, counterviolence and bloodshed for over a decade.[7]

Moreover, the ISI used their local Sikh partners for operations in East Punjab. Terrorist training for young Sikhs was strengthened, while the *gurudwaras* on both sides of the border were converted as rest, retreat and preparation areas, but also as depots for weapons and ammunition storage. During Operation Blue Star, the storming of the Golden Temple in Amritsar in June 1984 by Indian army units, the full magnitude of this phenomenon became visible. The besieged Sikh insurgents proved to be well-led and well-trained; they also had plentiful supplies of weapons and ammunition.

Operation Blue Star and its Consequences

Many critics in India see Operation Blue Star as an erroneous decision even today, because they feel that moderate elements of the Sikh community were humiliated by what happened, a grievance that lingers till this day. However, for Indian Prime Minister Indira Gandhi the time to act had come. Counterintelligence reports had stated that Balbier Singh Sandhu, Subheg Singh and

Amrik Singh, all three prominent heads of the Khalistan movement, had made at least six trips to Pakistan between 1981 and 1983.[8] The Home Secretary, T. N. Chaturvedi, had also submitted Intelligence Bureau reports to her stating that weapons training was taking place in gurudwaras in Jammu and Kashmir and Himachal Pradesh, the states bordering Punjab. The Soviet KGB, which cooperated closely with the Indian external intelligence service, R&AW, had also relayed a tip-off that the CIA and ISI were working together on an operation plan for Punjab, code-named Gibraltar. The KGB report also referred to the movement of 300,000 Pakistani troops into the Poonch–Rajori sector in the Pakistani part of Kashmir (Azad Kashmir) with the intention of bringing the Kargil–Leh road under control.

The then R&AW chief R. N. Kao had interrogated a Pakistani Army officer in the top secret Counter-Intelligence Center, situated in the Red Fort in New Delhi, and reported afterwards that Pakistan had despatched over 1,000 highly trained men from its Special Service Group (SSG) into Indian Punjab "... to aid the mad monk Bhindranwale in his fight against the Indian Government."[9] Additionally, it was ascertained that the ISI had activated the India–Pakistan smugglers' syndicate which operated in the south, primarily in the Kutch region of Gujarat, and in northern Jammu and Kashmir. By interrogating captured smugglers they established that Pakistan wanted to push developments in Punjab to a climax and that a large number of Pakistani agents had seeped over the desert border, through the Rann of Kutch, into India, in order to prepare sabotage schemes. The report was rounded off with reference to the discovery of sophisticated electronic cameras with photographs of military installations and other strategic objectives.

On 1 June 1984, Indira Gandhi agreed to Army units sealing off the Golden Temple at Amritsar, and the first skirmishes started on 5 June. The resistance held out for three days till 8 June. The Army then applied clean-up operations throughout Punjab, known as Operation Woodrose. The total number of those killed in Blue Star and Woodrose was estimated to be 700 Army personnel and 5,000 Sikh insurgents and civilians.[10] Indira Gandhi paid for her decision only a few months later when her Sikh bodyguards turned their guns on her. Her assassination led to the Congress-led pogrom of Sikhs in New Delhi and other cities in November 1984, which cost many thousands of lives.

The 1984 atrocities, spanning Operations Blue Star and Woodrose and the November outrage, were milestones in the evolution of the Khalistan movement. Young Sikhs followed the heightened calls by extremist groups, and new and even more radical groups emerged. The government's attempts to find a political solution after Blue Star and Woodrose by winning hearts and minds failed, due to ignorance and half-heartedness. The Indian successes of 1984 were therefore squandered. By spring 1986 the Golden Temple was restored and controlled by Damdami Taksal, representing a radical group. The violence and the killing of innocent civilians increased. In the two years 1990–1991 there were 5,058 civilian deaths, a similar number to the whole twelve-year period 1978–1989, during which there was a total of 5,070 fatalities.[11]

Assistance from the ISI

The ISI contributed to the high number of fatalities in Punjab. Thanks to their military support, the AK-47 found its way into the Sikh extremists' arsenal from May 1987 onwards. Due to its manageability and reliability, it was the ideal weapon for guerrilla fighters, as it increased their firepower and hit ratios. The Indian police and para-military forces, by contrast, were equipped with Second World War vintage rifles: only a few had Self-Loading Rifles (SLRs), and these were no match for the Kalashnikov. Only after Indian police stations and vehicles were provided with Light Machine Guns (LMGs) was there a near balance of firepower on both sides. Besides the Kalashnikov, the ISI also delivered modern explosive materials. Former Police General K.P.S. Gill reports:

> Though crude bombs extracted a steady toll of innocent lives, it was only after 1990 that sophisticated explosives became an essential component of the terrorist combat gear supplied by Pakistan. The scale of killing, consequently, was directly connected with the gun power available to the terrorists.[12]

One intriguing revelation about the training of Khalistan insurgents in Pakistan came from a member of the Babbar Khalsa[13] who was arrested and interrogated by Indian authorities in the early 1990s. He described the ISI inviting him to join a flight training school in Bombay. At an advanced stage of his training, during a solo flight he was to crash his plane into an offshore oil rig. He rejected the plan, however, as the Sikh faith forbids suicide assassinations. This statement by a Sikh source is credible as the ISI had organised a series of plane hijackings by Sikhs between 1981 and 1984. In one of these actions a pistol had been passed to one of the hijackers in Lahore. The West German Intelligence Service (BND) reported in 1984 that it was part of a delivery from a German manufacturer to the government of Pakistan, thereby tracing the weapon back to Islamabad. The US, who were then Pakistan's partner in the anti-Soviet operation in Afghanistan, reacted angrily to the news and conveyed a serious warning to Islamabad. Thereafter, this particular series of plane hijackings came to an end. Suicide missions by Sikh insurgents would indeed have been a perfect military tactic had not Sikhs objected to them on religious grounds.[14]

Dr Jagjit Singh and the Sikh Movement

The fight for Khalistan continued not only in India, but also in the international arena. Where large Sikh migrant communities had settled, principally in Canada and the United Kingdom, the ISI and R&AW were also present. Toronto, for instance, which had a Sikh population of 50,000 at the beginning of the 1980s, became a hotly contested area of action. The figurehead of the Khalistan movement abroad was Dr Jagjit Singh Chauhan, a former physician turned politician who had served a short stint as a minister in the Akali Dal government in Punjab.[15] After that he left for London, in his self-appointed position as Khalistan President, in order to win global support for the Sikh cause. He travelled on a UN document and was supported financially by his followers. Chauhan drew large crowds to events in London, Washington and New York, in various Canadian cities and other Western metropolises. Even Henry Kissinger listened to him. Soon New Delhi was forced to take countermeasures, as Chauhan had foreseen. His experienced eye had noticed the Indian agents shadowing him on his arrival at or departure from international airports and he warned his followers of infiltration by secret service personnel disguised as refugees or businessmen. Indeed, the Indian Home Minister Zail Singh announced in April 1981 that the government had started "a surveillance operation against expatriate Khalistanis in places such as Canada."[16] As *India Today* wrote in 1985:

> Indian Government intelligence on external groups has increased dramatically in the last two years, mainly because of the additional intelligence operatives from RAW and the IB that have been posted under diplomatic cover in key embassies like Toronto, Vancouver, London, Washington, New York, Bonn and Paris.[17]

According to Zuhair Kashmeri and Brian McAndrew, two Canadian journalists, they described in their book *Soft Target*, published in 1989, how:

> [the Sikhs became] victims of manipulations and disinformation carried out by the Indian Government. With the aim of discrediting the Sikhs and undermining the campaign for an independent Punjab, Indian agents have infiltrated the

Sikh community in Canada, formenting hostility towards India and even pro-
voking violent incidents... Along the way, India has also played a devious game
with the Canadian Government ... exploiting the Canadian desire to maintain
good relations with India, Indian diplomats and agents erected a steady stream
of phony tips on the Sikhs to the Canadian government.[18]

The book mainly concerns the destruction of the ill-fated Air India Flight
182 in 1985, for which the authors blamed R&AW. In their mind India's
intelligence agency was trying to discredit the Khalistan movement. The
Boeing 747, *Emperor Kanishka*, was blown up in mid air by a smuggled bomb
concealed inside a passenger's suitcase, killing 329 people.[19] Kashmeri and
McAndrew make concessions for the Indians, saying that such a high number
of victims were not intended. Under AI182's normal flight schedule, the aircraft would have been parked at London Heathrow at the time of the explosion; but the flight was delayed for an hour and forty minutes, by which time
it had a full complement of passengers.[20]

The ensuing court case was heard in Canada under Judge Ian Bruce
Josephson. The accused consisted of six main suspects, all of whom belonged
to the Babbar Khalsa group, created in 1978.[21] Eventually the last two accused,
Ripudaman Singh Malik and Ajaib Singh Bagri, were acquitted due to a lack
of evidence. The long-drawn out investigation into Flight 182 was closed on
16 March 2005 and those who perpetrated the attack remain at large.

The Pacification of the Situation

In India, Rajiv Gandhi succeeded his mother as Prime Minister (1984–9)
after her assassination, and ordered an aggressive series of counter-measures
against the ISI's involvement in Punjab. In R&AW, the desks of CIT-X and
CIT-J were kept very busy.[22] In the mid 1980s, a series of bombings rocked the
cities of Karachi and Lahore, spelling out to the Zia-ul-Haq regime that New
Delhi was ready to fight terrorism with terrorism. This had the desired effect
on Rawalpindi, which began to weigh the cost-benefit considerations. With
the assistance of Jordanian Crown Prince Hasan bin-Talal, whose wife Sarvath
is from Pakistan, ISI Chief Hamid Gul and R&AW Director A. K. Verma met
in Amman and Geneva to find a way out of the precarious situation. Gul is
said to have promised to stop the Khalistani groups from attacking Indian
cities, and in return Verma promised a halt to the bomb attacks on Pakistan.
However, Gul could not keep his promises: the political resistance and turmoil in East Punjab kept churning, and the ISI continued their assistance to

the Khalistan secessionists. In 1989 Rajiv Gandhi came to Islamabad under the auspices of the SAARC summit. In a meeting with Benazir, the ISI's activities in Punjab were one of the topics touched upon. There are still rumours that Pakistan betrayed their Sikh allies by handing the Indians lists of names, topographical maps and other intelligence information, a claim that Benazir and her then Minister of the Interior Aitzaz Ahsan vehemently denied.

In response to the ongoing unrest in East Punjab, in 1990 the government in New Delhi once again called out the Army. In a coordinated series of actions, the Army, police and other security services took on the Sikh separatist political underground in a no holds barred manner. In 1990/91 3,497 terrorists were killed; and in 1992 the number was 2,911. The ranks of Khalistan commandoes began to shrink rapidly in the face of this onslaught and some of their leaders fled to Pakistan. For example, the ISI had to play host to Wadhava Singh and Mehal Singh from Babbar Khalsa, Paramjit Singh Panjwar from KCF, Pritam Singh Sekhon from KHL and Narain Singh from KLA.

In Indian Punjab, the terror slowly started abating from 1993 onwards, though a last major terrorist strike occurred in 1995. External events also contributed to this state of affairs. In August 1988, the Zia-ul-Haq era came to an end; and in December of that year a democratically elected government once again held office in Islamabad. The political unrest in East Punjab calmed down over time, but a cell within the ISI still keeps an eye on the Sikh resistance. The Khalistan chapter is not yet fully closed.

14

THE ISI IN NORTH-EAST INDIA

India's Troubled North-East

North-east India, with its scenic diversity, is one of the most attractive parts of the country. The states of Arunachal Pradesh, Assam, Manipur, Meghalaya, Mizoram, Nagaland and Tripura cover 8 percent of India's national territory, but account for only 4 percent of its total population.[1] The "Seven Sisters", as the north-east states are known, are characterised by ethnic, linguistic, cultural and religious cleavages; but roughly speaking, the hill tribes are mainly Christian and the plains-dwellers mostly Hindus and Muslims.

Bordering China, Bhutan, Bangladesh and Myanmar (Burma), these states are connected to mainland India by a stretch of territory 130 km long by 20–30 km wide at Siliguri in the north of West Bengal. The north-east represents a geo-strategic challenge for India: security experts call the corridor bordering Tibet and Bangladesh the country's "chicken neck": easy to sever, easy to bleed dry.

The aforementioned ethnic, religious and cultural differences, combined with economic underdevelopment, political ignorance and corruption, encouraged political resistance to develop in north-east India soon after Independence. This gave rise to a political underground which launched an insurgency in the early 1950s with acts of terrorism. A so-called Federal Government of Nagaland (FGN) became strong enough to spread into the four Naga districts in neighbouring Manipur in 1956. Some of these underground organizations in north-east India were soon being supported by

Pakistan and other neighbouring states; these included the National Socialist Council of Nagaland (NSCN), the United Liberation Front of Assam (ULFA), the People's Liberation Army (PLA) and the National Liberation Front of Tripura (NLFT).

The NSCN, active since the early 1950s, maintained its headquarters in North Burma, where they received support from the local Kachin Independent Organization (KIO). The PLA, founded in 1978, moved into north Burma in order to develop training camps and sanctuaries with the help of the NSCN. The ULFA from Assam already had previous contacts in Burma, who provided training and logistics. KIO helped all three organizations with training and supplied them with weapons from the Burmese Army. Over many years, they all felt relatively secure in Rangoon, from counter-measures by New Delhi.

In the early 1990s, ULFA established an additional fourteen camps in Bangladesh.[2] These served as safe havens for fighters and families, as training grounds and also as drop off points for weapon supplies.[3] Not only ULFA, but also the NSCN and PLA established a presence in the border regions of Bangladesh. NSCN set up a base in Masalong; and the PLA had two camps in Burma plus a further five in Bangladesh.

Assistance from Friends

In 1990, via the Pakistan embassy in Dhaka, the NSCN and ULFA developed contacts with the ISI. As far back as the 1960s, undivided Pakistan had supplied weapons for the Naga fighters. However, the turbulent developments in East Pakistan and the birth of Bangladesh in 1971 led to a temporary halt in this weapons pipeline. Relations were never completely broken off, however, and in the 1980s they were revitalised.

In January 1991, with the help of the ISI, several high-ranking ULFA leaders travelled to Pakistan to sign a training agreement for ULFA cadres. In the same year, two 6-member ULFA groups arrived in Islamabad for training; a third 10-member group followed in 1993. The ISI's auxiliary support for operations of this kind covered more than just the training courses in Pakistan. Well in advance, new identities and fake passports had to be procured, travel routes determined and the financing of the whole operation had to be secured. In this way, the Pakistan embassy in Dhaka became an important ISI station, the hub of its operations in north-east India.

In the ISI directorate in Islamabad, they must have been content with the results of the first training courses for ULFA fighters, since they continued through the 1990s and were extended to include other underground groups. The Indian security forces at one point arrested and interrogated a member of the NLFT, who revealed that between 1997 and 1998 some of their top brass had gone for training with the ISI in Pakistan. The detainee mentioned the names of NLFT leaders, thereby uncovering the whole structure of task distribution and kinship within the top echelons of the group.[4]

Parallel to the Muslim resistance in Kashmir, other Islamist organizations in north-east India were also increasingly active in the 1990s. The main militant Islamist resistance groups in north-east India were: Muslim United Liberation Front of Assam, Muslim United Liberation Tigers of Assam, Islamic Liberation Army of Assam, United Muslim Liberation Front of Assam, United Reformation Protest of Assam, People's United Liberation Front, Muslim Volunteer Force, Adam Sena Islamic Sevak Sangh, Harkat-ul-Mujahideen and Harkat-ul Jihad.[5]

The ISI was always ready to help their friends in north-east India procure weapons. In Thailand, after the collapse of the Khmer Rouge regime in Cambodia from the 1980s onwards, light weapons and light machine guns awaited prospective buyers, so new supply opportunities opened up. Thus in 1991 the ISI provided weapons from Thailand to a group of 240 NSCN members. Small boats brought the cargo to Cox's Bazaar, a port in Bangladesh, which became the hub for weapon supplies in the region. Consequently, two more deliveries were made. In week-long treks the NSCN and ULFA fighters themselves fetched weapons from Bangladesh and brought them back to their bases. On the land route there was the ever-present danger of interception by the Indian Border Security Force, the police in the individual states and by Army units. In fact the fourth delivery was ambushed and the group involved was mostly wiped out. They then switched to longer and more difficult routes, in an attempt to make their delivery paths more secure.

In the initial years of the new arms supply channel, the ISI was obliged to procure and finance the weapons. According to Tara Kartha, one prominent Naga fighter, imprisoned by the Indians, in the 1990s he received three instalments totalling US$ 1.7 million from the ISI for weapon purchases. Later on, the rebels often funded the purchase themselves. Bank robberies, tax extortions, blackmail and the drug trade supplied the means; thus terror began to be self-financing. Such weapons supply routes were running throughout the 1990s and into the new millennium, with Bangladesh as the main trans-shipment point.

In arms procurement the ISI also received support from their Chinese colleagues. As far back as 1993, ULFA had contacts with the Chinese military.

The first weapons supply came from a Chinese ship in 1995, another in 1997 by a land route through Bhutan. The end of the 1990s saw the revival of NSCN contacts with China, which had lain dormant in the 1980s. In 2000, high-ranking officials of the organization negotiated with the Chinese authorities in Kuming province regarding new weapons assistance.[6] In December of that year, NSCN-IM received a delivery valued at US$750,000 via Cox's Bazaar; and that same month a delivery by road reached the Burmese border town of Tamu, conveniently situated opposite Moreh in Manipur. The Chinese supplies were fully paid for by the underground fighters. This was proven by India, which successfully traced back a transaction of US$1 million to a Chinese state company.[7]

Outlook

In the second decade of the new millennium, underground terrorist groups remain active in north-east India. New recruits, mainly students or those from a Muslim background, continue to join the original outfits. The offer of a monthly stipend of 2,000 to 3,000 Indian rupees per person at a time of mass unemployment is one enticing incentive. Moreover, the numbers of madrasahs has multiplied in Assam and the Shiliguri belt and some youths there have begun to be drawn to more extreme versions of international Islamist politics.

Of the seven states in the north-east, four are still considered to be disturbed; only Arunachal Pradesh, Meghalaya and Mizoram have proven to be politically stable so far. However, they are also experiencing increasing problems due to crossborder incidents. China's territorial claims on Arunachal Pradesh, particularly the Tawang Tract, demand New Delhi's special attention towards the state.

The most powerful and most active underground group in north-east India appears to be NSCN-IM (National Socialist Council of Nagaland—Isak-Muivah), which today numbers between 3,000 and 5,000 armed fighters. It is organised into a political and a military wing. Its rival, NSCN-Khaplang, has at its disposal over 2,000 active members. Its headquarters lie in "eastern Nagaland", namely Myanmar.[8] ULFA and PLA also continue to operate, and numerous other groups have emerged too. Occasionally, since 1997, fragile armistices between New Delhi and the NSCN have taken hold. Discussions take place abroad, on neutral ground. New Delhi woos the separatists with promises of political integration and amnesties; but it can only make such offers within the framework of the Indian Constitution. As long as ULFA leaders believe their independence is the only honourable solution, and declare north-east India to be one of the few regions in the world which yet remains to be liberated from colonial rule, such discussions will bring no permanent solutions.

Assam's size and population make it the key state for the pacification of north-east India. It accounts for more than half of the total landmass of the north-east, and with over 26 million inhabitants it also constitutes the majority of the population.[9] Here and in Nagaland, progress towards peace has proved particularly difficult to achieve. NSCN-IM demands all Naga areas, roughly 120,000 square km^2 of Greater Nagaland, including parts of Assam, Manipur, Arunachal Pradesh and Myanmar. The states concerned reject such demands, hence the long term outlook is for further demonstrations and political unrest.

In April 2000, Chief Minister Prafulla Kumar Mahanta submitted to the State Assembly of Assam a 16-page report regarding ISI operations in Assam, which covered the following points:

1. Promoting indiscriminate violence in the state by providing active support to local militant outfits.
2. Creating new militant outfits along ethnic and communal lines by instigating ethnic and religious groups.
3. Supplying explosives and sophisticated arms to various terrorist groups.
4. Sabotaging oil pipelines and other installations, communications lines, railways and roads.
5. Promoting fundamentalism and militancy among local Muslim youths by misleading them in the name of Jihad.
6. Promoting communal tension between Hindu and Muslim citizens by way of false and highly inflammatory propaganda. Promoting indiscriminate violence in the state by providing active support to local militant outfits.

These indications suggest that the ISI is still present and active in north-east India. In August 1999 Assam police announced the arrest of two ISI officers and two local agents, whose identification were proven without a doubt. The officers came from Karachi and Lahore, the agents from Kashmir and India. Reports of this kind regularly appeared in the Indian press. The ISI uses such agents for special missions, constructs sleeper cells, infiltrates local organisations, brings counterfeit money into the region[10] and is responsible for acts of terror. Nor could they pass up the chance to expand their influence over madrassas in north-east India through their network of contacts and confidants.

Some Muslim youth organization members were allegedly covertly invited to Pakistan where they recived religious instruction along with training in weapons and explosives. In 2001, the Assam police arrested thirty-four returning members of the Harkat-ul-Mujahideen (HuM), hereby exposing the ISI's new support group. Moreover, in early 2000, it was revealed that members of the United Liberation Front of Seven Sisters (ULFSS) had been instructed how to use weapons and explosives in ISI camps in Bangladesh.

15

STRUCTURE—PERSONNEL—BUDGET

Organizational Structure

In the period when General Zia-ul-Haq was COAS, 1976–88, the ISI underwent a large scale and profound reevaluation. Zia had no political power base, apart from the Army, hence he utilised the intelligence service to observe and control his opponents and the wider political scene. Thus, the intelligence service developed its own political agenda and its personnel gained power, prestige and self-confidence

It was the Soviet invasion of Afghanistan in December 1979 rather than the *coup d'état* by the Pakistan military that benefited the ISI, allowing them to develop into a regional player with activities and goals, not supervised or coordinated by any other authority, whether parliament or the foreign, internal, finance or defence ministries.

According to the Federation of American Scientists, in the 1980s the ISI was structured as follows:[1]

Joint Intelligence X (JIX):

JIX was the largest main department of the ISI. The secretariat and administration were located here while coordination of all other ISI wings and field organizations were undertaken by the secretariat. The analysis section was also located here.

Joint Intelligence Bureau (JIB)

JIB was considered the most influential department and consisted of three sections, one assigned to operational work in India, another being entrusted with keeping political control over Pakistan.

Joint Counter-Intelligence Bureau (JCIB)

JCIB had little in common with JIB. Its working area covered Asia, Afghanistan and the Middle East. Over many years there was a close cooperation with the CIA on the China issue. After the disintegration of the Soviet Union, Russia and the Central Asian states became the new main places of interest. Monitoring of Pakistani diplomats stationed abroad was also undertaken here. JCIB was responsible for the reports to the political leadership, and a JCIB director was always stationed in the Prime Minister's Secretariat as a contact.

Joint Intelligence/North (JIN)

JIN was responsible for all operations in Jammu and Kashmir, including infiltration, exfiltration and propaganda. It was headed by a two-star general, thereby highlighting the significance of Kashmir. Apart from analysts, the so-called cloak and dagger staff are found here, divided into operative cells and trained for special missions. The Afghanistan Bureau created during Zia's time was within JIN. After Jalalabad it was reduced in importance and was downgraded to a cell. The East Punjab cell still exists today.

Joint Intelligence Miscellaneous (JIM)

JIM was responsible for espionage in the remaining foreign countries.

Joint Signal Intelligence Bureau (JSIB) comprises the departments of wireless, monitoring and photography which were headed by a deputy director. JSIB maintained a chain of listening posts along the border with India and was responsible for contact with militant groups. According to New Delhi, JSIB has had approximately 200 underground stations operating in India since the early 90's.

Joint Intelligence Technical (JIT) deals with developments in science and technology to advance all aspects of intelligence gathering.

In this set-up, the DG ISI was assisted by three two-star generals from the Army, Air Force and Navy as DDGs, who were in charge of political, external and administrative matters respectively.

In the 1990s the ISI underwent reorganization. Up to the beginning of Musharraf's tenure as COAS in 1999, the structure was as in the following chart on p. 169.[2]

After the departure of DG ISI Mahmood Ahmed in October 2001, structural adjustments and personnel cuts were again made in the ISI.

In pursuit of accuracy the author submitted questions about the structure of the intelligence service to ISI HQ in Islamabad. These were very carefully answered. Joint Intelligence North (JIN), whose field of operations covers South Asia and Afghanistan, as well as Joint Intelligence Miscellaneous (JIM), covering the remaining world, were ommitted from the picture. The

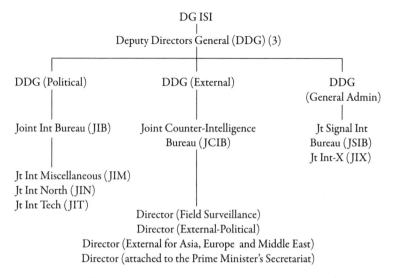

DG ISI
|
Deputy Directors General (DDG) (3)

DDG (Political)	DDG (External)	DDG (General Admin)
Joint Int Bureau (JIB)	Joint Counter-Intelligence Bureau (JCIB)	Jt Signal Int Bureau (JSIB) Jt Int-X (JIX)
Jt Int Miscellaneous (JIM) Jt Int North (JIN) Jt Int Tech (JIT)		

Director (Field Surveillance)
Director (External-Political)
Director (External for Asia, Europe and Middle East)
Director (attached to the Prime Minister's Secretariat)

Special wings of ISI:
1. ISI Academy
2. Military Liaison Section (MLS)

author was forwarded the ISI structure as follows: Secretariat Director General ISI, Administration and Personnel, Finance, Training, Analysis, Internal, Counter Terrorism, Technical, Information and Media. The ISI's interlocutors of course made no mention of the Internal Wing, which observs Pakistan's domestic political situation: its focus is on politicians, political parties, professors and students, the media, journalists and foreign diplomats.

It was the Analysis wing that was presented to the author as the heart and mind of the ISI, its areas of responsibility covering national security and ongoing international issues. Nowadays, this analysis is organised by region, with terrorism being the core issue.

Since 9/11, the cooperation between the CIA and ISI runs mainly through the Counter-Terrorism wing. Internally, there is cooperation with the country's other security agencies. Additionally, there is also an interface between the MI and the ISI. The MI is often supported by the ISI, especially in their operations in border areas and the tribal belts. A newly established Counter-Terrorism Center, the largest in Asia, is the core of the department. It has outstations in the country's provinces and is staffed with trained specialists. A sophisticated database has permitted successful cooperation with other intelligence agencies worldwide since 9/11, and has contributed to acknowledged results: up to spring 2007, a total of 689 al-Qaeda members were seized by the ISI, 369 of which were handed over to the CIA.[3]

The Technical wing received extensive material and training assistance on information gathering from the US after 9/11, in return for the ISI's assistance in person-to-person contacts; this helped alleviate the year-long neglect of human intelligence (HUMINT) by the US services.

The contemporary internal organization of the ISI is as follows:[4]

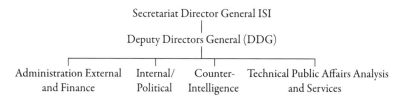

As of spring 2015 the following officers were holding leading posts within the Directorate of the ISI:

Lt. Gen. Rizwan Akhtar (DG ISI); Maj. Gen. Amer Aslam Khan (DG Personnel); Maj. Gen. Ahmad Mahmood Hayat (DG Analysis); Nasir Dilawar Shah (DG Counter Intelligence); Maj. Gen. Sajjad Rasul (DG Security); Maj. Gen. Tariq Qaddus (DG Counter Terrorism); Maj. Gen. Amir Azeem Bawa (DG Technical); Sector Commanders: Maj. Gen. Naveed Ahmeed (Sindh); Maj. Gen. Raja Aftab (Punjab) Maj. Gen. Ifthikar Amir (Balochistan); Maj. Gen. Tayab Azam (KP).

After the February 2008 elections, the Zardari/Gilani government pushed for intensified political control of the ISI. A first attempt in summer 2008 to subordinate the ISI to the Ministry of Interior by decree was blocked by GHQ. In November 2008, the shifting of the Internal wing's working area to the IB was ordered, and its closure within the ISI was announced. The intention of this first step was the democratization and control of the intelligence service. Local observers are certain that in the light of the unstable domestic political situation the ISI will nevertheless continue to work internally and will remain the eyes and ears of the military.[5]

Personnel Structure

Until 1966, a brigadier led what was then a relatively small and efficient intelligence agency. From the 1970s, its increasing size and importance called for a two-star general at its helm who during his term in the ISI would receive his third star. Today, it is usually the rank of lieutenant general that leads the ISI from the outset.

Today, two-star generals, the majority from the Army, are the directors of the main wings within the Directorate of the ISI in Islamabad. Two-star generals are also posted as Sector Commanders in the capitals of the provinces. Other higher positions in the ISI structure are held by active officers from the brigadier, colonel, major or captain ranks. For some of them their assignment of two to three or even more years runs still as extra-regimental duty. Altogether, they make up approximately half of the entire staff.

The total number of ISI personnel is unknown. In Zia's time it was estimated to be c 20,000, including informants and procurement assistants. In the 1990s and 2000s there were cuts, so that today the ISI is estimated to have a core strength of approximately between 4,000 and 5,000 people. Any higher figures published elsewhere are probably over-estimates.

In 2006, under duress, Musharraf announced his intention of returning responsibility for the appointment of the Director General to the Federal Public Service Commission (FPSC).[6] However, this move failed due to strong resistance on the part of the ISI. At the end of 2006, an Amendment of the FPSC legislation was accepted by both houses of parliament, with the result that:

> The candidates for the posts of Directorate General of ISI pass through a transparent and systematic process comprising written tests, interviews, medical examinations and in some cases, intelligence and psychological tests also. Security clearance of the selected candidates is carried out by the vetting agency of the ISI keeping in view the standards and peculiar requirements in accordance with the mandate of its Directorate. A panel of highly qualified senior officers select the candidates keeping in view the sensitive nature of jobs to be assigned/performed, and the candidates are tested/interviewed with particular emphasis on their potential, trends, zeal, devotion, dedication and psychological suitability required for the job. It is, therefore, in the larger interest of the country to make the recruitment of the posts of Directorate General ISI by the department itself instead of the FPSC.[7]

In 2009, under Kayani, there were changes in the personnel policy. Two-star generals continue to come directly from the Army, Air Force or Navy, with the remainder from the Army Intelligence Corps.[8] The career officer starts his military life in combat weapons, and not in the medical or engineering services. After completing basic training, there is an intelligence exam, to which only selected candidates are admitted. The successful candidate becomes an officer in the Intelligence Corps, and undergoes further training. Later on, he may join the ISI. Thus, the ISI is not threatened by bureaucratization or controversy over promotions and seniority as is seen in other agencies, like R&AW.

The proportion of civilian members in ISI is now between 40 and 50 percent. Vacancies are advertised by the FPSC, and invited applicants must undergo a test on current affairs, English and analytical skills at the FPSC. A list of successful applicants is forwarded to the ISI for a personal security check. After this difficult round, a joint interview by FPSC and ISI is the last hurdle. Civilian ISI employees come under the Ministry of Defence.

The remaining 5–10 percent of ISI staff are former military personnel on a contract basis. This personnel structure conforms to the formal official position that the ISI is not dominated by the Army. In fact it is the key positions that are occupied by the Army, while the desk officers are generally area specialists.

A brigadier heads the ISI units in the provinces. Here an important interface exists with the Army. The nine corps commanders have intelligence battalions led by a lieutenant colonel at their disposal. Contacts to the police Special Branch are also held here. Under the battalion level there are Field Security sections, Special Task teams and Field Interrogation teams, which replaced the former Field Intelligence unit and Field Intelligence team.

Budget

The ISI's budget is officially and secretly set by the Ministry of Defence; only a few people know the exact figures. The author was told of an allegedly accurate auditing system, which guarantees professional practice and prevents criminal scheming. The "official" ISI budget is estimated to stand today around US$ 300 million, but there are various ways of raising extra funds. For example, Indian experts believe the ISI deployment in Kashmir is financed by four sources: the drug trade, counterfeit money, donations from abroad and some compulsory input from the economy.

Since the 1980s, the ISI seems not to have experienced any budgetary problems. The Afghanistan adventure proved to be a golden option for the organisation. Financial inputs from the US and Saudi Arabia totalled around US$6 billion, with additional private donations and support from other countries. By the early 1990s, over US$10 billion had been earmarked for Afghanistan. As coordinator and distributor for US and Saudi Arabian aid, the ISI could divert a considerable proportion of these funds to their own ends.

Another source of case was the profitable trade in heroin. Poppy had always been cultivated in Afghanistan and previously also in Pakistan's North West

Frontier Province (NWFP). In Afghanistan between 1982 and 1991, opium production rose from 250 to 2,000 tons.[9] In Pakistan between 1983 and 1992, the income from the drug trade rose from c US$384 million to c US$1.8 billion.[10] The ISI was on board with both trends. Since the mid-1980s, a special cell in the ISI financed operations in Afghanistan through the profits of the drug trade; indeed, the CIA was considered to be behind the idea.[11] In 2001, B. Raman wrote the following about the ISI's new sources of finance:

> This cell promoted the cultivation of opium and the extraction of heroin in Pakistani territory as well as in the Afghan territory under Mujahideen control for being smuggled into the Soviet controlled areas in order to make the Soviet troops heroin addicts. After the withdrawal of the Soviet troops, the ISI's heroin cell started using its network of refineries and smugglers for smuggling heroin to the Western countries and using the money as a supplement to its legitimate economy. But for these heroin dollars, Pakistan's legitimate economy must have collapsed many years ago.[12]

In July 1991, the Bank of England ordered the closure of the Bank of Credit and Commerce International (BCCI), the largest Muslim-owned bank. It was proven that BCCI was financing Islamist and other terror organizations, money laundering and assisting with the global drug trade: "BCCI did dirty work for every major terrorist service in the world."[13] The ISI maintained connections with BCCI and right up until its shutdown carried out part of its financial transactions through them. Osama bin Laden was also a BCCI customer. Contrary to general perceptions, he not only operated his undertakings with his own fortune, which was limited, and after his return to Sudan in May 1996, actually non-existent; but was also deeply involved in the drug trade and arms trafficking.

After the Soviet retreat from Afghanistan, the ISI-backed drug trade went from strength to strength. The proceeds contributed to the purchase of weapons and the stabilization of Pakistan's budget, which would have been totally shattered without the heroin money, according to expert opinion. A group of Army and ISI officers also became very wealthy through their involvement in the drug trade some of whom were investigated by the National Accountability Bureau.[14] Experts estimate that an additional thirty or so high-ranking Army and ISI officers netted considerable sums from the drug trade.

In March 2003, the US Senate held a hearing of its Subcommittee for Asia and the Pacific, questioning the former American ambassador Nancy Chamberlin about her State Department report. After persistent inquiry, she was forced to admit to a substantial estimated value relating to the ISI's participation in the heroin trade from 1997–2003. A former DG ISI declared to the author that he had read part of Chamberlin's report, and attributed her statements to pressure, speculation and arrogance.

All in all, it must be said that even during the Taliban era a brisk drug trade existed. No one can believe the supposedly virtuous guardians of public morals who said that poppy cultivation had been eliminated. Although the Taliban did burn the opium fields in the first year of their rule, this stopped the following year for financial reasons. While smoking marijuana and use of heroin have remained punishable offences, there are no objections to drug exports being routed through Saudi Arabia to the "infidel" countries. Under American pressure, the Taliban destroyed poppy fields in a big propaganda extravaganza in 2000 and loudly forbade further cultivation. But the warehouses continued to fill for two more years, so the results were minimal. In today's Afghanistan, harvests once again reach record highs—and Kabul is fully aware of this. Washington's hopes that the government would prevent poppy cultivation were illusionary. Although Hamid Karzai issued a ban on growing and trading in opium,[15] it is widely known that high-ranking Afghans are among the leading drug traffickers in the country.

In different meetings with high-ranking ISI officers the author was told that some rogue individuals might have been involved in the narcotics trade in the past—but that the agency itself never has been and certainly is not involved in drugs in recent decades. But in the 2010 report of the United Nations Office of Drugs and Crime, heroin exports from Afghanistan each year amount to some 3,750 tons, half of which is exported via Balochistan. Since the killing of Nawab Akbar Bugti in summer 2006 the province is defacto under control and run by Pakistan's Military and Intelligence Agencies. It would be naive to believe that the routes of the drug trade through Balochistan are not well known to them. And it might be even more naïve to expect that some ISI operatives are not cashing in. From 2014 an additional drug route emerged, as heroin is now transported in large quantities to Bangladesh and from there to India.

During the author's discussions in 2015 with leading ISI cadres the drugs trade was again on the agenda. The ISI insisted that the agency was in this respect totally clean. Written memoranda to this effect were also passed to the author:

> Why would ISI involve itself in drug trade, while it knew that it could harm its own country? Pak had made concrete efforts to curb opium production in FATA and drug trafficking from Afghanistan to Pakistan and beyond. In this

regard Anti Narcoting Force's efforts are always recognised by the international watch dogs... ISI's involvement in the drug trade is illogical. Conversely, Afghanistan being the neighbor of Pakistan is the main source of heroin trade in the region. The maximum poppy cultivation in Afghanistan is carried out in the Afghan provinces contiguous to Pakistan. Interestingly, while the Taliban were in power in Afghanistan (1996–2001), their regime had succeeded in eradicating the opium trade in Afghanistan in year 2000 and this has been acknowledged at the October 2001 session of the UN General Assembly. Now the logic is that if the Taliban were against the poppy cultivation in Afganistan during 1996–2001, how could ISI benefit from the heroin trade?

16

THE ISI UNDER PERVEZ MUSHARRAF

Lt. Gen. Mahmood Ahmed

The military's seizure of power in Pakistan on 12 October 1999 was constitutionally a *coup d' état*, even if the Supreme Court later legitimised it for three years on the basis of the doctrine of necessity. Prime Minister Nawaz Sharif had the legal right to replace the Army chief, but the absence of protests or large-scale demonstrations after his downfall heralded the end of the diminishing reputation and economic failures of the 32-month Sharif government.

For the execution of a successful coup, a COAS needs the assistance of two more generals, the Head of the General Staff (CGS) and the Commander X Corps stationed in Rawalpindi. On 12 October, the CGS was Lt. Gen. Mohammad Aziz Khan and the Corps Commander was Lt. Gen. Mahmood Ahmed. An important role fell to Lt. Gen. Muzaffar Hussain Usmani, Commander of the V Corps Karachi, while Musharraf was on board his now infamous PIA flight from Sri Lanka to Karachi.

Under Karamat, Mahmood Ahmed had been promoted to a three-star general and was made Commander of NDC—an appointment which disappointed him since he had expected a corps command.[1] His desire was fulfilled a short time later when Karamat's successor Musharraf gave him the X Corps, a post only open to someone in whom an Army general has full confidence. Both were artillerymen. During their careers they had occasionally been in the same unit and trained together. Their political views were similar too. Mahmood Ahmed's family originated from Ludhiana in India, and like Pervez

Musharraf he was a Mohajir. After the coup, Musharraf promoted him to DG ISI in October 1999, therefore giving him the second most powerful position in Pakistan.[2]

It was about this time that Mahmood became a born-again Muslim. He announced to his friends, "I have seen the light," and he criticised those who, according to him, were not good Muslims. In contrast to CGS Aziz Khan, who as a religious man was not troubled by the lack of faith amongst his peers, Mahmood became a problem for all those officers who were not averse to the odd single malt and did not pray regularly. Besides his demonstrative piety, Mahmood showed an increasing arrogance in his demeanour.[3] So among his comrades Mahmood was popular only until he became a brigadier, when his behaviour changed.

For Mahmood Ahmed, 9/11 was the beginning of the end of his career. At the time of the terror attacks he was in Washington, holding meetings with the CIA, the White House, the Pentagon and with members of the NSC.[4] But he was stranded for three days in Washington, due to the closed air traffic, and was on the receiving end of Deputy Secretary of State Richard Armitage's famous threat to Pakistan: you are either "with us or against us". To the surprise of the Americans, Mahmood immediately agreed to all their demands, without consultating Musharraf. When questioned, he explained that Musharraf would also see things his way and therefore would reach the same decision. According to rumours, Mahmood also used his longer than expected stay in Washington to recommend himself as future Vice COAS to the Americans.

Musharraf did in fact make a political U-turn and became a US ally in the fight against international terrorism. However, he did not make Mahmood the Vice Army chief, with access to the Army units. There has been much speculation about why he did this. One opinion prevalent amongst the military in Rawalpindi was that if Mahmood Ahmed became Vice-COAS, he could send Musharraf into retirement at some point and take Pakistan's fate into his own hands. Musharraf became aware of this and reacted quickly: he restructured the top military positions on 7 October 2001, offering Mahmood Ahmed the post of CJCSC, primarily a representative one, gilded with a fourth star but without the accoutrements of a power base. Mohammed Yousuf[5] got the newly created post of Vice-COAS. Both Yousuf and Mahmood had been course mates, but Mahmood had a longer service term than Yousuf. In crucial discussions between Musharraf and Mahmood, the latter insisted "let's stick to seniority," meaning that he (Mahmood) should become Vice-COAS. Musharraf rejected this and used the singular authority of a Pakistani Army chief to dismiss a three-star general without reason and without the involvement of an internal committee.[6]

For the next two years Mahmood lived in seclusion in Lahore and was inaccessible to foreign visitors. Early in 2003 he wrote a letter of apology to Musharraf, who then on 3 March arranged his appointment as chief executive of the Fauji Fertiliser Company. Later in Rawalpindi adverse remarks by former ISI staff were made about Mahmood's prostrations.[7] Mahmood's critics commented that Musharraf had been clever in giving Mahmood the Fauji position, as it meant having him under his watchful eye.

But there were still unanswered questions about Mahmood's tenure. According to observers, Pakistan's surprisingly rapid switch to the American side in September 2001 was made for good reasons. On the one hand, Musharraf and his generals were afraid the US might insist that Pakistan forfeit its nuclear weapons. This stockpile was the highest priority for the Pakistani military. Today, Pakistan's atomic weapons are safe and cannot be rendered inactive in a first strike, neither by the US nor by India. On the other hand, there may have been more pressing reasons for Musharraf to move immediately to George W. Bush's side. According to intelligence reports, after 9/11 the Bush government was informed quickly and accurately about Pakistan's relationship with the Taliban and Osama bin Laden and al-Qaeda. The Pentagon's Defence Intelligence Agency (DIA) had reported on 23 September, just twelve days after the terror attacks, that:

> Bin Laden's al-Qaeda network was able to expand under the safe sanctuary extended by Taliban following Pakistan directives. If there is any doubt on that issue, consider the location of bin Laden's camp targeted by US cruise missiles in August 1998. Positioned on the border between Afghanistan and Pakistan, it was built by Pakistani contractors, funded by Pakistan's ISI Directorate and protected under the patronage of a local and influential Jadran tribal leader, Jalaluddin Haqqani. However, the real host in that facility was the Pakistani ISI. If this was later to become bin Laden's base, then serious questions are raised by the early relationship between bin Laden and Pakistan's ISI.[8]

DG ISI Mahmood Ahmed soon came under the searchlight of American security analysts, as his close proximity to the Taliban and al-Qaeda was evident. In particular, his visit to Mullah Omar on 17 September 2001 gave cause for speculation.[9] During this meeting with the Taliban leadership Mahmood was hypocritical about extraditing Osama bin Laden to the US. Musharraf had recommended the extradition, but in Mahmood's private discussion with Mullah Omar he advised against it. Musharraf was informed of this by the Taliban, and once America confronted him with ISI's entanglement with the Taliban and al-Qaeda, he had no alternative but to send Mahmood into retirement.

To this day the ISI is trying to polish Mahmood's and its own reputation. The reply given to the author in 2015 in this particular case was: "The assertion is totally baseless. The fact is that although Lt. Gen. Mahmood had tried to convience the Taliban to extradite OBL, the Taliban Shura, which was the final decision-making authority, had refused to extradite him. The Shura was of the view that in light of Pashtun traditions they were required to protect their guest. One needs to understand that the Taliban were fiercely independent, when it came to arriving at a decision. In this context, there were many other occasions when the Taliban ignored Pakistan's demands. The destruction of Buddha statues in Bamiyan during their rule in Afganistan, despite Pakistan's requests to refrain from doing so, clearly reflects the adamant attitude of the Taliban regime."

Mahmood now sports a beard and is once again inaccessible to visitors.[10] For the time being, it seems impossible for him to address the incidents of his tenure as DG ISI; for example, the case in summer 2001 when Egyptian investigators located the leader responsible for the Egyptian embassy attack in Islamabad in 1995.[11] The Canadian Egyptian Ahmed al-Khadir was discovered living in Peshawar, enjoying high level patronage. The Egyptians informed DG ISI Mahmood Ahmed and he assured them he would deploy an ISI command and arrest the terrorist the next morning. However, that night, instead of ISI personnel, Taliban fighters in cars with diplomatic plates brought al-Khadir across the border to safety in Afghanistan. The ISI obviously had no interest in blowing their agent's cover and revealing everything.

The Case of Ahmed Omar Saeed Sheikh

Indian observers believe they know the particular reason for Musharraf's speedy separation from Mahmood Ahmed. On 9 October 2001, the *Times of India* reported that American and Indian investigations discovered that US$100,000 had been transferred in summer 2001 to Mohammed Atta, the leader of the 9/11 attacks. The transfer, allegedly on DG ISI Mahmood Ahmed's instructions, was carried out by Ahmed Omar Sheikh, via a contact in Dubai.

Much is now known about the connection between the British-born Omar Sheikh and the ISI. The son of Pakistani emigrants, he left the London School of Economics in 1993 for the ISI and al-Qaeda camps in Pakistan and

Afghanistan to learn the fundamentals of terrorist attack planning. His ISI handling officer was allegedly Brigadier Ijaz Shah, who was the ISI contact dealing with senior figures in the Taliban and similar groups. Omar Sheikh appeared soon afterwards in Bosnia[12] and later in India, fighting on behalf of Islamist causes. His modus operandi was to kidnap tourists and demand ransoms for their release. He was arrested and condemned in 1994,[13] then spent some years in an Indian prison before being released with two other well-known jihadis in December 1999, as a result of a spectacular plane hijacking demand. Afterwards, he lived openly in Lahore, supporting himself by "providing training and weapons to kidnappers in exchange for a percentage of the ransom they collected."[14] His good ISI contacts made it possible for him to meet Mullah Omar and Osama bin Laden in Afghanistan in 2000 and 2001 and to visit his parents in Great Britain twice. According to his statements, he also met Mohammad Atta in Kandahar, who gave him some details of the planned attacks on the US. His former ISI contact Brigadier Ijaz Shah, a friend of Musharraf, had meanwhile left the ISI and become Home Secretary in Punjab. Sheikh continued to stay in contact with him and through Shah was in touch with Aziz Khan, the corps commander in Lahore, and with Ehsan ul Haq, the corps commander in Peshawar.

During his prison term in India, Omar Sheikh met Aftab Ansari, a contact he kept up with when freed. After Ansari's release in July 2001, he left for Dubai and took part in a kidnapping where a ransom of US$830,000 was extorted from an Indian shoe manufacturer. Ansari is said to have handed over US$100,000 to Sheikh, who then forwarded it to Mohammad Atta in August 2001 as uncovered by the FBI, with India's assistance. On 9 October 2001 the *Times of India* reported under the headline "India helped FBI Trace ISI-Terrorist Links":

> Senior government sources have confirmed that India contributed significantly to establishing the link between the money transfer and the role played by the dismissed ISI chief. While they did not provide details, they said that Indian inputs, including Sheikh's mobile phone number, helped the FBI in tracing and establishing the link.[15]

Two days later *Agence France-Presse* wrote:

> A highly-placed (Indian) government source told AFP that the 'damning link' between the General and the transfer of funds to Atta was part of evidence which India has officially sent to the US. 'The evidence we have supplied to the US is of much wider range and depth than just one piece of paper linking a rogue general to some misplaced act of terrorism,' the source said.[16]

Accusations from Pakistan's arch enemy India should be taken with caution. The psychological warfare between the intelligence services is fought with no holds barred and with all available strategies. Despite the origin of this information from Indian sources, an assessment that this is purely psychological warfare would be inappropriate. The circumstances of Mahmood Ahmed's dismissal by Musharraf in October 2001 were very unusual. Also unusual is the behaviour today of all those involved. Despite peace discussions and community-based monitoring between India and Pakistan, India has never retracted its accusations; and the US 9/11 Commission Report does not mention the connection. The ISI's written response given to the author in 2015 in this case, was short and simple: "Even the US has never made the accusation that Pakistan knew of 9/11 and kept it from them. It amounts to quoting someone else's conspiracy theory based on questionable input and logic".

Another unresolved event where Ahmed Omar Saeed Sheikh featured again was the Daniel Pearl case. Pearl was a *Wall Street Journal* correspondent stationed in New Delhi who came to Pakistan to investigate the extent to which jihadi organizations, banned by Musharraf, continued to enjoy the highest patronage; whether the ISI was involved in 9/11; and, if possible, to explore Osama bin Laden's whereabouts. Other sources say that Pearl wanted to research the so-called shoe bomber, the Richard Reid case,[17] and this is partially true.[18] But Daniel Pearl was kidnapped and murdered in January–February 2002 in Karachi. His dismembered body was found some weeks later.[19] The French philosopher Bernard-Henri Lévy wrote a book entitled *Who Killed Daniel Pearl?*[20] and Hollywood produced a film featuring Angelina Jolie as Pearl's wife.

The Karachi police were aware a few days after Pearl's disappearance that Sheikh was involved in the kidnapping, and started searching for him. Sheikh allegedly asked the then Home Secretary Ijaz Shah for protection, and Lt. Gen. Aziz Khan[21] for advice. He was also prepped in his statements by the Karachi police, in order to prevent a disclosure of his close ISI connections. Afterwards Omar Sheikh, who was promised a minor punishment, was transferred to the custody of the Sindh police. However, under interrogation Sheikh began to blab, having lost his nerve. Contrary to the arrangements made in Lahore, he revealed details of several jihadi operations in Kashmir and India in which the ISI had a hand.

The Karachi police had a mole leaking to the press and *The News* received information about Sheikh's confession and reported it, despite warnings from the ISI. The editor responsible was put under pressure, feared for his life and fled to the US for several years. On 10 April 2002, the Indian former intelligence officer B. Raman[22] listed details of Sheikh's statements to the Karachi police in an article titled "The man who knows & talks too much."[23] Sheikh admitted having resided in Lahore under the patronage and with the knowledge of the ISI. He had contacts with Corps Commanders Aziz (Lahore) and Ehsan ul Haq (Peshawar) and had also met Musharraf.[24]

Omar Sheikh's case was explosive for the ISI. A mild punishment and imminent release were out of the question after his confession, and he had to be placed in isolation. On 15 July 2002 an anti-terrorism court condemned him to death for the kidnapping and murder of Daniel Pearl.[25] Even though the top al-Qaeda terrorist Khalid Sheikh Mohammad is known to have murdered Pearl, Omar Sheikh has been languishing in a Pakistani prison for over eleven years. As a Class A prisoner, he lives quite well and maintains contacts with his jihadi friends.[26] However, his appeals are constantly deferred.

The ISI also did well financially through extraditing al-Qaeda suspects to the US. Amongst this group were high-ranking names such as Abu Zubaidah, Ramzi Binalshibh, Khalid Sheikh Mohammad and Abu Faraj al-Libbi.[27] However, one suspect they cannot afford ever to have questioned or extradited is Omar Sheikh, irrespective of the sum offered.

In the background lurks the explosive question as to whether the ISI leadership knew in advance of the 9/11 attacks on the US and did not warn Washington.[28] For the supporters of this conspiracy theory, there is a clear chain of proof, which goes as follows. In 2000 or 2001, Omar Sheikh was brought into the planning of 9/11 by Mohammad Atta in Kandahar, and later spoke about it with Corps Commanders Aziz (Lahore) and Ehsan ul Haq (Peshawar), without necessarily giving away any operational details. Both Musharraf and Mahmood Ahmed were apparently aware of this. After the terror attacks, Washington quickly uncovered these alleged connections and decided to use them to exert pressure on Pakistan. Ergo, Musharraf's quick move to the US side. The misfortune was that a disclosure of the actual circumstances was inconvenient for the George W. Bush government. All that mattered now was to have Pakistan as an ally on the American side in the fight against terrorism, as well as to secure American interests in the Middle East and Central Asia.

Interrogations of imprisoned Taliban and al-Qaeda leaders have revealed that in spring and summer 2001 there were discussions between the Taliban and al-Qaeda's leadership on whether attacks should be made on US targets. Mullah Omar's Shura was against this as they were waiting expectantly for payments from US companies for future pipeline contracts across Afghanistan.

Instead, for ideologial reasons, they pleaded for attacks on Jewish targets worldwide and the state of Israel. However, Osama bin Laden backed the plan and it was eventually accepted. An al-Qaeda Council decided "that Omar had no authority to stop jihads outside Afghanistan's border."[29] According to imprisoned Talibs, the ISI once again compelled Mullah Omar to limit al-Qaeda's operations to the Afghanistan area.[30] This circumstance permits this deduction, observed by Ridgeway:

> Given the Taliban's intimate knowledge of the plan for the 9/11 attacks—the debate within the top ranks of the Taliban and the Al Qaeda, a shura council meeting, and the suggestion that Pakistan was pressuring Omar to keep Al Qaeda inside Afghanistan—it seems evident that the ISI must have known what was about to happen. In a so-'called ally, this is treachery of the highest order.[31]

In 2007 and 2008, the author succeeded in speaking to the publicity-shy former ISI chief Mahmood Ahmed at his home in Lahore. Over three long conversations, the bearded general proved to be a genial host and interlocutor. When asked about his US visit and the local events in September 2001, he spoke vehemently of his conviction that 9/11, to quote him, "was an inhouse job." His alleged statement to Omar Sheikh about the US$100,000 transfer to Mohammed Atta he dismissed as Indian propaganda and slander.[32]

The further career of Brigadier Ijaz Shah, who had a special working relationship with Sheikh and probably knew him best, is also food for thought. After Musharraf's coup he was made Home Secretary of the Punjab Province, and then headed the IB from February 2004 to March 2008. Both appointments showed that there was a close relationship of trust between the two men. Added to this, Ijaz Shah tried to get out of the firing line when it was clear that Musharraf was losing power as a result of the Lawyers' Movement in 2007. Shah now declared his willingness to become Pakistan's next High Commissioner in Australia, which Musharraf rejected.

Lt. Gen. Ehsan ul Haq

Mahmood Ahmed's successor as DG ISI in October 2001 was Ehsan ul Haq, a Pashtun from NWFP.[33] He began his military career in 1969 in an air defence regiment, and then as DG MI was a trusted director of intelligence. Before his appointment as DG ISI he led the Army Corps in Peshawar for more than a year. It was then that he made contact with Omar Sheikh. To recap, Omar Sheikh had stated in the police interrogations that he allegedly informed the corps commanders in Lahore (Aziz) and Peshawar (Ehsan) about his meetings with Mohammad Atta in Kandahar. Washington apparently gave Ehsan ul Haq the benefit of the doubt. Ehsan was considered a politically moderate officer who was loyal to Musharraf. From America's point of view he was an acceptable replacement for Mahmood Ahmed[34] and was soon seen as a reliable ally. In Islamabad, Ehsan ul Haq became one of Musharraf's closest political, military and strategic colleagues. As DG ISI, he contributed substantially to the developments in Afghanistan and Kashmir. On the home front he became the eyes and ears of his President.

One consequence of Musharraf's decision to stand by America's side was that another substantial clearing out of the ISI became inevitable. Senior officers in the Afghanistan and Kashmir departments were let go, either by being retired or returned to barracks.[35] In addition, the priorities of the service were once again rearranged. Ehsan ul Haq received the order "to shift its approach from international horizons to the regional and domestic subjects in order to make its role more effective and useful for the country in general and the armed forces in particular."[36]

Further personnel reorganization in the ISI ensued. In the three years to spring 2004, the service was reduced by 40 percent to well under 5,000 personnel. This was followed by an effort to create a new reputation for the service. In March 2003, for the first time, the ISI invited Pakistan-accredited foreign journalists to its HQ where, over tea and cake, officers explained the political situation from the government's point of view.[37]

The next improvement in the ISI's image was to do with party affiliations within the new political system created in 2002. Before the 2002 parliamentary elections, the ISI was obliged to transform the PML-Q,[38] previously a part of Nawaz Sharif's PML, into a Musharraf supporting party, mockingly called the King's Party. Its duties were also to supervise and implement the compliance of the Legal Framework Order 2002 (LFO).[39] After the elections, which did not result in a clear parliamentary majority, it was the ISI's task to persuade a number of PPP parliamentarians to leave the PPP. Threats and enticement were used to obtain the necessary majority for the government camp in parliament. The Internal Political wing under DDG ISI Major General Ehtesham Zamir tackled the given tasks. The governments in the National Assembly in Islamabad, as well as in the provincial parliaments of Punjab and Sindh, managed to function in the subsequent years as Musharraf's political aides. However, in Balochistan a coalition had to be formed with the parliamentary mullahs, and in NWFP the situation spun out of control. Here, the religious electoral coalition, the MMA, whose accomplishments were monitored by the ISI, achieved a majority. They would began implementing a multitude of fundamentalist policies, and observers soon spoke of a threatening Talibanization of the province.

The ISI's decisive and calculating involvement before and after the 2002 elections was rated as a strategic mistake by its critics, precipitating a multitude of problems which Musharraf would confront in subsequent years. According to critics, the DG ISI and his deputies, in their efforts to eliminate both Nawaz Sharif and Benazir Bhutto politically, played into the hands of a religious fundamentalist strand. They argued that Ehsan ul Haq was not a fundamentalist; but his renowned personal friendship with Qazi Hussain Ahmed, Amir of the JI, proved that he underestimated or ignored the dangers posed to Pakistan by its religious zealots.[40] His critics also see a miscalculation by the ISI head in the military's deployment in FATA[41] in 2002. Here, a misjudgement of the situation by the ISI led to a disaster for the army and the Frontier Corps. As the monthly magazine *Herald* wrote in April 2006:

> Putting up a formidable front against government forces in the Wana and Azam Warsak areas between 2002 and 2004, the militants started proceeding in a systematic fashion to achieve two specific objectives: defeat and eliminate the intelligence network of the Pakistani and American forces and threaten the local population to force them into acquiescence... By early 2005, the military and the FC had been effectively confined to their barracks and stripped of whatever intelligence support they had in the area.[42]

According to the DG ISI's critics, this showed that he did not understand the tribal ways of thinking and actions, and nor had he cultivated a special relationship with tribal and clan leaders in NWFP, FATA and Afghanistan.[43] However, the journalistic clique behind Ehsan ul Haq wrote that his last year in the ISI directorate was his greatest, as in his decisions he placed the national interest above those of his Pashtun traditions and sentiments.

Musharraf blamed the failures in NWFP and FATA more on the Governor NWFP and the Corps Commander Peshawar than on his ISI chief. On the other hand he did not transfer the investigation of his assassination attempt in December 2003 to Ehsan ul Haq and the ISI. Its hindrance would have been a special case for MI and ISI. Instead he gave this responsibility to Lt. Gen. Ashfaq Pervez Kayani, Corps Commander Rawalpindi, who ten months later was to replace Ehsan ul Haq at ISI, in October 2004.

The last months of Ehsan ul Haq's tenure as DG ISI brought him a special assignment: a scandal that enveloped Pakistan's folk hero, Dr Abdul Qadeer Khan, which grabbed worldwide attention and had to be brought under control. The incident was to do with accusations of smuggling and selling nuclear technology, about which Washington presented evidence to Musharraf during his visit to Camp David in June 2003. During Musharraf's stay at the UN in New York in September 2003, CIA chief George Tenet handed over concrete evidence that highly sensitive information was being delivered by Dr Khan to Libya and Iran. The scandal was such that Musharraf had to act. The Heads of the ISI and the Strategic Planning Division received an order to examine the American information and to confront AQ Khan with the evidence.[44] A preposterous situation developed as the ISI, which over the years was the guarantor of Khan's security and assisted in his purchases in the international arms bazaar, now became his inquisitor.

The result was inevitable: Khan had to be the lone transgressor, the fall guy, so that the government could save face. However, the browbeaten Khan resisted and explained to Ehsan ul Haq that "every Army chief since Gen. Zia-ul-Haq knew of his activities,"[45] and therefore he was not the sole culprit. Unable to resist the ISI's pressure, in a televised speech in February 2004 he took the blame and asked the people for forgiveness. He was granted a presidential pardon and then placed under strict house arrest. Five years later the IHC declared Khan a free man.

But this was not the end of Ehsan's military career. He was appointed as Chairman Joint Chiefs of Staff Committee in October 2001, where he was fifth in seniority, and received his fourth star. He remained a further three years in uniform—obviously Musharraf wanted his former ISI head close by. However, this gave observers, including the author, new ways of interpreting the 9/11 events. The Corps Commanders Aziz (Lahore) and Ehsan (Peshawar) had been recipients of Omar Sheikh's information. The assumption that they would have informed Musharraf and Mahmood Ahmed is highly likely. In summer 2001 Musharraf and at least three of his generals may have been told at least one version of the rumour that planning for some terror acts in the US was afoot, and kept silent about them. Washington was soon aware of this. Mahmood Ahmed, who met with Mullah Omar after 9/11 and advised him not to cooperate with the US, had to go. Aziz Khan and Ehsan ul-Haq, as well as Musharraf, remained in the game.[46]

DG ISI Ashfaq Pervez Kayani, October 2004–October 2007

During Kayani's leadership, the background to the assassination attempts on President Musharraf in December 2003 was cleared up and those involved were apprehended.[47] Kayani managed to put an end to the rivalries between the individual intelligence services and made them cooperate with each other. This was precisely why he was appointed as ISI head in October 2004.

Kayani is from Jhelum in Punjab. His father was an army NCO who died relatively young. Kayani is considered by his comrades to be a disciplined, professional soldier without the backing of any political group. He was Director General Military Operations (DGMO) in GHQ and then appointed Commander X Corps in Rawalpindi.[48] Although he possessed no intelligence experience, he was seen as the perfect successor to Ehsan ul Haq.[49] Once in post, he endeavoured to pull the ISI away from the headlines, though not always successfully. The ISI repeatedly surfaced in newspaper columns regarding missing persons or mysterious arrests, even if their direct participation was mostly unproven.[50] People asked whether the ISI, IB, FIA or police were active in the respective cases, but these questions remain mostly unanswered. The press often reported only a version of the story sourced from security personnel. If victims were rescued, they were obviously still in shock; either they were guarded in their comments or more often did not talk about their experiences at all.

There then followed the affair of Chief Justice (CJ) Iftikhar Mohammad Chaudhry, which escalated rapidly into a question of political survival for Musharraf. The ISI did not appear in the forefront, for although Kayani was present at the crucial meeting between Musharraf and Chaudhry, he held back from the ensuing crisis. He did not provide an affidavit regarding this meeting to the judicial committee of inquiry, who examined and rescinded the CJ's dismissal by Musharraf, unlike the heads of MI and IB. Kayani was present at Musharraf's meeting with Benazir Bhutto in Abu Dhabi in summer 2007. On Musharraf's behalf, he held further negotiations with the PPP's leader in August 2007, in London. The topic discussed was her political comeback and future cooperation with the President. During Benazir's first reign, Kayani had been Deputy Military Secretary; they knew each other, which was beneficial to the discussions. In addition, both meetings between Kayani and Bhutto showed that the DG ISI held Musharraf's confidence.

Nor was the ISI directly involved in the spectacular Red Mosque (Lal Masjid) incident in Islamabad in summer 2007. The storming of the complex was led by the special forces of the Army, commandered by officers of the X Corps. The national and international press was keen to report on the geographical proximity of the mosque to the intelligence headquarters and capture evidence of ISI personnel praying in the mosque, but couldn't find any direct connection to the ISI. The agency was criticised for not recognizing the potential danger. Others believe the ISI was involved in this atrocity.[51] The French journalist Roger Faligot wrote that "departments of the ISI used the mosque for intelligence and put political pressure on President Pervez Musharraf."[52] He believed that:

– As Musharraf had little confidence in the ISI—particularly the counter-terrorism section—it was kept away from the operation to recapture the mosque and replaced by other military security and intelligence units
– Underneath the mosque, a secret transmission center was discovered with wires leading directly from the neighbouring ISI headquarters.

As his source, Faligot quotes the American secret service, although he does not actually name them. He writes:

> On September 21 (2007), Kayani was replaced as head of the secret services by someone more dependable, Lieutenant-General Nadeem Taj, Musharraf's former secretary and a relative of the president's wife. Another interesting related fact: the ISI's 'counter-terrorism' unit (considered compromised because of its links to certain members of pro-Taliban groups) has undergone a purge in the last few weeks.[53]

Faligot's report is an example of the kind of speculation that was aired after the storming of Lal Masjid. There was no transmission centre under the mosque. He also owes us an explanation as to why Musharraf appointed Kayani as Vice-COAS in October 2007, thereby making him his potential successor. Musharraf saw Kayani as a professional soldier and not a political general. As a civilian President, Musharraf would be responsible for the political arena, and Kayani for the military side. Hence, he didn't want Kayani to be involved in the Lal Masjid case, so the ISI had to be kept away. This was overlooked by Faligot.

Visits to the US were frequent during Kayani's term of office in the ISI. One of the main topics for discussion was probably the hunting down of the remaining al-Qaeda cadres based in the Federal Administrated Tribal Areas (FATA). For himself and the ISI, Kayani was able to mention the arrest of Abu Faraj Al-Libbi, in May 2005.[54] In the case of Osama bin Laden, however, total helplessness prevailed. For the author, with his thirteen years' experience in Pakistan, there is no doubt that some ISI personnel must have known bin Laden's place of residence; a continuous stay in FATA, allegedly untraceable, is pure myth. Political agents stationed in the border and tribal areas are well informed about what is happening in their section. They have informants in the towns as well as in the countryside. If shepherds chanced upon foreigners in their area, the news would find its way up to the village elders and from there to the government agent. Small payments and favours would keep such an information chain intact.

Most politicians, coloumists and journalists assumed that Osama bin Laden would probably be found in the border areas. People from these areas were not convinced that it would be possible to trace him there. They reckoned that the ISI knew better.

17

THE TROUBLED VALLEY

KASHMIR

Defenders of the Faith and Freedom Fighters

In the Indian state of Jammu and Kashmir (IJK), a new generation of political activists surfaced during the 1980s, inspired by Islam and antipathy towards India. From 1988, religious and nationalist extremists began throwing bombs. A series of explosions in Srinagar in 31 July 1988 heralded the beginning of a Kashmiri intifada, which is currently under control but not extinguished. From the outset, New Delhi reacted harshly and brutally. As the police in the Indian part of Kashmir were considered to have been infiltrated by the insurgents, military and special police were deployed. From 1989 on, Hindu pandits received threatening letters telling them to leave Kashmir; as the threats turned into terror acts and murders, the exodus of the pandits started in 1990.[1] In 1991, the Indian Prime Minister Chandra Shekhar was forced to ask his counterpart Pakistan's Nawaz Sharif for assistance in the release of Nahida Imtiaz, the kidnapped daughter of a parliamentary delegate. This request was humiliating for India.

By the beginning of 1990, there were more than thirty militant political-religious organizations in IJK. Some of them were aimed at radically Islamizing the country. Their attacks were directed against bars, cinemas, beauty salons, video shops and the like. The women in the Kashmir valley were soon forced to go veiled. Fanatics attacked unveiled women with ink or acid.

On 21 January 1990 the Indian Army began house searches, an action which caused an outcry among local Muslims. The often arrogant and insecure security forces over-reacted. The attacks, brutalities, rapes and killings by the military and special operation group increased and became a feature of everyday life for Kashmiris.

The anti-Indian forces in Kashmir started to coalesce around a common political platform from 1993. With the help of the ISI, the All Parties Hurriyat Conference (APHC) was created. This was a conglomerate of over two dozen groups. Their main goal was the right to self-determination in Kashmir. Their methods were to organise protests, boycotts and attacks. But because of the unstable political situation in Pakistan, a split occurred within the APHC. Apart from the groups demanding annexation to Pakistan, others started advocating Kashmir's independence. The 2002 elections revealed the limitations of the APHC. Despite boycotts and attacks, there was a respectable turnout of 45 percent for the IJK, which was a relatively free vote, according to independent observers. Afterwards, the APHC admitted that its political influence hardly extended beyond the Kashmir valley.

The APHC is now split more than ever. The leaders of the Kashmir and Pakistan parliamentary group argue about the speaker's role in the whole organization. The main demand of the APHC is to be fully involved in future negotiations on Kashmir. For a long time New Delhi showed little flexibility, but eventually they engaged in dialogue with the moderate forces of the APHC; however, two early meetings brought little progress. Meanwhile Islamabad continues to support the pro-Pakistan faction within the APHC.

The ISI and Kashmir

The mujahideen religious warriors are seen as terrorists on one side and freedom fighters on the other side. President Zia-ul-Haq had laid the foundation for what was to happen in Kashmir in the 1990s. From 1988, the ISI began to organise training camps for young militants from the Valley. At the beginning their partner was the Jammu Kashmir Liberation Front (JKLF), who were responsible for recruiting the fighters, while the ISI delivered training and equipment. Funding came from the Gulf region and the drug trade, and donations were collected in the mosques of Pakistan, US and Western Europe. All this ensured the recruitment and training of new young volunteers and the deployment of battle-hardened mujahideen from Afghanistan. The recruits came mainly from Punjab and NWFP, but young Muslims were also enlisted from abroad. The training camps for the volunteers from Jammu and Kashmir were located in Azad Kashmir, close to the LoC; the camps for the Pakistanis and the foreigners were in Punjab and NWFP.[2]

Once the JKLF, under their leaders Amanullah Khan and Yasin Malik, drifted ideologically towards independence for Kashmir, the party was dropped by the ISI in the early 1990s. It was replaced by the Hizbul Mujahideen (Party of the Holy Fighters), created in Pakistan in 1989. This became the militant arm of the Pakistani Jamaat-e-Islami (JI-Islamic Party), which vehemently demanded the annexation of Kashmir to Pakistan. Over the years, Hizbul Mujahidin became the strongest and most active resistance group in Kashmir. On 27 October 1990, the official accession date, Hizbul Mujahideen adopted a resolution regarding the annexation of Kashmir to Pakistan (Qarardad Ilhaq-Pakistan). Its goal was the creation of an Islamic society, enforcing the veil and prohibition; hence the acid attacks on women in IJK were largely carried out by Hizbul Mujahideen.

Another extreme group, Harkat-ul-Mujahideen (Movement of the Holy Warriors), was bolstered after the fall of Kabul in 1992 with fighters from Egypt, Tunisia, Algeria, Bosnia, Tajikistan, Chechnya, Myanmar and the Philippines. They then started to broaden their operations in Kashmir. The organization is based in Pakistan and led by Maulana Fazlur Rehman Khalil, who has links with Hizb-ul Mujahideen. Its splinter group, Harkat-ul-Mujahideen al-Alami, carried out bomb attacks against French naval contractors and the local US Consulate in Karachi. Between 1993 and 1997 Harkat-ul-Mujahideen emerged as Harkat-ul-Ansar (Movement of the Companions); banned as a terrorist organization in 1997 by the United States because of its links to Osama bin Laden, it reverted to its old name. In January 2002 it was outlawed as a terrorist organization by President Musharraf. Harkat-ul-Mujahideen reorganised themselves into Jamiat-ul-Ansar (Army of the Companions) and was reinforced by the inclusion of other splinter groups like the Harkat-ul Jihadi-e-Islami. At the insistence of the Americans, Jamiat-ul-Ansar was banned by Musharraf on 15 November 2002.

Other new militant organizations surfaced during the 1990s. Those of particular interest were Lashkar-e-Taiba (Army of the Pure)[3] and the Jaish-e-Mohammad (Army of the Prophet Mohammad), renowned for their successful recruiting and suicide assassinations. Both organizations grew rapidly and were soon the preferred partners of the ISI. Lashkar-e-Taiba proudly admitted responsibility for the terror attacks on the Indian Parliament in New Delhi in December 2001; Jaish-e-Mohammad, under Maulana Masood Azhar, had traceable connections to al-Qaeda.[4]

The apex of tensions between India and Pakistan came in 2002 when their armies were deployed to the LoC (Line of Control). Under pressure from the US, Musharraf announced the closure of the training camps in Azad Kashmir, which directly affected 1,500 jihadis.[5] By mid November 2003 most of the militant organizations were blacklisted by President Musharraf, some for the second time, since they tend to reorganise and rebrand themselves immediately afterwards.[6] Hizbul Mujahideen continues to survive and remains active; it is considered a purely Kashmiri organization and is therefore not prohibited by Pakistan. The same goes for the Lashkar-e Taiba, which now exists as Jamaat-ul-Dawa.

New Delhi reacted to the intensified cross-border terrorism in the 1990s with successive troop reinforcements. At any one time, up to half a million Indian soldiers were present in Kashmir. They furnished evidence of Pakistan's control and support of the riots in Kashmir and spoke of terrorism against India. Pakistan officially denies having provided either material or military assistance for the Kashmir resistance, but it does admit to political and moral support directed against what it terms an illegal annexation. They started propaganda counter-offensives denouncing the rampages of Indian soldiers, the suffering and victimization of the Kashmiris and the violation of their human rights by India. The target of the local propaganda offensive was the international community, especially the US, European Union and the UN, with the aim of precipitating their intervention. Pakistan's goal was also to internationalise the conflict, thereby forcing India to the negotiating table.

The number of victims of the Kashmir conflict is inaccurately stated by both sides: Pakistan statistics state there have been 80,000 casualties; the Indian side claim only 40,000.[7]

Kashmir in 2014

The opposing stances of India and Pakistan have given the Kashmir conflict a particularly symbolic function since its outset. Pakistan sees itself standing for the right to self-determination and the fellowship of Muslims in South Asia. It therefore supports the secession efforts of the Muslim Kashmiris, as Kashmir's release from India's hegemony would not only reverse a historical injustice, but also confirm Jinnah's two-nation theory. India, on the other hand, sees itself as a secular country which embraces all religious communities of the subcontinent, in accordance with the founding precepts of the state of India set out by Gandhi and Nehru.[8] Kashmir being the only Indian state with a Muslim majority is seen by New Delhi as proof of the correctness of the one-nation theory. In addition, the emergence of Bangladesh in 1971 is regarded in India as proof of the end of the two-nation theory.

New to the Kashmir struggle are its geo-strategic aspects, in particular those affecting water resources. Three of the six main rivers of the Indus basin flow through Kashmir.[9] Whoever possesses Kashmir controls and manages the use of most of the water flow. Since 1960, an agreement regulates its distribution through World Bank mediation.[10] However, the increasing demand for water for agriculture and electricity in India and Pakistan raises doubts as to whether the contract will still hold in the future.[11]

Over two decades, there have been many different proposals offering a solution to the Kashmir imbroglio. Experts talk of over a dozen models, but none is seen as practicable. India claims it is ready to accept a Kashmir solution on to the basis of the status quo, according to its Constitution, namely that IJK is now an integral part of the Indian state. For Islamabad, such a solution is not enough; the Pakistanis believe that at least the return of the Valley should be secured.

In the APHC, there are factions of "Pakistan friends" supported by the ISI who call for Kashmir's independence. New to the scenario is a group of realists who, aware of the years of suffering of the population, is committed to the improvement of the situation within the framework of the Indian Constitution. Thus, an agreement on Kashmir is still nowhere in sight.

For the ISI, therefore, Kashmir remains an area of activity *sui generis*. The necessary auxiliary troops continue to be available. The militant Hizbul Mujahideen groups of the 1990s continue to exist under their old name;[12] Lashkar-e-Taiba and Jaish-e-Mohammad are currently partially active under new names;[13] Al-Badar continues as a smaller group and is also active. New militant groups are merged in the Save Kashmir Movement and the United Jihad Council. According to Indian intelligence estimates, in 2007 there were 1,500 to 3,000 trained Kashmiri fighters active. They are based in five to six ISI-controlled camps located in Punjab. Additionally, there are half a dozen training camps in Azad Kashmir, where 300–500 jihadis are trained before they are despatched to smaller camps.[14]

Since the de-escalation on the LoC in 2003, due to pressure from the US, there have been only minor skirmishes along it. This was the situation more or less continuously until 2012, the reason being that Indian security forces have succeeded in now effectively controlling the area. Modern technical monitoring devices have been installed and the training of border troops intensified and refined. Infiltration over the LoC increasingly became a gamble. From 2003, agents and fighters trying to penetrate Kashmir and India from Pakistan went through a third country, the route through Bangladesh or Nepal proving to be a safer passage.

A compilation of individual reports in mid 2009 indicates that the ISI is strengthening its commitment in Azad Kashmir once again. There is evidence that they are trying to bring back experienced jihadis from Afghanistan and Pakistan to Azad Kashmir, to strengthen the local militant outfits. Other reports speak of ISI actively hiring new young fighters.

Finally, there are indications that psychological pressure is put on former soldiers or jihadis who had renounced holy war in order to reactivate them.

During 2013 there were violations of the ceasefire on the LoC, beyond the usual exchange of gunfire and artillery duels. Jihadis infiltrated and attacked police and military posts in IJK, over the LoC, leading to the beheading of some Indian prisoners. It is understood that the Indian side responded by sending commando troops via the LoC. This only confirms the fact that for Kashmir there is still no real and lasting solution in sight. In summer 2015 the author was given in writing the ISI's line on the ongoing Kashmir conflict as follows: "Kashmir dispute, the longest running in contemporary time, is the unfinished agenda of the Partition of the subcontinent. It is not merely a territorial dispute, as it involves the lives, wishes and future of over 17 million Kashmiris. Pakistan's claim over Kashmir is based on the principle of democratic choice; Kashmiri's right of self-determination; ages of old historical and cultural bonds, religious affinity and geographical location/connections. On the contrary, India's claim over Kashmir is based on a forced accession to India by the then ruler of the state, which was against all historical, cultural and democratics norms and principles. Freedom movement of Kashmiris in Indian Held Kashmir is due to the negation of grant of their right of self determination, human rights violations and mis-governance. India is a status quo player in Kashmir, which is not interested in conflict resolutions, whereas Pakistan has made several suggestions that lie between the status quo and new 'out of box thinking'. But India has never agreed to anything, not even to free movement of Kashmiris."

18

TURBULENT TIMES, 2007–2010

The Beginning of Change Afoot, 2007

For Pakistan, 2007 was a turbulent year in politics. In March, Musharraf dismissed the country's most senior judge, Iftikhar Muhammad Chaudhry, sparking a protest movement by the country's lawyers, which escalated into a wider campaign against Musharraf's rule. His dual function since 2001 as President and Army chief, including his intention to be elected for a further five-year term as President, were serious points of contention. Musharraf appeared to be badly advised about the protests and acted foolishly, thereby tarnishing his political reputation still further. On 20 July a Supreme Court Committee of Inquiry reinstated Chaudhry, and Musharraf suffered considerable loss of face.

The next challenge was when the aforementioned Red Mosque in the heart of Islamabad was occupied by religious fanatics. After much deliberation, Musharraf ordered the complex to be stormed by an Army commando.[1] The operation led to many casualties, among them many women and girls who were studying in the mosque's madrasahs. Consequently, there followed a wave of attacks across the whole country against the military and other security force targets.

In August, the Supreme Court decided that former Prime Minister Nawaz Sharif had the right to return to Pakistan and live there. Contrary to this judicial decision, the former Prime Minister was detained upon his arrival at Lahore airport on 10 September, and four hours later was forcefully deported to Saudi Arabia. On 5 October Musharraf declared a National Reconciliation

Ordinance, which stated that all charges against politicians made between 1 January 1986 and 12 October 1999 would be lifted. The main beneficiaries of this amnesty were Benazir Bhutto and Altaf Hussain. One day later, Musharraf was elected as President for a further five years. With 384 votes, he obtained 55 percent out of a total of 702 votes. Benazir Bhutto returned to Pakistan on 18 October after an eight-year exile. The triumphal parade in Karachi, arranged by the PPP leadership, ended in a bloodbath caused by a suicide bomber and snipers; 135 people were killed and over 400 injured. The returning Benazir was fortunate to escape death by a hair's breadth.

President Musharraf finally proclaimed a State of Emergency on 3 November 2007. According to the official version, the Constitution was partially and temporarily suspended, but parliament was not dissolved. On 16 November Prime Minister Shaukat Aziz stepped down, and the President swore in the former Senate President, Muhammad Mian Soomro, as head of an interim government; Musharraf justified his act by blaming it on the intervention of the judiciary in politics, threatening the fabric of Pakistan. In fact in the weeks prior he had been the target of a series of attacks and assassination attempts, resulting in many casualties, and for some while it seemed as if parts of the country were about to be plunged into anarchy.

The proximity of timing between the State of Emergency and the dismissal of Judge Iftikhar Chaudhry suggested a deeper motive for the President's actions. Musharraf feared a negative decision from the SC under CJ Chaudhry regarding the legality of his re-election as President. Six petitions were lodged against this election, or partially submitted before election day. The SC under CJ Chaudhry had approved of holding the elections. His legitimacy however depended on the success of the petition proceedings. The replacement of Chaudhry with another judge would finally secure his re-election. The new CJ was Abdul Hameed Dogar, a loyal man in the general's eyes.

The protests responding to the State of Emergency announcement resulted in the police being deployed, and they cracked down harshly on the demonstrating party members, lawyers and journalists. Prominent leaders of the protests were arrested, amongst them Hamid Gul. Over the years, the retired 70-year-old former ISI head had become Musharraf's professed opponent, accusing him of betraying Pakistan's interests. Hamid Gul challenged the proclaimed State of Emergency as being military law in disguise. Musharraf responded by arresting him; but in detention the now sickly former general was refused the medication he required.

Benazir Bhutto also joined the protests. She demanded the cancelling of the State of Emergency and the release and reinstatement of Judge Chaudhry.

Calling the people to the streets, she began preparations for large PPP demonstrations. She was also planning a march from Lahore to Islamabad. Benazir was then placed under house arrest for seven days. The reason given was her criticism of the alleged security shortcomings in the assassination attempt against her in Karachi. According to the authorities, information about new planned assassination attempts justified the prohibition of demonstrations and her enforced house arrest.

President Musharraf eventually bowed to the continuous countrywide protests and to pressure from Washington; on 9 November he announced the imminent removal of the State of Emergency and his intention to hold parliamentary elections at the beginning of January 2008. In addition, he let it be known that he had given strict instructions that no intelligence agency would be allowed to be involved in electoral manipulation. He also reaffirmed the wish to return to civilian life in the near future.

However, Benazir Bhutto felt that the power-sharing deal she had agreed with Musharraf during her exile would win little acceptance with the populace. She now banked on a PPP election victory, and explained that in the future she would no longer cooperate with a civilian President Musharraf. Thus, the key features of Pakistan's new political order proposed by Musharraf to the Bush government seemed to be collapsing. The year was nearing its end with political turbulence threatening the country's immediate future.

On 18 November, the Deputy US Secretary of State, John Negroponte, visited Islamabad. The US was afraid of state collapse and was concerned about the security of Pakistan's nuclear weapons. Negroponte pressured Musharraf for a speedy removal of the State of Emergency, and recommended the restoration of the agreement painstakingly negotiated between Benazir and the President. Musharraf still promised parliamentary elections at the beginning of January 2008, but he opposed the immediate removal of the State of Emergency. Benazir was more conciliatory after the meeting with Negroponte. She eschewed the other parties' demands for a rolling campaign of opposition against Musharraf and the appointed interim government. So Negroponte started his journey home having achieved only partial success. On 22 November the SC once again gave Musharraf their support. Eleven judges acknowledged the legality of the 6 October elections. For Musharraf, the road to a further five-year term of office seemed open, as long as he discarded his uniform.

Even if the ISI seemed outwardly calm, the directorate was on high alert. They knew from PPP circles that Benazir Bhutto was assuming that the government and the ISI had been informed in advance about the assassination attempt in Karachi. From Dubai, her husband Asif Zardari accused the ISI of being involved in it. It was also whispered that she had said that as future Prime Minister she would have no objections to the questioning of A. Q. Khan by the IAEA and the deportation of Dawood Ibrahim to India. Even the possibility of American air strikes against the Taliban and al-Qaeda from Pakistani territory were not totally over-ruled by her. And everyone knew that Benazir had plans to reform the Pakistan intelligence services should she return to power.[2]

The broader increase in attacks on the Army and ISI was alarming the generals in Rawalpindi, as did the bombing of Islamabad's Aabpara market. In September 2006 there had been a failed rocket attack on the ISI Directorate. In the first weeks of July 2007, after the storming of the Red Mosque, there were two assassination attempts in Rawalpindi targeting staff members of the GHQ and ISI. In a separate attack, a SSG officer was killed. On 4 September 2007 there were terrorist attacks on a vehicle carrying Army officers and a bus with ISI staff, resulting in twenty-five deaths. On 24 November, two more attacks took place in Rawalpindi: in front of the gates of the re-designed former Ojhri camp, a suicide bomber accounted for thirty-four casualties; and almost simultaneously another took the lives of two watchmen in front of an entrance to the GHQ. On 4 November, a woman set off a bomb outside the ISI's regional office in Peshawar; she perished, but there were no additional victims. Numerous other attacks on military, ISI and police facilities, almost always with high numbers of victims, followed in 2008, 2009 and 2010. Among the most spectacular attacks were that against GHQ in Rawalpindi in October 2009; one on the mosque near GHQ, which was mainly used by the military for Friday prayers; and one on the regional ISI headquarters and the police academy, both in Lahore.[3]

In mid November a complaint was lodged at the Supreme Court against Musharraf's re-election as President. The judges were to vote on the issue, so the ISI launched a surreptitious campaign of persuasion. At least three judges received secretly taped videos in which they were shown in compromising situations with certain ladies. The ladies, who were sent by the ISI, had been given as "thank you gifts" by clients for services performed, and the judges had happily helped themselves. There were also sensitive videos pertaining to the daughters of the other judges. The message was clear: that a positive vote was expected. As it turned out, the court judgement went in their favour; the ISI had won its campaign.[4]

However, for Musharraf the difficulties continued. On 25 November Nawaz Sharif returned to Pakistan, and thousands of his supporters prepared a large welcome for him in Lahore. The PML leader announced to the press that he would not recognise a civilian Musharraf as the legal President. He also demanded the reinstatement of the former SC judges, in particular CJ Chaudhry. Nawaz Sharif declared himself a staunch democrat and many Pakistanis cheered him. It was forgotten how during his term as Prime Minister the SC had been stormed by his supporters. It was also forgotten that he had wanted to abolish democratic structures and through a constitutional amendment had tried to become the Amir ul-Momineen.

DG ISI Nadeem Taj, 2007–2008

Lt. Gen. Nadeem Taj was appointed DG ISI by Musharraf on 21 September 2007. He had the reputation of being a cool-headed infantryman. Even more than Kayani, Nadeem Taj was seen as a Musharraf supporter and had been closely associated with him for many years. When a brigadier he was Musharraf's military secretary, and as such was part of the Army general's entourage on that fateful flight from Sri Lanka to Pakistan in October 1999. Nadeem Taj remained in this post when Musharraf became President, and was promoted to major general in February 2000. He was also in the car with the President during the first failed assassination attempt on Musharraf in December 2003. Directly after this he became DG MI, from which post he supervised the 2002 parliamentary elections, and thereafter initiated the confidential dialogue with Benazir Bhutto.

Taj left the MI in February 2005 and took command of the 11th Infantry Division in Lahore. His last post before the appointment as DG ISI was as head of the Pakistan Military Academy in Kakul. This showed that Musharraf had high hopes for him, namely the top post.

A few days before Nawaz's return to Pakistan in late November 2007, President Musharraf flew to Saudi Arabia accompanied by Nadeem Taj. The purpose of their journey to Riyadh has two possible explanations. According to the first, Musharraf tried to persuade the Saudis not to let Nawaz Sharif leave the country. The royal house opposed this unjustified demand.[5] Actually, in Riyadh they had an interest in repatriating Nawaz Sharif to Pakistan. They did not trust Benazir Bhutto because of her connections to Washington, and saw that Saudi interests would be better served with Nawaz Sharif in power. To persuade him, they gave Nawaz two armoured cars as a gift for his return home.

The second version suggests the visit was an attempt to arrange a meeting for the time after the return of the former Prime Minister. Distrust against

Benazir had continued to grow amongst Musharraf's advisors and in the Army leadership; they were looking for the means to cut her down to size and to prevent an outright PPP election victory in January 2008. When Nawaz Sharif returned to his PML group, it was reckoned that they would compromise the PPP vote bank and produce a divided election result which would make life easier for the civilian President Musharraf. The fact that the new DG ISI Nadeem Taj remained in Riyadh while Musharraf continued to travel to the Holy Places in Saudi Arabia speaks for this version of events. Obviously, detailed questions were still to be clarified.

A Military Farewell

On 26 November 2007 Musharraf began his farewell visits to the troops. He reminded the soldiers that they were the guarantors of Pakistan's existence. Two days later, he stepped down as COAS. President Musharraf was now a civilian.

For most of his seven years as President, Musharraf had enjoyed the support of the people. In 2006 popular backing for his policies stood at over 60 percent. Thereafter he began to lose his political sensitivity through the arrogance of power, and this is what led him into the crisis with the country's judiciary from 2007 and his eventual political demise.

His successor as COAS was Ashfaq Kayani, who had been Vice-COAS since October and had received his fourth star. Rumours soon arose that he was planning a reshuffle among the generals and ISI. Under the heading "Gen. Kayani to remove Mush loyalists," Amir Mir wrote:

> Kayani is all set to reshuffle the top brass, including the chief of the Inter Services Intelligence as well as several corps commanders loyal to Musharraf... According to well-placed military circles, besides changing the director of the ISI, General Kayani has also decided in principle to replace the sector commanders of the notorious ISI in the four provinces before the dawn of 2008.[6]

For Pervez Musharraf, political life continued for the time being. On 29 November he was sworn in by CJ Abdul Hameed Dogar for a further five-year term of office as President of Pakistan. According to the Constitution, he was also commander-in-chief of the armed forces and chairman of the National Security Council. Apart from the COAS's position, it seemed that after the January 2008 elections the new Prime Minister would also have to live with a President who was not politically powerless. The PPP leadership around Benazir Bhutto was aware of this and tried to take counter-measures. Their party's election manifesto demanded the abolition of the NSC and a reversion to the defence committee of the cabinet as it had been before the Musharraf era. In this set-up the balance of power would shift, with the Prime Minister heading the sole chairmanship and the President being partially deprived of political power.[7] The manifesto also contained a demand to bring the military dictators to justice. This was a clear challenge to Musharraf.

Assassination

On 27 December, Benazir Bhutto met Hamid Karzai for the first time, and was presented to him as the future Prime Minister of Pakistan. In the afternoon, she was in Rawalpindi for her election campaign. She spoke in the same place where once before in 1951 Prime Minister Liaquat Ali Khan had met a violent end. As usual she addressed a large crowd of listeners; and as always she sought contact with her public. Standing in an open car, she moved amongst the masses receiving their jubilant approval.

There is contradictory information about how the attack unfolded. There was at least one suicide bomber involved, but there was additional shooting from gunmen in the vicinity. The official versions remain inconsistent: either she was shot in the head, or else was killed by a head fracture resulting from the explosion. An autopsy was not carried out, at the request of her husband, Asif Zardari. In accordance with Islamic custom, the funeral took place the same day at the Bhuttos' ancestral seat near Lakarna in Sindh. Even now, the true identity of the perpetrators remains unknown.[8]

The government was quick to find a suspect. A recording of an alleged telephone call pointed to Baitullah Mehsud, leader of the Tehrik-i-Taliban (TTP) in South Waziristan, and his extremist supporters. Mehsud denied the claim and a large majority in Pakistan are willing to believe him. They accuse the establishment, the ISI or others close to Benazir of involvement in her murder.

Zardari and the PPP leadership avoided bringing the Army or the ISI under close suspicion. This was partly because Benazir had alleged in a letter that if she were to be assassinated then three names ought to be in the frame: Brigadier (retd.) Ijaz Shah, Director, IB; the Punjab Chief Minister, Pervez Elahi (PML-Q); and the ailing 70-year-old Hamid Gul.[9]

Exoneration for Musharraf and his supporters came from India. Five days after the attack, B. Raman wrote a first analysis. On the question whether Musharraf and the Army leadership were involved, his considered view was:

> Unlikely. Musharraf and other senior Army officers were unhappy with her confrontational style after the first attack on her at Karachi on October 18,

2007. They were also unhappy about her habit of making what they saw as wild allegations and taking her complaints to her friends in the US. They wanted to marginalise her and prevent her from becoming the Prime Minister again. They would have been able to achieve this through "normal" Pakistani methods such as manipulation and rigging of the polls. They did not have to resort to the extreme step of having her killed. Moreover, in the unlikely event of their wanting to have her killed, they would have got it done at some other place such as Peshawar and not in Rawalpindi, where there would have been little deniability.[10]

Collaboration between the military's middle and lower ranks without the knowledge of the President and the Army generals he considered a possibility, although he admitted there could be no proof.[11] B. Raman referred to the extremist Lashkar-e-Jhangvi (LEJ), the Jaish-e-Mohammad (JEM) and the Jundullah (Soldiers of Allah), all of whom they considered to be suspects. LEJ and JEM both had sniper-trained former military in their ranks, and both groups rejected the idea of a woman Prime Minister. Besides, the LEJ was still radically anti-Shia, and Benazir Bhutto's mother was a Shia.

As in the case of the deaths of her two brothers, the full truth about Benazir's murder will probably never be uncovered.[12] But after a exhaustive and detailed investigation it now seems highly probable that Baitullah Mehsud and his TTP were behind her killing.

For some days the country was in deep mourning. Afterwards, the humdrum daily political routine returned. President Musharraf postponed the elections from 8 January to 18 February and the politicians plunged into the election campaign.

Elections and Presidential Change

Whoever was responsible for the murder of the charismatic PPP leader in December 2007, the impact on Musharraf of the assassination was catastrophic. Any residual sympathy for him had ebbed away fast during the lawyers' campaign, and now he lost it completely. The overwhelming view in Pakistan was that the President's time had already expired in late 2007. It is interesting that Musharraf's former comrades, including reputable retired generals, now spoke openly against him. Even among the active officer corps, the opinion expressed privately was that the former general should withdraw from politics and leave the country.

Like Chief Justice Iftikhar Muhammad Chaudhry, the harassed Musharraf now showed his fighting spirit. He saw the forthcoming February 2008 elections for the National Assembly and Provincial Parliaments as a way of consolidating his Presidential office. In reality, this election proved yet another disaster for him; and his former protégé, General Kayani, contributed towards it. Days before the election, the leaders of the PML-Q, the so-called King's party, were convinced that they would win, believing they could rely on the requisite help from the MI and the ISI. However, Kayani saw the situation differently. He ordered the military not to interfere in the election preparations and officers were forbidden from contacting politicians, under threat of disciplinary action. Soldiers could only be deployed to maintain order in the polling stations The Military Intelligence service (MI) was pulled from involvement in electoral procedures, also a strong signal to the ISI, most of whose officers were wary of acting against the Army generals' wishes. Thus, the possibilities of electoral manipulation were limited[13] and Musharraf and his henchmen were unable to influence the last phase of the polling campaign as originally planned.

The results were significant: the biggest party was the PPP (124 seats); next was the PML-N (91 seats); in third place was the PML-Q (56 NA seats), which despite supporting the President ended up on the opposition benches, and in Pakistan's four provincial parliaments could not join any government.

But the palpable joy and relief in the country over the successful free and democratic elections was immense. Politicians and columnists vied to outdo each other in their enthusiasm, the mood was jubilant.

One of the first tests for the new government was President Musharraf's fate. While Nawaz Sharif sought his removal from office, the Zardari-PPP faction showed that they were ready to cooperate with Musharraf so long as his power was curtailed. However, Musharraf did not submit easily to being cut down to size. People everywhere were demanding impeachment, even in Washington. On 18 April 2008, Musharraf delivered an hour-long televised speech; he vehemently denied the accusations of having abused his office, but announced his resignation as President. Days later he travelled to London, where he lived in self-imposed exile until March 2013. His successor as President was the 52-year-old Asif Ali Zardari, selected by the national parliament and four provincial parliamentary elections on 6 September 2008 and sworn in on 9 September 2008.

The Difficult Years, 2009–2010

By spring 2009, it became clear that the lingering crisis regarding the judiciary had to be solved. In March 2009 the Bar Associations called for new protest marches in support of the former Chief Justice Chaudhry and colleagues. On 12 March a new "Long March" started from Karachi, which was due to reach Islamabad four days later. Nawaz Sharif, who had long remained uncommitted, joined up with his party just before the big showdown when the protest march moved nearer Islamabad, lending it additional impetus. President Zardari and his Prime Minister Yousuf Gilani were running into trouble. Kayani then intervened, increasing the pressure on an obstinate President by promising no Army intervention against the protestors. At the last moment Zardari caved in. On 16 March Prime Minister Gilani made a televised address in which he stated that Chief Justice Abdul Hameed Dogar would go into retirement on 21 March and his predecessor, Iftikhar Mohammad Chaudhry, would return to office. For the majority of lawyers in the country, the two-year struggle had reached a successful conclusion.

A special test for the new rulers of Pakistan was its policies against national and international terrorism, both a legacy of the Musharraf years. The ISI continued to be the focus of worldwide attention. The Obama administration in Washington, in office since early 2009, demanded Pakistan's full support in trying resolve the Afghanistan question. This meant that Islamabad had to bring back under its control its troubled border regions with Afghanistan. However, in spring 2009 Islamabad first had to clean up the Swat valley in NWFP, where 4,000–5,000 TNSM Islamists led by Maulana Fazlullah were now ruling the roost.[14] Their goal was complete implementation of Sharia law amid conditions similar to those introduced by the Afghan Taliban in the 1990s. At one point the Islamic fundamentalists announced that their sway now extended beyond the Swat valley, to Buner district in the Malakand Division, in relatively close proximity to Islamabad; this was the straw that broke the camel's back. From mid April, a military reconquest of Swat began, involving 5,000 troops with artillery, tanks and air support.[15] A large proportion of the population fled; at one time there were up to 1.5 million internal refugees. After three months the Army had cleared the valley, and one third of the local Islamists had been killed or captured. The others, among them a large part of the leadership, fled to FATA, to Afghanistan, and to the provinces of Punjab, Karachi and Azad Kashmir.

In mid October 2009 the Army launched Operation Rah-i-Najat in South Waziristan, a main base of the Pakistani Taliban.[16] It was the fourth military operation since 2004 and this time the GHQ was serious. About 30,000 military personnel came up against 15,000 Taliban, mainly from Mehsud's tribe, and 1,500 foreign fighters, including 1,000 Uzbeks. After heavy fighting, by late 2009 the Army had South Waziristan under control. The casualties included 500 TTP fighters, though most of them escaped to other parts of FATA; and 200 Uzbeks, while the rest of them fled and were scattered. The ISI Directorate recorded this as one of their special successes; they had known the exact whereabouts of the Uzbeks and passed this information on to the Army, sharing in their targetting.

19

REFORM ATTEMPTS

Personnel Changes

Pakistan experts assumed that after the change of government in Islamabad in 2008, there would follow fundamental changes in the ISI's role. The new regime in Islamabad was inclined to bring the country's prime intelligence service more under its control. The auspices were favourable till the military's reputation suffered a setback among the populace and Kayani ordered a retreat to barracks. Change seemed all the more necessary when the coalition found out through the press that the ISI continued to act subversively internally. Local journalists discovered that the head of the Internal Politics Division in the ISI, Major General Nusrat Naeem, had once again met the newly elected parliamentarians from FATA for political discussions. It was therefore clear that the ISI under DG Lt. Gen. Taj continued to represent the interests of President Musharraf.[1] Besides, it was known that the ISI was busy destroying sensitive data regarding the top people in the new government, the opposition, the judiciary and the media which had been collected over the years. The assumption was that the ISI was trying to cover up some of its recent activities.

The government tried to counteract these revelations. In May, the Pakistani press reported changes in the nation's intelligence and security apparatus. Thereafter the Political wing would be separated from the ISI and transferred to the IB. Also, new reporting procedures were announced in relation to the Prime Minister, President and Army: in future, the ISI and IB would report directly to the Prime Minister; the President would receive reports from the IB only every two weeks; and MI would only report to the COAS and the Corps Commanders.[2] However, these press stories were obviously a trial balloon, based on Benazir Bhutto's demands[3] dating from October 2007. In reality, nothing changed, for the time being at least.

There was also instability surrounding the position of the IB chief. In the middle of March 2008, Musharraf's trusted friend Brigadier (retd.) Ijaz Shah stepped down. His successor was supposed to be Tariq Lodhi,[4] a friend and confidant of President Zardari. Meanwhile in Sindh, the MQM opposed the appointment of Dr Shoaib Suddle as Inspector General of Police. The party leaders threatened to cross over to the opposition, so Zardari had to make new arrangements. Suddle was removed from Sindh at the end of June, after only a ten-week term of office, and was made the new Director of the IB. Lodhi remained in the IB as Joint Director, a post which he had held previously.[5] Then President Zardari and Interior Minister Rehman Malik set out to rebuild the IB and to increase its intelligence and internal political role. Its military personnel, both active and non-active, were removed and replaced by police officers. In May 2008 Javed Noor, who was previously IG Police in Azad Kashmir, became Director of the IB. Its staffing and budget were increased substantially and, since June 2008, the IB has been represented by a Director General as advisor on national security in the Prime Minister's Secretariat. Interestingly, aid in the form of money, material and expertise arrived from the US, as Washington was keen to counter the role of the ISI by strengthening the IB.

But the ISI was still proving successful in espionage. In April 2010 the Indian IB exposed Ms Madhuri Gupta, an Indian Foreign Service Second Secretary in the Indian High Commission in Islamabad, as a mole recruited by an ISI officer. The lonely 53-year-old had allegedly been entrapped and had, for at least two years, leaked secret information on Indian affairs to the ISI.

On 26 July 2008, the government took further steps to gain better control of intelligence gathering. By government notification, it was communicated that in accordance with the terms of Rule 3 (3) of the Rules of Business of 1973, the Prime Minister agreed that the IB and ISI would be placed under the administrative, financial and operational control of the Internal Division, with Minister of Interior Rehman Malik becoming the country's security czar. The government, keen to gain Washington's approval, felt they had picked a favorable time to seek their goal.

GHQ responded immediately and put a halt to the reform. Ostensibly, the point was made that a three-star general at the head of the ISI could hardly receive directives from the Minister for Interior, who as a civil servant rose to Deputy Director of the FIA and therefore was comparable to a two-star general rank. Besides, in the GHQ there were more pressing concerns. The ISI was hanging on to secret documents regarding the assistance of China and North Korea in nuclear and rocket armament procurement, and also documents relating to the questioning of A. Q. Khan on the transfer of nuclear technology.[6] GHQ and ISI were alarmed that Washington could now get access to this sensitive information.[7] They took action, and one day later another government statement was issued stating that the ISI would continue to report directly to the Prime Minister. The excuse was some misunderstanding, with a promise of detailed clarification to follow later, which never happened. To political observers it was clear that Kayani had prevailed and shown who held power in Pakistan. Zardari, Gilani, Malik and Washington had to take this into account.

In the wake of these events, the military tried to paint a rosy picture of democracy in action. The COAS and ISI chief called on the President and the Prime Minister to brief them on the country's security situation. Local newspapers were encouraged to report in detail on the development. One month after Zardari's election as President, a two-day briefing of news agencies took place behind closed doors in parliament. This was attended by the President, Prime Minister, COAS and the DG ISI. Later on, resident journalists in Islamabad were invited to the ISI Directorate and informed about the ISI's view on points of topical interest.

The public image of the ISI still needed to be improved, as the service remained under suspicion. They were said to have been involved in a terrorist assualt on the Indian embassy in Kabul, in July 2008, which left 58 dead and 141 wounded.[8] On 1 August, the *New York Times* published a report by an un-named US official accusing the ISI of helping out in the attack. The accusations were based on discussions intercepted beforehand between the ISI and the perpetrators, which only made sense after it had been carried out. However, only Washington and New Delhi received additional intelligence evidence, which prompted the Americans to arrest an ISI officer in Afghanistan. Prime Minister Gilani flew to Washington that July for talks with President Bush, who confronted him with the intercepts and threatened serious consequences if such atrocities were repeated.[9] The justification for the terror acts in Kabul articulated by the Pakistan military was their conviction that India had established itself politically and economically in Afghanistan, and was supporting secessionism in Balochistan.[10]

In September 2008, American pressure resulted in the replacement of DG ISI Nadeem Taj; in the wake of the terrorist attacks in Kabul, they felt he was no longer acceptable as an interlocutor.[11] For Kayani, the American reservations were convenient. Like all his predecessors, he was anxious to have people in whom he had confidence in place in all key roles. The leadership post at the ISI is one such position. The three-star general Taj was considered to be a Musharraf supporter, someone whom Kayani tried increasingly to keep at a distance. On 29 September 2008, one year after the beginning of his tenure, Nadeem Taj was replaced as DG ISI and transferred as a corps commander to Gujranwala. He remained a member of the commanders' circle but was kept at a distance from the political epicentre in Islamabad.[12]

Nadeem Taj's successor as DG ISI was Ahmad Shuja Pasha, who was therefore promoted to a three-star general. Born in 1952, the Pashtun Pasha was an infantryman and Director of Military Operations in GHQ, and as such responsible for operations against insurgent militants in FATA and NWFP. His ideas about further action against the insurgents were in broad alignment with those of the Army chiefs. Pasha was also considered a trusted ally of Kayani; his appointment as DG ISI was thus welcomed in Washington, so Pasha accompanied Kayani to meetings with America's top military chief.[13]

In November 2008, Kayani and Pasha began to get to grips with the leadership of the ISI. Four newly promoted two-star generals, namely Asif Yaseen, Mumtaz Ahmad Bajwa, Zaheer ul-Islam and Niaz Khattak, were appointed to the executive level of the service. Back in September, two major generals in the ISI, Nusrat Naeem and Asif Akhtar, had been bypassed for promotion; Naeem, who had headed the Internal Wing, now handed over to Zaheer ul-Islam and left the agency. One consequence of these actions was that Washington was tentatively satisfied; meanwhile the Pakistani commentariat was happy to write articles arguing that the ISI had been "cleansed".[14]

This seam of optimism seemed to be confirmed when, on 23 November, it was announced that the so-called Political Wing of the ISI had now ceased its activities and was to be abolished. In the future, the IB would be responsible for these matters. Minister of Foreign Affairs Shah Mehmood Qureshi announced the news to reporters on the eve of his journey to India.[15] However, one day later a local newspaper quoted a high-ranking unnamed official saying that the Political Cell's work was frozen but the department had not been dissolved. The very next day Prime Minister Gilani officially announced through his press department the closure of the ISI cell. The laconic reason given by the Prime Minister was that this streamlining was intended to increase the effectiveness of the country's premier intelligence service.[16] However, experienced local observers immediately reported their doubts. They knew that the truth of such a measure, if any, would be proven only over the course of time.[17] The whole debate was suddenly overtaken by events in Mumbai, which dominated the headlines not only in South Asia but globally.

The Mumbai Terrorist Attack

On 26 November 2008, a ten-man terrorist commando landed on small boats in Mumbai to spread terror and death. Their principal targets were two famous hotels, one of the city's major train stations and a Jewish centre. At the end of sixty hours of continuous terror, there were 173 dead and numerous wounded.[18] Of the ten terrorists, nine were killed and one, Ajmal Amir Kasab, from Pakistan's Punjab, was captured alive. He was later hanged. His interrogation brought the first insights into the attack. All ten perpetrators came from Pakistan, nine from Punjab and the leader from NWFP. They were a Lashkar-e-Taiba terrorist group, who had been trained and primed over months in two camps close to Muzaffarabad in Azad Kashmir and later in Karachi.[19] According to Kasab's statement, among the trainers were two former Pakistani military personnel. Indian officials and experts quickly made it known that an operation of this magnitude could hardly have been planned, prepared and accomplished solely by LeT. They pointed the finger at the ISI, and the Indian Prime Minister Manmohan Singh stated unequivocally on 6 January 2009 that "there is enough evidence to show that, given the sophistication and the military precision of the attack, it must have had the support of some official agencies in Pakistan."[20]

The ISI added fuel to these suspicions. As soon as the first pictures of the terrorists surfaced in the media, they tried to erase the traces. The ISI turned up in Kasab's village of Faridkot, in Okara district, and threatened his neighbours to swear silence. Kasab's parents also vanished from the village. Just how much the ISI felt under pressure was visible in the subsequent weeks. It invited international journalists to ISI headquarters to prove the alleged spuriousness of the accusations. DG ISI Lt. Gen. Pasha, who had formerly been based in Germany for military training and spoke German, granted an exclusive interview to *Der Spiegel*, in which he denied all accusations against the secret service. In the Pakistani press, articles and columns from commissioned writers were published, praising the agency and its role as the guarantor of Pakistan's security. Simultaneously polemic statements about alleged atrocities carried out by India's

R&AW surfaced on the internet. R&AW responded, and this led to a lively and interesting bout of psychological warfare between the two adversaries.

Any analysis of the Mumbai events must ask the question whether the leadership of the ISI and GHQ were informed beforehand about the planned terror attacks. One answer common among writers on intelligence matters is the idea of "an ISI within the ISI"; but the author thinks this is erroneous. This phrase might have been deliberately created by the ISI itself. Pakistan's prime intelligence service is a strictly led, efficiently run organization, with no room for groups pursuing their own secret agenda. An operation such as the Mumbai attacks, which needed expert technical assessment, money and time to prepare, could not have been carried out or kept hidden without the knowledge of the service's leadership. Considering the political explosiveness of the event, the COAS as well would have to have been informed.

The government in Islamabad was not accused of co-conspiracy or of having prior knowledge of the Mumbai attack by New Delhi, so they opted for damage limitation. As soon as the attacks became public knowledge, Zardari and Gilani spoke to their Minister of Foreign Affairs, Qureshi, who happened to be in India. He proposed to his Indian counterparts a visit by DG ISI Pasha to investigate the incident. But GHQ and the ISI quickly put a stop to this: Qureshi was recalled and flew home on a PAF plane that night. The government now began to toe the military line: all allegations were denied, evidence demanded and reports and information from India were explained as insufficient. Meanwhile the LeT was blacklisted, its offices closed and its bank accounts frozen. Allegedly only that part of the organization active in the social welfare was excluded, whereas all LeT base groups continue to have a free field of action. A number of LeT cadres were arrested, among them the masterminds of the Mumbai attacks, Zahir ur-Rehman Lakhvi and Zarrah Shah. During their interrogation, both spoke candidly about their role in the preparation of the terror atrocity, without regrets, without doubts.[21] Initially seven LeT cadres faced prosecution under the Pakistan Anti-Terrorism Act, to which two were later added. Initially the trial was closed. New Delhi realistically expects neither an accurate factual explanation of what occurred nor an appropriate sentence to be passed on its perpetrators.

In the US, India's battering coincided with the outgoing Bush government and the incoming Obama administration. They feared retaliatory strikes from India on Pakistan, in particular a real prospect of a bombing attack on the ISI HQ in Islamabad. Senator John Kerry, designated chairman of the Senate Foreign Relations Committee, flew to New Delhi, tasked with the mission of persuading India to adopt a more prudent response. He promised future American intervention in South Asia politics in a manner that might satisfy Indian expectations. In reply, India submitted intelligence data about the Mumbai attacks collated jointly between R&AW and CIA. Both services managed to obtain some of the intercepted communications between the terrorists and their backers. As in the Kabul embassy bombings, the possibility of a forthcoming high profile attack was known beforehand, but not where and when it might take place. Kerry's journey ultimately proved to be successful. New Delhi refrained from military retaliation.[22] They decided to erect no additional hurdles for President Zardari, who was more appreciated in India than he was in Pakistan, and to see what the Obama administration's new policies towards Pakistan would bring.

Nearly a year after the Mumbai attacks, in October 2009, David Coleman Headley was arrested in the United States. At birth the Washington-born US citizen was known as Daqood Sayed Gilani, but used his new Western name to erase his Pakistani roots and links to LeT. For Headley, it proved straightforward to travel five times to India, carrying a US passport with a business visa and to obtain local information for LeT before the planned outrage. During his interrogation he gave details of 26/11, as the Mumbai attack came to be known. According to Headley, the ISI was in constant contact with LeT over the preparations for Mumbai, at each and every stage of the operation. In addition, the ISI had prepared a list of four or five al-Qaeda members who they were to put in the frame as potential suspects involved in the attacks. This plan failed largely because of the self-confidence of the LeT leadership: they envisioned global interest in the 26/11 terror acts, which they regarded almost as a marketing opportunity for their brand of terrorism, an event that would help them obtain further financial assistance and recruit new fighters.

What were the motives for the Mumbai attacks? Experts trace them back to the Pakistan's military interest in three key areas: Kashmir, Afghanistan and nuclear armaments. Regarding Kashmir, Zardari's statements about a cooperative relationship with India rang alarm bells in Rawalpindi; the military were afraid that Pakistan's presence in Kashmir would be diminished. In the case of Afghanistan, the traditionally warm relationship between New Delhi and Kabul fed their obsessions that India was a serious competitor in Afghanistan and a challenge to Pakistan's strategic interests and security. Indian assistance was also linked to the secessionist movements operating for many years in Balochistan, which is not totally untrue.[23] And with regard to nuclear armaments, ultimately the military was afraid that Washington would receive access to all its sensitive data were the Pakistani government to cooperate with the US. All of the above was seen as counter-productive to Pakistan's interests. Thus, the Mumbai attack can be read as as a strong hint, in fact a simultaneous warning to Islamabad, New Delhi and Washington.

Indian intelligence was able to obtain many details about the 26/11 attacks in a relatively short space of time. In December 2008 Indian officials accused the LeT's Zakiur Rehman Lakhvi of being involved in planning and excecuting the attacks. The evidence provided was so strong that Pakistan had no other choice but to arrest him and six of his co-conspirators in December 2008.

However, on 25 May 2010, the High Court in Islamabad ruled that there was not enough evidence against Hafiz Saeed linking him to the Mumbai case and he was acquitted; this verdict confirmed the Lahore High Court's ruling in June 2009. The proceedings against the other accused LeT members were similarly thwarted. Evidence was declared insufficient and the accumulated facts and intercepts sent by India dismissed as irrelevant.

Nor did Zakiur Rehman Lakhvi and his accomplices face any hardship during their time in jail. In Adyala prison in Rawalpindi they stayed in relative luxury A-class rooms with television, mobile phones and access to the internet. They were able to welcome dozens of visitors every day, who were not even asked to identify themselves by the jail authorities.

On the order of the Lahore High Court, Zakiur Rehman Lakhvi was finally released on bail on 10 April 2015. There can be little doubt that this happened according to the wishes of GHQ and the ISI Directorate.

On the other hand, in New Delhi the remaining terrorist Ajmal Amir Kasab was convicted after a transparent court process, sentenced to death in May 2010 and hanged in November 2012.

Further Attempts at Reform

In January 2009, Prime Minister Yousuf Raza Gilani dismissed Mahmud Ali Durrani from his position as National Security Advisor, most obviously because of his comments on Mumbai. Durrani was asked on television whether Pakistani citizens "might have been" involved, at a time when the terrorists' origins were no longer secret. He was relieved from his post soon afterwards. Imran Gardaizi, the Prime Minister's press spokesman, laconically justified his sacking to journalists by saying: "He gave media interviews without consulting the prime minister."[24] In reality, Mahmud Durrani's dismissal was one of several attempts by Gilani to free himself from President Zardari's shadow. Durrani's appointment as National Security Advisor had been due to his previous advocacy of Benazir Bhutto's interests in Washington, as a result of which he was a close confidant of Zardari.

Another reason for his dismissal was Mahmud Durrani's split loyalties after Mumbai. For years, the retired major-general was seen as an "American man" by GHQ and the ISI. He had been suspected of close ties to the CIA ever since his early military service. In fact, Durrani never made a secret of his pro-American stance; and this might have been why he was never given his third, general's, star.[25] President Musharraf, heavily dependent on American assistance, exploited Durrani's reputation in the US and sent him as ambassador to Washington in 2005. When President Zardari, also strongly dependent on Washington, made Durrani the National Security Advisor with cabinet rank in February 2008, GHQ was discomforted. Then when America demanded that Pakistan's military be subordinated to the policy-makers and the ISI subject to greater democratic oversight. Rawalpindi felt Durrani was in too risky position. Prime Minister Gilani was aware of this, and in the aftermath of Mumbai he felt secure in his dismissal of the National Security Advisor.

On 24 February 2009 Gilani took a further drastic reform by instructing the Minister of Justice to prepare a bill to abolish the NSC. The National Assembly then only needed a simple majority to erase this relic of the Musharraf era. Although formally the NSC carried out a purely consultative role, during periods of crisis their recommendations and resolutions were of great importance.[26] The abolition of the NSC had already been suggested in the PPP's election manifesto for the February 2008 elections, with the objective of returning to the Defence Committee of the Cabinet, which was managed by the PM and did not come under the President. Also, the military were in the minority in the Defence Committee.[27] It is fair to ask whether the timing of the plan was meant to coincide with the absence of Kayani, who was on a one-week official visit to the US. As in the alleged abolition of the political wing of the ISI, the military were to lose very little; in fact they would continue to steer matters relating to national security.

One example is the control mechanisms over nuclear weapons. Their supervision is the responsibility of the National Command Authority (NCA), headed by the President. The NCA is divided into Employment Control Committee, Development Control Committee and Strategic Plans Division. The latter is the most important link in this chain of control. It is attached to the NCA Secretariat in Rawalpindi and works closely with GHQ.

More difficult still is the situation with the ISI. In this case far stronger democratic oversight of the agency was being sought by the government and by Washington,[28] against the wishes of the military. Compared to the experiences of the Musharraf years, voices calling for refom in the ISI have increased, and experts have put forward various possible changes. A columnist for the *Daily Times*, Shaukat Qadir, considers that the CJCSC post should be re-valued: the position of a four-star general as Chair of Joint Chiefs of Staff Committee should become the interface between the government and the military. The ISI and the commanders of the Army, Air Force and Navy would thus be subordinate to the CJCSC and report to him.[29]

Also noteworthy are the proposals for direct reform of the ISI. The service collects information from politics, economics, industry, diplomacy and the like. In fact, the ISI functions far beyond the military framework, and its current name is misleading. A name change, for example to Bureau of National Intelligence, is preferable and would make it possible for the appointment of civilian specialists as head of the service.[30] This would also be beneficial to the quality of its work. With the return to democracy in 2008, expectation of reform in the ISI were high.

20

CLOUDS ON THE HORIZON

Afghanistan—the Never-ending Story

On 9 March 2010, Kayani extended Ahmed Shuja Pasha's tenure for another year. His departure from military service had been pending and was slated for 18 March. In Washington, Pasha's continuing role was welcomed, as the ISI under Pasha was now seen as an important ally in seeking to eradicate jihadism in the region. A high profile report by an analyst at the London School of Economics in June 2010 on the ISI and the Afghan Taliban was sceptical: it claimed that ISI officers continued to attend meetings of the Quetta Shura, where they give tactical advice and coordinated ISI assistance (training and material) for the Taliban. The report was based on interviews with Taliban commanders in Kabul in spring 2010.[1]

It is well known that the ISI continues to assist the Afghan Taliban, trying to control them but thereby incurring setbacks along the way because of their proximity. This became clearer in early 2010 when Mullah Abdul Ghani Baradar, the number two in the Quetta Shura and its chief strategist, wanted to negotiate with Hamid Karzai in Kabul without the knowledge of Mullah Omar or the consent of the ISI. The latter picked him up during a routine check near Karachi, and Baradar was arrested. In this way the ISI signalled their insistence on being at the negotiating table where discussions about Afghanistan were concerned. The Americans eventually managed to interrogate Baradar, but he was not handed over to them. Baradar remained in custody until September 2013, and was then released.[2]

On the other hand, at the same time there were examples of close cooperation between the ISI and CIA. Thus, only ten days after Baradar's arrest, the
ISI and CIA jointly participated in capturing Mullah Abdul Salam and three
other Taliban commanders. Salam, regarded as the shadow governor of
Kunduz, had been on his way to a meeting with Baradar. In both cases, it was
apparent that in Afghanistan affairs the ISI would sometimes work with and
sometimes against the CIA—not unusual in intelligence work, and simply the
name of the game.

The Raymond Davis affair

In March 2011, Prime Minister Gilani extended Pasha's tenure at the top of the
ISI for another year: continuity was guaranteed until 18 March 2011. Kayani
was pleased with this development, as he foresaw troubled times ahead and
wanted Pasha by his side. Kayani knew about Washington's discontent with
developments in Afghanistan, attributed to there being insufficient involvement
on the part of the Pakistani military in FATA, where the TTP, the Haqqani
group and the smaller but still existing al-Qaeda were based. According to
Washington, these were the key sources of terror, and Pasha was the reason why
there was then no major offensive being prosecuted in FATA, especially in
North Waziristan. As DGMO, Pasha coordinated the Army's operations in
GHQ, 2006–8; as DG ISI, he also determined military strategy in FATA from
2008. For Washington's taste, he operated with too much restraint. This was the
background to the Raymond Davis affair, which erupted in early 2011.

On 27 January 2011, in Lahore, Davis shot dead two young Pakistanis who
had been tailing him on motorcycles and overtook him at a traffic light. It was
later found out that they were armed but did not have their weapons in their
hands. As the two men approached his car on foot, Davis immediately drew
his gun and fired. He was detained and interrogated in prison. Washington
demanded Davis's immediate release to the United States, citing diplomatic
immunity. After six weeks of imprisonment and the payment of blood money,
Davis was freed on 16 March. According to Sharia law, the sum in question
should have been over $2 million paid to the families of the victims. Davis was
flown by special flight to Bagram air base near Kabul, and then on to the US
naval base at Diego Garcia.

This event became the main topic of political debate in the country for
weeks on end. Even many years later there is no convincing explanation of the
circumstances. Possible scenarios ranged from two inexperienced petty crimi-

nals wanting to rob Davis, to the portrayal of Davis as a trigger-happy, paranoid CIA agent; but why would an alleged CIA agent be compelled to shoot two people in the city centre at midday, and why would the US embassy so quickly offer contradictory details regarding Davis's person and status, and why would the highest levels in Washington agitate for his immediate release? Even Obama and Hillary Clinton requested Davis's immediate transfer to the US, and the influential John Kerry flew immediately to Islamabad.

This did not spare Raymond Davis from a month and a half in jail. Pakistan doubted his diplomatic immunity. They stated he had not acted in self-defence, since one of the victims had been shot in the back. Also, the name of Raymond Davis was false and he was illegally carrying a weapon. In his camera were found photos of Pakistan's security institutions, and there were claims he had been in contact with the Pakistani Taliban (TTP), thereby voiding his diplomatic immunity. A legal case against him was prepared and Davis was interrogated in Lahore. What he admitted to remains unknown.

Who was Raymond Davis? It turned out that he was a former US Army Special Forces soldier, now working for a private US security firm, which was often contracted to carry out security tasks for the CIA, State Department and Pentagon. Davis had been sent to Pakistan and assigned to the US consulate in Lahore. In his visa, he was officially listed as an administrative consultant. According to the local press, he was fluent in Urdu and Pashto and his salary was much higher than that of a normal CIA undercover agent. Rumours arose in the first two weeks that his task was to keep contact with dissidents and saboteurs, as evidenced by the phone numbers found on Davis's mobile phone. This version of events is convincing, and most Pakistanis believe it to this today.

According to another plausible version, the ISI had Davis followed. Two men were briefed, allegedly by the police or the IB, but they were inexperienced and not up to the task. They might have observed Davis taking illegal photographs, meeting a third party, or handing over some items. They then tried to confiscate the objects that Davis was carrying, but he perceived this as a threat, grabbed his pistol and killed them both.

Another plausible explanation for what happened was given to the author by a high-ranking ISI officer. According to him both victems were carrying US$ notes with them. They were working as agents for Davies and on that fateful day had most likely been underpaid (or short changed) by him. Angered by their treatment they followed him and demanded payment in full. Davies, frightened for his life, killed them both.

Till today the background to the killing and what lay behind it remain unclear. Noteworthy also was the recklessness of Davies' colleagues from the

Consulate General, whom he called for help. In their rush to the scene they ran over a pedestrian, the third fatality of the day. Three days later there was another victim, when the wife of one of the two shot men committed suicide. The drama had reached its peak: leading politicians issued hyperbolic anti-American statements, the newspapers were filled with reports and commentary, and the general public was incensed.

At this point, a chronology of relations between the CIA and ISI will help explain events. After 9/11, there was close cooperation for some years between the two services in the hunt for al-Qaeda. The ISI tracked down terrorists and handed them to their CIA allies, receiving good remuneration. The deployment of drones from 2007 against targets in FATA reinforced this cooperation: the ISI provided the coordinates of the target and the CIA operated the drones.[3] However, from 2010 the ISI became reluctant to deliver such intelligence according to the US's wishes; while the American side was also becoming more independent. ISI information was proving increasingly unsatisfactory, so the CIA found and began cultivating its own sources of information. The Americans paid well to anyone who would yield intell, so the ISI lost its monopoly. This made the ISI feel not only under-appreciated but also deceived.

One example was in North Waziristan, and concerned the retreat of the Afghan Haqqani group. At the urging of the ISI, the Pakistani Army had agreed not to attack the Haqqanis in North Waziristan. The CIA took little notice of this and rained their drones on North Waziristan and other FATA agencies. The ISI found itself no longer master in its own house. In addition, there was collateral damage: almost every drone attack resulted in rising civilian anger and outrage. Journalists and columnists began to write about a violation of Pakistan's national sovereignty and communications between Langley and Rawalpindi deteriorated fast.

The Raymond Davis case resulted in yet further Pakistani animosity towards the US and the government and military had to react. They tried to present the halt in drone attacks during the six weeks of the Davis affair as their own small victory in terms of reclaiming their territorial integrity. In fact, the temporary ending of drone attacks was due to America's confusion over the Davis affair. Then on 17 March, the day after Davis left the country, a drone strike in FATA resulted in 44 people losing their lives. The Pakistani outcry was immense; in their eyes the Americans were taking revenge for the Davis case. Even Army chief Ashfaq Kayani made his displeasure known, saying it was highly regrettable that a *jirga* (tribal gathering) was so carelessly and callously targeted, with complete disregard for human life. On 11 March Pasha flew to the US, for several hours of conversation with CIA Director Panetta. He was unable to achieve a halt in the drone attacks, as demanded by Pakistan. On 23 April, despite COAS Kayani asking the US to reconsider their drone campaign, there was another attack in North Waziristan, resulting in a further twenty-five deaths. Washington's drone strategy remained undeterred.

In addition to the drone operations, there was another bone of contention between the ISI and CIA. During the Musharraf years, the CIA and half a dozen other US security services had maintained a foothold in Pakistan. Their personnel had risen over the years to nearly 3,000 by early 2011, police and military trainers included. After the Davis affair, under a Pakistani directive, a dozen American agents hastily left the country, followed by hundreds more in subsequent weeks. By mid 2011 the Pakistani authorities declared that the majority of the 3,000 American workers had left the country; only a much reduced number returned in subsequent years.

For DG ISI Pasha, the Raymond Davis affair cast a first shadow over his brilliant reputation as his country's spymaster. He and Kayani agreed not to force a complete break with the United States as a result of the Davis incident, since the ongoing modernization of the Pakistani military, as well as their plans for Afghanistan, depended on further cooperation with Washington. Thus it was that Shuja Pasha sought to get Raymond Davis out of the country as rapidly as possible, to the extent that he turned up in person at the decisive court hearing in Lahore concerning Davis's release, which was quite exceptional. It is known that during the session he sent text messages to the US Ambassador Cameron Munter, obviously appraising him of the course of the hearing.[4] Thus suspicions arose that he was proving more a pawn of Washington than a representative of Pakistani interests in the Davis case. This interpretation is however unfair: Ahmed Pasha Shuja's stand was always "Pakistan First." However, he certainly felt pressure from Washington. But all things considered, in discussion with Kayani, he came to the conclusion that Pakistan must give way on this issue. We still don't know whether all aspects of the Davis affair were revealed. A suspicion that there was an as yet undisclosed link to subsequent events in Abbottabad might be justified. The nervousness manifested in the very highest office in Washington makes one wonder.

The ISI, approached by the author about the Raymond Davis affair in summer 2015, gave in writing a simple explanation of his release: "The factual position is that the murder case was settled by the US authorities by contacting the near relatives of the deceased and paying them some amount as a Qasas, as per Islamic jurisprudence. Based on mutual agreement, the court had released Raymond Davies."

Abbottabad

The Davis affair faded into the background once one of the most significant global news stories of all time broke on 2 May 2011, namely the killing of Osama bin Laden in Abbottabad, Pakistan, by a US Navy Seals commando team. For the COAS and the DG ISI, "Operation Geronimo" was a worst-case scenario. Even in Pakistan, only a minority believed that both services knew nothing of bin Laden's presence in the country. The majority was convinced that the al-Qaeda leader's many years of successfully eluding capture owed something to the ISI. Pakistan's prime intelligence agency is deemed to be an effective one, one of the best, at least in Asia. It is strictly led and managed, and it contains no groups that pursue independent political agendas—no ISI within the ISI. There could hardly have been a branch of ISI protecting the al-Qaeda leader and his family successfully over the years without the knowledge of the leadership. Also, the claim that bin Laden lived with his family for five years in Abbottabad without coming into contact with the security services of this garrison town seemed absurd. In Abbottabad, the police, the ISI and MI are responsible for security. It is home to an ISI station, manned by half a dozen people. That they and the police never noticed bin Laden's house and its inhabitants seems implausible.

Today, official US reports and cover stories from various international magazines have shed some light on the origins and conduct of Operation Geronimo. On 8 August 2011, the *New Yorker* published an insightful article, "Getting bin Laden", by Nicholas Schmidle, who obviously benefited from inside contacts. In Pakistan, even the former military and security expert Brigadier (retd.) Shaukat Qadir authored an investigation, albeit from Pakistan's perspective, entitled "Operation Geronimo."[5]

But let us scrutinise some additional considerations. Firstly, the official statements about tracking down Osama bin Laden indicated they were based exclusively on CIA information. Protection of sources has the highest priority in all intelligence agencies. We should assume that in the tracking of bin Laden much has been concealed and will continue to be so. And secondly, the key conclusion of Shaukat Qadir's investigation is that Osama bin Laden was sold out, betrayed for money.

It is reasonably sure now that neither Kayani nor Pasha was informed by the Americans about Operation Geronimo, not even at the last moment. In the CIA in spring 2011 it was assumed that both of them know where Osama bin Laden was and who organised his protection. Perhaps they had read of Mohammed Ali Jinnah's reaction in December 1947 regarding Kashmir:

when Jinnah's staff tried to inform him that tribal warriors were deployed in Kashmir, he blocked it with the words, "do not tell me, my conscience must be clean." Jinnah wanted to know no details as he had to be able to look his British and Indian counterparts in the eye. In Langley, they probably realised that Musharraf and Kayani were following Jinnah's precedent; both officials tried to remain distant from the bin Laden case. But still, from 2002 onwards, the entire affair was within the hands and fell under the responsibility of the respective heads of the ISI, namely Ehsan-ul Haq 2001–4, Pervez Kayani Ashfaq 2004–7, Nadeem Taj 2007–8 and Ahmad Shuja Pasha 2008–12; all of whom were also trying to stay away from the case as much as possible.

It can be assumed today that they took none of their deputies into confidence. Each agency has a department for special (cloak and dagger) work. Within this department a small special cell, comprising two or at most three man—or perhaps even only one—was created. This cell was responsible for the protection of bin Laden and his family. No other individuals within the ISI were involved. Carlotta Gall's notion of a special cell consisting of a single protector, as set out in her book *The Wrong Enemy in Pakistan: America in Afghanistan 2001–2014*, might therefore be correct. Whether intelligence data retrieved from Abbottabad by the Navy Seals, revealing that a total of twelve people within the ISI were informed about the whereabouts of Osama bin Laden, are correct, remains to be seen.[6] To the author this number seems rather high.

The daily routine of the operation was evidently managed by the ISI. Whether the courier al-Kuweiti and his brother, living with their families within the same premises as the bin Laden family and known to the neighbours as Arshad and Tariq Khan, were the only civilian assistants, again seems doubtful. Existing indicators refer to some carefully selected cadres from the Harkatul Mujahideen, led by Maulana Fazlur Rehman Khalil or from the Jaish-e-Mohammad, led by Maulana Masood Azhar. Both groups are known for their close links to the ISI and their members are thought to be highly reliable.

In this scenario, two questions remain open. Firstly, was bin Laden sold out for money, and if so by whom? Reports of detention of some ISI personnel suggest that at least part of the betrayal emanated from within the ISI itself. In Islamabad and Rawalpindi, at different locations the author was presented with rumours about an ISI Colonel who disappeared directly after Abbottabad and now lives in the USA.

The trigger for betrayal might have been a sense that the time of Osama's concealment was coming to an end. There was a bounty of US$25 million and one or other of the helpers might have wanted in on the reward.

Secondly, the question arises as to why Pakistan's top military would burden themselves with a world-famous terrorist over so many years. In searching for the answer, one has to remember that Mullah Omar managed to stay under the protection of the ISI in Balochistan for more than ten years. He died in April 2013 and his death was made public only at the end of July 2015. Osama bin Laden most likely knew this to be the case. Omar Sheikh Mohammed, the former link between bin Laden and the ISI (see Chapter 16), should also be remembered here. Omar Sheikh has been held in prison in Pakistan since 2002; his appeal against the death sentence has been pending for many years now. Therefore, bin Laden's falling into American hands had to be prevented at all costs.

The liquidation of bin Laden was also out of the question. It would have been difficult to keep it a secret and no one in the top levels of the GHQ and ISI wanted to be remembered throughout Islamic history as the killer of the al-Qaeda icon. Ergo, all who were closely involved hoped to keep the issue at bay and trust in natural causes taking Osama bin Laden from them; but this option underestimated the will of the Americans to retaliate for the 9/11 attacks and hence could never succeed.

Pasha's farewell

Kayani and DG Pasha were both losers after Abbottabad. Among the corps commanders, there was strong criticism of them—a first in the history of the Army. Kayani seriously contemplated resigning, but such a step would have been interpreted as an admission of guilt over Osama bin Laden, so this option could not be considered. The political leadership in Islamabad reacted cautiously and kept their frustration under control. Pasha was therefore also spared, as his resignation would also have indicated that the ISI had protected bin Laden, which was inconceivable for them to admit.

Washington was also in favour of holding on to Kayani and Pasha. CIA Director Panetta made this clear when he announced before the US Senate in the second week of June that "continuing cooperation with Pakistan is critical to keep a tremendous amount of pressure on al-Qaeda's leadership and the networks that provide it support and safe havens at a time when it is most vunerable." Regarding Operation Geronimo, Panetta stated that "one of the key lessons from this operation is that we have seen no evidence to indicate that senior Pakistani leaders were involved in harboring Osama bin Laden or knew of his whereabouts." Thus, Washington was issuing a clean bill of health to Kayani and Pasha. America feared a revolt within the military and even greater scepticism towards the US among the populace. America's overall objective was the continuation of its strategic partnership with Pakistan beyond 2014.

Kayani's reputation revived after Abbottabad, albeit slowly and incompletely.[7] People began to remember the positive aspects of his military leadership. In addition to recalling the military to barracks and the advances made in training and equipment, Kayani's special merit was that Islamic fundamentalists were denied access to the higher ranks of the services. He interviewed every officer who came up for promotion to the rank of brigadier or above.[8]

Ahmad Pasha Shuja's reputation also recovered, but more slowly. In the opinion of many people, the DG ISI was one of the key individuals responsible for the success of Operation Geronimo, and therefore obviously did not have the ISI under control. There were hearings in parliament, before courts and commissions. In addition to Abbottabad, other operations were now investigated in which the ISI seemed to be involved. These included the murder of journalist Saleem Shahzad, the cases of missing persons and the scandal of Memogate in September 2011. High-ranking ISI people now had to testify, or at least submit a statement in writing.

In particular the murder of Syed Saleem Shazad created attention and protest not only in Pakistan but also within the international media. Shazad was a Pakistani investigative journalist writing for local papers, for the Hong Kong based *Asia Times Online* and for an Italian news agency. He specialised in security issues, in particular those relating to al-Qaeda. According to Shazad, Osama bin Laden was in 2010 still frequently moving around in Pakistan's and Afghanistan's Hindu Kush mountains to meet top al-Qaeda and Taliban commanders. In his writings Shazad often published interviews which he had conducted with al-Qaeda leaders. Shazad wrote also about links between some Islamists and the Pakistani military. In *Asia Times Online* he reported a background story about the terrorist attack on 22 May 2011 at *PNS Mehran*, the headquarters of the Pakistan Naval Air Arm in Karachi. In the assault 15 attackers killed 18 military personnel, wounded 16 others and destroyed two American-built P-3C Orion surveillance aircraft. According to Shazad the attackers were all from Ilyas Kashmiri's 313 Brigade of al-Qaeda and the attack was carried out after negotiations with the Navy for the release of officials, suspected of al-Qaeda links, had failed. Syed Saleem Shahzad disappeared in Islamabad on the evening of 29 May 2011 on his way to a TV show. His body, which showed signs of brutal torture, was found a day later some 150 km away from the capital.

In Pakistan a majority of journalists remain convinced till today that their former colleague was murdered by the ISI. International papers like the *New York Times* reported the story in similar fashion. In Washington Admiral Michael (Mike) Mullen, Chairman of the Joint Chiefs of Staff, stated his believe that Shahzad's killing was "sanctioned by the [Pakistani] government" but added that he did not have a "string of evidence" linking it to the ISI. In reaction Associated Press of Pakistan, the state-owned news agency, called Mullen's charge "extremely irresponsible."

The ISI's narrative of this case was presented to the author in 2015 as follows:

> Syed Saleem Shazazad, a prominent Pakistani journalist, was abducted from Islamabad on May 29, 2011. The Government of Pakistan constituted a Commission of Inquiry to probe the matter. The Commission comprised a Judge of the apex court, the Chief Justice of the Federal Sharia Court, Inspector Generals of Police from Punjab and Islamabad and the President, Pakistan Federal Union of Journalists (PFUJ). The commission was mandated to inquire into the background of this incident and identify the culprits involved in it. The commission was unable to identify the culprits behind this incident. The commission in its proceedings found, "no sufficient material has come out on the record to verify the involvement of the ISI in the incident and from the bare facts of the incident, no conclusion can be drawn that ISI has been instrumental in this regard".

Memogate was a case in which DG ISI Pasha also came under fire. The main character in this scandal was Mansoor Ijaz, an American citizen of Pakistani descent. In September 2011 Ijaz brought the public's attention to a letter which he claimed was written on the insistence of former Ambassador Haqqani and passed to Admiral Mike Mullen in Washington. The tenor of the letter was that President Zardari feared an impending military takeover and was asking for help from Washington to prevent this. In the new democratic Pakistan, Memogate quickly became a national affair, especially since Ijaz then claimed that Pasha had visited Arab countries seeking their consent to a planned military coup. The military refuted such allegations. Indeed no military takeover was in the pipeline and nor would support for a coup d'etat have been forthcoming from the Gulf monarchies. On the other hand, the allegations made by Ijaz aroused suspicion and put both Haqqani and President Zardari under great pressure.

In response to the author's enquiry about the "Memogate" affair, in August 2015 the ISI sent him the following statement:

> Mr Hussain Haqqani was not in line with the national interest and, therefore, his credibility to function as the Ambassador to serve Pakistan's interest had

become doubtful. Mr Haqqani was a political appointee and his appointment as Ambassador to the US was made by Zardari's government. The same government removed him from his post, proving that Ambassador Haqqani was working hand in glove with anti-Pakistan forces. Given the circumstances, the ISI played a positive role in this case and when the government decided to removed Mr Haqqani from his post, the issue came to an end. The claim made by the author [Hein Kiessling] that Gen. Pasha had visited the Gulf countries to get their consent for imposing Martial Law in the country also makes no sense.

In the PPP government camp, Memogate was seen as an attempt by the military to damage President Zardari's reputation in retribution for the Abbottabad case. The military of course saw it the other way around. Before the Supreme Court, Kayani and Pasha gave affidavits in which they contradicted Mansoor Ijaz's statements and refuted all his allegations. By a decision of the SC, a commission was formed which included the Chairman of the Balochistan High Court (Qazi Faez Isa), the Sindh High Court (Musheer Alam) and the Islamabad High Court (Iqbal Hameedur Rehman). Mansoor Ijaz was invited to give evidence in Islamabad, which he accepted, saying he wanted to testify against the ISI and the military. In an interview with the *Christian Science Monitor* he said that "whenever he testifies in the inquiry about the memo, he will not spare either the ISI or the military being an umbrella for the proliferation of extremism."[9] After obtaining a visa for Pakistan, he reneged on his travel for security reasons. In the end he gave his testimony in camera at the Pakistan embassy in London, but it contributed very little to a clarification of his actions.

Abbottabad and the Memogate affair contributed significantly to Lieutenant General Shuja Pasha's desire to leave the service. To clarify the Memogate case, Pasha had met Manzoor Ijaz on October 2012 at the Park Lane Intercontinental Hotel in London. The meeting brought no new findings for the military, but Pasha himself encountered new criticism from political quarters. This increased further when he met Musharraf in Dubai in January 2012 and advised him not to return to Pakistan for the time being, because of the unfavourable sentiment towards him in the country.[10] In Islamabad, the Senate responded with a resolution calling for Musharraf's arrest upon his return. Interior Minister Malik announced that Musharraf would be detained should he return home.

At the end of January 2012, there were signs that Pasha's service might be coming to an end, although there were also speculation in the papers about a third extension. Kayani still kept his options open. He hinted to Pasha about the possibility of another extension of one more year but gave at the same time to the Prime Minister three possible names as Pasha's successor: Zaheerul Islam, Commander V Corps Karachi; Rashid Mahmood, Commander IV Corps Lahore; and Raheel Sharif, Commander 30 Corps Gujranwala. In response, Pasha asked to be relieved from the post of DG ISI on 9 March. Hours later, Zaheerul Islam's name as the future DG ISI was announced.

It was unclear whether another posting for Pasha would be forthcoming. The country's newspapers reported that he was to succeed Lieutenant General (retd.) Khalid Ahmad Kidwai as head of the Strategic Plans Commission (SPC). Such an appointment would have been given in recognition of services rendered and also as a sign of trust in Pasha's future commitment. According to other newspapers, the top post in Fauji Fertilizer was earmarked for Pasha, which would have guaranteed him financial security. Neither of the two options materialised. The internal political situation militated against an appointment to the SPC post. Elections were due in one year and the possibility of a change of government was in sight. Among the generals at GHQ, the view was that the highly respected Kidwai should continue in the SPC. This would make it easier for the new head of government to appoint someone of his choosing to the SPC.[11] The denial of the Fauji Fertilizer post was obviously a final punishment by the generals for Abbottabad.

Ahmad Shuja Pasha retired as a Lieutenant General from the Army on 18 March 2012. A short time later he became advisor to the United Arab Emirates intelligence services, with residence in Dubai before returning quietly to Pakistan in late 2014. It is said that COAS Raheel Sharif persuaded him to come home. Pasha is now active in social and educational work in his home area of Chakwal in Punjab.

21

QUO VADIS, ISI?

DG ISI Zaheerul Islam Abbasi, March 2012–November 2014

Zaheerul Islam Abbasi, from the Punjab Regiment (commissioned in April 1977), belongs to a military family. His father was a colonel, and three brothers and a brother-in-law were also officers. Pakistan's press regarded him as a hard-working and upright person—a soldier trusted by his superiors and comrades. In his military career he worked as Chief of Staff Army Strategic Force Command 2004–6; as a two-star general, he was head of Internal Security in the ISI 2008–10; his appointment as commander of the Army Corps in Karachi in 2011 showed COAS Kayani's respect for him. His position at the top of the list as Pasha's successor was therefore no surprise. In March 2011 Kayani had twenty months of service left as COAS, and wanted Zaheerul Islam at his side.

There was some controversy over Kayani's list of ISI would-be successors. After it was submitted, Defence Secretary Nargis Sethi demanded a list of all two-star generals eligible for promotion. It was argued that the Prime Minister should see all those eligible for DG ISI. As such a list must have already existed in the ministry, this was clearly an attempt to snub the COAS. This led to a meeting between the President, the Prime Minister and the COAS, at which Kayani stuck with his panel and Zaheerul Islam was appointed. One particular aspect helped the government to save face: Zaheerul Islam had no personal contacts in America; he had been on business trips to the US but had no close friends there.

Zaheerul Islam went to Washington for the first time as DG ISI for three days, 1–3 August 2012. The visit should have taken place two months earlier, but was cancelled at short notice in protest over the drone attacks on 24 and 28 May, which resulted in fourteen deaths.[1] Islam's visit to Washington was the first US trip by a senior Pakistani official in a year. Its urgency became clear when a renewed drone attack just days before his departure did not lead to another cancellation.[2] In the meeting with CIA Director David Petraeus, defense and security matters were highest on the agenda. The drone attacks were a main theme. In Pakistan, it was bitterly noted that just a few days after the lifting of the NATO blockade on supply routes, there was a US drone attack in North Waziristan on 4 July 2012 that claimed twenty-one lives.[3]

In Washington, Zaheerul Islam called the US drone campaign "a violation of Pakistan's sovereignty." He claimed they disregarded international law and were contrary to the American commitment to support liberalism and democracy in Pakistan. Their continuation would have a negative impact on other areas too. In Pakistan they would lend incentives to fundamentalists and extremists, and in FATA would help to recruit more militants. In his opinion, this called for a new mechanism for intelligence-sharing and counter-terrorism cooperation between the two countries. Basically, Zaheerul Islam did not rule out further attacks in FATA, but asked for Pakistan's direct involvement in their detailed planning. The French news agency AFP quoted him as follows: "We need this precision strike capability to avoid collateral damage and its political fallout. The idea is that the US develops the target and tells us, and we destroy it ourselves." According to the DG ISI, as long as the previous practice continued, Pakistan would not be able to assist in efforts to achieve stability and security in Afghanistan. This would also affect the planned withdrawal of NATO troops.

Other issues raised by the ISI delegation were cross-border incursions of militants from Afghanistan into Pakistan; violations of the protocol of diplomatic conduct, by using it as an excuse to support the CIA's unilateral espionage operations in Pakistan; the duty of diplomats to obtain permission from the Pakistan government in order to bear lethal weapons, all of which should be licensed; and that CIA agents were again entering Pakistan under diplomatic cover.

The US did not agree with Pakistan's proposal on the delivery of drone technology. After the meeting of the two intelligence chiefs, the drone attacks remained solely in CIA hands. However, there was now a reduction in the attacks and more cautious identification of targets.[4]

During Zaheerul Islam's term as DG ISI, in April 2014, the gun attack on the respected journalist Hamid Mir occurred, resulting in enormous political and judicial pressure on the agency in its aftermath. Some sections of the local media also started a campaign against the ISI. Interestingly, among those who rallied to the agency's support was Imran Khan, who called the press criticism unjustifid. Adressing a party convention on the occasion of the 18th anniversary of the PTI he said: "There is no second opinion that the attack on Hamid Mir is deplorable but eight-hour long media's malicious campaign against Inter-Service Intelligence (ISI) by a TV channel would not have even done by an enemy country... what ever was done with the army and ISI, this might not have been done with the enemy" (*The Nation*, 02. May, 2014). He also criticised the respective media combine (Jang group) for protecting its business interests in the name of freedom of expression. A day before Imran Khan came out with his personal statement the Core Committee of the PTI had already condemned the media bashing of ISI by a TV channel.

In a written statement given to the author in 2015, the ISI presented its view of the Hamid Mir case:

> Hamid Mir in his TV programmes had been undermining the ideology of Pakistan, distorting Army's image, especially senior leadership. Due to his perceived thinking, supported by the dubious role of Geo TV network, he was degrading the Armed Forces by twisting facts and blaming ISI and Army for different things. ISI had maintained an intimate interaction with Hamid Mir, so as to give him the true picture of national/regional environment and has been asking him not to compromise national security or state institutions. ISI had no role in his shooting incident and had extended all the help to the civil government in investigating the case by being part of the Joint Investigation Team. But unfortunately the investigations have been unable to find the culprits. Geo TV Network had subsequently apologised accepting that it had blamed ISI/Gen Zaheer without proof.

Against this background the role of the ISI during the PTI and PAT demonstrations in Islamabad from August 2014 onwards remains unclear even today. Local political observers have little doubt that the agency was backing it, in spirit and financially. For them the countdown to the whole operation had already begun during Shuja Pasha's term in office; they see him as its godfather. This view gets credit from the fact that Pasha, already retired and living in Dubai, came over to Pakistan in October 2014 to meet Khan at the house of PTI member Shafqat Mahmood. According to Imran Khan, the issues of terror and drone attacks were discussed. His political opponents mocked his statement, and even his own followers were unhappy about it.

What part was played by DG ISI Zaheerul Islam during the demonstations is still unknown. Realising that neither camp was able to bring the proposed one million people on to the streets, he might have—in accordance with the COAS—backtracked and advised both Imran Khan and Tahir-ul-Qadri to steer their followers away from violence and to let the whole undertaking peter out slowly. Ex-DG ISI Pasha was obviously displeased with what his successor was doing, otherwise he would not have returned from Dubai for discussions with Imran Khan during such a politically sensitive period? In March 2015, in Islamabad and Rawalpindi, the author heard several times the view that Zaheerul Islam should never have become DG ISI—obviously a reaction of the Pasha and government camps to Islam's performance during the siege of Islamabad by PTE and PAT in August 2014.

Two months before Lt. Gen. Islam handed over the ISI command to his successor the agency again suffered again a high-ranking casualty due to terrorism. ISI-Brigadier Zahoor Fazal Qadri, who was posted at the ISI-Directorate in Islamabad, was killed by the newly launched South Asia Branch of al-Qaeda. He was murdered on 6 September together with his brother while off duty and attending a religious ceremony at a Sufi shrine near Sargodha. Before being transferred to Islamabad Brigadier Zahoor had been posted to Waziristan on an important assignment which earned him a prime position on al-Qaeda's hit list.

Déjà Vu: Prime Minister Nawaz Sharif for the Third Time

In the Pakistan elections on 11 May 2013, most voters opted for a change of government but shied away from a real new beginning. They decided not to risk any new political experiments. Thus, the PML-N won 157 seats in the NA, making them the ruling party; and there was a similar result in the Punjab government. The PPP lost the elections, even if it remained the strongest political force in Sindh and formed the government there. In the National Parliament PPP was the second strongest, though far behind with 39 seats. Imran Khan, who had promised a political tsunami, won 35 seats in the NA for the PTI; in KP province, his party became the strongest political force and formed the new ruling party there.

On 18 May, COAS Kayani met with Nawaz Sharif, on Kayani's initiative. The meeting was held in Lahore at the home of Shahbaz Sharif, who was also present. Over the past five years Kayani had met the CM Punjab several times, but not Nawaz Sharif. The Army chief was now working "to brush aside the past propaganda of certain quarters about the future Nawaz–military relations."[5]

Just days later, the press reported that Zaheerul Islam had also expressed a desire to speak to the future head of government. Nawaz Sharif was invited to a detailed in-camera briefing about the security challenges confronting Pakistan and the role of the premier intelligence agency in countering them. Nawaz Sharif accepted the invitation and on 11 July arrived at the Directorate in Aabpara Market with some of his ministers, staying there for five hours. On the host's side, apart from DG ISI Zaheerul, were his deputies: Maj. Gen. Sahibzada Asfandyar Patodi; Maj. Gen. Naveed Mukhtar (Counter-terrorism); Maj. Gen. Sajjad Rasul (Security); Maj. Gen. Nasir Dilawar Shah (Counter-Intelligence); and the sector commanders Maj. Gen. Naveed Ahmed (Sindh), Maj. Gen. Raja Aftab (Punjab), Maj. Gen. Tayab Azam (Khyber Pakhtunkhwa) and Maj. Gen. Iftikhar Amir (Balochistan). Thus almost the entire ISI leadership was present. General Kayani also participated, and in a carefully orchestrated move the Prime Minister paid an official visit to GHQ in Rawalpindi. Clearly the military wanted to present the new political leadership with their views on Pakistan and the politicians showed willingness to listen. But mistrust between both sides was evident even then and would deepen in the months ahead.

A Change in Army Command

The new head of Pakistan's Army was installed on 29 November 2013, in a ceremony at a sports stadium near the GHQ. COAS Parvez Kayani Ashfaq handed over the command stick (*malacca*) to his successor General Raheel Sharif, who had been selected by Prime Minister Sharif three weeks previously. According to eyewitness reports, Kayani seemed relaxed: he had been DG ISI for three years, and COAS for six years, managing a force 700,000 strong and a nuclear weapons arsenal. He has various additional credits to his name: the order to retreat to barracks in 2008, so that democracy in Pakistan would be given a chance; and the improvement of training and equipment standards in the Army. However, the complete security of the country eluded him during his tenure. Kayani managed to rid the Swat valley of extremists, but failed in a similar operation in North Waziristan. Terrorism by the TTP, mainly directed against the military and other security forces, continue to this day. He also leaves his successor an unsolved problem in Afghanistan, a fragile relationship with the USA and a brittle nuclear cooperation arrangement with Saudi Arabia.[6]

COAS Raheel Sharif is an infantryman from a Punjabi military family. There is no relationship between himself and Prime Minister Nawaz Sharif, although both families have Kashmiri roots. As Inspector General for Training and Evaluation, he was responsible for improvements and changes in training programs. He is regarded as a pioneer in counterinsurgency training and strategy; the TTP hardly saw his appointment as cause for celebration.

Like Kayani, Raheel Sharif will need information and advice from the ISI for planning and decision-making. Zaheerul Islam's term of office in the Directorate lasted till November 2014. Soon it became clear that Raheel Sharif wanted him to stay on, as Islam's experience from four years within the ISI was a great asset. Nawaz Sharif voiced no objections to this step. Prime Minister Sharif showed no objections. Islam's experience from four years within the ISI was needed.

The external and internal challenges facing Pakistan are continually being reassessed by the agency. India has stepped up its cooperation with Iran and Afghanistan,[7] to which Saudi Arabia responded by seeking to enhance its nuclear cooperation with Pakistan. The Kashmir issue remains still on the ISI's agenda, including the preservation of water rights for Pakistan. The drone attack phenomenon is also unresolved, though the United States now operates more cautiously than hitherto. For the ISI, it is determined to keep its information monopoly in FATA intact and to strengthen its own HUMINT further in neighbouring countries.

Within Pakistan, the ISI has over the last five years been confronted with a situation different from that which obtained during the Musharraf era. Parliament and the courts no longer hesitate to make inquiries and to demand written or oral statements from ISI personnel in public or in camera. Furthermore, the new government has sought to extend its control over the ISI. For instance, in November 2013 the Interior Ministry set up a committee to investigate money allegedly paid by the ISI to politicians.[8]

Demands for reform and stronger democratic control of the ISI have also became more insistent. The question arose as to whether it was essential for a military officer to head the intelligence service? After all, ISI activities now included large areas that were not military in nature. A civilian expert at the top of the agency was therefore seen by many politicians as more appropriate than a man in uniform. The opponents of such changes feared a loss of efficiency on the part of the ISI and are against it. They still see the military and the ISI as guarantors of the existence of the state of Pakistan, which will only be weakened by excessive reforms.

The officers in GHQ and ISI are keeping an eye and ear on such discussions. They are aware of the sensitivity of such thoughts and plans. For the military, the

ISI is an important tool for information-gathering and decision-making; they do not want to lose an iota of control over it. But any serious changes would require restructuring the whole military leadership. Proposals in this regard, for example, a serious revaluation of the JCSC position, have been raised in the past; they have been acknowledged but never tackled. It remains to be seen whether this government has the will and the power to considering implementing the necessary reforms in their remaining years in office.

POSTSCRIPT

As the cabinet of Prime Minister Nawaz Sharif began work in June 2013, its members thought they were beginning a stable five-year parliamentary term. The PML-N, led by Sharif, had won an absolute majority in the National Assembly (NA), with the former ruling party PPP as the second strongest force. The PTI of Imran Khan, who had predicted a landslide victory for himself and his party in the election campaign, was the third strongest party, even if it was second in the total number of votes cast. In addition, in the important state of Punjab, the PML-N was able to form the provincial government under CM Shahbaz Sharif. For Nawaz Sharif, the foundations of a secure period in office seemed to be in place. Reports by election observers from the EU, Commonwealth and other organizations had declared the elections on May 11 as free and democratic. Also, the donor countries—active since the 2008 elections as "friends of the new democratic Pakistan"—were satisfied.

However, in August 2014, slightly more than a year after the elections, the situation changed dramatically; the stability of the Nawaz Sharif government was no longer secure. Thousands of protesters camped out in Islamabad and demanded the government's resignation. They blocked parts of the government area, got close to the Prime Minister's house and occupied Pakistan Television for hours. The situation was chaotic for many days, as the world press reported in detail. Beijing cancelled the scheduled mid-September visit of the Chinese President, Xi Jinping, and the Friends of Democratic Pakistan were no longer particularly pleased with the political situation.

The former cricketer turned politican, Imran Khan (PTI), and the Islamic cleric, Tahir-ul-Qadri (PAT), were responsible for this change in fortunes. In mid-August, they had mobilised their followers and supporters to march on the capital. Imran Khan demanded the government's resignation and a review of the May 2013 election results. His goal was new elections in the near future. Personally he had never accepted an opposition role for himself for the next five years. PAT leader Tahir-ul-Qadri, who normally lives in Canada, spoke openly of a revolution and the need to create new political structures. Although the PTI and PAT were unable to bring a million people to march on Islamabad as announced, they rallied approximately 50,000 protesters during the first week. After that, their numbers decreased: a nucleus of between 5,000 and 10,000 supporters held out for a month. During the first four weeks there were also two fatalities and about a dozen injuries in skirmishes with the police.

Initially the government responded without an overall strategy, and then tried to de-escalate the situation. Parliamentary and government delegations met with the leaders of the protesters, and concessions were offered. But Imran Khan's main demand, the resignation of the Prime Minister, was rejected. Nawaz Sharif knew that the majority of parliament was behind him.

At the request of the government, the Pakistani military took over the security of important government buildings ahead of the protest, but otherwise they kept their distance. COAS Raheel Sharif was informed of the situation by the Prime Minister, and meetings with leaders of the protest were also undertaken. In the GHQ, the corps commanders' circle discussed the security situation. Through a press release, the public was informed that the situation could only be solved politically. In the background, there were concerns and warnings from the US and other Western countries against damaging Pakistan's precious democracy. Washington continued to classify the Nawaz Sharif government in Islamabad as legitimate.

The GHQ in Rawalpindi had no wish to interrupt ongoing American aid from the Kerry Lugar Bill. Furthermore, the Army and Air Force were engaged in fighting TTP Islamists in North Waziristan. One consequence was the presence of a million internal refugees (IDP), aid for whom was precarious and inadequate. In addition, there were major floods in the country that monsoon season. There was no question of the military taking over political power in this situation. But there was still not much political sympathy for Prime Minister Sharif within the military, including the top-ranking generals; the predominant feeling was serious antipathy. Since May 2013 there had often been deep disagreements and tensions between both sides.

Firstly, there was the Musharraf case. Since his return to Pakistan in April 2013, the former President and Army chief had been held under house arrest.

Later on, the military and the government came to an informal understanding. The plan was to indict the former President, to show that no one was above the law, to be followed by bail and a deletion from the Exit Control List. Musharraf would then be allowed to visit his ailing mother in Dubai, but not return. However, this understanding was ultimately not upheld by the government. Nawaz Sharif obviously wanted Musharraf to face similar humiliation as was meted out to him previously. He had been imprisoned from October 1999 to December 2000, treated poorly and finally convicted. Afterwards, he was allowed to go into exile in Saudi Arabia.

Ever since then, Nawaz Sharif has had a difficult relationship with the military. With aggressive statements emanating from other cabinet members towards the military and the ISI, his views were gaining support. The generals and their legal advisers felt deceived and under threat. Since mid-June 2014, the Army and PAF had been fighting the TTP in North Waziristan (Operation Zarb-e-Azb). For the military, the attitude of the government in the Musharraf case complicated this costly campaign. The former COAS Musharraf continues to elicit sympathy among many of the serving ranks and officers. Why then, asked the soldiers, should we risk our lives in Waziristan for politicians who do not respect our opinions and feelings and do not keep their word?

Moreover the military was generally dissatisfied with the attitude of the government towards the TTP. Nawaz Sharif's preference is to solve the long-standing conflict with the Pakistani Taliban through negotiation. However, the military, who have born the brunt of attacks by the group in recent years, are less keen on talks. They know that negotiations with the fanatical TTP leadership will only succeed if they have been weakened by battle, which is why they put Nawaz Sharif under pressure till he agreed to a major offensive in North Waziristan in the summer of 2014 The major terrorist attack on a Christian church in Peshawar in September 2013, in which more then eighty worshippers were killed and many others wounded, had obviously not been anough to convince the political leadership in this regard.

Further developments proved the military right. In September 2014 an Al Qaeda commando team tried to highjack a Pakistani Navy frigate in order to attack US Navy ships in the Indian Ocean. Of the ten attackers six were killed before boarding, but four stormed the ship and the ensuring gun battle lasted several hours. It was the second big attack on the Pakistan Navy. In May 2011 terrorists assaulted the large Pakistan Navy base *PNS Mehran* in Karachi. One alarming aspect of the two incidents was that former or currently serving

Pakistani Navy personnel were involved. Al-Qaeda is clearly able to recruit from within the Pakistan military.

The key event in this sequence of events occurred on 16 December 2014, when seven TTP gunmen attacked the Army Public School in Peshawar, resulting in the deaths of 145 people among them 132 children. Sharif was now forced to act. A national action plan to crack down on terrorism was established in January 2015, and a committee and fifteen sub-committees for the implantation of this plan came into being. The moratorium on execution of death sentences, in place since 2008, was lifted and the hangman got busy. Up till mid April 2015, some sixty or so convicted terrorists have been executed. COAS Raheel Sharif accepted this outcome and was grateful to the political leadership for its decision to rid Pakistan of this menace through such measures.

The second major rift was Nawaz Sharif's proposed South Asia policy, observed by the generals with definite suspicion. Pakistan's new Prime Minister was seeking to reduce tension in the internal politics of South Asia. Increased economic cooperation, especially with neighbouring India, would be one option. Sharif accepted the invitation from New Delhi, sent to all SAARC heads of government, for the swearing-in of Prime Minister Narendra Modi on 26 May 2014. Within the military, there was little approval for this: they classified the new Indian Prime Minister as a seasoned political hardliner. In their mind, his Pakistani counterpart is not of the same calibre. Overriding the objections of the military, Nawaz Sharif nevertheless took the flight to India. His entourage included his son, Hussain Nawaz, Sartaj Aziz (Adviser on National Security and Foreign Policy), Tariq Fatemi (Assistant to the Prime Minister on Foreign Affairs), Javed Aslam (Prime Minister's Principal Secretary) and Foreign Secretary Aizaz Ahmed Chaudhry. The entourage demonstrated his intention to make his own mark on Pakistan's India policy. But the Pakistani hopes for policy discussions during this trip did not materialise, which drew malicious comment from the government's critics.

The third issue was that the GHQ was worried about what the new government might concede in the upcoming crucial political negotiations in Afghanistan. For over three decades Pakistan's Afghan policy had been the domain of the ISI and the military, and both wanted to remain in charge. After the withdrawal of ISAF troops from Afghanistan, Pakistan's generals anticipate new security problems emanating from its western neighbour, including infiltration into Pakistan.

When the LeT attacked the Indian Consulate-General in Herat on 23 May 2014[1] political analysts in both countries saw this as an ISI warning directed at two audiences. First, it was a signal to the government to leave Afghanistan policy to the military. Second, it was a message to India and Iran to take Pakistan's interests in Afghanistan into account. The city of Herat is located within Iran's sphere of interest in Afghanistan. Tehran and New Delhi have been cooperating since 2013 in developing Iranian coastal areas while Indian experts are involved in upgrading Iranian seaports as gateways to Central Asia's markets. The Indian Navy also hopes to establish a base on the Iranian coast as a balance to Pakistan's port in Gwadar. Given the background to these developments, the attack in Herat was seen as an unambiguous warning to Tehran.

Then followed a terror attack by two teenagers in the dining hall of the Serena Hotel in Kabul on 20 March 2014, killing nine people; this too was ascribed by experts to the ISI. President Hamid Karzai released a statement saying this terrorist attack had been conducted "by an intelligence service outside of this country." In an interview given to an Indian TV channel, Karzai became even more direct: he spoke of terrorism, which was "nurtured" and "supported" in Pakistan, where the militants had their "ideological roots."

Over a month of controversy between government and military ensued, with the ISI remaining the eyes and ears of GHQ. At the beginning of General Raheel Sharif's tenure as COAS, in November 2013, he had decided to allow corps commanders and the DG ISI to complete their service in their positions. DG ISI Zaheerul Islam returned the favour in his own way. As reported by the Pakistani media, in February 2014 the ISI bugged the telephone conversations of some parliamentarians. Though the chiefs of ISI and MI were called before a Senate committee, there were no untoward consequences.

A more serious matter for the ISI was the above mentioned attack on Hamid Mir, news anchor of the Jang Media Group and host of *Capital Talk*, a popular TV show, who was targeted in Karachi in April 2014. Mir, who was travelling in a car, was shot in the legs and abdomen by a motorcycle-born assassin. The journalist survived the shooting, as the gunman deliberately fired low. Several observers thought the attack was obviously intended as a warning. Over the previous few months, Hamid Mir had reported critically on the military and the ISI—evidence that the Jang Group stood firmly in the government camp. Prime Minister Sharif immediately ordered a judicial inquiry into the incident, and personally rushed to hospital to visit the victim.

Hamid Mir and his brother, Amir Mir, openly accused the ISI, and in particular DG Zaheerul Islam, of instigating the attack. Against this background, the much publicised dash by Sharif to the Karachi hospital was an open provocation towards the military. Their reactions were inevitable—a demand for a shutdown of Geo TV, the TV channel of Jang media group. As a result, Geo TV was unavailable for several weeks in some areas. At the same time, journalists who were closely affiliated with the political opposition or the military felt provoked. Geo TV was accused of running a smear campaign against the ISI and the military. For months, the country experienced a media war, in which ARY News, a news channel based in Dubai and Karachi, became the main opponent of Geo TV.

In Islamabad a few thousand followers of Imran Khan (PTI) and Tahir-ul-Qadri (PAT) continued their demonstrations till October 2014. Qadri was the first one to call a halt to the entire undertaking. He told his supporters to go home as the "sit-in has achieved its purpose, it has awakened the nation and played its role in the path of revolution." Imran Khan's followers camped out a few weeks longer. An understanding between the government and the PTI was finally reached, a recount of the election results will take place and a judicial commission will oversee the recounting process. In April 2015 the PTI National Assembly members returned to the Parliament and no calls were heard for mid-term elections.

During the siege of Islamabad the nucleus of both camps of protestors were paid a modest daily allowance. Political analysts are still asking where this money came from. Although evidence is lacking, many believe that the protesters' march, which began in mid-April, was initiated by the ISI. This may or may not be true—but at least it was tolerated by the agency and the GHQ. Due to the lack of political alternatives, Pakistan's military finally did not wish to overthrow the Nawaz Sharif government. But their aim, to weaken the Prime Minister, had been fully achieved.

DG ISI Lt. Gen. Rizwan Akhtar

Lt. Gen. Rizwan Akhtar was promoted to three star general on 22 October and took over as DG ISI on 8 November 2014. He was known as a close ally and aid to COAS Raheel Sharif and his promotion and new posting therefore came as no surprise. Prime Minister Sharif endorsed the move as he had never felt comfortable with Akhtar's predecessor Zaheerul Islam.

Rizwan Akhtar is regarded politically as being more neutral and less engaged. Analysts see him belonging to a new generation of political generals who understand that the military can perform successfully only in cooperation with the country's political leadership. He is an infantryman from the Frontier Force Regiment, commissioned in the Pakistan Army in 1982, who graduated from the Command and Staff College Quetta, the National Defence University Islamabad, and the US Army War College. During his career he commanded an infantry brigade and an infantry division in FATA, gaining valuable experience in counterinsurgency. Before taking over the ISI Directorate in Islamabad he had been DG Sindh Rangers. As such he commanded the Karachi operations against terrorists and criminal elements, jointly undertaken by Rangers and Police. Though the Karachi operation was still in full swing, Akhtar was called back to GHQ in preparation for his new posting.

It is most unlikely that under the leadership of DG ISI Rizwan Akhtar the ISI's policy on Afghanistan and India will change significantly. In Afghanistan the ISI will try to start a reconciliation process between the Government and the Taliban. On Akhtar's first visit as Chief of the ISI in February 2015, this again topped the agenda. It will be a difficult task as many of the commanders in the meantime are going their own way and the influence and power of Mullah Akhtar Mansour, who succeeeded Mullah Omar in 2015 (Omar died in April 2013) remains unclear.

During his first three months in office the new ISI chief visited Afghanistan on three occasions, and in mid January 2015 met President Ashraf Ghani for the first time. In the light of what happened at the Army Public School in Peshawar, joint efforts to fight terrorism and extremism were on the top of the agenda. For example, training of Afghanistan Army officers is already under way at the Pakistan Military Academy in Abbottabad.

In late February Lt. Gen. Rizwan Akhtar went for the first time officially as ISI chief to Washington where he met his counterpart, CIA Director John O. Brennan, and other senior members of the National Security Council. Regional security and mutual affairs were on the table. The situation in Afghnistan was foremost in all the rounds of talks as the need for a reconciliation process between the government in Kabul and the Afghan Taliban has in the meantime been accepted in Washington as inevitable if not desirable.

Meanwhile in Pakistan, the ISI is supporting the Army in its ongoing Zarb-e-Azb operation against TTP, which is still in full swing. The number of eliminated "hard core terrorists" amounted to 263 by April 2015, according to ISPR, but the operation's main target to secure FATA and staunch TTP-terrorism is still far from having been achieved.

In New Delhi, security circles are fully aware of the ISI's continuing efforts to diminish India's influence and engagement in Afghanistan. One also does not expect any substantial changes in Pakistan's Kashmir policy. In contrast, one New Delhi analyst believes that the ISI remains in contact with the al-Qaeda chief Ayman al-Zawahiri and is helping him to set up a new al-Qaeda branch in South Asia by drawing new recruits to the terror organization. This may or may not prove to be a reliable prediction; only al-Qaeda's future operations will bring us closer to the truth.

(There follow two official ISI statements that were sent to the author in August 2015. These have not been edited and are presented to the reader with the same stylistic conventions as in the original documents.)

APPENDIX 1

REALITIES vs MISPERCEPTIONS—BALOCHISTAN

1. Due to economic potentials, Balochistan has become a venue of geo-politics and battlefield of economic interests between global and regional power players. Balochistan was becoming prone to terrorism and sectarian violence, however these tendencies have been sufficiently contained. An analysis of summary of terrorist incidents since 2011 establishes that 4618 terrorism incidents occurred in Balochistan resulting into killing of 2407 civilians/Security Forces and 5229 injured. However, owing to effective counter measures by LEAs and restricting the role of dubious INGOs the situation is improving.

2. A misperception is widely prevalent that ***thousands of innocent persons are missing in Pakistan particularly in Balochistan***. This highly exaggerated figure has been propagated by various interest *groups having vested agendas*; these include nationalists, relatively less informed politicians, foreign funded media and few human rights organizations, both domestic and international.

3. The issue of Missing Persons (MPs) *date back to October 2006*, when agitations gained momentum against the issue and Supreme Court of Pakistan (SCP) took suo moto notice. In the backdrop of agitations and different high level meetings, a committee in Ministry of Interior (MoI) was formed

by the Federal Government, which laid down the criteria of enforced disappearance, which *"means such persons as has been picked up/taken into custody by one of the law enforcement/intelligence agencies, working under the civilian or military control, in a manner, which is contrary to the provision of law"*.

4. By the end of year 2009, the list of MPs had *swelled to 2390* and after detailed scrutiny by the said committee, *2201x cases were dropped* from the given list being *misreported/failing to fulfill the criteria* of enforced disappearance.

5. To further institutionalize the system, *in April 2010, 1ˢᵗ Commission of Inquiry on Enforced Disappearance (ColoED)* compromising 3x retired judges was formed by the Federal Government of Pakistan. This was an *independent commission* having all the judicial powers of SCP. Commission was given the *mandate under laid down Terms & References to trace out the whereabouts of MPs*. After a detailed scrutiny by the committee, *only 189x cases from the entire country were considered as MPs* and in this list *only 52x persons were from Balochistan*. The said list was handed over to 1st Commission of Inquiry and this Commission duly assisted by law enforcement and intelligence agencies *made a substantial progress in tracing out 134x MPs (including 32x MPs from Balochistan)*. A report to this effect was submitted by this Commission to the Federal Government of Pakistan.

6. In *March 2011, 2ⁿᵈ judicial Commission was formed*, which is performing its duties till to-date. Since March 2011, the Commission *has traced 1233x individuals (including 78x individuals from Balochistan)*. Presently, there are *only 121x individuals still missing from Balochistan*.

7. The said Commission *regularly holds judicial proceedings on daily basis* and also presents its report on quarterly basis to the basis to the Federal Government of Pakistan. In addition to Commission of Inquiry, general public has all the rights and access under the Constitution to file writ petitions before higher courts including High Courts and SCP. Higher courts to provide relief to general public, as deemed necessary and appropriate.

8. **Realities vis-à-vis Misperception**
   a. Sizeable Baloch *majority is still neutral*, but vulnerable to militants/ separatists influence.
   b. There is a *systematic* insurgency in Balochistan augmented with *propaganda* clearly *engineered* by *professionals*.
   c. There are around 105 *Ferrari camps active in remote and mountainous terrain*.

d. The terrorists, while fighting against LEAs, are also killed during action. In many such cases, dead bodies are taken away by their accomplices, who bury them at unmarked places. The families in few cases are also not informed about the deaths for obvious ramifications.

e. As regards to enforced disappearances, following types of individuals are also included/propagated in the category of MPs:-

(1) *Suicide bombers and unidentified persons*, who die in suicide attacks.

(2) *Victims of sabotage incidents*, whose bodies could not be recognized.

(3) *Mentally retarded individuals*, who leave their homes and move into other parts of the country.

(4) *Individuals, who die in Ferrari Camps* and information for their death is not known to the families.

(5) *Proclaimed offenders* many a times are also reported as MPs by the relatives.

(6) Incidents have also come to light where persons, who are serving sentences in various jails are also included in the list of MPs.

(7) Most of the purported MPs, having links with various terrorist outfits and fearing arrest, have taken refuge in the far-flung areas of KPK/FATA and Ferrari Camps of Balochistan. In addition, many have fled to other countries mainly Afghanistan. To mislead the authorities their families purport them to be MPs.

APPENDIX 2

INDIAN/RAW's INVOLVEMENT IN PAKISTAN

1. *General Overview.* Indian/RAW's involvement in internal matters of Pakistan is a well-established fact manifested through sponsoring terrorism by proscribed terrorist organizations and Sub-nationalist Militant Organisations. **RAW in collusion with other intelligence agencies; especially Afghan National Directorate of Security (NDS) is fomenting instability in Pakistan by providing financial support, training, weapons**

and explosives and sanctuaries on foreign soil. RAW's patronage of Mutahidda Qaumi Movement (MQM) to vitiate fragile ethno-political environment of Karachi through MQM's offices in London, destabilizing financial capital of Pakistan is no more a secret. **Indian Embassy and consulates in Afghanistan are directly involved in funding, coordinating and supporting Balochistan Sub Nationalists (BSN) miscreants and Techrik-e-Taliban Pakistan (TTP).** Fake identity & travel documents and passports are also being provided to facilitate their international travel. **Disproportionate number of Indian consulates and their location closer to Pak-Afghan Border** duly stagged with RAW officials reflects Indian intent and design to meddle in the internal affairs of Pakistan. **Sufficient and irrefutable evidence is available to establish Indian/RAW's involvement in Pakistan.**

2. *Violation of International Law.* UN Charter and international law comprising treaties, conventions and various UNGA/UNSC resolutions **prohibit states from interventions and interfering in internal matters of other states.** On the contrary, Indian/RAW's involvement in internal matters of Pakistan has been continuous phenomenon since inception. The most recent admission by Prime Minister Narendra Modi's of Indian Involvement in dismemberment of **Pakistan in 1971** constitutes self-indictment of India's unlawful intervention. On 7 Jun 2015 of Dhaka University (Bangladesh), while reiterating his participation in rallies in support of Bangladesh he also stated '**Remember the days of 1970, tell our coming generations, that it was us. That each and every Mukti Jodha (freedom fighter) sitting here, I bow to you. Standing shoulder to shoulder, the Indian Army sacrificed in blood with them. And none would be able to say that this blood belonged to a freedom fighter and that to an Indian soldier, no distinction could be witnessed.'** Moreover, Mr Ajit Doval, Indian National Security Advisor (NSA) has repeatedly reiterated for providing financial support to terrorist entities operating against Pakistan. Excerpts from his statement on adopting defensive-offensive strategyare 'Now when we come into defensive offence, we **start working on the vulnerabilities of Pakistan**, it can be economic ... it can be political ... it can be **defeating their policies in Afghanistan, making it difficult for them to manage internal political balance or internal security** ... Pakistan's vulnerability is many times higher than that of India ... **You do another 26/11, you lose Balochistan ...'** (available on social media) is

reflective of Indian intent and policy of using terrorism to weaken and destabilize Pakistan.

a. Going further, India is violating by aiding and abetting TTP and its leadership. **Senator Chuck Hagel's** statement at Cameron University— 2011 states **'India has always used Afghanistan as a second front against Pakistan. India has over the years been financing problems in Pakistan.'** This affirms that India is responsible for **obstructing Pakistan's obligations in fighting terrorism under UNSC Resolution—1267 & 1373** by providing support to proscribed terrorist entities and its leadership. In the similar vein, Mr Manohar Parrikar's statement vividly manifests Indian design of perpetrating terrorism and meddling in Pakistan **'We have to neutralise terrorism through terrorists only. Why can't we do it? We should do it. Why does my soldier have to do it?**

b. To sum it up, it is a well-known fact that India is relentlessly pursuing terrorism as a matter of undeclared state policy while decrying being a victim of terrorism emanating from Pakistan. In fact, India needs to address woes of people of India who are subjugated and suppressed with powerful security apparatus of the state with due backing of draconian laws like Prevention of Terrorism Act (POTA) and Armed Forces Special Powers Act (AFSPA). This is not consistent with proclaimed image and stature of India, especially while claiming its enlarged role in the international order as the largest democracy and rising economic power. Pakistan reserves the right to seek internal justice for violation of internal laws and covenants against India.

3. *RAW's Signature in Afghanistan.* Officially India is maintaining the same number of Council Generals as of Pakistan. Contrarily, large number of Indian Diplomatic staff is present in Afghanistan. A substantial number of RAW agents are performing the duties under diplomatic guise and pursuing an anti-Pakistan agenda. Statements by Senator Chuck Hagel cited above and **Christine Fair's statement;** who is considered to be a biased and anti-Pakistan journalist states 'Having visited the Indian mission in Zahedan, Iran, **I can assure you they are not issuing visas as the main activity!** Moreover, India has run operations from its mission in Mazar (through which it supported the Northern Alliance) and is likely doing so from the other consulates it has reopened in Jalalabad and Qandahar along the border. **Indian officials have told me privately that they are pumping money into Balochistan.** Kabul has encouraged India to engage in provocative activities such as using the Border Roads Organisation ...'. Such

statements substantiate Pakistan's stance of Indian/RAW's involvement in fomenting terrorism in Pakistan through her consulates in Afghanistan and Iran.

4. *RAW Fomenting Instability in Balochistan.* RAW in collaboration with Afchan intelligence agency NDS is actively providing convert financial, terrorist training, weapons and explosives to Baloch militant groups such as the Balochistan Liberation Army (BLA), Baloch Republican Army (BRA), Balochistan Liberation Front (BLF) etc for conducting terrorist activities in Balochistan. These militant outfits are involved in militant activities treading the separatist's agenda and are responsible for causing mayhem in the province. Irrefutable evidences also suggest that Baloch militants are being harboured at various places and **training camps located** in Afghanistan by **RAW in concert with Afghan intelligence agency NDS for over a decade.** Some of the Baloch militants who have recently surrendered have also validated Indian hand in fomenting insurgency in Balochistan.

a. RAW is also providing sustained financing and monetary support to Baloch feudal & militants both in Afghanistan and Balochistan. Besides, RAW with the complete support and patronage of Afghan authorities is also involved in provision of Arms & ammunitions to Baloch militants for conducting terrorist activities inside Pakistan. Some sources privy to confined circles also point out about the evidences held by them regarding RAW's involvement in provision of fake identity and travel documents to Baloch militants for moving out of Afghanistan to India, UAE and Western countries (Switzerland, UK ect). RAW recruited and arranged visits of hundreds of militants of Pakistani origin to India, where they were briefed and trained by RAW for terrorist activities. It is pertinent to mention that these militants are **involved and legally nominated in numerous acts of killings of Punjabi and Pashtun settlers in Balochistan, blowing of gas pipelines, railway tracks and IED blasts.**

b. RAW in collaboration with prominent Baloch sub nationalists round the globe is also persistently utilizing various international forums, NGOs and think tank organizations like forum of United Nations Human Rights Council (UNHRC) etc for maligning Pakistan through arranging stage managed events such as preplanned anti-Pakistan intervention, media briefings, protests and demonstrations. **"Their convergence, facilitation (lodgment, travel expenses etc) and subsequent** media (including vibes) propagation in manages/funded by RAW". RAW is also actively involved in unleashing massive propaganda and disinformation campaign on Balochistan issue vis-à-vis maligning Pakistan on internet and social media by launching anti-Pakistan blogs, web pages with fake identities.

5. *RAW—NDS Support to TTP.* It has been substantiated that NDS with the active support of RAW has been/is involved in providing all out support to the TTP elements to operate from Afghanistan against Pakistan. Huge funding, training camps where recruits are trained and equipped for sabotage/subversion against Pakistan are patronized by the nexus. A huge quantity of ammunitions and explosive is being inducted in the garb of reconstructions and protection of Indian nationals working on various projects in Afghanistan. RAW has also provided financial support to TTP through NDS as well as Indian cover offices.

a. As per Austro D. Agnelli, Italian Journalist, 'India has established training camps in Tajikistan at Farkhor Airbase and Ayni Airbase where the young recruits of Uzbekistan and Tajikistan are trained and sent to Pakistan for terrorist attacks.' According to the reports of Italian journalist, the members of Indian Secret Services at Farkhor Airbase and Ayni Airbase are recruiting underage unemployed youth from different under-developed backgrounds and offer them handsome money. During this period RAW agents preach religion based on extremism, terrorism and hate against Pakistan and after the training they are offered an ordinary job or fight against Pakistan for Islam and get entry into Jannah (Paradise).

b. RAW in collusion with NDS has been actively involved in providing financial support, weapons, explosives and harbouring of TTP on Afghan Soil. High value commanders with approximately 2000 to 2500 TTP militants of various chapters are being harboured in the province of Nangarhar, and Nuristan.

6. *RAW's Backing to MQM.* Enough substantive evidence of training and funding of MQM by RAW, is available to establish collusion of RAW with MQM to foment instability in the economic capital of Pakistan. Judicial confessions of target killers and criminals have revealed that RAW in convert with MQM leaders is organizing their movement to India through third countries like Singapore and Thailand/Bangkok, conducting specialist training in India, re-insertion into Pakistan and financially supporting militant wing of MQM. All these criminals have killed hundreds of

innocent citizens and terrorized society; duly validated by the First Information Reports lodged against them and judicial process being followed.

APPENDIX 3

ORGANISATIONAL STRUCTURE OF THE ISI

Joint Intelligence X (JIX)
It serves as the secretariat which coordinates with and provides administrative support to the other ISI wings and field organisations. It also prepares intelligence estimates and threat assessments.

Headed by a Director, JIX looks after general administration and accounts of the ISI directorate. The Director is assisted by five Deputy Director, handling administration, budget, accounts, transport and miscellaneous work. It is one of the largest wings of the ISI Directorate.

Joint Intelligence Bureau (JIB)
It is the largest wing of the ISI Directorate with about 60 per cent of the staff of the Directorate on its rolls. The DDG is assisted by a Director who has under him five Assistant Directors in charge of the subject of Labour, Students, Political parties, Anti terrorism and VIP Security.

In addition, there are three sub-sections dealing exclusively with the political and economic developments in specified regions of the world:

(a) Sub-section 1—deals with India and the Far East.
(b) Sub-section 2—deals with communist countries.
(c) Sub-section 3—deals with East Asia and Africa.

There is also a separate Special Wing dealing exclusively with Afghanistan, headed by a Director. The Section has three sub-sections, each looked after by a Deputy Director, dealing with:

(i) Training and operations
(ii) Arms distribution and logistic support
(iii) Training of Afghan refugees and psychological warfare.

JIB also controls the positioning and functioning of the Pakistani Military Attaches/Advisors in missions abroad.

Joint Counter Intelligence Bureau (JCIB)

It is responsible for field surveillance of Pakistani diplomats stationed abroad, as well as for conducting intelligence operations in the Middle East, South Asia, China, Afghanistan and the Muslim republics of the former Soviet Union. DDG (External) controls the JCIB for surveillance of foreign diplomats and nationals, political leaders and ISI personnel. DDG (External) is assisted by four Directors, as follows:

(a) Director—field surveillance and foreign diplomats and foreigners
(b) Director—External (Political)
(c) Director—External for Asia, Europe and Middle East
(d) Director—attached to the Prime Minister's Secretariat.

This Wing also has a unit called Inter Services Security Section (ISSS) which maintains surveillance on ISI personnel. Detachments of JCIB are stationed at Lahore, Karachi, Peshawar, Kohat, Rawalpindi, Mardan, Nowshera, Attock, Murree, Jhelum, Kharjan, Gujranwala, Sialkot, Sahiwal, Multan, Sargodha, Hyderabad, Muzaffarabad, Tulbul and Gilgit. These detachments carry out counter intelligence tasks, apart from collecting internal political intelligence.

Joint Intelligence North (JIN)

It is responsible for carrying out special operations in Jammu and Kashmir, including infiltration, propaganda and other covert operations. It is also tasked with collection of intelligence on Jammu and Kashmir. It provides training and supply of arms and ammunition and funds to Kashmiri militants to carry out sabotage and subversion.

Joint Intelligence Miscellaneous (JIM)

It conducts espionage in Europe, America, Asia and Middle East—directly from the ISI Headquarters, through agents and indirectly through its officers posted abroad under cover assignments. It also operates trained spies in India and Afghanistan to carry out offensive intelligence operations.

JIM is headed by Director (Operations) who has under him two Deputy Directors for operations in Europe/America and in Asia/Middle East. There are eight Assistant Directors of the rank of Majors in this wing.

Joint Signal Intelligence Bureau (JSIB)

Its main function is to provide communication network for the ISI and to collect intelligence through monitoring of communication links of neighbouring countries, particularly India and Afghanistan.

This wing also produces signal codes for the use of Services. A sizeable number of officers and men from the Army Signal Corps have been taken here. JSIB has detachments at Karachi, Lahore and Peshawar. Each headed by a Deputy Director.

It is headed by Director (Technical), who is of the rank of a Colonel and is assisted by three Deputy Directors for Wireless, Monitoring and Photos. It operates a chain of signals intelligence collection stations along the border with India and provides communication support to militants operating in Kashmir.

Joint Intelligence Technical (JIT)
It deals with technical aids for intelligence operations. It handles all the electronic gadgets required for ISI's intelligence operations.

Special Wings of the ISI:

ISI Academy: It was renamed in April 1989 as 'Defence Services Intelligence Academy'. It is headed by a Deputy Director (Training) who is assisted by Officer Commanding (Language) and Officer Commanding (Technical Training).

Military Liaison Section (MLS): Though the MLS is a part of Pakistan's Ministry of Interior, it functions directly under the control and command of the ISI Directorate. MLS is represented by all the civilian security agencies, para-military organisations, Federal Investigation Agency and Passport and Immigration Directorate.

In addition to these main elements, ISI also includes a separate explosives section and a chemical warfare section.

APPENDIX 4

ISI DIRECTORATE

As at Spring 2010

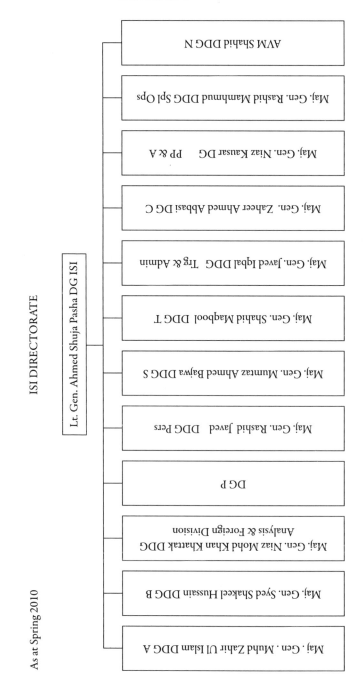

Lt. Gen. Ahmed Shuja Pasha DG ISI

AVM Shahid DDG N

Maj. Gen. Rashid Mamhmud DDG Spl Ops

Maj. Gen. Niaz Kausar DG   PP & A

Maj. Gen. Zaheer Ahmed Abbasi DG C

Maj. Gen. Javed Iqbal DDG Trg & Admin

Maj. Gen. Shahid Maqbool DDG T

Maj. Gen. Mumraz Ahmed Bajwa DDG S

Maj. Gen. Rashid Javed DDG Pers

DG P

Maj. Gen. Niaz Mohd Khan Khattak DDG Analysis & Foreign Division

Maj. Gen. Syed Shakeel Hussain DDG B

Maj . Gen . Muhd Zahir Ul Islam DDG A

APPENDIX 5

DIRECTOR GENERALS ISI

Major General R. Cawthorne	1948	1948
Brigadier Syed Shahid Hamid	July 1948	June 1950
Brigadier Mirza Hamid Hussain	June 1950	May 1951
Colonel Muhammad Afzal Malik	May 1951	April 1953
Brigadier Syed Ghawas	April 1953	August 1955
Brigadier Sher Bahadur	August 1955	September 1957
Brigadier Muhammad Hayat	September 1957	October 1959
Brigadier Riaz Hussain	October 1959	May 1966
Major General Mohammad Akbar Khan	1966	1971
Lt. General Ghulam Jilani Khan	1971	1978
Lt. General Muhammad Riaz Khan	1978	1980
Lt. General Akhtar Abdur Rahman	1980	March 1987
Lt. General Hamid Gul	March 1987	May 1989
Lt. General (retd) Shamsur Rahman Kallue	May 1989	August 1990
Lt. General Asad Durrani	August 1990	March 1992
Lt. General Javed Nasir	March 1992	May 1993
Lt. General Javed Ashraf Qazi	May 1993	August 1995
Lt. General Naseem Rana	1995	October 1998
Lt. General Khawaja Ziauddin	October 1998	October 1999
Lt. General Mahmood Ahmed	October 1999	October 2001
Lt. General Ehsan ul Haq	October 2001	October 2004
Lt. General Ashfaq Pervez Kiyani	October 2004	October 2007
Lt. General Nadeem Taj	October 2007	October 2008
Lt. General Ahmad Shuja Pasha	October 2008	March 2012
Lt. General Zaheerul Islam	March 2012	September 2014
Lt. General Rizwan Akhtar	September 2014	Present

ABBREVIATIONS

ACR	Annual Confidential Report
AIG	Afghan Interim Government
AISSF	All India Sikh Student Federation
ANP	Awami National Party
APMSO	All Pakistan Muhajir Student Organization

ABBREVIATIONS

ARC	Aviation Research Centre
ARD	Alliance for the Restoration of Democracy
APC	Amoured Personnel Carrier
ATTF	All Tripura Tiger Force
BADO	Baloch Armed Defence Organisation
BAKSAL	Bangladesh Krishak Sramik Awami League
BCCI	Bank of Credit and Commerce International
BCP	Bangladesh Communist Party
BDM	Baluchistan Dehi Mahafiz
BDR	Bangladesh Rifles
BLA	Balochistan Liberation Army
BLF	Balochistan Liberation Front
BLO	Bangla Liberation Organization
BLUF	Balochistan Liberation United Front
BLT	Bodo Liberation Tigers
BND	Bundesnachrichtendienst (Federal Intelligence Service)
BNP	Bangladesh Nationalist Party
BRA	Baloch Republican Army
BRO	Border Road Organization
BSF	Indian Border Security Forces
BTFK	Bhindranwale Tiger Force of Khalistan
CBI	Central Bureau of Investigation
CGS	Chief of General Staff
CHT	Chittagong Hill Tracts
C-in-C	Commander-in-Chief
CIA	Central Intelligence Agency
CJ	Chief Justice
CJCSC	Chairman Joint Chiefs of Staff Committee
CMI	Corps Military Intelligence
CMLA	Chief Martial Law Administrator
COAS	Chief of Army Staff
CPI	Communist Party of India
CSIS	Canadian Security Intelligence Service
DDG	Deputy Director General
DESTO	Defence Science & Technology Organization
DG	Director General
DGFI	Directorate General of Forces Intelligence
DGMO	Director General of Military Operation

DGS	Directorate General of Security
DIA	Defence Intelligence Agency
DIB	Directorate of Intelligence Bureau
DIP	Domestic Inland Product
DRI	Directorate of Revenue Intelligence
EC	Election Commission
EOW	Economic Offences Wing
EU	European Union
FATA	Federal Administrated Tribal Areas
FC	Frontier Corps
FGN	Federal Government of Nagaland
FIA	Federal Investigation Agency
FIU	Field IntelligenceUnits
FO	Foreign Office
FPSC	Federal Public Service Commission
FRIENDS	Foundation for Research on International Environment, National Defence and Security
FSF	Federal Security Force
GHQ	General Head Quarters
HNLC	Hynniewtrep National Liberation Council
HuA	Harakat-ul-Ansar
HuJ	Harakat-ul-Jehad
HUJI	Harkat-ul-Jihad-al-Islami
HuM	Harakat-ul-Mujaheddin
HUMINT	Human Intelligence
IAEA	International Atomic Energy Agency
IAF	India Air Force
IAS	Indian Administrative Service
IB	Intelligence Bureau
INCP	India National Congress Party
IFAS	Indian Frontier Administration Service
IFOR	Implementation Force
IG T&E	Instructor General Training and Evaulation
IHH	Insani Yardim Vakfi
ILAA	Islamic Liberation Army of Assam
IISS	International Institute of Strategic Studies
IJI	Islami Jamoori Ithad
IM	Indian Mujahideen

IMF	International Monetary Fund
IP	Indian Police
IPS	Indian Police Service
IRS	India Revenue Services
ISAF	International Security Assistance Force
ISI	Inter Services Intelligence
ISS	Adam Sena Islamic Sevak Sangh
JCIB	Joint Counter Intelligence Bureau
JCO	Junior Commissioned Officer
JCSC	Joint Chief of Staff Committee
JEM	Jaish-e-Mohammad
JI	Jamaat-i-Islami (also Jamaat-e-Islami)
JIB	Joint Intelligence Bureau
JIC	Joint Intelligence Committee
JIM	Joint Intelligence Miscellaneous
JIN	Joint Intelligence North
JIT	Joint Intelligence Technical
JIX	Joint Intelligence X
JKLF	Jammu & Kashmir Liberation Front
JMJ	Jagrata Muslim Janata
JSIB	Joint Signal Intelligence Bureau
JUF	Jamaat-ul-Fuqra
JUM–B	Jamiat-ul-Mujahideen Bangladesh
KANUPP	Karachi Nuclear Power Plant
KFC	Khalistan Commando Force
KGB	Komitjet Gosudarstvjennoj Bjezopasnosti (Committee for State Security)
KHAD	Khadamat-e Etela'at-e Dawlati (State Information Agency)
KIO	Kachin Independent Organization
KLA	Khalistan Liberation Army
KLA	Kosovo Liberation Army
KLF	Khalistan Liberation Force
KNA	Kuki National Army
KRL	Kahuta Research Laboratories
LEJ	Lashkar-e-Jhangvi
LeT	Lashkar-e-Toiba (also Lashkar-i-Toiba)
LFO	Legal Framework Order
LMG	Light Machine Gun

LoC	Line of Control
LTB	Liberation Tigers of Bengal
LTTE	Liberation Tamil Tigers of Eelam
MEA	Ministry of External Affairs
MI	Military Intelligence
MMA	Muttahida Majlis-e-Amal
MNA	Member of National Assembly
MNF	Mizo National Front
ML	Martial Law
MOSSAD	HaMossad leModi'in uleTafkidim Meyuhadim (Institute for Intelligence and Special Operations)
MULFA	Muslim United Liberation Front of Assam
MULTA	Muslim United Liberation Tigers of Assam
MQM	Mohajir Qaumi Movement (currently Muttehida Qaumi Movement)
MS	Military Secretary
MTCR	Missile Technology Control Regime
MVF	Muslim Volunteer Force
NA	Northern Areas
NAB	National Accountability Bureau
NCB	Narcotics Control Bureau
NCO	Non Commission Officer
NCP	National Congress Party
NDC	National Defence College
NGO	Non Government Organisation
NIA	National Investigation Agency
NLC	National Logistics Cooperation
NLFT	National Liberation Front of Tripura
NSA	National Security Advisor
NSI	National Security Intelligence
NSC	National Security Council
NSCN	National Socialist Council of Nagaland
NSCS	National Security Council Secretariat
NTRO	National Technical Research Organisation
NWFP	North-West Frontier Province
PAEC	Pakistan Atomic Energy Commission
PAF	Pakistan Air Force
PINSTECH	Pakistan Institute of Technology

ABBREVIATIONS

PLA	People's Liberation Army
PM	Prime Minister
PMO	Prime Minister's Office
PML	Pakistan Muslim League
PML-Q	Pakistan Muslim League Quaid-e-Azam
PNA	Pakistan National Alliance
PNCA	Pakistan Nuclear Command Authority
POK	Pakistan occupied Kashmir
PPP	Pakistan Peoples Party
PSO	Principal Staff Officer
PULF	People's United Liberation Front
PSC	Public Service Commission
PSYWAR	Physiological Warfare
RAAM	Riyast-i-Amoor-o-Amanat-i-Milliyah
R&AW	Research and Analysis Wing
RAS	Research and Analysis Service
retd	retired
RSSO	Ruchika Social Service Organisation
SAAG	South Asia Analysis Group
SAARC	South Asian Association for Regional Cooperation
SAVAK	Khadamat-e Etela'at-e Dawlati (National Intelligence and Security Organization)
SC	Supreme Court
SDECE	Service de Documentation Extérieure et de Contre-Espionnage (External Documentation and Counter-Espionage Service)
SFF	Special Frontier Force
SFOR	Stabilisation Force in Bosnia and Herzegovina
SGPC	Shiromani Gurudwara Prabhandhak Committee
SIB	Subsidiary Intelligence Bureau
SIMI	Students Islamic Movement of India
SLR	Self Loading Rifle
SSF	Special Frontier Force
SSG	Special Services Group
SSP	Sipah-e-Sahaba
TECHINT	Technical Intelligence
TJ	Tableeghi Jammat
TMVP	Tamil Makhal Viduthalai Pulikal

TNA	Tamil National Alliance
TNSM	Tehreek-e-Nafaz-e-Shariat-e-Mohammadi
TTP	Tehrik-i-Taliban Pakistan
ULFA	United Liberation Front of Asom
ULFSS	United Liberation Front of Seven Sisters
UMLFA	United Muslim Liberation Front ofAssam
UNOCAL	Union Oil Company of California
UPSC	Union Police Service Commission
URPA	United Reformation Protest of Assam
USMAP	United States Military Aid to Pakistan
VCOAS	Vice Chief of Army Staff

NOTES

INTRODUCTION

1. In summer 2015 the ISI made known its views on the matter to the author: "Pakistan is in favour of the de-nuclearization of South Asia but no unilateral act or specific waiver is acceptable. India's "No First Use" policy is just for political purposes, as she has retained the "First Use" option by including in her nuclear doctrine that in the event of a major attack against India or Indian forces anywhere by biological and chemical weapons, India will retain the option of retaliating with nuclear weapons. So on the pretext of the use of chemical weapons by an adversary, India can resort to nuclear weapons."

2. The ISI's view on the matter was communicated to the author in 2015: "Our nuclear weapons are safeguarded by a robust command and control system, as Pakistan has established the improved Personnel Reliability Programme for all scientists and officials working on sensitive projects, along with a Human Programme for all military personnel involved with the nuclear forces. The concerns expressed seem to be based on Indian and Western propaganda regarding the safety of Pakistan's nuclear installations and weapons. The fact remains that Pakistan's nuclear assets are well protected by impregnable defence arrangements and it is impossible for terrorists to reach the distant vicinity of those locations. Pakistan's position is also shared by senior members of the US military, including Admiral Mike Mullen, the former Chairman of the US Joint Chiefs of Staff, who in 2007 said that he did not see any indication that security of those wapons was in jeopardy. It is wrong to say that the operational control of Pakistan's nuclear weapons is in the hands of the Army."

3. In August 2015 the ISI sent the author a statement setting out its views of the situation in the province and of alleged R&AW activities there. This is found in the appendix at the end of the book.

4. The others involved were Sheikh Abdullah-Azam, Abu Hafs al-Masri, Abu Ubajdah, Dr Fadl (Sajid Imam), Wael Dschuleidan and the Kurd, Abu Had.

5. Approximately 200 al-Qaeda fighters participated, of whom eighty or so died.

6. Besides Osama bin Laden, the Fatwa was proclaimed by the Egyptians (Dr Ayman Al-Zawahiri and Rifa' i Taha), the Pakistanis (Sheikh Mir-Hamza and Fadl Al-Rahmen) as well as Bangladeshis (Sheikh Abdul Salam Mohammad Khan). Every one of them belonged to the leadership of an active jihadi group.

265

7. There was a time of close cooperation between the Indian IB and CIA in the 1960s and between R&AW and the CIA in the 1970s. After separating from IB in 1968, R&AW Director R. N. Kao garnered a lot of help from the CIA in structuring R&AW and developing ARC. There were also covert operations by R&AW and the CIA in Himalayan Tibet. This kind of cooperation came to an end in the 1980s.

8. Ghazala Wahab, "Fighting a Ghost—When it comes to national security, who dare argue," *FORCE*, February 2007, p. 71.

1. THE FIRST DECADE

1. See Winchell (2003, pp. 374–88): "In 1948, following Pakistan's loss of the first Indo-Pakistani War, and the abysmal intelligence performance of Pakistan's intelligence service, the Intelligence Bureau, the then Deputy Army Chief of Staff General R. Cawthorne formed the Inter-Services Intelligence (ISI) agency." Also Hamid Hussain (*Covert Action Quarterly*, no. 73, Summer 2002, p. 18) saw the founding of the ISI as a result of the war: "after Pakistan found itself without sufficient intelligence during its first war with India over Kashmir." In the renowned German weekly paper *Die Zeit* (no. 4, 17 January 2002, p. 6) Michael Schwelien wrote: "Actually the ISI was created in 1948... by a British major .... The army leadership in Pakistan in the first Indo-Pak War in 1947–8 had amassed incorrect information regarding the opponent."

2. Azad Kashmir (Free Kashmir) is Pakistani parlance for the areas under their control, which are known in India as Pakistan-Occupied Kashmir (POK).

3. For the historical Great Game see John Keay, *The Gilgit Game*, Oxford, 1993. For a newer perspective on this political game see Ahmed Rashid, *Taliban*, London, 2000.

4. Sarila (2005), p. 325.

5. Cohen (1984), p. 7.

6. Lal (2000), p. 6.

7. Ghosh (2000), p. 15.

8. At that time his decision for Pakistan was shaped by Cawthorne's friendship with Pakistan's future leaders, Sikander Mirza and Ayub Khan.

9. Wilson (2002), p. 165.

10. Cohen (1984), p. 17.

11. Information from Rizvi (2003), p. 60.

12. Besides the ISI and MI there are also civilian intelligence and security agencies existing in Pakistan, from which the Intelligence Bureau (IB) and the Federal Investigation Agency (FIA) are noteworthy. The total staff in all the intelligence services is approx. 100,000, with a yearly budget of US$ 150 million.

13. From an interview between the author and the Pakistani historian Col. (retd.) Mohammad Effendi, who headed the research department of the ISI in the 1980s-90s.

14. Winchell (2003), p. 375.

2. THE ERA OF THE FIRST GENERALS, 1956–1971

1. Altaf Gauhar, "How Intelligence Agencies Run our Politics," *The Nation*, 17 August 1997.

2. Ibid. Sir Feroz Khan Noon was the last Prime Minister of the first democratic period of the

country, 1953–8. His term of office lasted less than a year, from 16 December 1957 to 7 October 1958.

3. President Mirza came from the military. He was also Defence Secretary. However those generals he later deposed saw him more as a bureaucrat and a politician than belonging to the Army.

4. Mirza (2000).

5. Ibid., p. 400, fn 55.

6. General Ayub Khan took over the Presidency immediately after the coup.

7. *Herald*, August 1994.

8. Quote from Umar Cheema, *The News*, 2 May 2007. Six navy officers under the guidance of the Gurjati Faiz Hussain had planned to kill Ayub Khan and assume power.

9. Altaf Gauhar, "How Intelligence Agencies Run our Politics," *The Nation*, 17 August 1997.

10. Altaf Gauhar (1998), p. 320.

11. Ibid., p. 321. Another version of this event exists, in which the author of Operation Gibraltar is President Ayub Khan. He instructed the deputy ISI chief Brigadier Jan to plan the operation, while ISI Chief Brigadier Riaz was not informed. Later on Ayub Khan feigned his ignorance and tried to conceal his authorship. ISI chief Riaz opposed the concept of Operation Gibraltar, arguing that no insurgency operation could succeed without preparations. His affront was so great that he wanted to dismiss his deputy Jan, but was not permitted to do so. Director of MI Brigadier Irshad initially sided against Operation Gibraltar, but when he realised that Ayub Khan was the author, he supported it.

12. Operation Grand Slam brought the use of force to the internationally recognised border between India and Pakistan. Originally it was intended as one of several additional options for a successful Operation Gibraltar. Their goal was the disruption of road links between India and Kashmir, with specific objectives being the capture of a strategically important bridge at Akhnur and the conquest of Rajauri. After Operation Gibraltar proved a failure, Grand Slam was supposed to relieve the troops in Kashmir.

13. Ibid., p. 318.

14. *Herald*, August 1994.

15. Altaf Gauhar, "How Intelligence Agencies Run our Politics," *The Nation*, 17 August 1997.

16. One lakh is 100,000 rupees. One US$ is currently 105 rupees.

17. Haqqani (2005), p. 59.

18. Ibid., p. 61.

19. Gauhar, ibid. Maj. Gen. Rao Farman Ali was from 1970 Advisor to the Governor of East Pakistan. In this capacity during the elections in the 1970s he promoted the Jamaat-e-Islami, whose militant branch Al-Badar was responsible for the killing of numerous Bengali intellectuals. The general, who died in 2005, is known by his critics even today as the architect of this persecution and killings.

20. Winchell (2003), p. 377.

21. See Ziring (1997), here quoted in Altaf Gauhar, ibid.

22. Manekshaw was the Indian Army chief.

23. Arif (1995), p. 32.

24. Jilani Khan was a major-general when he was made DG ISI. Bhutto promoted him in 1972 to a three-star general.

25. Andrew/Mitrokhin (2005), p. 341.
26. Indo-Soviet Treaty of Peace, Friendship and Cooperation.
27. The headquarters of Eastern Naval Command of the Indian Navy is located in Vizag, the fourth largest port of the country, located in Andhra Pradesh on the Indian east coast.
28. The movement led by Charan Singh Panchi, in exile in London, the name of which was later changed to the Khalistan Movement, led by Jagjit Singh Chauhan.

3. ZULFIKAR ALI BHUTTO 1971–1977

1. Ikram Sehgal, "Intelligence happenings," *The Nation*, 24 November 1991.
2. Balochistan remains politically volatile to this day and the ISI sees the hand of India's R&AW agency in seeking to destabilise the province. In response to a request from the author, in August 2015 the ISI sent him a policy statement on alleged Indian involvement in Balochistan. See Appendix 1.
3. The Baluchistan Dehi Mahafiz (BDM) was one of the recruited civilian police forces of the Home Ministry in Quetta and consisted of 1,100 political loyalists.
4. The discovery of the arms was due to Major Shahid Tirmizi, then attached to the ISI. In his career, he would later make it up to three-star general.
5. Wolpert (1993), p. 161.
6. Unpublished manuscript, "The Shadow War—The Great Game replayed," Preface, p. 3, which was shown to the author in March 2002.
7. Ibid.
8. Quoted from Wolpert (1993), p. 263. Chishti resigned from the Army in March 1980 having expected a promotion; its non-appearance perhaps affected his opinion of Zia.
9. Statement by the Pakistani historian Professor Dr Aslam Syed to the author in June 2004.
10. Anwar (1998), p. 11.
11. K. M. Arif (1995), p. 44.
12. Tirmarzi (1995), p. 44.
13. Haqqani (2005), p. 114.
14. Local observers estimated that about 35 to 40 constituency results had been manipulated.
15. Arif (1995), p. 78.
16. Tirmazi (1995), p. 34.
17. Arif, ibid., p. 71.
18. Haqqani (2005), p. 115.
19. Arif (2005), p. 86.
20. Shaikh (2000), p. 79.
21. Arif (1995), p. 93.
22. Wolpert (1993), p. 302.
23. Prof. Aslam Syed to the author, August 2004.
24. *Newsline*, October 1992, p. 25.
25. Shortly before his own death, Justice Dorab Patel, one of the three judges who declared Bhutto not guilty in the legal proceedings (four judges charged him guilty), in an interview in 1994 called the verdict "a judicial slaughter of Bhutto."

4. AN INTERIM BALANCE SHEET OF 30 YEARS, 1948–1977

1. Akhund (2000), p. 136.
2. Quote from Asghar Khan (2005), p. 287.
3. Liaquat Ali Khan was killed on 16 October 1951 in Rawalpindi by an Afghan refugee living in Pakistan.
4. *Newsline*, October 1992, p. 25.
5. Jones (2002), p. 228, expounds: "That Bhutto used the FSF to scare his opponents is beyond dispute, but establishing the extent of the force's excesses is difficult. Certainly, at the time, many Pakistanis believed that the organization was routinely carrying out murders, and leading independent historians have concluded that the FSF was involved in several incidents in which Bhutto's political enemies were harassed and even killed."
6. The first Director General of FSF was Haq Nawaz Tiwana, soon replaced by the more rugged and more experienced Masood Mahmood, who became a confidant of Bhutto and later became "approver ... whose evidence would help send Bhutto to the gallows." (Wolpert, 1993, p. 223).

5. THE ISI UNDER ZIA-UL-HAQ, 1977–1988

1. *Newsline*, October 1992, p. 25.
2. Quoted from Abbas Nasir, "The Inside Story," *Herald*, January 1991, p. 29.
3. K. M. Arif (1995), p. 109. Arif, who under Ayub Khan gained work experience in the CMLA, himself became PSO and as Zia's Chief of Staff one of the closest assistants of the military dictator.
4. Tirmazi (1995), pp. 13 and 311.
5. For information on American–Pakistani relations, 1947–2000, see Kux (2001).
6. Ibid.
7. Global Policy Forum, "Al-Qaeda and the War on Terrorism," www.globalpolicy.org/empire/terrorwar/analysis/2008/0120history.htm.
8. Yousaf appointed Mark Adkin as his co-author, a former major in the Royal Anglian Regiment. Adkin was stationed in Germany, Malaysia, Mauritius and Aden. After his active military service he had several years in the Overseas Civil Service, and finally five years as contract officer for the Barbados Defence Force. While he was the Caribbean Operation Staff Officer he participated in the US invasion of Grenada in 1983.
9. Raza Ali, "The Shadow War" (unpublished manuscript), p. 3.
10. Ibid., introduction, pp. 5ff.
11. Kux (2001), p. 246.
12. Similarly seen by Agha Shahi, Secretary in the Foreign Office. The future Minister for Foreign Affairs felt the Soviet Army's invasion of Afghanistan was a simple act of aggression and as such could not be accepted.
13. Raza Ali, ibid.
14. Yousaf (1991), p. 32.
15. Yousaf/Adkin (1992), p. 22.
16. Tirmazi (1995), p. 344.

17. Raza Ali, ibid.
18. Yousaf (1997), p. 27.
19. Ibid., p. 29.
20. "White Book—Pakistan's subversive activities against the Afghan revolution," Kabul, 1984, pp. 48ff.
21. *US News and World Report*, Washington, 16 June 1986, p. 30.
22. *Chalees* means forty, referring to the Prophet's forty companions.
23. Julius Mader (1988), pp. 47ff.
24. Peterzell (1984), p. 9.
25. Ibid., p. 12.
26. In 1987 some Stingers fell into Russian and Iranian hands.
27. Yousaf (1992), p. 207. The statement of an old ISI hand contradicts that of the author. According to him Akhtar Rehman maintained immense influence over the ISI until his death; up to August 1988 Hamid Gul was in reality only Rehman's deputy.
28. These were the 107mm Chinese single-barrelled rocket launcher SBRL and the 122mm Egyptian rocket launcher.
29. Yousaf (1992), p. 189.
30. Interview with Syed Raza Ali in March 2004.

6. TURBULENCE AT THE END OF THE 1980s

1. In interviews a Pashtun described his people as follows: "likes freedom, money, religion—loyalty goes first to the tribe!"
2. Interview with Hamid Gul in March 2005 in Rawalpindi. Gul's statement is unreliable. According to former military personnel, during his ISI tenure Gul favoured Hekmatyar as he had the best infrastructure for the distribution of weapons. Years later he admitted being influenced by the Jamaat-e-Islami in giving preference to Hekmatyar.
3. Yousaf (1992), p. 206.
4. According to different sources, there were up to 30,000 various rockets in Ojhri Camp.
5. Another reason for Junejo's dismissal was that he was growing in stature and had questioned Zia's choice of promotions to three-star rank. Zia used to recommend people in his capacity as COAS, and then approved them as President, but this had to be routed through the Prime Minister, and Junejo began asking questions. In 1985 Zia recommended Major General Pirdad Khan for promotion, but bypassed Major General Shamin Alam. Pirdad was commander of the Frontier Constabulary of the Northern Areas (FCNA) when Indian troops occupied Siachen. Shamin Alam, on the other hand, had an unblemished record. By way of compromise, both were promoted. Shamin Alam made four stars before retiring as CJCSC.
6. K. M. Arif (1995, pp. 394–5) writes that, as DG ISI, Akhtar got the ISI to bug the telephone calls of Zia's daughter and submitted the tapes to the President as IB schemes, allegedly authorised by Junejo. The constantly distrustful President suggested that the PMPrime Minister should spy on him through the IB. Manufactured photographs from the ISI showing the arrival and departure of visitors' cars to the President served the same purpose. Akhtar's avowed goal was the resignation of Prime Minister Junejo.

7. In particular, reference is made here to the wealth accumulated by Zia-ul-Haq and Akhtar Rehman in the 1980s.

8. On 29 May 1988 Zia dismissed Junejo, dissolved parliament and set up a caretaker government with some ministers but no Prime Minister. The Senate, the second parliament chamber, continued to function further with Ghulam Ishaq Khan as President.

9. The background to this theory is that in 1988 a rebellion by Shiites occurred in Gilgit, the suppression of which led to hundreds of deaths. By 1977 a majority of Shiites settled in the Kurram agency in FATA and the Northern Areas (Gilgit and Baltistan). Starting from 1977 the government increasingly settled Sunni Muslims here. There were rebellions by the Shiites in 1983, 1988, 1996 as well as in April and November 2007 against this policy. Zia-ul-Haq crushed the 1988 unrest, spilling blood and leading to acts of revenge by the Shiites.

10. Quoted from Khalid Hasan, "The Zia-ul-Haq murder mystery," *Friday Times*, 16–22 June 2006, p. 9. A summary by Hasan brings out all the current well-known and accessible aspects of the incident. Among other things he refers to comments by Maj. Gen. (retd.) Mahmud Ali Durrani, then an observer at the crash and later Pakistan's ambassador to Washington, who nullifies John Gunther Dean's accusations of Israeli involvement as far-fetched.

11. A. K. Verma, "Siachen: An Episode to Remember," South Asia Analysis Group, paper 1859, 26 June 2006.

12. *New York Times*, 22 May 1991, here quoted from A. K. Verma. The then *NYT* correspondent Barbara Crosette reported from South Asia and the UN.

13. Former Pakistan Air Forces chief Air Marshal (retd.) Zulfiqar Ali Khan in a discussion with the author in 2005.

14. The opinion of Air Vice Marshal (retd.) Mian Sadruddin, former F-104 starfighter pilot and flight instructor, in discussion with the author in 2005. For example as a cause of error he considers it possible that the hydraulic link was blocked by moving luggage: three crates of mangoes were brought on board shortly before take-off and could have slipped to cause a hydraulic blockage. Alternatively the passanger capsule inside the plane could also have slipped due to inproper installation and the shearing of the bolts holding it in place.

15. Khalid Hasan, ibid. However, Durrani was also at the scene of the catastrophe.

16. A similar tragedy is the death of two Americans who wanted to fly back from Bahawalpur to Karachi in their own plane but were persuaded by Zia to accompany him aboard his flight up to Rawalpindi.

17. According to other sources there were five battalions that the ISI trained for Hekmatyar.

18. See Coll (2004), p. 192.

19. Quote from a text delivered by Beg in a talk to officers at the army auditorium in Rawalpindi, 28 January 1991.

20. Ibid.

21. Beg's remarks in discussion with the author, April 2007.

7. AN INTERNAL POLITICAL SCENARIO, 1988–1991

1. Arif (1995), p. 399.

2. Lt. Gen. Shamir Alam, who as CGS participated in the armed tanks demonstration, communicated, "No need to come—all ashes."

3. Accompanying Beg among others was Major General Jahangir Karamat, who years later became COAS.

4. Abbas (2005), p. 133.

5. According to Beg he had explained to his division commander that the army had done all it could and now a political process was required in order to save the situation. The commander's reply had been "Get Out."

6. Interview with Beg in April 2005 in Rawalpindi. According to Beg, in April 1988 Zia-ul-Haq asked him to prepare a report on the political development of the country. Beg once again recommended that Pakistan should quickly be led back to democracy. Zia laughed and answered, "You don't know what all the problems are."

7. Abbas (2005), p. 136. The informative book is written in a friendly tone towards the Bhuttos, thus the description of Beg is not the praise of a party loyalist.

8. Zahid Hussain, "General Glasnost: A Final Salute?" *Newsline*, August 1991, p. 39.

9. Imranullah Khan was Commander of the 10th Corps in Rawalpindi; Imtiaz Warraich and Jehangir Karamat belonged to GHQ; Hamid Gul was ISI chief.

10. Arif (1995), pp. 402–3. From 1977 General K. M. Arif belonged to the closest staff around Zia until he obtained his fourth star in 1984 and was appointed Vice-COAS.

11. On 29 May 1988 Zia-ul-Haq had recalled Junejo's government and dissolved the National Assembly and the four Provincial Assemblies.

12. Adnan Adil, "Beg: The Inside Story," *Newsline*, February 1993, p. 28.

13. Benazir Bhutto *vs*. Federation of Pakistan, Constitutional Petition 2 R-1987, dated 2 June 1988.

14. Quoted from Arif (1995), p. 397.

15. In Pakistan until the end of the 1990s the "establishment" was largely understood as the state bureaucracy, which was predominantly structured and trained according to the British colonial model. Since Ayub Khan's time, it had largely reflected the wishes of the military and the large feudal landlords, and shaped and decided on essential issues, albeit according to its preferences. After the takeover by General Musharraf in 1998, however, the "establishment" shifted to mean the military alone.

16. Muhammed Ali Shaikh (2000), p. 110.

17. Present were the IJI leader Ghulam Mustafa Jatoi, the caretaker chief ministers of the four provinces, Minister for Interior Akhtar Ali G. Kazi, Professor Ghafoor Ahmed of the Jamaat-e-Islami, and the DG ISI Hamid Gul.

18. IJI = Islamic Democratic Alliance.

19. *Herald*, August 1994, p. 42. In *Newsline*, the second largest political monthly magazine in Pakistan, Gul was quoted as follows: "It was necessary to create a countervailing force to the PPP; otherwise democracy could not have been restored."

20. *Herald*, January 2001, p. 43.

21. *Newsline*, October 1992, p. 28.

22. The PPP obtained 93 seats, against 54 for the IJI, and the seats for the minorities amounted to the ratio of 7:2. Altogether the parliament had 207 seats, so coalition arrangements were necessary with smaller parties and independent parliamentarians.

23. Shaikh (2000), p. 120.

24. It was soon whispered that General Aslam Beg had ambitions on the Presidential office. According to the Constitution, such an intention would only be possible two years after retirement from the military service.

25. Shaikh, ibid.

26. List according to Iqbal Haider in a discussion in Karachi in 2005.

27. PNCA consisted of five members: the President, Prime Minister, COAS, Director Kahuta Research Laboratories and Chairman Pakistan Atomic Energy Commission. The respective meetings were chaired by the President and Prime Minister together.

28. Quoted from Khalid Hassan, "Benazir took power 1988 under deal with army: CIA," *Daily Times*, Lahore, 3 July 2007.

29. Akhund (2000), p. 138.

30. Interview with Agha Shahi in Islamabad, March 2004.

31. Still under Zia, Hamid Gul met with his Indian counterpart in R&AW, A. K. Verma, in Amman and Geneva. The meeting came at the suggestion of the then Jordanian Crown Prince Hasan bin Talal, whose wife was from Pakistan. The topics discussed were Khalistan and Siachen, but concrete results were not forthcoming.

32. Abbas (2005), p. 137.

33. Kallue was a comrade of Imtiaz Ali Khan in the Army school of war. Both of them came from the armoured division and were friends. Benazir might have selected Kallue as DG ISI on recommendations from her Defence Adviser.

34. Maleeha Lodhi and Zahid Hussain, "Pakistan's invisible Government," *Newsline*, October 1992, pp. 22–3.

35. Quote from a contemporary witness in *Newsline*, ibid., p. 29.

36. Ibid.

37. In secondary sources such as newspapers the two are often referred to as Brigadier Imtiaz Billa and Major Amir.

38. Quoted from Khaled Ahmed, *Friday Times*, Lahore, 1–7 June 1995, p. 9.

39. *Newsline*, August 1992, p. 70.

40. *Newsline*, October 1992, p. 37.

41. Ibid., p. 33.

42. Imtiaz and Aamer did not make statements concerning this in the investigation proceedings, therefore COAS Beg, even had he wanted to, could not wield any measures against Gul.

43. Ibid., p. 37.

44. *Friday Times*, vol. XII, no. 48.

45. Quoted from *The Nation*, Lahore, 21 November 2005.

46. *Newsline*, October 1992, p. 38.

47. See also Altaf Gauhar (1998), p. 20.

48. *Newsline*, ibid., p. 38.

49. *Herald*, January 2001, p. 49.

50. General Imtiaz died in 2003.

51. *Herald*, January 2001, p. 44.

52. A summary of the Commission's report can be found in the Appendix.

53. Maleeha Lodhi and Zahid Hussain, "Pakistan's Invisible Government," ibid.
54. Discussion with Aslam Beg in Rawalpindi, April 2007.

8. THE ISI AND NAWAZ SHARIF, 1990–1993

1. Interview with Aslam Beg.
2. ACR = Annual Confidential Report, the evaluation report of the officers which was a condition for possible promotions and advancements.
3. The Pakistani contingent consisted of 10,000 non-combatants.
4. Interview with Aslam Beg in Rawalpindi, April 2007.
5. Ibid.
6. Ibid.
7. Haqqani (2005), p. 200.
8. *Herald*, June 1991, p. 24.
9. *Newsline*, 1991, p. 42.
10. Interviews with Beg, Rawalpindi (2003, 2004 and 2005).
11. Taken from a statement by Beg to the author in 2006.
12. In a discussion with the author in April 2005, Gul played down these contacts. The Afghans offered their condolences on the death of his daughter; the second time Afghans visited was as guests at military manoeuvres in Pakistan where Gul was the adjudicator.
13. In all fairness it must be mentioned that Asif Nawaz tried to reach a modus vivendi with Hamid Gul and to transfer him for the rest of his Army tenure. He sent no fewer than four letters to Gul in which he wrote: "my old friend, please don't let me down."
14. *Herald*, June 1991, p. 24.
15. Discussion with Ross Masood Hussain, founding director of the Institute of Strategic Studies Islamabad, in 2007.
16. Durrani had already started reforming the MI and had laid the foundation for the Corps Military Intelligence (CMI) as it exists today.
17. Discussion with Durrani in Rawalpindi, April 2005.
18. Statement by a former ISI member to the author.
19. Durrani later vehemently denied these meetings (discussion with Durrani, 2008).
20. See Coll (2004), p. 218.
21. Ibid., p. 220.
22. The Army's Promotion Board had already decided on Durrani's promotion at the end of 1991.
23. A witness later explained to the author that "within months of his assuming office, Asif became disillusioned with Sharif." In Army circles it was commonly rumoured that he was planning a coup.
24. Quote from General Mirza Aslam Beg to the author.
25. According to Iqbal Haider, minister in the second Benazir Bhutto cabinet and expert on the Karachi political scene, "Altaf Hussain was created, trained and equipped by the ISI."
26. For example in 1995 the official number of dead stood at 2,000, including those killed by the security forces.
27. Verkaaik (2004), p. 83.

28. From the outset, the assistance for the formation of the Haqiqi group was an open secret. The DG ISI Javed Nasir, who took over the post from March 1992, later openly claimed for himself the sponsorship and the temporary heyday of the MQM-Haqiqi.

29. More than two dozen accusations were raised against Altaf Hussain

30. *Herald*, January 1993, p. 56a.

31. Koch (2005), p. 213. According to Koch, the North Koreans functioned as wholesale dealers for the Russians. For this isolated country, international arms traffic represented the only source of lucrative foreign exchange.[32] In the Pakistani embassy in Pyongyang was 3rd Secretary Capt. (retd.) Shafqat Cheema, acting liaison officer of the ISI 1992–6, who also occasionally officiated as ambassador. The captain, with help from Col. (retd.) Ghulam Sarwar Cheema, a relative and well-known PPP politician, joined the ISI and was sent to North Korea. When he returned to Pakistan, there was a preliminary investigation against him in the ISI Directorate. Shafqat Cheema fled to Xinjang in west China where he sought political asylum. Because of cooperation with Pakistan in the fight against their insurgent Uyghurs, Beijing extradited him, but his fate afterwards is unknown.

33. Javed Nasir supplied some information about this later when he sued the Pakistani daily *The News*. According to Indian intelligence reports, Javed Nasir flew twice to Bosnia.

34. Dhar (2006), p. 284.

35. Quoted from Amit Baruah, "U.S. came close to declaring Pakistan a 'terrorist' State in 1992," in *The Hindu*, New Delhi, 30 April 2006. Baruah cites Haqqani, who is now in the US after his former services for Benazir Bhutto, Nawaz Sharif and Pervez Musharraf.

36. Ibid.

37. Ibid., p. 249.

38. In fact President Ghulam Ishaq Khan and COAS Waheed had asked Nawaz Sharif to recall Javed Nasir before. Initially he refused, but at the same time assured them he would control Nasir's activities more strictly in future.

39. Zhob, the former Fort Sandeman, lies in northern Balochistan close to the border with Afghanistan.

40. Iftikhar Ali Khan wanted his own promotion delayed so that he would be the most senior nominee for the COAS post when Kakar's successor retired. Waheed Kakar favoured Ali Quli Khan and transferred Iftikhar against his wishes.

41. Army chief Waheed Kakar made no friends in either the PML or the PPP camp in his dismissal of Nasir and Durrani. Javed Nasir was a close friend of Sharif's father, at the time when Sharif was still firmly under his father's thumb. In Asad Durrani's case the PPP camp lost a valuable confidant and advisor. A former military member later commented to the author on the reaction in the Army towards the situation: "Javed Nasir's dismissal was widely welcomed by senior officers but Durrani had a considerable following within the army."

42. Maleeha Lodhi, "The ISI's New Face," *Newsline*, May 1993, p. 56.

43. Ibid.

44. In a GEO TV program on 30 April 2006 the former caretaker Prime Minister Mir Balakh Sher Mazari protested that Javed Nasir's dismissal was unwarranted. It was not because of the US but "many brotherly Islamic countries complained that he was harbouring terrorists

and was using them to enable the ISI to make trouble in those countries." Mazari alleged that he informed the President and the COAS of his intention to remove the DG ISI. Both agreed and after a few days Waheed Kakar sent him a list of four potential successors, from which he selected Lt. Gen. Ashraf as the new ISI chief. Khaled Ahmed ironically commented on Mazari's remarks in the *Daily Times* 18 July 2006: "This was breaking news that no one noticed. Everyone in Pakistan thought bearded General Javed Nasir was thrown out because of his Islamic zeal and his reckless adventures in India in 1993. Now it develops that the "brother" states of the Islamic world were more upset with him and wanted his scalp."

45. Lodhi, ibid., p. 57.
46. Ibid.
47. Remarks from Aslam Beg to the author.
48. Lodhi, ibid.
49. The Ojhri Camp was a transit depot where weapons and ammunitions flown into Rawalpindi were stored before they went by truck towards Afghanistan. On that fateful day 200 trucks were parked in the camp and numerous people were at work. The fire broke out where gunpowder was stored; it quickly spread and ignited ammunition and rockets. TNT did not explode, otherwise the disaster would have being substantially worse. In the camp there was no fire-fighting equipment because, as was later explained, Ojhri was designed as only a temporary storage facility. In the first 24 hrs after the fire, no one entered the burning camp. Fire brigades were called to assist from 300 km away and used tanks to flood the camp, which was located on a slope. On the second day of the disaster Javed Nasir was deployed as director of the rescue operation. Nasir instructed his people to pray and to put on the Muslim mourning shroud. Afterwards, he was the first person to enter the camp to save what had not yet burned or exploded.
50. Comments by Javed Nasir to the author in Lahore, 2005.
51. Ibid.
52. *Washington Post*, "Attacking Iran May Trigger Terrorism," 2 April 2006.
53. Javed Nasir, ibid.

9. HISTORY REPEATS ITSELF

1. The alleged so-called Surrey mansion scandal should also be mentioned here. It concerned the purchase of a luxury house south of London by Benazir Bhutto and Zardari.
2. In the vehicle was a brigadier and Qazi Saifullah Ahktar, the Amir of HUJI.
3. Maloy Krishna Dhar, then Joint Director of the Indian Intelligence Bureau, had observed Abbasi receiving military documents from an Indian Army officer in a hotel lobby in New Delhi.
4. Abbasi and Musharraf were friends; as brigadiers they were stationed in the northern areas at the same time. According to unproved Indian claims, the rebels wanted to offer Musharraf the Presidency after the successful coup.
5. *Dawn*, 12 March 1997.
6. Iqbal Akhund (2000), p. 298.
7. Ibid., pp. 299–300. What Akhund omitted to mention was that during Benazir's first term Zardari was known as "Mr Ten Percent", which significantly contributed towards the fall of her government.

8. Zahid Hussain, "Targeting the President," *Newsline*, June 1994, p. 27. A former military witness later commented to the author that "indeed my impression was also that she learnt only this one lesson: steer clear of the army. However, she unlearned the lesson she began her first term with: provision of good governance."

9. Quoted from B. Raman, "A revamp of Pakistani Intelligence Community is underway," *SAPRA*, 18 December1998.

10. Apart from General Rafaqat, the election cell base in the Presidency contained other top bureaucrats like Roedad Khan, Ijlal Zaidi and Chaudhry Shaukat.

11. While Beg explained that the money was never in his possession and he had immediately forwarded it, rumours soon circulated that he had kept more than half for himself. Even after Beg's version was later confirmed by GHQ, the accusations lingered; so the goal of damaging his reputation had been achieved.

12. Quoted by K. N. Daruwalla in Sharma (2001), p. 129. The question here is whether there was a higher authority than the Army chief at that time.

13. Ibid., p. 130.

14. Interview with Durrani, April 2005.

15. Among them were Asif Zardari; opposition leader Nawaz Sharif; former Chief Minister of Sindh, Muzaffar Hussain Shah; PPP Chief Minister in NWFP, Altaf Ahmad Sherpao; Anwar Saifullah, Cabinet Minister under Benazir and son-in-law of former President Ghulam Ishaq Khan; V.A. Jaffery, financial advisor to the Prime Minister; and the retired generals Mirza Aslam Beg and Asad Durrani.

16. Zahid Hussain, "Targeting the President," *Newsline*, June 1994, p. 26.

17. The PML had the majority in the Senate and chose their candidate Wasim Sajjad as chairman.

18. Ikram Sehgal, "Intelligence Happenings," *The Nation*, Lahore, 24 November 2001. Indeed, Javed Qazi replaced almost all the Afghanistan experts with new and largely inexperienced individuals; according to his critics, one of them was Ikram Sehgal who would later have difficulties with the pre-programming of the Taliban in the ISI.

19. Interview with Javed Ashraf Qazi in Islamabad, March 2007.

20. Ibid.

21. Ibid.

22. The accused Omar Sheikh in the Daniel Pearl case was one of them.

23. B. Raman, "Daniel Pearl and the London Blasts," SAAG Paper no. 1458, 15 July 2005, wrote: "By then, the Arabs of Afghan vintage had already started creating mayhem across the world after the end of the Afghan Jehad. So, these agencies wanted to avoid the use of the Arabs in Bosnia. They turned to Pakistanis, particularly Pakistanis living in the UK and other countries of West Europe. Thus began the radicalization of the Muslim youth of Pakistani origin living in West Europe."

24. Ibid.

25. Dhar (2006), p. 286.

26. Ibid., p. 287. Here Dhar relies primarily on the observations by the Polish journalist Marek Popowsky, who belongs to SFOR and IFOR and travelled extensively in the Balkans.

27. The Amir Munawaid Camp developed by Hekmatyar in the 1980s was taken over by al-

Qaeda in the second half of the 1990s after Hekmatyar was dropped by the ISI. In Muridke near Lahore the training of the Chechens took place in the Markaz-al-Dawa-al-Irshad Camp.

28. Dhar (2006), p. 293. Former military and ISI personnel doubted or denied to the author that the ISI was involved. They thought it possible that individuals or former ISI could be involved.

29. See Ayesha Siddiqa, "The New Land Barons," *Newsline*, July 2006, p. 29 for an exact location of the properties. According to her, in principle every Army general at the time of their retirement possessed properties valued between 150 and 400 million rupees (US$ 2–6 million), and this is a cautious estimation.

30. Interview with Rana in Rawalpindi, spring 2005.

31. Ibid.

32. A former retired military officer gave this version of Murtaza's murder to the author: "My take on this is from a Sindhi Wadera as follows. You might recall that Zardari until September 1996 used to sport a rather magnificent moustache which suddenly disappeared in early September. This Sindhi Wadera, whom I will not name, claims he was present when Zardari was intimidated in the presence of Murtaza around September 10 or so, who was drunk. Zardari was terrified as Murtaza proceeded to abuse Zardari and some of his henchmen beat him up. Finally Murtaza ordered that one half of Zardari's moustache be shaved off as the ultimate humiliation. This Wadera asked permission of Murtaza to drop Zardari home. According to this Wadera (feudal lord) Zardari wept all the way home and swore on his mother that Murtaza would pay."

33. Statement by Shoaib Suddle, Deputy Inspector-General of Police, Karachi, quoted in the daily paper *Jang*, London, 10 October 1996.

34. Quoted from Raja Anwar (1998), p. 208.

35. For the establishment and progress of Al-Zulfikar, see Raja Anwar, *The Terrorist Prince*, Lahore, 1998. Anwar was advisor to Zulfikar Ali Bhutto, and after Bhutto's execution belonged to Murtaza's followers in Afghanistan. In Kabul, in October 1980, there was discord between them both. Murtaza was afraid that his experienced comrade would become a political competitor. According to Murtaza's wishes, and with the help of KHAD boss Najibullah, Raja Anwar spent until May 1983 in a Kabul prison. Anwar's book, although written to settle things with Murtaza Bhutto, is a very good source about Al-Zulfikar. The book was written in Urdu, translated into English in 1998 by Khalid Hassan, and published in Lahore.

36. Ibid., pp. 138–9.

37. In the second attempt, it was the pilot's quick thinking which saved the day.

38. Anwar (1998), p. 70.

39. B. Raman, SAAG paper no. 287. According to Raman, the poisoning of Murtaza's younger brother Shahnawaz Bhutto in 1985 in southern France must be attributed to the ISI as a reaction to the existence of Al-Zulfikar and their activities.

40. *Defence Journal*, Karachi, January 1999.

41. Coll (2004), p. 315.

42. The author lived with his family for over three years in Quetta, cheek by jowel with the concerned families, and had a close relationship with the male residents, who were all Pashtuns. Having been a guest in their houses, the author thinks it highly unlikely that Kansi was hid-

ing there. As the author and his family were only able to meet their neighbours' womenfolk after a couple of years, readers can imagine the shock and anger that was unleashed by the CIA–ISI actions.

10. FOREIGN POLICY AND THE ISI

1. *Herald*, December 2001, p. 48.
2. After the departure of the Soviet Army, many of them saw themselves God-appointed warriors in the fight against world communism. Also as an intelligence agency they estimated themselves far higher than their colleagues in CIA and KGB.
3. Quoted from Ahmed Rashid, "Coming in from the Cold," *Herald*, June 1993, p. 57.
4. Gul Hasan represented his country first in Vienna and afterwards in Athens. Rahim Khan became ambassador to Spain.
5. It is interesting that there was initial resistance in Riyadh to Durrani's posting. The Saudis were obviously not happy with the thought of having such an experienced intelligence expert as ambassador within their walls.
6. Karamat was again removed after approximately two years.

11. NAWAZ SHARIF, SECOND TIME AROUND, 1997–1999

1. Lt. Gen. Ali Kuli Khan, a Pashtun, was CGS in GHQ and seen as first in line for the COAS post. Corps Commander Lt. Gen. Khalid Nawaz, a Punjabi, stood in second place. Ali Kuli Khan was not acceptable to Nawaz Sharif because he was a protégé of Kakar, who had forced Sharif to resign in 1993. Lt. Gen. (retd.) Iftikhar Ali Khan opposed Khalid Nawaz. Iftikhar Khan was Secretary for Defence from May 1997 to October 1999 and had personal grounds against Khalid Nawaz, who as Quarter Master General (QMG) refused to change a plot allotted to Iftikhar. This finally led to appointing Musharraf as the new COAS.
2. Ziauddin had the following academic qualifications: Masters Degree in Strategic Studies; BSc (Hons) in War Studies; 1st Class Bachelor Degree in Physics and Mathematics; BSc (Hons. 1st Class) in Construction Engineering, receiving a gold medal for 1st place; Post Graduate Diploma in Topographic Engineering from Defence Mapping School (DMS), US. In his military career, apart from the mentioned commandership, he was also Private Secretary to COAS (as brigadier for three years), DG Combat Development of the Pakistan Army (as a major general) and Adjutant General in GHQ (as a lieutenant general).
3. CGS Lt. Gen. Aziz came from the Pakistan-controlled area of Kashmir (Azad Kashmir). Since his time in the ISI he had close connections with extremist organizations such as Harakat-ul-Mujaheddin/Harakat-ul-Ansar (HuM/HUA), Lashkar-e-Taiba (LeT) and Al Badr.
4. In particular Maj. Gen. Ghulam Ahmed Khan went against Ziauddin's leadership style and goals. He tried to tone down many of Ziauddin's arrangements and carried them out with the thought of a resignation. Musharraf made him a three-star general after the coup. The death of Ahmed Khan in a car accident on 24 August 2001 was a sad loss for Musharraf.
5. Coll (2004), p. 440. Steve Coll, a Pulitzer Prize winner in 1990 and 2005 and then managing editor of the *Washington Post*, obviously had good contacts with CIA sources.
6. The CIA had succeeded in setting up Afghan tracking teams, whose task was to ferret out Osama bin Laden and to monitor his movements.

7. Coll (2004), p. 442.

8. They were Corps Commanders Tariq Pervez and Saleem Hyder. Pervez was relieved of his post by Musharraf, and Hyder was made Master General Ordnance, or in other words he was neutralised. After the failure of Kargil, Prime Minister Nawaz Sharif wanted four generals to be sacked: apart from CGS Aziz and Commander X Corps Mehmood, these were Major Generals Tauqir Zia (DGMO) and Javed (Commander FCNA). Musharraf successfully resisted the government's wishes.

9. A widespread opinion in Pakistan today is that, due to the Kargil incident, the commanders had considered replacing Nawaz Sharif with his younger brother Shahbaz Sharif, who as Chief Minister in Punjab demonstrated successful leadership. The Prime Minister knew about this and tried to stop such a development with Musharraf's dismissal.

10. Soon after 12 October 1999 selective rumours were already in circulation that the group was primarily formed as a security force for Sharif and Ziauddin and the hunt for Osama bin Laden was secondary or a pretext; the truth probably lies in the middle.

11. Jones (2002), p. 47. Jones gives a detailed description of the events of the day. According to him, Ziauddin failed to become COAS because he was unable to replace the key positions of CGS and Commander X Corps. The majority of the three-star generals refused to agree to such a change in the absence of Musharraf.

12. The assassination took place three days before Raad's closing arguments. Four gunmen drew up in a car, and three of them stormed the office and shot the lawyer, his assistants and the landlord of the premises, who happened to be there.

13. The declaration from Acting PML President Javed Hashmi on 18 December 2000 that Saudi Arabia and the other Islamic countries paid US$ 83 million to Pakistan for the departure of the Sharif family still requires verification, but could well be possible.

14. On 13 December 2000 Musharraf explained that the Sharif brothers had been sent into a decade-long exile and there was no possibility of their return during this time.

15. In the opinion of observers, the appointment was only a small compensation for Ziauddin. During his arrest he was told to testify against Nawaz Sharif and that by doing so he would be permitted to retire with his pension and benefits intact. Ziauddin refused. A higher post, for example as Chair of the Punjab Public Service Commission, would have been more appropriate.

12. AFGHANISTAN IN THE 1990s

1. For an excellent overview of the situation see Ahmed Rashid (2000), p. 21. Rashid addressed a book-launch at the Institute for Strategic Studies in Islamabad in 2000 and encountered both intense criticism from conservative forces there as well as interested queries from the numerous diplomats present. The book was so well-received for its questions regarding Pakistan, its relationship with the Taliban in 2000 and the events of September 2001 that it became an international best-seller. From the quantity of literature published meanwhile on Afghanistan and the Taliban, reference should be made to Lt. Gen. (retd.) Kamal Matinuddin, *The Taliban* (2002); and Kathy Gannon, *I is for Infidel* (2005).

2. The northern, shorter route to Central Asia went from Peshawar via Jalalabad to Kabul, then through the Salang Tunnel to Mazar-e-Sharif and onwards through Tirmiz to Tashkent.

3. For this, Pakistan needed to muster US\$ 300 million from foreign donors.

4. Figures according to Rashid (2000), p. 28.

5. Ibid., p. 29.

6. Rabbani was the former number two of the Taliban, and later became Minister of Foreign Affairs.

7. Studying in madrasahs offered a way out of the dreary living conditions inside Afghanistan, since most madrasah heads supported the Talibs during their stay, in a bid to increase adherents to their particular sect.

8. B. Raman, "The Terrorist Pearl Harbour," South Asia Analysis Group Paper, 11 September 2001.

9. Abbas (2005), p. 195. Abbas recalled this in an interview he conducted with an ISI colonel.

10. Minister of Interior Babar had his input in the return of bin Laden from Sudan to Afghanistan in May 1996. At the suggestion of Burhanuddin Rabbani and in agreement with the ISI, he won Benazir Bhutto's consent to allow Osama bin Laden to travel through Pakistan to Jalalabad. The condition for bin Laden was not to act against the US or against Saudi Arabian interests in the future.

11. The Kashmiri Muhammad Aziz Khan had been CGS in the GHQ as a three-star general since the beginning of 1999. As such he stood by Musharraf in the unsuccessful Kargil affair; even today many people imply that he was the actual initiator of Kargil. Apart from Mahmud Ahmed, Commander X Corps in Rawalpindi, Aziz became Musharraf's most important supporter in his political *coup d'état* on 12 October 1999.

13. PUNJAB

1. Quote from K. P. S. Gill, "Endgame in Punjab: 1988–199," *Faultlines*, vol. 1, New Delhi, April 1999.

2. Quote from Kshitji Prabha (2000), p. 84.

3. It was a macabre political joke that Bhindranwale, who came from a humble background and who died in a hail of bullets in Operation Blue Star in 1984, was initially supported and developed by New Delhi, in other words R&AW, at the onset of his bloody career against the Akali Dal.

4. Prabha, ibid., p. 109.

5. The members of the Panthic Committee in Indian Punjab were selected from the Sikh groups of Akal Takht of Amritsar, Anandpur Sahib, Damdama Sahib, Patna Sahib and Nanded Sahib.

6. In Indian Punjab the Sikhs make up 60 percent of the population, whereas in Pakistan it is a tiny fraction.

7. Kshitij Prabha, ibid., p. 112.

8. Subheg Singh had made a name for himself as major general in 1971 as the trainer of the Mukhti Bahini. However, later accused of corruption and dismissed from the Army, he became the strategic head of the Sikh extremists. Amrik Singh was President of the All India Sikh Student Federation (AISSF).

9. Chand Joshi (1984), p. 24. Jarnail Singh Bhindranwale, seen by India as a prophet of terror, was the religious leader of the Khalistan movement.

10. Joshi, ibid., p. 161.

11. K. P. S. Gill, ibid., p. 51.

12. Ibid.

13. Babar Khalsa was regarded as the oldest and a well-organised Khalistan group. In the ISI, Waqar Ahmad was dealing with them. He organised the operation K2, which aimed at linking the drug smugglers in Mumbai with the terrorists in Punjab and Jammu and Kashmir. The operation was not successful as two of the key players, Manjit Singh and Mohammad Sharif, were quickly arrested. However Operation K2 was successful in the field of weapons smuggling. They managed to bring numerous weapons to Gujarat, India that were used in subsequent terrorism acts, like Mumbai in 1993 through the Rann of Kutch. See Swami (2007), p. 154.

14. Only at end of the 90's did the ISI's hand in hijacking become visible again. After the forced landing of an Indian plane, originating from Kathmandu, in Kandahar on 24 December 1999 the interaction between air piracy, the Taliban and ISI agents could not to be ignored.

15. Akali Dal was the prominent political party of the Sikhs.

16. Kashmeri and McAndrew (1989), p. 9.

17. Ibid., p. 45.

18. Ibid., back cover page. "Soft Target' is a synonym often used in intelligence circles for a target object which can be easily infiltrated.

19. Out of these, 60 of them were children under the age of 10. Among the passengers were 22 Americans, 160 Canadians and 100 Indians.

20. The experts' report regarding the crash came to the conclusion that the ignition of the bomb was adjusted to 25 minutes after the scheduled landing time.

21. By the time of the court case in 2005 two of the suspects were dead and one went successfully underground. Interesting is the case of Inderjit Singh Reyat, who on 10 May 1991 was sentenced for 10 years due to his participation in the terror attacks in Tokyo and Flight 182. In a second hearing, the sentence was reduced to five years. Reyat was supposed to be the principal witness in the case against Malik and Bagri. However, in court he could not remember anything.

22. Praveen Swami (2007), p. 153.

14. THE ISI IN NORTH-EAST INDIA

1. According Wikipedia the population in 2011 was 44,98 million or 3,7 per cent of India's total.

2. Besides this, ULFA established camps in south Bhutan and in the Samdruk Dzonkha area. In one of these bases, Indian authorities later found indications of previous ISI training activities.

3. NSCN and ULFA were not the only groups with camps in Bangladesh. NLFT, another underground group, had accommodation camps for its fighters and families there. Besides that, they maintained safe houses in Cox's Bazar, Chittagong and Dhaka. Other groups with bases in Bangladesh are the All Tripura Tiger Force (ATTF) and one that is registered in the Indian state of Meghalaya as Hynniewtrep National Liberation Council (HNLC).[2] See P.V. Ramana, "Networking the Northeast: Partners in Terror," *Faultlines*, vol. 11, New Delhi, 2002, p. 109.

4. Ibid.

5. Tara Kartha, *Tools of Terror: Light Weapons and Indian Security*, New Delhi: Knowledge World-IDSA, 1999, p. 260.
6. According to Indian findings, in 2001 NSCN possessed a fully-fledged liaison office on Chinese territory close to the border to Arunachal Pradesh.
7. The bank draft for this was issued "for unspecified goods."
8. Information from Sashinungla, "Nagaland: Insurgency and Factional Intransigence." *Faultlines*, vol. 16, New Delhi, January 2005, p. 95.
9. In reality, the expression "seven sisters" is incorrect; rather Assam is the mother of northeast India while the other six states are her descendants.
10. "ISI pumping counterfeit currencies into State," *Assam Tribune*, 25 February 2000.

15. STRUCTURE—PERSONNEL—BUDGET

1. Intelligence Resource Program Federation of American Scientists (www.fas.org).
2. Details of the structure in appendix.
3. See Musharraf (2006), p. 237. Musharraf's acknowledgement that the ISI took hundreds of millions of US$ as bounty, was foolish and counter-productive. In a discussion regarding Musharraf's recent memoirs *Into the Line of Fire*, a Pakistani critic also condemned the ISI as a "purely mercenary agency chasing up bounty money by handing over al-Qaeda suspects to the CIA circumventing all legal channels. Significantly, how many innocents are still being handed over to the CIA for money reasons outside the due process of law?" In the Urdu version of the book the relevant remarks were omitted, and Musharraf later admitted to having made an error here.
4. An organisational chart as at April 2010 given to the author by Indian sources is in the appendix.
5. This also applies to MI, regardless that COAS Kayani announced in September 2010 that the political cell had been closed. This explanation is for the previous announcement of a cash grant to the ISI in the amount of Pakistani rupees 5.5 billion in the financial year 2007–2008. So far the only explanation is that it was intended for operations. Obviously the declaration should counteract future MI abstinence in the questions of principle and legality of the payment to the ISI.
6. This covers Grade16 and above in the Internal Service Intelligence Bureau, the Pakistan Ordnance Factories and the ISI.
7. See 'Senate okays ISI recruitment bill, *The News*, 27 November 2004.
8. Every army corps has an intelligence battalion which has detachments at the divisional and occasionally at brigade level. During wartime it is in charge of battlefield intelligence. In peacetime it undertakes the observation of security and developments in their own ranks. Together the intelligence battalions build the so-called intelligence corps of the army.
9. In Paul Thompson, "Pakistani ISI and/or opium drug connections", Center for Cooperative Research 2002, (www.historycommons.org/timeline.htm), one could read: "Afghan opium production skyrockets from 250 tons in 1982 to 2,000 tons in 1991, coinciding with CIA support and funding of the mujahideen. Alfred McCoy, a professor of Southeast Asian history at the University of Wisconsin, says US and Pakistani intelligence officials sanctioned the rebels' drug trafficking because of their fierce opposition to the Soviets: "If their local allies

were involved in narcotics trafficking, it didn't trouble CIA. They were willing to keep working with people who were heavily involved in narcotics." For instance, Gulbuddin Hekmatyar, a rebel leader who received about half of all the CIA's covert weapons, was known to be a major heroin trafficker. The director of the CIA in Afghanistan claims later to be oblivious about the drug trade: "We found out about it later on.'"

10. Napoleoni (2004), p. 160.

11. In an interview a former army man commented that, "in fact, for a few years, CIA vehicles bringing in arms used to return with opium—as they did in Nicaragua. The ISI learnt very quickly."

12. B. Raman, "Heroin, Taliban and Pakistan", *SAAG* Paper, 6 August 2001.

13. *Detroit News*, 9/30/01.

14. B. Raman, "Heroin, Taliban and Pakistan", *SAAG* Paper, 6 August 2001.

15. Karzai offered US$500 bonus per acre of destroyed poppy plants, however the market proceeds to the farmers amounted to US$6,400.00 per acre.

16. THE ISI UNDER MUSHARRAF

1. The disappointment over the appointment as NDC commander was so great that Mahmood refused to receive congratulations from his comrades on the occasion of his promotion to a three-star general.

2. At a project demonstration by a brigadier at GHQ in 1998, Musharraf and Corps Commander Mahmood Ahmed appeared 40 minutes late; among those waiting patiently were CGS Aziz and DG ISI Ziauddin.

3. A good example is his well-known rude reprimand to the Information Minister Javed Jabbar in front of the Cabinet.

4. Mahmood had been in the US since 4 November 2001. The journey was a routine visit in the context of mutual relations. Supporters of the numerous conspiracy theories surrounding 9/11 try to insinuate that Mahmood consciously attempted to dissociate himself from the forthcoming assassination attempts through his US stay.

5. As a Lt. General, Yousaf was CGS. At the beginning of 1999 he replaced A. Khan, who was transferred to Corps Commander Lahore by Musharraf.

6. The post of the CJCSC rejected by Mahmood was taken up by Mohammad Aziz Khan in 2002; he was previously CGS and afterwards Commander IV Corps in Lahore.

7. The explanation given to the author was: "If you have been sacked over differences of policy, you don't accept jobs."

8. http://nsarchive.gwu.edu/NSAEBB/NSAEBB97/.

9. Mahmood travelled in the company of high-ranking Muslim clerics, three of them would die by September 2007 in political-religious motivated assassinations. They were Maulana Mohammad Hassan Jan, Mufti Nizamud Din Shamzai and Mufti Mohammad Jamil.

10. An exception was Peter Goss who as designate CIA chairman was able to meet him in August 2004 in Islamabad. The topic for discussion is said to have been international terrorism.

11. In the attack embassy buildings were destroyed and 15 people were killed.

12. From Great Britain approx. 200 Muslims of Pakistani descent went for training to Pakistan. They were trained in HUA camps and afterwards went on to strengthen the HUA contin-

gent in Bosnia. Both the British and American intelligence services were fully informed about this.

13. In May 2002 the *Washington Post* reported that as early as 1994 the ISI had paid for Sheikh's defense counsel in India.
14. Quote from Ridgeway, (2005), p. 144.
15. Manoj Joshi, *Times of India*, 9 October 2002.
16. *AFP* report, "India Accuses Ex Pakistan Spy Chief of Links to US Attacker", 11 September 2001, here quoted from James Ridgeway, (2005), p. 144. Ridgeway's book *The 5 Unanswered Questions About 9/11* elevates itself amongst the writings about the possible background of the 11 September attacks through objectivity and good research.
17. Reid was supposed to have received the order to carry out a suicide operation from the Lahore-based Jamaat-ul-Fuqra (JUF). The JUF leader in Pakistan was Ali Shah Gilani. Daniel Pearl had, among other things, the intention of interviewing this Gilani.
18. Pakistani authorities hinted after the murder of Pearl that he was a R&AW agent. If anything, Pearl would have had contacts to the CIA or Mossad. In fact, the ISI should have been more afraid that Pearl would acquire information about Dawood Ibrahim, who was living in Karachi.
19. The perpetrators were jehadis from Harkat-ul-Mujahideen (HUM) and Harkat-ul-Jehad-al-Islami (HUJI).
20. Bernard-Henri Lévy, *Qui a tué Daniel Pearl?* Paris, 2003.
21. Up till October 1998 Aziz was Deputy DG ISI and therefore responsible for the Taliban, the Harkat-ul-Mujahideen and for the Arab mercenaries.
22. B. Raman gets his information from his former working group. His reports in the South Asian Analysis Group (SAAG) appear to be well-founded, even if they are usually biased against Pakistan.
23. *South Asia Terrorism Portal*, 13 March 2002.
24. A listing of Sheikh's statements is in the Appendix.
25. Three more co-defendants were condemned to life imprisonment. Today it seems certain that Khalid Shaikh Mohammad was the one who committed the act and Sheikh was only an accomplice; however, they were all murderers.
26. B. Raman, in his South Asia Analysis Group
27. (SAAG) paper, no. 1458, 15 July 2005, "In the meanwhile, Omar Sheikh is as active as ever from the jail keeping in touch with Jehadi terrorists not only in South Asia, but also in the UK and other countries of Europe. Last year, through his lawyers and with the connivance of his jailers, he had statements disseminated all over Pakistan and Afghanistan condemning the US for the alleged desecration of the Holy Koran by the US guards at Guantanamo Bay in Cuba. Well-informed sources in Pakistan claim that two of the perpetrators of the London explosions of July 7, 2005, had met him in jail during their visit to Pakistan and that it was he who had motivated them to launch the terrorist strike in London."
28. Khalid Sheikh Mohammad is considered to be the chief architect of 9/11; Abu Faraj al-Libbi planned the assassination attempt on Musharraf in December 2003.
29. In "From BCCI to ISI" Abid Ullah Jan goes on to charge the ISI as an accomplice in the planning and execution of 9/11; however, he portrays the ISI as an ignorant victim of the CIA—a view which is laughed at, even in New Delhi.

30. Ridgeway (2005), p. 139.

31. Ibid.

32. Ibid.

33. For accuracy and fairness here, some evidence should be noted from a high-ranking former R&AW officer who told the author that the Indian authorities had a first notification of the US$ 100,000 transfer shortly after 9/11, when it was reported in a Pakistani Urdu newspaper. They researched further and presented the results to the Americans. Ehsan, who comes from Mardan, speaks Pashto. His family was active in the bazaar trade and thus he had no connection to Pashtun tribal structures.

34. For confirmation see a report in the *Frankfurter Allgemeine Zeitung* on 2 November 2001 which is absent any reference that Mahmood Ahmed could select his successor and settled on Ehsan ul Haq.

35. It is still unclear whether Washington's request to interview a number of these officers was carried out.

36. Quote from Muhammad Saleh Zaffir, *The News*, 6 October 2004.

37. In the following years, 2004–6, the ISI organised trips to Pakistan for small groups of journalists from Europe. A ten-day tour was arranged with meetings with ministers, parliamentarians, politicians, mullahs and also ISI representatives. Behind it all was the intention to abolish the negative image of Pakistan and to portray a friendlier picture of the country.

38. Pakistan Muslim League—Quaid-e-Azam.

39. LFO = Code of Conduct for Political Parties and Contesting Candidates for General Elections, 2002.

40. It was acknowledged that it was Ehsan who overcame Qazi Hussain's resistance against Musharraf's first visit to India in July 2001and therefore made the Agra summit possible.

41. The Federal Administered Tribal Areas (FATA) have a population of approximately 6 million. The area is divided into the Bajaur, Mohmand, Khyber, Orakzai, Kurram, North and South Waziristan agencies.

42. Intikhab Amir, "Whose Writ Is It Anyway?" *Herald*, April 2006, p. 81.

43. According to a high-ranking Pashtun, because of the incorrect situation assessment and advice given to Musharraf, the DG ISI is responsible for the loss of the Frontier Province to the mullahs.

44. Heading the Strategic Planning Division was Lt. Gen. Khalid Ahmed Kidwai who, together with Ehsan ul Haq, was instructed to bring the A. Q. Khan affair under control.

45. *The News*, Karachi, 5 May 2007 with reference to the dossier published by the London International Institute of Strategic Studies (IISS) on 2 May 2007 titled "Nuclear Black Markets: Pakistan, AQ Khan and the rise of proliferation—A net assessment."

46. Zahid Hussain wrote in *Newsline* in October 2004: "The retirement of General Aziz Khan has removed the last of Musharraf's accomplices in the coup, while the exit of Lt. General Javed Hassan has put the Kargil legacy to rest... General Ahsan Saleem Hayat is considered close to General Musharraf and his appointment to the second-most important position did not come as a surprise.... General Ehsan ul-Haq, the new Chairman Joint Staff Committee, has been a key member of General Musharraf's decision making coterie. He was made head of ISI following the October 2001 purge. His position assumed even greater significance as

the premier spy agency became a major instrument in the hunt for Al-Qaeda fugitives. Compared to his predecessors, Haq maintains a low profile, despite his high profile job."

47. Among those involved was a low-ranking member of the elite troop SSG. The remainder came from the Islamic crowd. A military court sentenced five of the perpetrators to death. The judgments have been only partially carried out.

48. Therefore, among other things, he was responsible for the hotline to the Indian leadership in the military operations sector.

49. Interviews by the author in Rawalpindi and Islamabad, March 2007.

50. According to data received from human rights organizations, more than 1,000 people had disappeared since 2001. Intelligence services and police argued over who is involved. However, according to Asma Jehangir of the HRCP there is concrete evidence that federal agencies were involved and many of those arrested were brutally tortured; *Daily Times*, 6 October 2007. Those released later stated that they were in military detention.

51. A plausible explanation was offered by a former Army member. Apparently during the Lal Masjid episode Musharraf told Kayani in March 2007, "Stay out of this matter. It is none of your business."

52. Roger Faligot, "Pakistan: the hidden side of the attack on the Red Mosque," *Rue 89, Votre Revolution de L'Info*, 8 October 2007.

53. Ibid.

54. After the arrest of Khalid Sheikh Mohammad on 1 March 2003, Abu Faraj al-Libbi became the new number three of al-Qaeda. Among other things he was responsible for planning the assassination attempts on Musharraf in December 2003 as well as the attack on the Prime Minister designate Shaukat Aziz in 2004.

17. THE TROUBLED VALLEY: KASHMIR

1. The Pandits in the Kashmir valley made up approx. 4 percent of the population. The data on the number of the Kashmiri Pandits vary; the authorities estimate that 250,000 of them became refugees.

2. Robert Gates, who later became head of the CIA, visited Pakistan and later referred to thirty-one such camps (*The Nation*, Lahore, 13 June 1990).

3. Lashkar-e-Taiba (LeT) is considered to be the military arm of Markaz Dawa wal'Irshad (Center for Proselyzation and Preaching), established by Professor Hafiz Mohammad Saeed. Its main office is in Muridke near Lahore. Over the years LeT has called openly for donations to the Kashmir Jehad. Prof. Hafiz Mohammad Saeed led a rally in Karachi, proclaiming, "There can't be any peace while India remains intact. Cut them, cut them." The Indian paper *The Pioneer* wrote on 1 January 2003: "The Lashkar-e-Taiba is buying land across Pakistan, especially in Sind and Punjab to expand its base. Hafiz Saeed, not long ago kept under house arrest, is busy touring the country gathering support, recruits and funds for his terrorist ambitions in Kashmir and elsewhere in India."

4. Attested connections exist with Khalid Sheikh Mohammad. Besides, the Jaish-e-Mohammad members were involved in the kidnapping of the journalist Daniel Pearl.

5. Observers speak of 5,000 to 8,000 fighters who had been through the camps in Azad Kashmir.

6. See Imtiaz Alam, "Banning the banned," *The News*, 17 November 2003: "Re-emergence of

former Tehrik-iJafaria, Sipah-i-Sahaba Pakistan, Jaish-i-Mohammed and Lashkar-i-Taiba with new names only showed the limits of legalistic measures against very well organised and firmly rooted militant outfits.... Keeping Jamaatul-Dawa on watch and letting All Parties Hurriyat Conference divide in favour of one faction, however, show, how far away we are from reviewing a wrong policy."

7. Figures as at 2007. According to data from a German South Asian expert, between 1988 and 1996 the losses in the Kashmir civil war stood at 13,000 civilians, 1,800 military personnel and 7,000 rebels; among the latter were 400 foreigners, mainly from Afghanistan. The number of arrested fighters was 25,000 and an additional 2,500 surrendered. The number of seized weapons was sufficient to equip more than one infantry division. Dietrich Reetz, "Optionen für Indien und Pakistan in Kaschmir," in *Indien 2000*, published by Draguhn, Hamburg.

8. Indian politicians repeatedly refer to the fact that in today's India there are as many Muslims residing there as in Pakistan.

9. The Indus Basin's river system originates in the Himalayas and descends to the Arabian Sea in the south; it supplies approx. 450,000 square miles, equal to the total land area of Germany, France and Italy. See Rene Klaff, "Wasser-Konfrontation oder Kooperation," in *Der Induswasserkonflikt*, published by Jörg Barandat, Nomos Verlag, Baden-Baden.

10. On 19 September 1960 the Indus Water Agreement was signed in Karachi by Ayub Khan, Jawaharlal Nehru and a representative of the World Bank. It regulates the allocation of the right to use the Indus water system. The Indus, over 3,000 km in length, is one of the longest rivers of the world. Its two most important tributaries are the Kabul River and the Kurram, both originating in Afghanistan. In the water dispute between India and Pakistan, they play no role. More contentious are the western tributaries of the Jhelum, Chenab, Ravi, Sutlej and Beas. The Sutlej originates in Tibet, the Jhelum in Indian Kashmir. The sources of the remaining three lie in the India Himalayan region.

11. Therefore there are differences in opinion between both states over the building of a new hydroelectric power station on the Indian side. Islamabad accuses New Delhi of exceeding its rights of use here.

12. On 1 November 1989 the JI-founded Hizbul Mujahidin, which was considered to be a purely Kashmiri organization and for this reason was not blacklisted by Islamabad.

13. Lashkhar-e-Taiba has split into al-Mansurin and al-Nasirin.

14. According to India's data, in 2008 there were a total of 36 camps with 3,660 militants. The information is credible since New Delhi could identify the names and location of the bases. The largest camps are located in Muzaffarabad and Kotli, which operate basic training for newly recruited fighters who would later be distributed to other camps. Camp Danna and Abdul-bin-Masud in Muzaffarabad and Camp Badli in Kotli belong to LeT. The Hizbul Mujahidin operates Camp Jangal Mangal in Muzaffarabad and another at Mangla.

18. TURBULENT TIMES 2007–2010

1. Among military circles a plausible explanation for Musharraf's procrastination made its rounds: that Musharraf was under pressure from the self-created judicial crisis; he deliberately allowed the extremists to take over the complex and amass weapons until there was no alternative

except to storm it; he hoped to impress the West that he alone stood against the religious extremists.

2. See "PPP chief calls for restructuring of ISI," *Dawn*, 27 October 2007.

3. Outside the military sphere, the terrorist attacks that made world headlines were those on the bus carrying the Sri Lankan cricket team in March 2009 in Lahore; at the courthouses in Lahore and Peshawar; and the spectacular attacks on the Hotel Marriot in Islamabad, mainly frequented by foreigners, in September 2008; and on the Pearl Continental Hotel in Peshawar.

4. The ISI operation became known after one of the judges concerned entrusted a British colleague with information that got passed on to the press.

5. Two weeks earlier, the Saudi Minister of Foreign Affairs visited Islamabad to discuss with Musharraf the return of Nawaz Sharif. Since Musharraf rejected the idea, no agreement could be obtained. Thus the flight to Riyadh would have been an attempt by Musharraf to correct things with the Saudis.

6. dnaindia.com on 3 December 2007. The Pakistani journalist Amir Mir is considered a man with good contacts within the Army and ISI circles.

7. The manifesto requires the assumption of the military under the policy. It also mentions bringing even the MI under civilian control.

8. Many articles and books have been written with the aim of exploring the tragedy and answering who the real culprits are. The latest book is *Getting Away with Murder*, written by Heraldo Munoz, who headed the UN commission assigned to investigate the assassination.

9. While Ijaz Shah and Pervez Elahi held powerful positions, Hamid Gul hardly had the means and manpower at his disposal for the planning and execution of such an assassination. In suspecting Gul, it seems that Benazir was still emotionally affected by her fall in 1991.

10. *South Asia Analysis Group* paper no. 2533, 2 January 2008.

11. B. Raman, ibid., as follows: "There are two kinds of complicity—active and passive. Active complicity at the lower and middle levels would mean active participation by elements in the planning and execution of her assassination. Passive complicity means officers at lower and middle levels were probably aware of plans being made by terrorists or opponents of Mrs. Benazir Bhutto to have her killed, but they did not sound the alarm bell. They told themselves "it would serve her right" and kept quiet. The possibility of a passive complicity is higher than that of an active complicity. But no evidence either way so far."

12. It seems that no real explanation on the offender or the background to the events was forthcoming from the Commission of Inquiry set up by the UN in 2009.

13. The decision was not solely Kayani's, though he pushed it through. He consulted with his commanders, from whom he got full support. The basic fact was that Musharraf had to go. In fact by late 2007 even Musharraf's loyalists like Nadeem Taj were of the opinion that he should vacate the Presidency.

14. In Swat, Fazlullah's supporters from NWFP never exceeded 1,500, but he continued to bring in Uzbeks and Tajiks. In 2009, when the Army went in, a realistic estimate of foreign support was around 3,500. Their goal was the complete implementation of Sharia and conditions similar to those of the Taliban in Afghanistan in the 1990s.

15. Sufi Mohammad is the founder of Tehrik-e-Shariat-e-Nifaz-e-Mohammad. He fought in the Swat Valley.

16. A security risk analysis by the ISI indicated that there was the risk of increased Taliban activities in 47 percent of the Punjab province. In the North West Frontier Province, the government controls only 38 percent of the territory; the Taliban already has 24 percent. Moreover, they had established a permanent foothold in 38 percent of NWFP. In the parliament in Islamabad the PPP, ANP, MQM, PML-N and some independent parties voted for the deployment of the Army. JI and Imran Khan's party, which are not represented in the NA, rejected a military operation and have called for further talks.

17. The Tehrik-e-Taliban Pakistan are Islamist tribesmen in FATA, which was renamed as the Pakistan Taliban after the storming of the Red Mosque in Islamabad in 2007. Most of them follow the native South Waziristani Mehsud. Their leader, Baitullah Mehsud, was killed in August 2009; his successor Hakimullah Mehsud was killed by a drone strike in November 2013.

19. REFORM ATTEMPTS

1. *The News*, 17 March 2008, "Two Fata MNAs-elect admit meeting ISI official." The Deputy DG ISI had spoken with a total of seven FATA delegates, who later confirmed the meetings with journalists but only wanted to speak about development questions in their constituencies.

2. *Daily Times*, 6 May 2008, "ISI political wing to be handed over to IB."

3. See "PPP chief calls for restructuring of ISI," *Dawn*, 27 October 2007.

4. Lodhi came from the PAF and left as Wing Commander. During his service he was also in the ISI.

5. The reason for the MQM resistance against Suddle goes back to Benazir Bhutto's second reign. Suddle worked in a team led by Minister of Interior Maj. Gen. (retd.) Babar, who cracked down harshly on MQM supporters during the pacification of Karachi and Sindh.

6. The investigation was undertaken by the then DG ISI Ehsan ul Haq.

7. B. Raman, "ISI within the ISI: Empire strikes back," SAAG paper, 2008.

8. The majority of the victims were Afghan civilians. From the embassy personnel, those who lost their lives were the military attaché, the press spokesman and two security members of the Indo-Tibetan border police.

9. Prime Minister Gilani and his Minister of Foreign Affairs Qureshi contradicted all accusations levelled against the ISI. For political analysts, however, it was clear that the hasty attempt to bring the ISI under government control before the beginning of the US trip was an attempt to calm the American side.

10. For the ISI's current views on Balochistan and allegations of R&AW meddling there, see their official statements sent to the author in August 2015. These are found in Appendixes 1 & 2 at the end of this book.

11. In *Newsweek*, Mark Hosenball wrote on 4 October: "Two US counter terrorism officials, who asked for anonymity when discussing sensitive information, said they believe that US complaints about alleged collaboration between ISI to one of the officials, the US presented Pakistan with a dossier outlining alleged treachery inside ISI, including purported contacts between ISI representatives and Taliban militants who attacked India's embassy in Kabul on July 7."

12. At the end of May 2008 there were rumours in Rawalpindi that President Musharraf's intention was to replace Kayani with Nadeem Taj. The plan was only thwarted by quick retaliatory action from the COAS, placing a determined Musharraf under protective Army custody on 28 May for five hours. Meeting between 11 p.m. and 1 a.m., the COAS then told the President his decision to send him into exile and set out the procedures to do so. A special plane was on standby; first stop would be London, where Musharraf would initially find shelter in the house of Brig (retd.) Imtiaz. Half a dozen people would be involved in the plan but none could keep a secret, and so it leaked out. London and Washington were made aware of the events. The US ambassador rushed a message to Kayani saying, "Wait, don't do it now!"

13. Pasha also accompanied Kayani on his unusual meetings with the mullahs in August 2008 on the carrier *Abraham Lincoln*.

14. Ejaz Haider, "Kayani clears the decks ahead of battle," *Rediff News*, 6 October 2008.

15. See *Daily Times*, 24 November 2008, "ISI Political Wing disbanded: FM."

16. *Daily Times*, 27 November 2008.

17. At least until mid 2010 the abolition of the Political wing was still unclear.

18. Among the dead were 138 Indians and 25 foreigners; nine of the foreigners were from the US or Israeli-born Jews.

19. Later reports also mention an Indian camp in Afghanistan whose connection to the ISI would be reinforced.

20. Literally Manmohan Singh stated, "There is enough evidence to show that, given the sophistication and the military precision of the attack, it must have had the support of some official agencies in Pakistan."

21. Zahir ur-Rehman Lakhvi is considered the Operations Chief of LeT, Zarrah Shah the Communications Chief.

22. Kerry's visit may have contributed towards the spring 2009 Indian elections and the Prime Minister's inevitable heart operation.

23. In an interview in Rawalpindi at the end of 2010, a local observer said, "I have heard young, unemployed men, hundreds of them, saying "What else can we do? $50.00 a day from the Indians is much better than Rs. 200.00 a day that I will receive as a manual labourer. So I will have a short life, but I will live it well. So what if the dollars come from India?""

24. *Hindustan Times*, 25 February 2009. The official notice from the Prime Minister's office directly after Durrani's dismissal stated: "for his irresponsible behaviour [of] not taking Prime Minister and the other stakeholders into confidence and lack of coordination on matters of national security" (quote from *India of Times*, 7 January 2009).

25. According to a former Army man there is another reason: apparently "Durrani had risen far beyond his level of competence. He has always boasted that he was the only serving officer as a Brigadier, who was permitted by Zia to participate in the 'second track' dialogues with India. This boast cost him his third star."

26. The NSC comprises the President, the Prime Minister, the opposition leader in the NA, the Chairman of the Senate, the Speaker of the NA, the four provincial chief ministers, the commanders of the Army, Air Force, Navy and the CJCSC. The President plays a decisive role.

27. On 9 February 2009, Pakistani newspapers reported for the first time on a meeting of DCC. They were advised about the situation in FATA and NWFP. Apart from the Prime

Minister, the participants were the Ministers of Defence, Defence Production, Foreign Affairs, Information and Broadcasting and Law. In addition, there were the advisors for Finance and Interior and the State Secretaries for Cabinet, Foreign Affairs, Defence and Interior. From the military there were the three service chiefs from the Army, Air Force and Navy and from the intelligence services the directors of the IB and the ISI.

28. In December 2008, Senator John Kerry demanded that the ISI be brought under control. Previously, the US Assistant Secretary of State Richard Boucher had requested reforms of the ISI.

29. Proposals of a similar nature had been submitted in the past. In the 1970s, Zulfikar Ali Bhutto appointed a commission to make proposals to reform the structure of the military elite. The former proposals were implemented only half-heartedly by Bhutto. In 1991, Aslam Beg proposed the revalution of the Joint Chiefs of Staff Committee position. President Ghulam Ishaq Khan and Prime Minister Nawaz Sharif rejected this, fearing that Beg was looking for a new job for himself.

30. Shaukat Qadir, "Restructuring ISI-II," *Daily Times*, 11 October 2008.

20. CLOUDS ON THE HORIZON

1. The LSE report was prepared by the then Harvard analyst Matt Waldmann and garnered considerable attention in the press and TV in June 2010. It is based on interviews with nine Taliban commanders in Afghanistan, as well as with various ambassadors. The report stated, "as the provider of sanctuary and substantial financial, military and logistical support to the insurgency, the ISI appears to have strong strategic and operational influence—reinforced by coercion. There is thus a strong case that the ISI orchestrates, sustains and shapes the overall insurgent campaign."

2. Baradar would continue to reside in Pakistan in the Khyber Pakhtunkhwa province.

3. The consensual use of drones was expressly confirmed by Shuja Pasha in a hearing before the Supreme Court in Islamabad in February 2014.

4. See Mark Mazetti, *The Way of the Knife*, New York: Penguin Press, April 2013.

5. Shaukat Qadir, *Operation Geronimo—The Betrayal and Execution of Osama Bin Laden and its Aftermath*, HA Publications, May 2012.

6. See Damien McElroy, "Osama bin Laden was in routine contact with Pakistan's spy agency," *The Telegraph*, 27 February 2012.

7. One of his brothers was allegedly involved in questionable business dealings which were later the subject of an official probe, according to the *Express Tribune* (9 Jan. 2016).

8. Observers see the proportion of Islamists in the Pakistani Army as currently between 5 and 10 percent. Many others may be orthodox Muslims but are not Islamists. It is said that Islamists can only be controlled and kept in check by the Muslim Orthodox not by the liberals.

9. Ijaz was asked whether Pakistan's traditionally pro-military judiciary should be doing more to probe his claim that General Pasha met with Arab leaders to discuss the possibility of a coup against the elected Pakistan People's Party government in Islamabad. He responded, "You're damn right they ought to ask that question. If the SC is not willing to, you can be sure I will."

10. It remains unclear whether Kayani approved the meeting in Dubai. A majority of local

observers have the opposite view; for them, Pasha's closeness to Musharraf during his London exile was an additional reason for the cooling of trust between the COAS and ISI chief after Abbottabad.

11. Khalid Kidwai continued to lead SPC till 2013, followed by Lt. Gen. Zubair Mahmood Hayat till 2015. In April 2015 the latter became Chief of General Staff (CGS), the second most important posting within the Army's GHQ. The new DG of SPC is now Lt. Gen. Mazhar Jamil, who got his third star already in 2013. In 2011, at the time of Operation Geronimo, Mazhar Jamil was as Major General the Commandant of the Pakistan Military Academy in Abbottabad and also its Garrison Commander

21. QUO VADIS, ISI?

1. The cancellation revealed they would not bow to American pressure for Dr Shakeel Afridi's release. Dr Afridi was sentenced to thirty-three years' imprisonment by a special tribunal for cooperating with the CIA in the detection of Osama bin Laden. His release may one day come about in exchange for the US-imprisoned physician, Dr Aafia Siddiqui.

2. The attack took place on 23 July in North Waziristan, killing 12 people.

3. The blockade of NATO logistics routes to Afghanistan was in response to the American air attack on 26 November 2011 on the Pakistani border post of Salala, in which 24 soldiers were killed. The drone attacks continued during the eight-month-long negotiations on the lifting of the blockade, causing 70 deaths in North Waziristan.

4. According to a study by the Bureau of Investigative Journalism, a maximum of four civilians were killed by drones in 2013. The London-based NGO published the study in January 2014.

5. One reason for Kayani's request to meet the future Prime Minister immediately was because his election portfolio was to use the Kargil Commission and to share their findings with Indian authorities. This must have alarmed the military.

6. In 2004, a secret defence pact was allegedly signed, by which Riyadh purchased nuclear weapons and ballistic missiles from Pakistan which are stored there for safety and reasons of secrecy. In 2012, the Saudis asked for the transfer of these weapons.

7. At the end of November 2013, New Delhi announced the dispatch of an expert working group to the Iranian port city of Chabahar. The port is to be extensively developed and will serve as an Indian naval base on the Arabian Sea. It will be a counterbalance to China's naval base in Pakistan's Gwadar. For Teheran, Chabahar will also offer the shortest route to sea, through Afghanistan. Regardless of what the Taliban in Kabul say in the future, Chabahar will strengthen Indo-Iranian cooperation and be a competitor for Gwadar.

8. Mehrangate comes into play here. The investigation is being carried out on the instructions of the Supreme Court. It is headed by FIA Assistant DG Muhammad Ghalib Bandeesha with a committee consisting of three more FIA directors. The final report will go to Minister Chaudhry Nisar Ali Khan, whose task will then be to keep his Prime Minister out of it. PML-N politicians also received money from Mehrangate.

POSTSCRIPT

1. President Hamid Karzai himself spoke of clear evidence linking this attack to the LeT.

SELECT BIBLIOGRAPHY

Abbas, Hassan, *Pakistan's Drift into Extremism*, New York: East Gate Books 2005.

Ahmed, Akbar S., *Jinnah, Pakistan and Islamic Identity: The Search for Salauddin*, London: Routledge, 1997.

Akhund, Iqbal, *Trial and Error*, Karachi: Oxford University Press, 2000.

Ali, Syed Raza, "The Shadow War: The Great Game Replayed", unpublished manuscript.

Andrew, Christopher, and Mitrokhin, Vasili, *The World Was Going Our Way: The KGB and the Battle for the Third World*, New York: Basic Books, 2005.

Anjum, Shakeel, *Who Assassinated Benazir Bhutto?*, Islamabad: Dost Publications, 2010.

Anwar, Raja, *The Terrorist Prince: The Life and Death of Murtaza Bhutto*, Lahore: Vanguard Books, 1998.

Arif, Gen. K.M., *Working with Zia*, Karachi: Oxford University Press, 1995.

Ashraf, Fahmida, *RAW, Covert Instrument of Indian Ambitions*, Islamabad: Institute of Strategic Studies, 2002.

Bose, Sumantra: *Kashmir—Roots of Conflict, Paths to Peace*, Cambridge, MA: Harvard University Press, 2003.

Stephen P., Cohen, *The Pakistan Army*, Karachi: Oxford University Press, 1984.

Coll, Steve, *Ghost Wars*, New York: The Penguin Press, 2004.

Collins, Larry and Lapierre, Dominique, *Freedom at Midnight*, London: HarperCollins, 1997.

Das, Gautam, and Gupta-Ray, M.K., *Sri Lanka Misadventure: India's Military Peace-Keeping Campaign 1987–1990*, New Delhi: Har-Anand Publications Pvt Ltd., 2008.

Datta, Sreeradha, *Bangladesh A Fragile Democracy*, New Delhi: Shipra Publications, 2004.

Dhar, Maloy Krishna, *Fulcrum of Evil ISI-CIA-Al Qaeda Nexus*, New Delhi: Manas Publications, 2006.

SELECT BIBLIOGRAPHY

Fischer, Louis, *The Life of Mahatma Gandhi*, New York: Harper Collins, 1983.

Gannon, Kathy, *I for Infidel*, New York: Public Affairs, 2005.

Gauhar, Altaf, *Ayub Khan, Pakistan's First Military Ruler*, Lahore: Sang-e-Meel Publications, 1993.

Gauhar, Atlaf, *Ayub Khan*, Lahore: Sang-e-Meel Publications, 1998.

Gauhar, Atlaf, *Thoughts and after thoughts*, Lahore: Sang-e-Meel Publications, 1998.

Ghosh, S.K., *Pakistan's ISI: Network of Terror in India*, New Delhi: A.P.H. Publishing Corporation, 2000.

Gill, K.P.S., and Sahni, Ajai (eds), *The Global Threat of Terror*, New Delhi: South Asia Terrorism Portal, 2002.

Gohari, M.J., *The Taliban Ascent to Power*, Karachi: Oxford University Press, 1999.

Gunaratna, Rohan, *Indian Intervention in Sri Lanka: The Role of India's Intelligence Agencies*, South Asian Network on Conflict Research, 1993.

Haqqani, Hussain, *Pakistan: Between Mosque and Military*, Washington: Carnegie Endowment for International Peace, 2005.

Hazarika, Sanjoy, *Strangers of the Mist*, New Delhi: Viking, 1994.

Hussain, Hamid, *Covert Action Quarterly*, No. 73, Summer 2002.

Jaisingh, Hari, *Kashmir—A Tale of Shame*, New Delhi: UBS Publishers, 1996.

Jiwa, Salim, *The Death of Air India Flight 182*, Vancouver: Star Books, 1986.

Bennett Jones, Owen, *Pakistan: Eye of the Storm*, New Delhi, Penguin Books, 2002.

Joshi, Chand, *Bhindranwale-Myth and Reality*, New Delhi: Vikas Publishing House Pvt Ltd, 1984.

Karan, Vijay, *War by Stealth—Terrorism in India*, New Delhi: Viking, 1997.

Karlekar, Hiranmay, *Bangladesh: The Next Afghanistan*, New Delhi: Sage Publications India Pvt Ltd, 2005.

Kashmeri, Zuhair and McAndrew, Brian, *Soft Target: How the Indian Intelligence Service Penetrated Canada*, Toronto: James Lorimer & Company, 1989.

Keay, John, *The Gilgit Game*, Karachi: Oxford University Press, 1993.

Khan, M. Asghar, *We've Learnt Nothing from History*, Karachi: Oxford University Press, 2005.

Koch, Egmont R., *Atom Waffen für Al Qaeda*, Berlin: Aufbau Verlag, 2005.

Kohli, M.S., and Conboy, Kenneth, *Spies in the Himalayas*, New Delhi: HarperCollins, 2005.

Kux, Dennis, *The United States and Pakistan 1947–2000: Disenchanted Allies*, Karachi: Oxford University Press, 2001.

Lal, Bhure, *The Monstrous Face of ISI*, New Delhi, Siddharth Publications, 2000.

Lamb, Alastair, *Kashmir-A Disputed Legacy 1846–1990*, Hertingfordbury: Roxford Books, 1991.

Levy, Adrian, and Scott-Clark, Catherine, *Deception, Pakistan, The United States and the Global Nuclear Weapons Conspiracy*, London: Penguin Books, 2007.

Julius Mader, *Geheimdienstaktivitäten im ungeklärten Krieg der USA gegen Afghanistan*, Berlin: Militärverlag der DDR, 1988.

Matinuddin, Gen. Kamal, *The Taliban Phenomenon*, Karachi: Oxford University Press, 2002.

Mirza, Humayun, *From Plassey to Pakistan*, Lahore-Rawalpindi-Karachi: Ferozsons, 2000.

Mukarji, Apratim, *The War in Sri Lanka*, New Delhi: Har Anand Publications, 2000.

Musharraf, Gen. Pervez, *In the Line of Fire*, London: Simon & Schuster, 2006.

K. Sankaran Nair, *Inside IB and RAW, The Rolling Stone that Gathered Moss*, New Delhi: Manas Publications, 2008.

Napoleoni, Loretta, *Die Ökonomie des Terrors*, München: Verlag Antje Kunstmann GmbH, 2004.

Peterzell, Jay, *Reagan's Secret Wars (CNSS Report)*, Washington, DC: Center for National Security Studies, 1984.

Prabha, Kshitji, *Terrorism An Instrument of Foreign Policy*, New Delhi: South Asian Publishers, 2000.

Raina, Ashok, *Inside RAW: The Story of India's Secret Services*, New Delhi: Vikas Publishing House, 1981.

Raman, B., *A Terrorist State as a Frontline Ally*, New Delhi: Lancer Publishers and Distributors, 2002

Raman, B., *Intelligence: Past, Present and Future*, New Delhi: Lancer Publishers and Distributors, 2002.

Raman, B., *The Kaoboys of R&AW*, New Delhi: Lancer Publishers and Distributors, 2007.

Rashid, Ahmed, *Taliban*, London, IB Tauris Publishers, 2000.

Ridgeway, James, *The 5 Unanswered Questions about 9/11*, New York: Seven Stories Press, 2005.

Rieck, Andreas, *The Shias of Pakistan: An Assertive and Beleagured Minority*, London: Hurst, 2016.

Rizvi, Hasan-Askari, *Military, State and Society in Pakistan*, Lahore: Sang-e-Meel Publications, 2003.

Rushd, Abu, *RAW in Bangladesh, Portrait of an Aggressive Intelligence*, Dhaka: Abu Rushd, 2001.

Sarila, Narendra Singh, *The Shadow of the Great Game: The Untold Story of India's Partition*, New Delhi: HarperCollins, 2005.

Schofield, Victoria, *Kashmir in Conflict*, London: I.B. Tauris, 2000.

Shafqat, Saeed, *Contemporary Issues in Pakistan Studies*, Lahore: Azad Enterprises, 1998.

Shaikh, Muhammed Ali, *Benazir Bhutto*, Karachi: Orient Publishing House, 2000.

Rajeev Sharma (ed.), *The Pakistan Trap*, New Delhi: UBS Publishers' Distributors Ltd, 2001.

V.K. Singh, Maj Gen., *India's External Intelligence: Secrets of Research and Analysis Wing (RAW)*, New Delhi: Manas Publications, 2007.

Sinha, B.M., *The Samba Spying Case*, New Delhi: Vikas Publishing House, 1981.

Small, Andrew, *The China-Pakistan Axis: Asia's New Geopolitics*, London, Hurst, 2015.

Swami, Praveen, *India Pakistan and the Secret Jihad*, London: Routledge, 2007.

Timarzi, Brigadier Syed A.I., *Profiles of Intelligence*, Lahore: Fiction House, 1995.

Verkaaik, Oskar, *Migrants and Militants*, Princeton, NJ: Princeton University Press, 2004.

Wilson, Sir James, *Unusual Undertakings—A Military Memoir*, London: Leo Cooper, 2002.

Winchell, Sean P., "Pakistan's ISI: The Invisible Government", *International Journal of Intelligence and Counter Intelligence*, Vol. 16, No. 3, Fall, 2003.

Wolpert, Stanley, *Zulfi Bhutto of Pakistan*, New York: Oxford University Press, 1993.

Yousaf, Brig. Mohammad, *Silent Solider The Man behind the Afghan Jehad*, Lahore: Jang Publishers, 1991.

Yousaf, Brig. Mohammad, and Adkin, Maj. Mark, *The Bear Trap*, Lahore: Jang Publishers, 1992.

Newspapers/Periodicals/Websites

Pakistan:
Daily Times
Dawn
Defence Journal
The Friday Times
Herald
The Nation
The News
Newsline
Weekly Independent
www.paktribune.com

India:
Assam Tribune
Covert Action Quarterly
Daily India
Faultlines
Hindustani Times
The Indian Express
Times of India
Outlook
The Pioneer
South Asian Analysis Group (SAAG)
South Asian Terrorism Portal

Times of India
www.dnaindia.com
www.rediff.com
sushantsareen.blogspot.com

Others:
Asian Times
Financial Times, Asian Edition
Newsweek
The Independent (London)
The Observer
Detroit News
Janes Intelligence Digest
New York Times
Star Tribune
Cicero
Der Spiegel
Frankfurter Allegmeine Zeitung
Stratfor
US News and World Report
Vanity Fair
Washington Post
www.longwarjournal.org
www.therearenosunglasses.worldpress.com
www.thepeoplesvoice.org
www.rue89.com
www.wikipedia.org
www.kashmir.net
Eurasianet.org

SUGGESTIONS FOR FURTHER READING

Siddiqa Agha, Ayesha, *Pakistan's Arms Procurement and Military Build-up*, 1979–99, Lahore: Sang-e-Meel Publications, 2003.

Arney, George, *Afghanistan: The Definitive account of a Country at Crossroads*, London: Mandarin Paperbacks, 1989.

Baweja, Harinder (ed.), *Most Wanted: Profiles of Terror*, New Delhi: Lotus, 2002.

Bodansky, Yossef, *Bin Laden, The Man Who Declared War on America*, California: Prima Publishing, 1999.

Cloughley, Brian, *War, Coups & Terror*, Barnsley: Pen Sword and Military, 2008.

Dhar, Anuj, *CIA'S Eye on South Asia*, New Delhi: Manas Publications, 2009.

Wilson, John, *The General and the Jihad*, New Delhi: Pentagon Press, 2008.

Joshi, P.C., *Main Intelligence Outfits of Pakistan*, New Delhi: Anmol Publications, 2008.

Khan, Maj. Gen Akbar, *Riders in Kashmir*, Karachi: Pak Publishers, 2008.

Amir Rana, Muhammad & Gunaratna, Rohan, *Al-Qaeda Fights back Inside Pakistani Tribal Areas*, Lahore: Pakistan Institute for Peace Studies, 2007.

Rashid, Ahmed, *Descent into Chaos*, London: Allen Lane, 2008.

Singh Sarila, Narendra, *The Shadow of the Great Game*, London: Constable and Robinson, 2006.

Swami, Praveen, *India, Pakistan and the Secret Jihad*, Abingdon: Routledge, 2007.

Seminar Papers, *Afghanistan, Unabated Turmoil*, Islamabad: Institute of Regional Studies, 2008.

Wright, Lawrence, *The Looming Tower, Al-Qaeda and the Road to 9/11*, New York: Alfred A. Knopf, 2006.

INDEX

INDEX